Inside Networks

 James K. Hardy

Humber College

Prentice Hall

Upper Saddle River, New Jersey   Columbus, Ohio

Library of Congress Cataloging-in-Publication Data

Hardy, James K.
    Inside networks / James K. Hardy.
      p. cm.
    Includes bibliographical references and index.
    ISBN 0-02-350091-3
    1. Local area networks (Computer networks). I. Title.
TK5105.7.H373   1995
005.6'8—dc20   94-28536
                                     CIP

Editor: Dave Garza
Production Editor: Mary Ann Hopper
Text Designer: STELLARViSIONS
Cover Designer: Jill E. Bonar
Production Buyer: Patricia A. Tonneman
Electronic Text Management: Marilyn Wilson Phelps, Matthew Williams, Jane Lopez,
   Karen L. Bretz
Illustrations: James K. Hardy

This book was set in Times by Prentice Hall and was printed and bound by Book Press. The cover was printed by Phoenix Color Corporation.

 © 1995 by Prentice-Hall, Inc.
A Simon & Schuster Company
Upper Saddle River, New Jersey 07458

Printed in the United States of America

10 9 8 7 6 5 4 3

ISBN: 0-02-350091-3

Prentice-Hall International (UK) Limited, *London*
Prentice-Hall of Australia Pty. Limited, *Sydney*
Prentice-Hall of Canada, Inc., *Toronto*
Prentice-Hall Hispanoamericana, S. A., *Mexico*
Prentice-Hall of India Private Limited, *New Delhi*
Prentice-Hall of Japan, Inc., *Tokyo*
Simon & Schuster Asia Pte. Ltd., *Singapore*
Editora Prentice-Hall do Brasil, Ltda., *Rio de Janeiro*

**Dedicated to Blanche,
a wonderful, strong, and caring woman**

■ Preface

This book, as its title implies, is about the inner workings of local area networks (LANs). The emphasis is on the lower layers, where there is a mixture of well-defined hardware and software that forms the support for all other network features. The book will complement other texts that concentrate on the upper layers and explore user commands, particularly NetWare user commands.

It is assumed that the reader has a slight technical interest or at least an interest in details. Some electrical terms are used, but an understanding of them is not vital. A few brief definitions are included in the glossary at the end of the book. Some previous exposure to assembly language and C language programming would also be a definite asset in following the programming examples.

Many chapters cover hardware and software details that are relatively easy to experiment with. For a modest amount of money, a school or even an individual can assemble a few cards and cables, add some readily available software, and then experiment. A full network operating system is not needed. There is a lot that can be learned from such a simple configuration. But please don't experiment on someone's fully operational network. Your mistakes (or mine) won't be appreciated.

If you want to experiment on your own, I would suggest either ARCnet or thin coaxial cable Ethernet cards—in that order. While these cards wouldn't be my first choice for a full installation, they are relatively inexpensive and they are the easiest cards to work with. Both, if used in small numbers, avoid the expense of a hub or concentrator. In particular, ARCnet, if kept to four or five stations, is the cheapest to use and the easiest to program. If you check first for the availability of Packet Drivers or other interface software, the cards will be of greater use. NetWare Lite and Packet Driver compatible software are two possibilities to explore.

As you will notice when you start reading, other than layer numbers and names, I don't rely heavily on OSI definitions of layers and what they do. Instead, my preference is to examine concrete situations, typically relying on Novell's NetWare, DOS workstations, and common adapter cards. OSI standards are important, but I feel that a deep understanding of them is not necessary for at least the initial understanding of how networks operate. For completeness, they are described in the appendix.

This isn't a book on programming. Although many samples are included, the intent is to illustrate various aspects of a network's operation, not to demonstrate correct network programming techniques. For that you will need much more complete documentation. The philosophy was to keep programs short and simple so that key details could be readily seen. In many cases when developing these examples I became totally stymied and I would think, If only *something* would work then I could add features later. That's what these programs are—a starting point. They need some user interface polishing and added error checking. These are for you to add.

If the reader has any suggestions, corrections, or additions for this book, please contact me through the publisher. However, if you are thinking of major additions, consider what will have to be cut first.

Now our philosophy for the day. The topic of local area networks is of great interest to me. Part of my daily work and also my teaching revolves around networks. However, sorting out conflicting details, writing sample programs, attempting to locate a publisher, and soliciting help from industry led to a great deal of frustration. On more than one occasion the whole project ended up in a cardboard box which kept edging closer to the garbage can. But it did all work out in the end.

The message then is, If you believe in something, do it! There will likely be obstacles. And, if you have to take a break, that's OK, but make sure you return to the original task.

Every author has those he or she wishes to thank. This isn't just a courtesy; these individuals and companies were a huge help.

My family: Rebel, John, Lara, Shawna, and Sandra, who undoubtedly often wondered which pile of paper I was under.

John Parsonage, my mentor for many years of teaching and writing.

Kathy Warren and Mike Lake of Humber College.

Russ Nelson of Clarkson University.

Colleagues who reviewed the final manuscript: Albert L. McHenry of Arizona State University; Gary Boyington of Chemeketa Community College; Robert Mikel of Cleveland State University; S. Ron Oliver of California Polytechnic, San Luis Obispos; and Anup Kumar of the University of Louisville.

Texas Instruments Incorporated, Houston, Texas.

3Com Corporation, Santa Clara, California.

Pure Data Limited, Toronto, Ontario.

Gandalf Data Limited, Nepean, Ontario.

Colleen Brosnan of Phoenix and Mary Ann Hopper of Prentice Hall, who made sense of my words and endured my changes.

And to my students, who often served as guinea pigs.

My thanks,
Jim Hardy

Contents

Chapter 4

ARCNET   79

Chapter 5

ETHERNET   113

Chapter 6

TOKEN RING (IEEE 802.5)   151

Chapter 11

TCP/IP   277

Chapter 12

MULTIPROTOCOL DRIVERS   289

Chapter 13

APPLETALK   307

Chapter 14

HUBS, BRIDGES, AND ROUTERS   323

Appendix
THE SEVEN LAYERS OF ISO-OSI   345

Glossary   351

Index   355

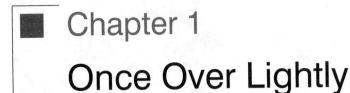

Chapter 1

Once Over Lightly

This is a fairly technical book—full of nuts and bolts and descriptions of how things work. However, we are going to begin with a gentle cruise through the topic of Local Area Networks (LANs). This will define some of the terminology, provide a little background, and build a foundation for the following chapters.

We will also explore how a user interacts with a network. This is important because the average users don't want to know what goes on inside the system—they just want to get on with their own job. Anyone installing, programming, or administering a network must constantly keep the end users in mind. The system must be easy to use for all levels of expertise.

Later, we will explore in more detail how a network functions.

THE BASIC NETWORK

While networks are available in many forms, the type we will concentrate on most closely is a dedicated server system, shown in Figure 1.1. This system is based on one computer that is used only as a server for the other personal computers (PCs) that are linked to it—no one works at its keyboard. The operating system software used for dedicated servers is usually Novell's NetWare or a similar software. In fact, this book will lean heavily on NetWare examples.

WHY NETWORKS?

The most basic reasons for connecting personal computers into a network are:

- Files can be stored and shared. The central server is then simply a high-performance warehouse. Its function is to guard these files and control who can access them and under what conditions.
- Diverse computers can be linked. The network will enable data files to be moved between OS/2, UNIX, Macintosh, VMS, and DOS machines.

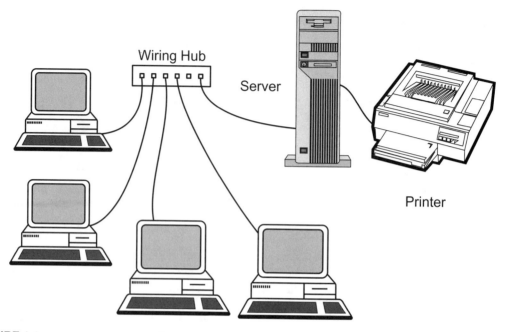

FIGURE 1.1
A network of personal computers with a dedicated file/print server. Once connected, the users' PCs turn into workstations.

- Printers, FAX connections, and mainframe links can be shared. This is the most common application for networks.

In the simplest situation, application programs (i.e., wordprocessors, spreadsheets, etc.) do not execute (run) on the server. Instead, they are simply stored on its disks. This makes licensing control and periodic updating of user software simpler.

To start an application program, the user would switch to a network drive (we will see what this means shortly) and then type the normal command to run the program. The application program files would then move over the network cables to the individual's PC and be executed there. In this situation, the server is nothing more than a glorified warehouse—a file server.

Most installations will also run a printer-sharing program on the server machine and attach one or more printers. The server now operates as both a file server and a print server.

Moving up in complexity, servers may also operate as database servers, communication servers, and FAX servers. All that is required is the addition of extra programs specifically written to run on the server operating system. For NetWare 2.x, these programs are called Value Added Programs (VAPs). For NetWare 3.x and 4.x, they are called NetWare Loadable Modules (NLMs).

It should now be obvious that the core of the server's software has to be a multitasking operating system. It must be able to perform many tasks at the same time.

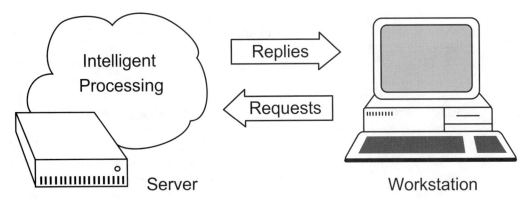

FIGURE 1.2
The client–server model. A workstation asks for some intelligent processing on the server.
Only selected replies return through the cable.

As more executing programs are added, the server will definitely slow down. Therefore, as the load expands, separate servers could be added that would be dedicated to print serving, database serving, etc. Novell's SQL database program for server use, for example, is sold with a minicopy of NetWare so that it can be run on a separate server machine if desired.

Server-based networks appear to mimic the old central mainframe system. The difference is that the relatively dumb terminals connected to a mainframe have been replaced by very sophisticated personal computers or workstations. These PCs are just as capable of running software as is the server. Now the customer can choose where programs run. Using the client–server model (a badly misused term), some application programs can even be split in half for more efficient operation (see Figure 1.2).

Server-based programs are becoming increasingly important for heavily used (queried) databases. With a split database operation, the server disk holds the database files and a "back end database engine" program runs in the server's **RAM**. This program is intelligent enough to process requests sent to it from "front end" programs running on a user's personal computer. A client PC could then make a request for a list of "all men with green hair," and this would be processed at the server. Only the answers would be sent back to the client machine. A more traditional database program would have to move the entire data file to the user's PC and make the selection there. With a split operation, the result is less network traffic, higher processing speeds, and better security for the database information.

USING A LAN

Let's follow a user on a modern network. Normally, many of these operations are automated and hidden from the user. However, we will get our user to perform each of the steps manually so they will be more obvious. The examples are taken from Novell's NetWare but would be typical of many different network operating systems. The actual hardware isn't important at this point because the user doesn't see it.

To begin, the user would turn on his or her personal computer. While the PC is performing its power-on tests and its operating system is being loaded, the network card inside the machine probably is also doing a self-test. In the case of a Token Ring card, this would also include tests of the local cabling (workstation to **concentrator** box).

Token-passing ARCnet cards will also join the network by themselves during this time. This disrupts network operations for a few milliseconds until the new adapter card is recognized. The card will periodically be receiving "invitations to transmit." Token Ring adapter cards will wait for a software command before joining. Ethernet cards don't need to "join." We will explain these details shortly.

The adapter card is now on the network in an electrical sense, but the workstation and the user aren't. The normal PC operating system (usually MS-DOS, DR-DOS, or PC-DOS) will have been loaded by this time and the user will have access to any local disk drives, but nothing more.

To continue the procedure, the local portion of the network software must now be loaded by the user. For NetWare, the user must execute (cause to run) the IPX.COM and then the NET5.COM (if DOS 5.x or 6.x is being used) files. These files stay resident in the computer as long as it is turned on and reduce the memory available for other applications. These two NetWare files use a total of about 60K **bytes** beyond the requirements of DOS itself. With DOS 5.x or 6.x or other memory management software, the two network files can be loaded into higher areas of memory and so will be less of a problem. However, they still consume valuable memory.

Now the server software can talk to the new user. The local PC is now on the network, but the user isn't. By typing F:, the user will find that a new "virtual" disk drive has appeared in addition to the local drives (A: through E:). This is the first of many potential network drives. The others aren't available yet and may not even be needed. At this point, the user has found the guard at the "front gate" of the server and can start limited communications with the server operating system.

Figure 1.3 shows a NetWare server disk's directory structure. Files appear in many directories and subdirectories just as they would on a local hard disk. Although the view from the user's PC will look and feel like a DOS environment, the file control actually belongs to the server's operating system. Server disk drives, for example, do not use drive letters such as A: or C:. They use volume names instead, such as SYS:, VOL2:, or DISK3:.

Confused? It is DOS that uses single-letter drives, and most DOS programs expect this. One of the functions of the NETx.COM or "shell" program at each workstation is to make the translation from DOS drive lettering to the server drives. Lotus 1-2-3, for example, could be working with a spreadsheet on the J: drive, but the network would understand that this was really the SYS:CHARLIE\DATA\LOTUS subdirectory. As long as the user, the workstation, and the application programs are happy with the illusion, everything works.

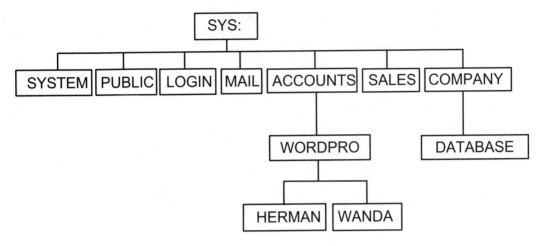

FIGURE 1.3
Subdirectories on a Novell server. The four on the left are part of the network operating system itself. Those to the right are added by the users and their supervisor. All except the LOGIN subdirectory are protected and require a name, password, and assigned rights to access.

NETWORK ACCESS

The user must now try to get access to some of these subdirectories. However, the server subdirectories are protected (that is, access to them is restricted), except the one named LOGIN. The user can connect his or her F: drive to only the LOGIN subdirectory. Any attempts to connect to other subdirectories would initially be futile.

If the user were to display a directory (by typing DIR) of the new F: drive, it would show a small number of files, one of them named LOGIN.EXE.

Modern networks are all about information sharing, and much of this information could be sensitive and valuable. Prospective users must, therefore, have a user name and password before they can login. Permission to use certain programs and information files is also needed. The user might be allowed full access to some files, permission to view, but not change, others, and denied any access to the rest. A network supervisor will create a suitable user name and initial password and enter these, along with the user rights, into the user database.

Now the user can attempt access to the server files by typing LOGIN followed by his or her assigned user name, for example, LOGIN WANDA. The first word, "LOGIN," will cause the LOGIN.EXE file to execute. This means the file first moves through the network cables to the user's PC and then runs in the PC's RAM (memory). The LOGIN program then takes the second word, "WANDA," and checks to see if it matches anything in a list of authorized users (Novell's Bindery, version 3.x, or NetWare Directory Services, version 4.x) on the server. Even if no entry is found, the LOGIN program will continue and ask for a password; it keeps unauthorized people guessing.

Once the correct combination of user name and password is entered, the login is complete. The server now knows that the user is active, what workstation he or she is using, and what limitations (rights) he or she has.

For the remainder of the day, our user will have a "logical connection number" assigned. Tomorrow that number will likely be different. NetWare uses this number in all its packets to and from that station. Supervisors use the number to see who accessed the system first this morning. The numbers start at one and climb as high as the license allows—10 users, 25 users, etc.

The only network drive at the moment will be the F: drive. This might be sufficient and can be reattached to any subdirectory that the user has access to by using the normal DOS Change Directory (CD) command.

If needed, additional virtual drives can be created and connected to various directories by typing something like Novell's "MAP" command.

```
MAP  G:=SYS:ACCOUNTS/WANDA
MAP  H:=SYS:ACCOUNTS/WORDPRO
MAP  J:=SYS:COMPANY/DATABASE
```

A typical network will allow about 21 extra "virtual drives" to be created by each user. They can be arbitrarily labelled F: through Z:. Drive letters A: through E: are usually reserved for local drives. (Novell's NetWare Lite requires an extension of "local drives" using the DOS LASTDRIVE command.) To the user, the files in these directories will simply appear as three extra disk drives in addition to the local floppy and hard drives (see Figure 1.4). If two or more users were going to share an information file, they would all connect to the same directory. Users can independently decide which drive letter to use on their individual workstations. Whether their particular wordprocessor or spreadsheet will then support file sharing is a separate issue.

Automating the Login

In a real office situation, the users would see very little of the previous operation. The network supervisor would likely have created special batch and script files to automate the startup. As a result, the users would only see a slight delay and then a request for a name and password. Their preassigned files would then be immediately available. Most of the network details would be totally invisible. This is the way it should be. The average office worker has enough to worry about without having to know a long procedure and special commands for using a network.

Most user-oriented network operations are handled with standard DOS commands—DIR, COPY, CD, DEL, etc.—provided users limit themselves to files with a DOS origin. In other words, very few new procedures need to be learned. Copying OS/2, Macintosh, and UNIX files, however, will require more careful procedures.

To automatically have a workstation access, or boot, onto the network, the supervisor would simply add the required network files to a local disk and then modify the PC's AUTOEXEC.BAT file. The essential files are shown in Figure 1.5. These could be on the workstation hard disk, if it has one, or even on a floppy.

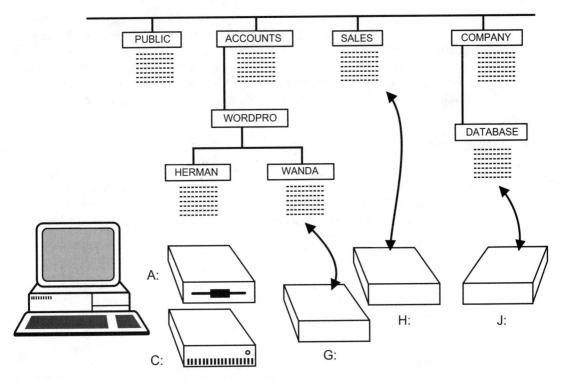

FIGURE 1.4
Once all connections are made, a workstation user sees the network simply as many disk drives. Some will be local ones while others will be virtual drives connected to various subdirectories on the server.

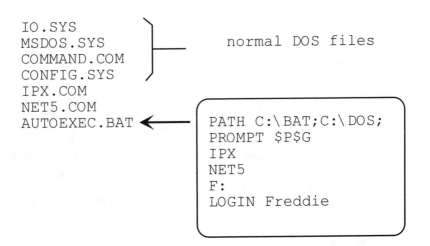

FIGURE 1.5
Minimum files needed to boot a personal computer and place it on the network. The content of a simple AUTOEXEC.BAT file is also shown. The user will still have to type his or her password.

A workstation can operate without a floppy (diskless workstations) if an extra memory chip is added to the network adapter card. This would contain just enough code to initiate the transfer of the three DOS files and any other required files from the server. Diskless workstations are not cheaper but are often used for security reasons so that the user cannot copy data onto floppies for personal or illegal use or introduce unwanted and possibly damaging software viruses into the network.

WHAT'S INSIDE?

Now that we are finished with outward appearances, what is really happening inside the workstations? After all, that's what this book is supposed to be about.

As indicated, the workstation portion of Novell's networking software consists of two files that use about 60K bytes of memory. This is in addition to the normal DOS system files—MSDOS.SYS and IO.SYS.

The NETx.COM file is often called the "shell." It contains several parts, one being a REDIRECTOR. It monitors all disk drive and printer requests that the user makes and decides whether they are for local or network devices. To continue with our "MAP" drive example started before, requests to use the A: or the B: drive are processed as they would be in any standard PC. They make the local floppies spin. Any request for the H: drive would be redirected instead to the network card.

The remainder of the NETx.COM file takes the redirected requests and creates special, short messages for the server using Novell's NetWare Core Protocol (NCP). These messages are sent to the lower IPX function for further processing (see Figure 1.6).

The IPX function resides in the memory resident image of the IPX.COM file. It is the packaging and delivery mechanism that controls source and destination addresses and several other details. It wraps an NCP message in its own IPX protocol and sends it to the adapter card. The card adds its own information, sets the destination address to the server, and puts the message on the network cable. In a server-based network, there is very little direct communication with other users (peers).

Because the IPX.COM file communicates directly with the adapter card, it must be carefully matched to the specific card. To accomplish this, the file is shipped in two parts. The first is the protocol part, which does the packaging of messages. The second is specific to the network card used and is often supplied by the card manufacturer as a "card driver." During the installation of the network, the two parts are glued together (linked) to form one file. This means that if your company uses two separate networks—one with Ethernet cards and the other with ARCnet cards—there will be several different files labeled IPX.COM. Be very careful not to interchange these files.

Alternatives to the use of NETx and linked-IPX will be provided in Chapter 12.

Layers

Data moves over a network in chunks or packets. These will have a maximum length that depends on the adapter cards used and the networking software. A good gen-

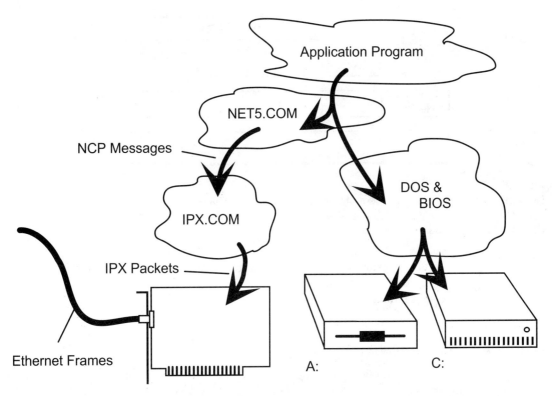

Application Program

NET5.COM

NCP Messages

IPX.COM

DOS & BIOS

IPX Packets

Ethernet Frames

A: C:

FIGURE 1.6
A redirector program intercepts requests made by the application program and decides
whether they are for local or network resources.

eral number to keep in mind is 500-byte chunks. Many network packets are simply
control messages and tend to be less than 100 bytes long.

In most networks, at least three levels of encapsulation or layering are used.
This means that extra bytes of information are added at the front and, sometimes,
the back end of the application program's data. The first level of encapsulation is
performed by Novell's shell. It builds and decodes NCP messages. If you are sending
a document to the server for storage or printing, it will be contained within NCP
messages, several hundred bytes at a time.

The IPX layer then adds 30 bytes in front of the "shell data." This header contains full source and destination addresses, sequence numbers, and message lengths,
to name only a few items. An exact description will be found in Chapter 10.

The lowest layer of encapsulation is provided by the specific adapter card being
used. Ethernet, for example, adds 22 bytes at the front of the IPX data and four
bytes at the end. IBM's Token Ring adds 15 at the front and six at the end. The front
portion usually contains adapter card addresses (these could be structured differently from the addresses contained in the inner layers). At the other end of the
packet, the adapter card will add some form of error detection code.

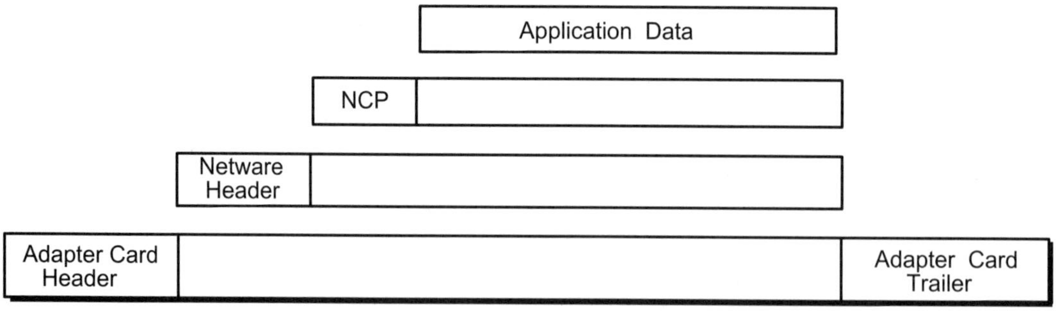

FIGURE 1.7
Networks generally add three layers of headers to their data. The first two levels will be characteristic of the network software—NetWare, in this case. The lowest layer will be determined by the adapter cards.

Total encapsulation can reach a theoretical maximum of six layers when the **ISO** standards are fully implemented. However, currently, three software layers are much more typical on a DOS workstation LAN (see Figure 1.7).

HARDWARE AND SOFTWARE

As we have seen, a network design needs two, somewhat separate, purchasing decisions—what server software to use and which adapter cards to use. If asked what type of network you have, you might answer, "My network cards are twisted pair (10BaseT) Ethernet, and the network software is Novell's NetWare 4.0."

Customers can select the overall capability and cost that meets their requirements. The hardware and software pieces must obviously work together, but most manufacturers support a variety of combinations.

Because network designers want even more flexibility, software has been developed that follows the seven-layer OSI standards. With more capable workstation operating systems such as UNIX, OS/2, and VMS, the ability to mix and match is attractive. However, because of limited memory availability, this capability isn't yet of major interest for DOS personal computers.

The OSI layers are discussed in the appendix. Although the software is not yet common, the layer names and numbers are often used as references. It would be wise for the reader to memorize these.

Server Software

Up to this point, we have concentrated on what was happening inside the workstation and ignored the server. Servers (and the resulting networks) come in two basic forms. The server's software defines this form.

If the server is like any other personal computer and runs standard DOS as its main file control system, then it will be part of a network of "peers." All of the PCs will be more or less equals. In fact, peer networks typically have many machines operating as part-time servers. Users will continue to perform normal work at the keyboards of these peer servers. A typical user might obtain an executable file from one machine, a data file from another, and print on a third. DOS peer networks work best if limited to about ten machines.

One of the earliest and best examples of a peer network system is provided by the Macintosh AppleTalk system. Other examples are Personal NetWare from Novell and LANtastic from Artisoft.

The advantage of sharing in a peer system is lower cost and higher flexibility. The disadvantage is lower performance on each machine as other users make demands on it. Peer networks will also have limited security. In a larger network of peer machines, the servers will often be set up as servers only—dedicated servers but still running DOS.

The previous discussion of peer network may leave the impression that all peer systems have poor performance. This isn't the case. If, for example, several Windows NT or OS/2 machines are interconnected, performance and security will increase. The removal of DOS from the picture makes the difference.

The other form of network is much more focused. Only one or two servers per network segment control all files and all printing. More importantly, this form of network server runs a completely different operating system and rarely accommodates a direct user at its keyboard. Both security and performance are improved.

The reasons for the operating system switch are many. DOS runs its microprocessor only in "real" mode, which limits direct memory addressing to one megabyte. Other operating systems use the 286, 386, 486, or 586 microprocessor's protected mode to greatly expand available memory and make more efficient instructions available. A second reason is the total lack of any file protection in DOS itself. This means that files on a peer network server can always be accessed by anyone who can physically get at the server and reboot it. Another reason is the low efficiency of the subdirectory structure when high-speed access by many users is required. Finally, as an operating system, DOS can only perform one task at a time. It cannot have one task interrupted and allow another task to use the same internal subroutines. DOS is single threaded, its code is non-reentrent, and so is inefficient when asked to look after multiple users or run multiple server-based programs.

A mixture of peer and central server networks is possible. Five PCs within an office, for example, could operate as peers with some sharing of general files. This "workgroup" could also be connected to a central server for corporate database operations.

NETWORK THROUGHPUT

A big concern of new network purchasers is the number of bits or bytes that can pass through a network in one second. The answer seems simple. Consider the following adapter cards and their advertised data rates:

FDDI	100.0 megabits/sec
ARCnet plus	20.0 megabits/sec
IBM new Token Ring	16.0 megabits/sec

Ethernet	10.0 megabits/sec
IBM Token Ring	4.0 megabits/sec
ARCnet	2.5 megabits/sec
IBM broad/baseband	2.0 megabits/sec
STARlan	1.0 megabits/sec

Real life is far more complex. Consider Figure 1.8. A user request at a workstation must pass through many steps before the requested information appears. There are software layers and network cards at both ends plus a hard disk at the server end. Each introduces delays and rate limits.

Some typical real-life figures using NetWare, a medium network load, and various cards are:

10 megabits/sec Ethernet	400–525 kilobytes/sec
4 megabits/sec Token Ring	150–250 kilobytes/sec
2.5 megabits/sec ARCnet	100–225 kilobytes/sec

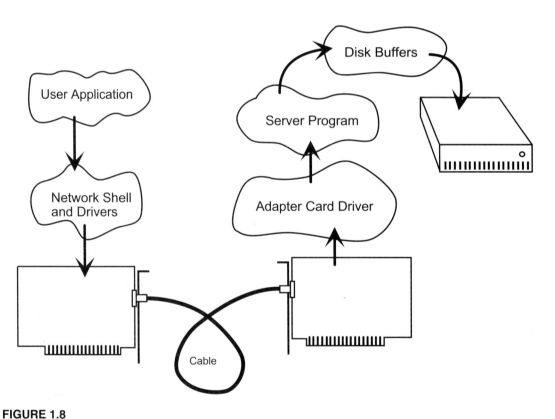

FIGURE 1.8
There are many factors that limit the flow of data over a network. The physical signaling rate on the cable is only one of them.

Software and the physical interface to the card are usually the biggest limiting factors. Some specific problems will be explained in later chapters.

PROTOCOL SUITES

If we move in for a closer look at how data is packaged for network transmission, we find a surprisingly small number of variations. These are the lower-layer protocol stacks or protocol suites. These protocols define how data is packaged inside, for example, an Ethernet packet and what action will be taken should some information be lost.

A comparison among three common lower-level protocols is made in Figure 1.9. The names of the seven ISO layers are included as a very rough reference. (See the appendix for a description of these layers.) None of the popular protocols for PC use is fully broken into the ISO layers, so the comparison here will be very rough.

Figure 1.9 shows that there is a clean break between the hardware—the adapter cards—and the network software. Cards such as Ethernet, ARCnet, and Token Ring are typical of the hardware layer. There are many variations of each. The software layers and files take over where the hardware leaves off.

Novell

Novell's protocols are a derivative of Xerox XNS (Xerox Network Systems), the software developed simultaneously with Ethernet hardware. A programmer creating a net-

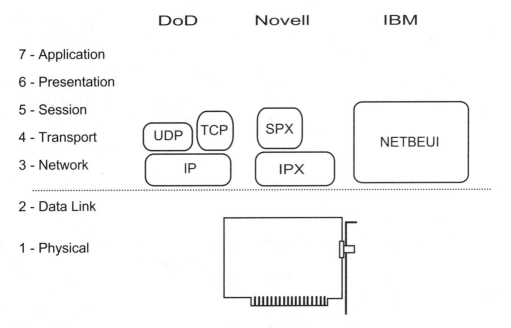

FIGURE 1.9
Approximate comparison of various commercial protocol stacks referenced to the seven ISO layers.

work application in a Novell environment could interface directly with either the IPX (Internetwork Packet eXchange) or the SPX (Sequenced Packet eXchange) layers.

To use the IPX layer, the programmer must break the application data into chunks no larger than 546 bytes and pass them to the IPX protocol code. This function, using information supplied by the application program, adds a header containing addresses, etc. With its new header attached, the packet is then passed to the network card for transmission. At the receiving end, the remote adapter card does its own checking and passes valid packets up to the remote IPX code. More checking is done, the IPX header is removed, and then the remote application is presented with up to 546 bytes of data.

If a packet is not delivered or happens to be out of sequence, IPX couldn't care less—it is "unreliable." This is not a criticism of the protocol; it is a specific term that means the application programmer has decided to do his or her own error checking and sequencing and therefore the IPX transport mechanism was most efficient.

The IPX addressing in the header is designed to cross network boundaries; it is "routable." It identifies networks and stations as separate entities.

Another programmer might decide to use the SPX layer instead. This layer performs certain operations and automatically passes information to the IPX layer. The ultimate transport mechanism is the same as before, but the programmer isn't concerned with it. The SPX layer adds "reliability" and is "connection oriented." The maximum amount of data handled in one packet is reduced to 534 bytes because the SPX operation adds 12 additional bytes of header information before passing the combination to IPX.

Before sending any data, SPX first "opens a connection." This means it does some initial communicating with the destination to see if it will be OK to send some important information. SPX performs its own numbering and checking. If it does not receive confirmation back from the remote station within a specific time that packets were received intact and in the proper order, it will retransmit several times. If that still fails, the user's application program will be notified. Even without data, SPX will send test packets over each of its "connections" to check that all is well.

Novell networks can also handle IBM's NetBIOS interface if an optional file is loaded at each workstation (more memory down the drain). However, NetBIOS is not Novell's preferred programming interface and so is only used to accommodate other application programs that specifically require it.

Novell's software will be more fully described in Chapter 10.

TCP/IP

The protocols generally referred to as **TCP/IP** were developed for the Department of Defense (DoD) and the ARPAnet that is used for defense research communications. They are now widely used in several environments, especially UNIX. The full suite consists of much more than TCP and IP.

The basic packaging mechanism is the internet protocol (IP). An IP "packet" can carry up to 64,000 bytes of data but typically is set to a much lower limit—typically 576 bytes, the same as Novell and XNS. The IP header is usually 20 bytes long.

IP, like IPX, is "unreliable" and so doesn't care if your packets aren't delivered. The main function of IP, like IPX, is to control addresses and deliver individual messages even to machines on distant networks.

In the next layer above IP, several choices are possible. The two most common are TCP and UDP.

TCP (Transmission Control Protocol)

TCP adds its own 20-byte header to the data before passing it down to the lower IP layer. TCP adds reliability in the same sense that SPX does. It is connection-oriented, which means that a lot of continuous checking is done regarding packet delivery.

UDP (User Datagram Protocol)

UDP is an unreliable, connectionless technique. The use of the word **datagram** indicates that short messages are to be carried; no technique is available for sequencing pieces of longer messages. UDP adds an 8-byte header before passing data down to the lower IP layer.

IBM

Much of IBM's network software did not originate with IBM. Some portions came from Microsoft and others from Sytek, Inc. (now Hughes LAN Systems, Inc.).

The core of IBM/Microsoft's network philosophy is the NetBIOS interface and the NETBEUI file that implements it. NetBIOS itself is not a protocol because it defines a programmer's interface, not what happens inside these layers. NETBEUI is the name commonly used for the associated protocol. It is, however, a limited protocol because large area network addressing is not fully defined. This means there are potential problems in multiple network routing.

MEDIA ACCESS

Now we move down into the adapter cards and the cabling.

A network's cabling system is common to all cards, and so there must be some agreed-upon procedure for sharing. LANs are totally unlike the telephone system where a user can dial a number to acquire the personal use of some wires and then stay "on the line" for hours at a time. For fair sharing of LAN cables, only one machine must be able to transmit at a time, and all others must listen. The length of time for each transmission must also be very limited, about a millisecond or two.

Two fundamental sharing mechanisms exist. Each requires that a large message be cut into short packets, and each machine must get a chance to send one packet. This prevents any one machine from monopolizing the network. Long messages are sent by successive packets.

The cable-sharing mechanism can be either the orderly Token Passing system or the "wilder" CSMA/CD technique.

Token Passing

At a noisy business meeting, some order can be established with a tennis ball. (A baseball bat also works wonders, but for a different reason.) Only the person who holds the ball can speak, but only a few sentences; all others must listen. When a speaker finishes his or her statement, the ball is passed to the next warm body. If that person has nothing to say, the ball is simply passed again. The ball or "token" may have to pass around the table many times before any one person has had his or her full say, but at least everyone will get an equal chance. ARCnet, MAP (an industrial automation network), and IBM's Token Ring use this technique. Special, short packets called "tokens" are constantly passed around a logical ring of workstations to invite each to transmit in turn.

CSMA/CD

"Carrier Sense Multiple Access with Collision Detection" (**CSMA/CD**) may appear to be a very chaotic system, but it works very well. To understand why, let's go back to our noisy business meeting.

With this access method, if someone decides to say something, he or she doesn't have to wait. However, the person must listen first. If the room is quiet, then he or she may speak. Should the speaker detect another attempt to talk (or the president snoring) he or she must immediately stop, wait for a random length of time, take a deep breath, and try again.

The "carrier sense" part means that everyone must listen to see that the room is quiet before talking. "Multiple access" means that there is no specific order; each user has a random chance of using the channel at any given time. "**Collision** detection" means that any speaker immediately stops if another noise is detected—there is no sense in continuing because the message will already be garbled. Just wait for the laughter and echoes to die down, and then try again.

Ethernet, STARlan, and IBM's older Broadband and slightly newer Baseband Networks use CSMA/CD.

Token Passing versus CSMA/CD

Which of these two systems—Token or CSMA/CD—is best? The answer can be found by looking at the marketplace. Both techniques sell equally well. The manufacturer's name and the card price are often more important to many purchasers than any performance advantages or disadvantages. Speed has more to do with card design than the media access technique. ARCnet was originally designed, many years ago, for 2.5 megabits/sec and recently moved to 20.0 megabits/sec. Token Ring was initially introduced at 4.0 megabits/sec and then raised to 16.0 megabits/sec. Ethernet, in its commercial forms, has always used a 10.0 megabits/sec data rate. Some present designs will move this to 100 megabits/sec.

The token system guarantees that any one station will not have to wait more than a certain amount of time before it gets its chance to talk. It, therefore, has a very predictable throughput. However, with many machines on one network, a cer-

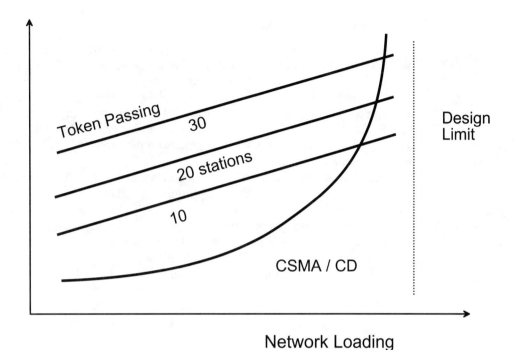

Network Loading

FIGURE 1.10
CSMA/CD and Token networks have changing time delay characteristics as more stations
are added and the overall network load approaches the design limit.

tain amount of time is used in simply passing tokens even when no one wants to talk.
Token networks will then show a predictable lag as more machines are added.

A CSMA/CD network gives each machine a statistical chance to talk but gives
no guarantees. The typical time delays do not depend on the number of machines on
the network but, instead, on the number of packets that are waiting to be sent at any
given time. Sometimes this can be much more efficient; in other cases, it isn't. It all
depends on how busy the average workstation is. Figure 1.10 illustrates some of the
differences in time delays between the two systems.

With other factors equal, such as data rates, a group of workstations that occasionally need to move large files will benefit from a CSMA/CD system. On the other
hand, a similar group that frequently wants to move small files will work better with
a token system.

If a network is being used to interconnect factory machines instead of personal
business computers, then the guaranteed maximum time delay of a token ring network becomes attractive. The reason is that people are more tolerant of occasional
delays than machines are. On an assembly line, for example, it is always nice if the
paint can is in place before the filling machine dumps several gallons of "raspberry
red" all over the conveyer belt. The MAP—Manufacturing Automation Protocol
(don't confuse this with Novell's MAP command)—network uses token passing with
a limited number of machine nodes for this reason.

BASEBAND VERSUS BROADBAND

Baseband and *broadband* aren't terms that are frequently associated with "local" networks, but they should be explained. The words describe the underlying frequencies used to carry the information on the cables.

All modern network techniques use special encoding methods to combine data with timing pulses (clock) to form a special waveform for the cable. The specific details about these are provided in later chapters. This waveform is effectively a form of modulation. It raises the frequencies on the cable above what the data itself would normally contain.

The result of this clock/data combination is that very low frequencies don't exist on the cables—at least not as a direct portion of the data. As we will see in the chapter on cabling, this is good. So what is a baseband and what is a broadband network?

With a baseband system, the highest cable frequency won't be much greater than the data rate itself. With 10-million-bits-per-second Ethernet, for example, the highest frequency component is roughly 12 MHz.

However, there are times when it is beneficial to have the data ride on (modulate) a much higher frequency. Broadband techniques will allow one cable to carry several different types of information—video as well as data, for example. The trick

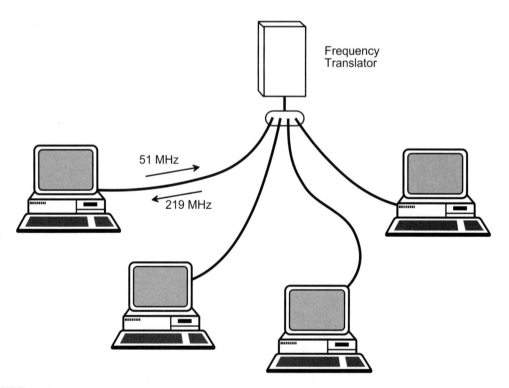

FIGURE 1.11
IBM's Broadband Network uses 6-MHz-wide channels and a translator unit. It is a CSMA/CD network.

is to make sure that each uses a different "carrier" frequency. In any broadband system, the signal frequencies are much higher than the data rate.

All of the major network hardware covered in this book are inherently baseband systems. This, however, doesn't prevent installers from adding higher frequency modulators for special applications.

IBM's old 2 megabits/sec Broadband Network and some versions of the MAP factory automation network are inherently broadband networks. Their 75 ohm cabling and amplifier systems are borrowed from cable TV equipment. The frequency components of IBM's Broadband system are shown in Figure 1.11. Notice the large difference between the 2 megabits/sec data rate and the actual carrier frequencies used.

TOPOLOGY

The topology of a network describes the cable layout. The three physical cable arrangements are shown in Figure 1.12: star, ring, and bus.

A network's "topology" can be considered in two ways. Physical topology describes what a human sees. Logical topology describes what the network software thinks is happening. The two can be quite different. We will look at physical topology first.

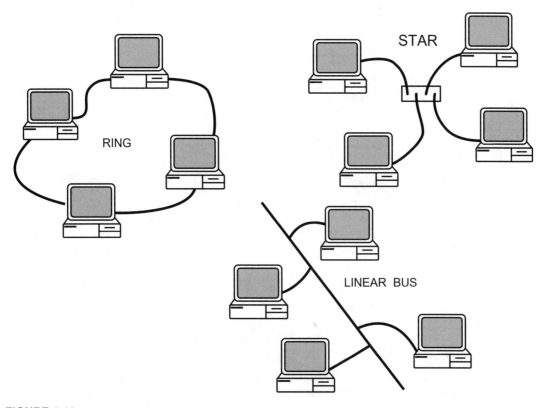

FIGURE 1.12
Three general patterns of wires are possible: star, ring, and bus.

Physical Topology

Physical topology used to be fully decided by the choice of network card. Ethernet was always a bus, and ARCnet was always a star. Now many cards provide several options. With ARCnet and Ethernet, the customer has a choice of either star or bus topology.

Physical topology is important when cabling is being attached to or removed from a workstation. It determines how difficult it is to get to the central wiring and whether other stations will be interrupted when a connection is changed. Physical topology can also affect the cable cost in a minor way if greater lengths must be run or if more wires are involved in each run. However, labor costs will usually make material costs insignificant.

Star

Because an emerging concern involves the ability to troubleshoot and manage a network, one topology has a definite advantage. The star or distributed star layout of cables is easiest to control and troubleshoot because few wires are shared and all wires tend to lead to a central point. This reduces the chance that one failure will upset a major portion of the users.

Star wiring brings all the cables together at some central box. Each machine will have only one cable (containing either two or four wires) leading to a central box of some sort. This is the preferred topology for troubleshooting, and newer networks build a lot of troubleshooting aids into this central **hub** or "concentrator."

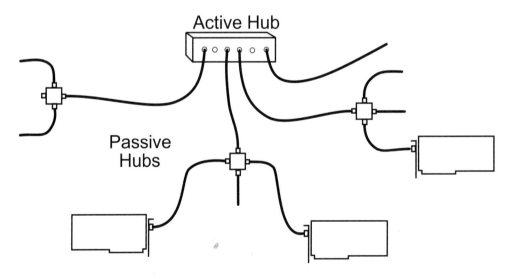

FIGURE 1.13
The more common version of Datapoint's ARCnet uses a distributed star with multiple connections made through active (amplifier) hubs and passive (resistor) hubs.

ARCnet uses a variation on the simple star called a "distributed" star (see Figure 1.13). A collection of active (amplifier) and passive (resistor) hubs are used, and the resulting pattern looks like several stars joined at random. As long as the signal can get from one machine to any other without following more than one path and getting too weak, the setup works.

The recent twisted pair (10BaseT) Ethernet standard also connects its stations in a distributed star pattern.

Ring

With a ring topology, each station has two cables: one going in, and the other going out. The last machine in the lineup connects back to the first to form a ring. All of the stations are effectively in series. One advantage is that each station acts as an amplifier; no separate amplifiers are needed except for abnormally long cable runs.

However, if built exactly as described, a ring is a very difficult configuration in which to connect or remove a station. Since each station is needed to complete the ring, either each station will have to be always turned on or the two ring ends will have to be "jumpered" when a station is turned off or removed.

The Token Ring network, as its name implies, really is a ring of wire, but it is laid out in a different shape. The input and output wire pair for any one machine are placed in a four-wire "lobe" cable (see Figure 1.14). This connects the individual station to a central box or wiring concentrator. Special relays are used in the wiring concentrators to automatically bridge the gap if any machine is turned off or removed. While the wire itself still forms a ring, the visible cabling resembles more of a star.

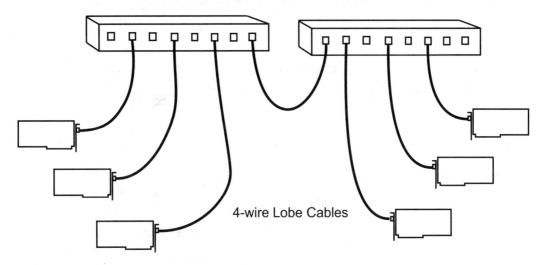

4-wire Lobe Cables

FIGURE 1.14
IBM's Token Ring keeps the ring separate from the machine so that only one cable assembly must be connected or removed.

Bus

A bus topology uses one long central cable. Machines connect to this cable at tap points. The two ends of the main cable simply end in terminating resistors (see Figure 1.15). The two initial Ethernet designs and a modified version of ARCnet use a bus. A physical bus can be somewhat difficult to troubleshoot because each connection point is at a different physical location, often in the ceiling or inside a wall. Any failure in the central bus cable will often disconnect half, if not all, of the users.

A variation on the bus is the "daisy chain." Each adapter card has two identical connectors that are directly connected within the card. They are arbitrarily labeled IN and OUT. The next machine in a line will have a cable connected from its IN connector to the OUT of the previous machine. The end machine usually has a terminating resistor connected to its OUT connector. Intervening machines can be turned off without upsetting the operation since the internal connection is direct. AT&T's StarLAN and the LocalTalk connectors of Macintosh use this arrangement.

Logical Topology

What network software thinks is happening can be quite different from what the physical layout of the wires might suggest. In other words, the logical topology doesn't always match the physical topology.

For example, the more common form of ARCnet is a physical star. However, when the "token" is passed, it follows a very definite order from one machine to the next. All stations actually receive the electrical signal, but only the one with the matching address reacts to it. It is, therefore, acting as a logical ring. The order of the token passing is determined by network addresses and not by physical proximity.

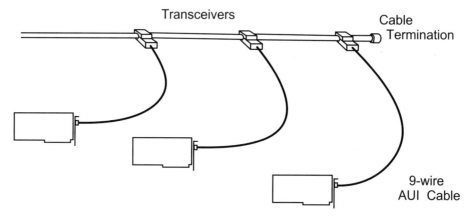

FIGURE 1.15
Ethernet's single bus cable is terminated at each end with resistors. Workstations connect with high **impedance** taps.

Token Ring could look, at first glance, like a physical star. However, when the individual wires are examined, a physical ring will be seen to exist. When tokens and messages are passed, they follow this ring, and so the network is also a logical ring. The passing of the token is controlled by physical order.

Ethernet, in any of its cabling forms, is a logical bus as dictated by its access method. There is no predefined station order. All machines are effectively in parallel, and each one hears all the messages. The transmission scheduling appears to be random, meaning that any machine can transmit any time it wishes—unless someone else gets going first.

SOME FINAL DETAILS

Here are some possible pitfalls to avoid when learning about networks.

First, data inside each packet is carried as individual bytes. All networks insist only that these be complete bytes, not 47.5 bytes, for example. In some descriptions of networks, the term "octets" will appear. In this text, the word is treated the same as a byte. The term octet was necessary a few years ago when some computers used 10- or 12-bit "bytes." Today, a byte is generally accepted as meaning eight bits. But, beware.

Another potential problem is the order of transmission and the numbering of bits within a byte. All serial port data transmission (COM1, COM2, etc.) on a personal computer sends the least significant bit of each byte first. ARCnet and Ethernet do the same. Token Ring reverses this and transmits the most significant bit first. To make life even more confusing, some documentation (IBM's) may label the bits being sent as 0, 1, 2, 3, ... even though it is the most significant bit being sent first. Again, be careful.

This bit order and numbering is only important if you are examining bits on the cable with an oscilloscope (which displays cable **voltage** versus time) or are reading specific documents. Bit order does not normally affect programmers or the use of protocol analyzers.

A related problem is the order of bytes in 16- and 32-bit numbers. Even within one protocol, there will be some variations. In some places, the most significant byte is placed first in a packet; in other cases, the least significant byte comes first. This problem does affect the programmer. Be careful also to determine whether a diagram is describing the network order or the programmer's order of partial-byte fields.

Chapter 2

Personal Computers

This chapter looks inside the generic MS-DOS personal computer—the PC. This machine can be converted from a stand-alone computer to a network workstation with the addition of an adapter card and some software. We aren't going to describe the overall operation of a PC but will concentrate instead on those hardware and software portions that are relevant to network operations. We will also see how added network software modifies the normal operation of the PC.

A TYPICAL PC SYSTEM

A functional block diagram of a typical 80x86-based system is shown in Figure 2.1. The microprocessor is connected to two different memory areas over a data bus. Depending on the microprocessor used, this bus could have 8, 16, or 32 wires. The 80286 and 80386sx, for example, use 16 wires or circuit board traces. The 386, 486, and 586 Pentium chips use 32 wires.

Address bus lines are also shown in Figure 2.1. Again, depending on the microprocessor model, there could be 20 lines (8088), 24 lines (80286), or 32 lines (80386, 80486, and 80586). Combinations of High and Low voltages on these lines identify the exact memory location being written to or read from.

Although not shown in Figure 2.1, there are still more lines in the total bus, for example, Read and Write and data size select lines.

MEMORY

Main Memory

The larger of the two memory areas shown in Figure 2.1 is the computer's main memory. It is further detailed in Figure 2.2. This area, filled with RAM chips, is where programs execute and work on data. This is also where packets are assembled before transmission and disassembled on receipt. Most of the microprocessor's instructions work with this main memory. For example, in assembly language, MOV

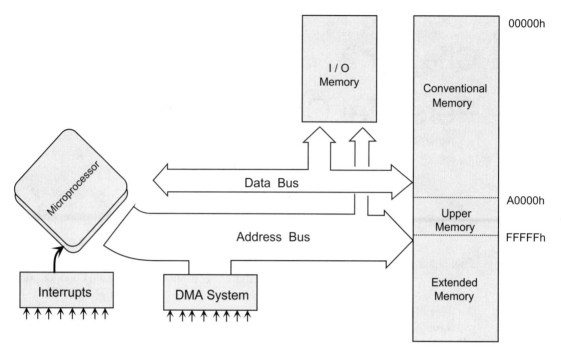

FIGURE 2.1
Real mode block diagram of an MS-DOS personal computer.

AX,[2000] will move 16 bits of information from location 2000 in main memory to the AX register of the microprocessor.

The maximum amount of main memory available depends on the processor model and the mode in which it is running. With all models running in the "real" or DOS mode (the 8088 doesn't have a mode choice), the maximum amount of main memory is one megabyte (1024K or 1,048,576 bytes). Using hexadecimal notation, the corresponding addresses range from 00000 to FFFFFh.

The lower 640K (addresses 00000 to 9FFFFh) will be RAM that is available to DOS and to application programs for reading and writing.

The remaining 384K (A0000h to FFFFFh) is termed "upper memory" and is reserved for specific purposes. The 128K range from A0000h to BFFFFh is reserved for display adapters (a fully loaded multi-megabyte display card uses this area 128K at a time). The next 128K portion, between C0000h and DFFFFh, is a "catch-all" area for hard disk controllers, video BIOS ROMs (Read-Only Memory chips), and network adapter cards. The final 128K is reserved for the system ROM chips. These contain the code that runs when the PC is first turned on. These ROMs are located between E0000h and FFFFFh.

One "quirk" of this 384K block on computers with the traditional ISA or AT bus is that each 128K bytes above A0000h must use either an 8-bit (byte) or a 16-bit (word) access, not a mixture. This isn't a major problem for the first group (A0000h to BFFFFh) because that is usually occupied by a single display adapter. However,

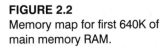

FIGURE 2.2
Memory map for first 640K of
main memory RAM.

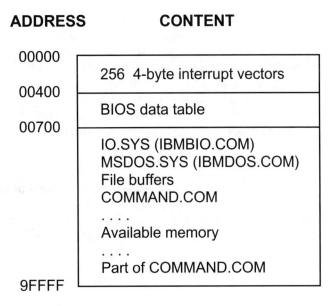

ADDRESS   **CONTENT**

00000

256 4-byte interrupt vectors

00400

BIOS data table

00700

IO.SYS (IBMBIO.COM)
MSDOS.SYS (IBMDOS.COM)
File buffers
COMMAND.COM
. . . .
Available memory
. . . .
Part of COMMAND.COM

9FFFF

the next 128K group could pose a problem. If several cards are installed in this group, they must all use the same access width. An 8-bit network card, for example, will not tolerate a 16-bit hard disk controller. Many video display cards also place their ROM chips in this block. (Some VGA cards place their ROM at C0000h to C7FFFh.) Therefore, the choice of video display card can affect the speed of the network.

To compound this problem, it is possible on 386-and-above machines to reassign RAM from the "above-one-megabyte" range down into unused portions of the 384K block. The access width of this "backfilled" memory for both Read and Write must stay consistent with existing cards.

Extended Memory

All processors used in PCs (except the 8088) have more than 20 address lines. This means they can handle more than 1,048,576 bytes (2 raised to the power of 20). The 386sx processors, for example, have four extra lines and so can theoretically handle 16 megabytes. However, with one odd exception, these lines are not available in the real or DOS mode of the microprocessor. The pure DOS world ends at one megabyte.

What happens when you plug one megabyte of RAM chips into your 286-and-above motherboard? This will result in 640K of memory from 000000h to 09FFFFh and then 384K from 100000h to 15FFFFh—beyond the range of normal DOS. A few years ago very few software programs took advantage of this extra memory, and so it was either unused or converted to a "RAMdisk" to speed hard disk access. However, DOS extender software and MS Windows can temporarily escape from the real mode, move into the protected mode, and access this memory. Whether this is of any value to you depends on the commercial application software you are using.

Because early DOS programs did not use it, the area within the first one megabyte became premium address space and the area below 640K even more so. If programs can run in higher areas of memory, it is important to move them up and free lower areas for programs which aren't as flexible.

The addition of network software on a personal computer can eat into the available DOS memory. For example, an extra 60K is potentially lost with Novell drivers. Fortunately, newer versions of NetWare workstation software can be moved up into higher memory areas to reduce the squeeze on lower memory.

High Memory

The "one odd exception" referred to above is the almost 64K block of memory from 100000h to 10FF0Fh. If the Segment:Offset address FFFF:000Fh is loaded into an address register pair of the 80286 (or higher) processor and then incremented, the

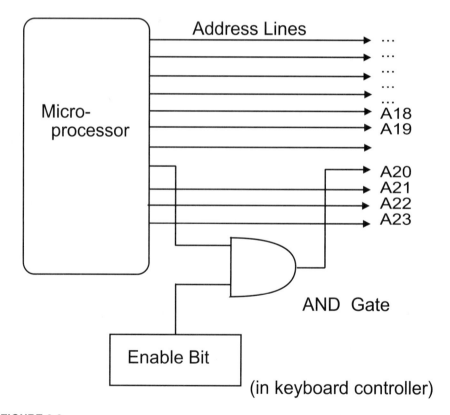

FIGURE 2.3
Extra disabling gate added to the A20 address line of personal computers (except for 8088/86 XTs).

A20 address line will turn on (remember that the first 20 address lines are A0–A19). This makes almost 64K of extra memory accessible in the Real mode and can be used by some software. (There was a speed advantage to grabbing extra memory within the Real mode of a 286 processor. Moving in and out of the 286 Protected mode was slow and clumsy. The 386-and-above processors are much more efficient at this.)

When IBM was developing their AT computer in 1985, this A20 address line quirk was known. They therefore added an external gate in the A20 line to make certain it stayed off when using DOS (see Figure 2.3). DOS extender programs that use the extra 64K must first enable this line, generally by writing a special code to, oddly enough, the keyboard controller.

I/O PORTS

The other portion of memory shown in Figure 2.1 is the Input/Output block of "ports." Only two instructions can be used to access this block: IN and OUT (and the corresponding string versions INS and OUTS). The microprocessor itself can handle a maximum of 64K bytes in this I/O block, but normally only about 4K bytes are used on the PC. These are numbered 000 to FFFh. This small block is rarely used for storing any quantity of data. Instead it contains control registers for display adapters, disk controllers, serial and parallel ports, and network cards. Typical uses are shown in Figure 2.4.

FIGURE 2.4
Memory map for personal computer's I/O block.

I/O PORTS	CONTENT
000-00F hex	DMA controller 1
020-021	Interrupt controller
040-043	3-channel Timer
060-063	Keyboard
080-083	DMA page register
0A0-0AF	Interrupt controller
0C0-0DF	DMA controller 2
. . . .	
200-20F	Games adapter
278-27F	Parallel printer 2
2F8-2FF	Serial COM 2
378-37F	Parallel printer 1
3B0-3BF	Display adapter
3D0-3DF	Display adapter
3F0-3F7	Diskette controller
3F8-3FF	Serial COM 1

INTERRUPT CONTROLLER

In addition to the two groups of memory, the block diagram in Figure 2.1 shows that the processor is also connected to two other circuits: an Interrupt Controller and a Direct Memory Access (DMA) controller.

Hardware Interrupts

The interrupt controller handles interrupt requests from various hardware sources such as a printer, network card, or the keyboard. When these circuits need attention, they will ask the processor to stop what it is doing and provide some processing time. Hardware interrupts are used, for example, when a packet is received by a network card. If the card's buffer isn't read promptly, the data could be lost when a following packet arrives.

Hardware interrupts are generally used in time-critical situations. The processor can then concentrate on some program without having to do a continual check on other functions. When an external event does occur, however, the processor can respond immediately.

The controller accepts requests on 15 individual pins (eight pins on the older "XT" class machine). The interrupt process is initiated when one of these pins first goes Lo (triggering occurs on the falling edge). If two or more are activated at the same time, the controller uses a priority system to select only one. The controller then signals the processor that a hardware interrupt has occurred. When the processor is ready, it will acknowledge the interrupt, and the controller will then pass it an eight-bit "vector number." This number more or less identifies the original source of the interrupt.

The original XT interrupt circuit consisted of one controller with eight request lines. These were labeled IRQ0, IRQ1, . . . IRQ7. All lines were preassigned except IRQ-2. As a result, many add-in cards competed for this "available" interrupt. The AT design, as shown in Figure 2.5, added one more controller chip with eight more input pins. It cascades into the original chip via IRQ-2 and so provides a net gain of seven lines.

As shown in Figure 2.6, the eight original IRQ pins are provided with vector numbers between 08h and 0Fh. The newer IRQ pins (8–15) use vector numbers 70–77h.

Software Interrupts

We have been looking at hardware interrupts. They occur at totally random times and are caused by external events—keys pressed on keyboards or network packets received. Software interrupts, in contrast, occur at predictable points—the programmer simply places interrupt instructions such as INT 21h in the program code.

Whereas a hardware interrupt generates a vector number in the interrupt controller chip, software interrupts carry their vector number with them, for example, INT 21h. After extracting this vector number from the instruction, the microprocessor proceeds in exactly the same manner as it does with a hardware interrupt.

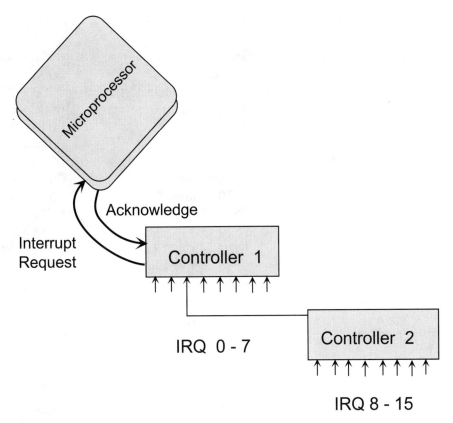

FIGURE 2.5
Hardware interrupts occur when one of the input pins of an interrupt controller abruptly
goes Lo. The XT bus uses only one controller, whereas the ISA/AT bus uses two.

The hardware and software vector numbers are shown in Figure 2.6. Notice how
these numbers have been intermeshed as the PC has developed. With the exception of
"05 - Print Screen," the first eight interrupts are generated within the processor when
unusual conditions occur. Intel had originally "reserved" the lowest 32 interrupt vectors (00h–1Fh) for hardware situations, but IBM decided to ignore this and assigned
many within that range to DOS and BIOS operations. This has resulted in some compatibility problems, particularly with Windows and OS/2 on older AT machines.

Interrupt Response

When the processor is successfully interrupted (many of the hardware interrupts can be
ignored or "masked"), it will immediately save its current program location on the stack
(an arbitrary area of memory). Later, when the entire interrupt operation is completed,
the processor will retrieve this information and then continue from that location.
   When the stacking is complete, the processor will start working with the interrupt vector that was obtained via either software or hardware. The processor multi-

Vector	Source	Vector Address
00	Divide by zero	0000 - 0003
01	Single step	0004 - 0007
02	Non maskable interrupt	0008 - 000B
03	Breakpoint	000C - 000F
04	Overflow	0010 - 0013
05	Print screen	0014 - 0017
06	Invalid opcode	0018 - 001B
07	Co-processor	001C - 001F
08	IRQ0 - Timer 0	0020 - 0023
09	IRQ1 - Keyboard	0024 - 0027
0A	IRQ2	0028 - 002B
0B	IRQ3 - COM2 serial	002C - 002F
0C	IRQ4 - COM1 serial	0030 - 0033
0D	IRQ5 - Printer 2	0034 - 0037
0E	IRQ6 - Floppy controller	0038 - 003B
0F	IRQ7 - Printer 1	003C - 003F
10	. . . .	0040 - 0043
	Software Interrupts	
6F	. . . .	01BC - 01BF
70	IRQ 8 - Clock	01C0 - 01C3
71	IRQ 9	01C4 - 01C7
72	IRQ10	01C8 - 01CB
73	IRQ11	01CC - 01CF
74	IRQ12	01D0 - 01D3
75	IRQ13 - Co-processor	01D4 - 01D7
76	IRQ14 - AT hard disk	01D8 - 01DB
77	IRQ15	01DC - 01DF
	. . . .	
	Software Interrupts	
FF	. . . .	03FC - 03FF

FIGURE 2.6
Interrupt vectors, their sources, and the address at which each vector is located. The actual vector stored at each vector address will depend on the application programs in use, the DOS version, and the location of the network software.

plies this vector number by four to form an address that will be near the beginning of main memory. IRQ-2, for example, will result in vector number 0Ah being given to the processor. This will identify a 32-bit segment:offset vector starting at address 0000:0028h in the "interrupt table" (4 × 0Ah = 28h).

The processor then loads its code segment and instruction pointer registers with the four bytes found at this location. The execution of the new code then begins. At completion, the processor returns to the original program that was interrupted by retrieving its address off the stack.

DMA CONTROLLER

The second circuit shown in Figure 2.1 is the Direct Memory Access (DMA) controller. Its purpose is to provide a high-speed data transfer service to move chunks of data between main memory and an I/O location. DMA is frequently used for information transfer to and from floppy disks and, in some cases, for hard disks. It is also used by some network cards to move packets of information between the controller card and main memory. The PC's DMA system was the forerunner of the "Bus Mastering" system introduced in IBM's line of Micro-Channel computers.

During a DMA transfer, the host processor is put on hold; all addresses and Read/Write signals are provided by the DMA controller instead. This controller literally grabs and controls the full bus. A possible advantage of using the DMA system may be improved speed, although 80386 and 80486 processors with higher clock rates and more efficient instructions can usually outdo most DMA chips. A bigger advantage is that the host doesn't really have to stop what it is doing, save information on the stack, switch to a new program, run it, and then return. Instead, the processor is momentarily stopped and when it "wakes up," proceeds with its instructions as if nothing had happened. Meanwhile, a block of data has been moved into or out of main memory (see Figure 2.7).

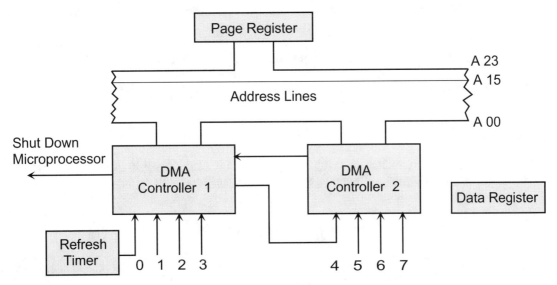

FIGURE 2.7
Direct Memory Access controller.

The DMA system on the older XT had four separate channels, each with a matching request pin. The 286-and-above computers use seven channels. In either case, one channel is dedicated to the dynamic memory refresh system. Every 15 microseconds, channel-0 of the controller halts the microprocessor and uses a few clock cycles to "read" one address in memory. It doesn't use the data for anything, but the act of examining a location causes the voltages across the tiny capacitors that form a memory location to be renewed. If at least 256 consecutive memory locations can be "read" in less than two milliseconds, then all RAM chips will maintain their tiny stored charge and so remember data. The remaining six DMA channels are available to the adapter card installer.

Each channel (except DRQ-0 refresh) can independently move data from a main memory location to a single I/O block location (DMA Read mode) or vice versa (DMA Write mode). In either mode, the channel can be programmed for either one byte (or word) to be transferred per hardware request or a full block of bytes per request (burst mode). When the appropriate request pin is activated, the controller will shut down the host processor and then send out a 16-bit address for main memory. The transfer will then take place between main memory and a no-name I/O location. This location doesn't have an I/O address. Instead, it is selected by logic gates in response to a DMA acknowledge signal. Several other control signals are also involved to ensure that normal I/O locations are not used.

The programmer must supply the appropriate channel with a 16-bit starting address and a byte count value. The mode would then be selected as either Write or Read, and the transfer set to either a single byte or burst for each request. Then, to complete the PC address requirements, an additional four bits would be placed in a separate Page Register by the programmer.

Finally, when the card (floppy or hard disk controller or local area network) is ready, it will make the DMA request by moving the appropriate DRQ pin Hi, and the transfer will begin. That card must be capable of moving bytes to or from the single I/O location.

Chapter 5, on Ethernet, provides a detailed example of a DMA transfer. The procedure will look very involved, but once set up, the operation is totally transparent to the processor and any program it may be running.

NETWORK CARDS

The four areas just mentioned are important to the local area network installer. When a network card is plugged into an expansion slot in a PC, it will require some or all of the following:

- several thousand bytes in main memory
- a few bytes in the I/O block
- one of the interrupt pins
- possible use of the DMA service

Other cards added to the computer will also be competing for these same facilities. Network installers often have problems figuring out what resources the other

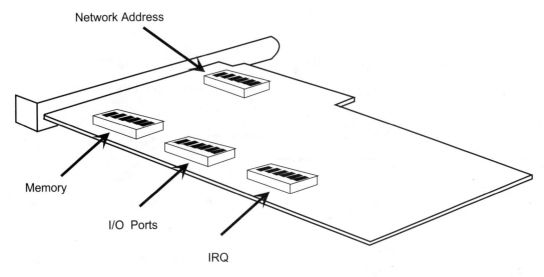

FIGURE 2.8
Selecting configuration options before installing a network card. Although switches are
shown here, the latest method is to set "switches" electronically from the keyboard.

cards are already using and determining what is left for the network card to use.
Most plug-in boards are provided with several choices for each of the above, either
by setting DIP switches or jumper blocks or using software settings (see Figure 2.8).

As an example, a typical ARCnet card might use the following settings:

2K of main memory	D000:0000–07FF
16 bytes of I/O memory	2E0–2EF
Interrupt Request	IRQ-2
DMA	none used

TIMERS

All MS-DOS computers include some sense of time. This is important to networking
software. Time, while a machine is running, is provided by a single integrated circuit
with three separate timers: Timers 0, 1, and 2 (see Figure 2.9). When a computer is
turned off, a separate, battery-powered CMOS clock chip takes over until the power
is turned back on.

- Timer 0 interrupts the computer 18.2 times each second. This is the
  timer "tick" generator that increments a counter in RAM. Programs can
  access this five-byte counter (RAM location 0000:046C) to see how many
  "ticks" have passed since midnight.
- Timer 1 operates the DMA system every 15 microseconds to refresh one
  more memory location.

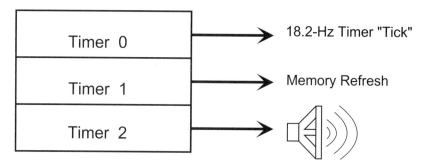

FIGURE 2.9
Three-channel timer used for memory refresh, timer "tick" operation, and the tone for speaker Beeps and Phasers.

- Timer 2 is connected to the speaker and generates the beeps or very essential "Fire Phaser" noise of Novell fame.

THE OPERATING SYSTEM

What is an operating system, and why does a computer need it?

A computer doesn't really need an operating system—at least single-user machines don't. Some early games written for personal computers were totally independent of extra software and included complete machine code to read keyboards, make disks spin, and put words and images on the screen. Their method of holding information on floppy disks was often incompatible with other types of software (this "happened" to make the software slightly more immune to copying).

For normal business software, the developers could have followed the same route—each manufacturer providing stand-alone code. However, hardware variations exist from computer to computer, and this could have required separate versions of software for some machines. In any case, each software developer would have needed to write code for reading disks and keyboards, etc. Program costs would have been higher, and any minor variations in their techniques would have been disastrous. The software would work, but it would have prevented such simple operations as passing a data file from a spreadsheet to a wordprocessor or even organizing application programs on a hard disk.

It is therefore advantageous to create a common set of routines to perform these and many other "low-level" operations. These services have been described in numerous books and are used by software developers most of the time. All programs, therefore, work with a common support system.

Because many of these standard functions have to do with disk operation, it is usually referred to as a "disk operating system" (DOS). This underlying layer of DOS must be loaded into memory before any business software will run because it supplies missing portions of the code. This code stays resident and uses significant portions of memory.

Application programs run "on top of" the DOS layer. Some software descriptions will describe programs as running "under" DOS. They mean the same thing. It all depends on how illustrations such as Figure 2.10 are drawn. I prefer the "on top of" description because it parallels the order in which the seven network layers of the ISO standard are drawn—hardware at the bottom, service software in the middle, application programs on top.

To be more specific, the layer referred to as DOS actually consists of several components. Two of these are loaded from disk into RAM, and the third is permanently in ROM. To be perfectly correct, only the top layer should be called DOS; the two components of the lower layer form the Basic Input Output System (BIOS). The BIOS layers do not understand file names but deal instead with sector, track, and head numbers on the disks. Networks must intercept requests long before they get down to this level.

What role does the COMMAND.COM file play? COMMAND.COM is the program that puts the familiar C:\> prompt on the screen. It is only present when no other application program is running. The Command file simply lets the user do menial tasks such as displaying file names and copying and deleting files. In that sense, it is simply another utility.

FIGURE 2.10
The resident portions of the personal computer's software form several layers between the hardware and the application program.

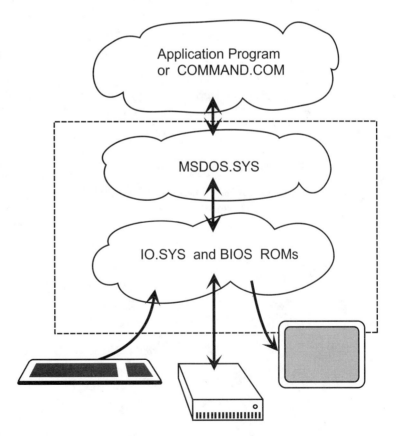

COMMAND.COM is the typical user's perception of DOS. Most are unaware of the other resident portions unless they have been playing with MEMORY commands to see where their memory has gone.

When an application program such as a wordprocessor needs a file, it simply tells the underlying DOS layer, "Please open the file on the A: disk called PAYROLL.ABC." This is very similar to a boss–secretary working relationship. The boss usually has no knowledge of the company's filing system (many employees think that the first six words of this sentence are sufficient) and relies instead on the secretary to retrieve file folders and keep them organized.

Actually, computers don't speak English very well so the request by the application program to the resident DOS layer is done as a software interrupt. Once the file name is established:

```
MOV  AX,3D00h  ; code 3D00 means open a file
INT  21h       ; software interrupt for microprocessor
```

Once opened, a file can then be read from or written to by an application program.

To digress for a moment, using a software interrupt to access DOS is inefficient and slow. This is the only technique with the MS/PC-DOS operating system. However, newer operating systems, such as OS/2 and Windows NT, use CALL instructions to specific memory locations for better performance. In later chapters, we will see a similar technique used for some types of network access. Now back to our DOS discussion.

This separation between the application program code and the DOS function code is the key to most network operations. If a program included all of its own code to spin disks and print characters, it would not be able to use network drives and printers. A program will only cooperate with a network if it requests the help of a DOS function rather than performing the task itself.

DOS Functions

All of the low-level DOS and BIOS operations are accessed by an application program by using software interrupts. Most of what are called the DOS functions use INT 21h. The remaining DOS and all BIOS functions use other interrupts between INT 05 and INT FFh. The DOS INT 21h Functions are accessed by first placing a value in the microprocessor's AH register and then executing INT 21h. For example, to find out what time the computer thinks it is:

```
MOV  AH,2Ch
INT  21h
```

The answer will be returned in the microprocessor's CX and DX registers.

CH = Hour (0–23)

CL = Minute (0–59)

Interrupt	AH Register	Function
INT 17		Print a character
INT 20		Terminate program
INT 21	3C	Create a file
"	3D	Open a file
"	3E	Close a file
"	3F	Read from a file
"	40	Write to a file
"	41	Delete a file
"	42	Move file pointer
"	4B	Load and execute a program
"	5C	Lock/unlock part of a file
INT 27		Terminate but keep in memory
INT 2F		Multiplexer/printer function

FIGURE 2.11
A sample of operating system services that may be of interest to a network.

DH = Second (0–59)

DL = Hundredths of a second (0–99)

A greatly abbreviated list of DOS services provided through software interrupts is shown in Figure 2.11. If you are interested, pick up a copy of any book describing DOS and BIOS function calls.

FILE OPERATIONS

The most common network operation involves moving information to and from disk files. How this is done in a non-network environment is explained here; later chapters will describe how the network performs the operation.

DOS now processes disk files using file "handles." The handles method is necessary if files are to be shared on a network, and all recent software uses it. An older and now obsolete method required the creation of a "file control block." The handles method has been available since DOS 2.0. The ability to share a file and lock small portions of it was added in DOS 3.1.

The smallest element of file storage on the disk is the sector. A sector consists of two parts, one permanent and the other changeable. The permanent part is shorter and consists only of a set of numbers that describe the platter surface, track, and sector. This "permanent" portion is created at the time the disk is low-level formatted and remains unchanged (until reformatted). The second portion is longer and contains 512 bytes of whatever information is being stored on the disk. This portion will be rewritten frequently as changes are made to its contents.

The disk controller card works with these sectors. It uses the permanent portion to locate the desired sector and then either reads the entire sector into a buffer or writes 512 bytes from the buffer back to the disk (see Figure 2.12). Remember that the sector is the smallest element of disk usage. If an application program wants to change even one byte, the full sector is read into a DOS buffer, the change is made, and the full sector is rewritten to the disk. There is a small gap between the permanent and the changeable portion of the sector to accommodate timing variations in subsequent Writes.

At the DOS interface level, this mechanism is completely obscured. Application programs and the upper layers of DOS itself have no idea which sector to use. They only know a file by its name and size. It is the lower BIOS layers that worry about sectors, clusters, and file allocation tables.

File Open

To use a file, a programmer must first ask DOS to "open" the file. This opening causes DOS to find the file and load the first few sectors into a transfer buffer located in main memory (see Figure 2.13).

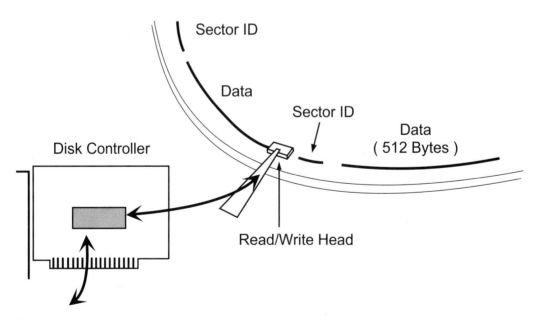

FIGURE 2.12
Disk controller card locates the correct sectors on the disk surface. The sector is read as
a serial bit stream and converted into bytes by the adapter card.

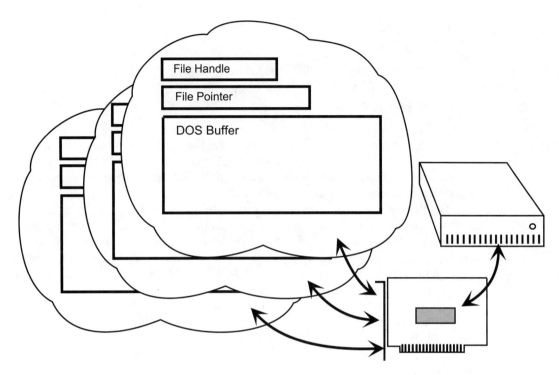

FIGURE 2.13
File transfer from disk using file handles.

To open a file, the programmer first prepares a string of ASCII characters that fully describe the disk drive, subdirectory path, and file name. An example might appear as:

```
"J:\DBASE\DATA\JUNK5.DBF", 00h
```

DOS requires that an extra Zero byte (00h) be added to the end to form a "Zero terminated ASCII string." The DOS command to open the file is:

```
MOV AX,3D00h
MOV DS,segment_address_of_string
MOV DX,offset_address_of_string
INT 21h
```

The code inside the DOS layer will then return a 16-bit "file handle" and initiate a 32-bit file pointer. The handle will be returned to the source program in the AX register. For all future access to that file, only that reference number need be used. File handles 0 to 4 are reserved by DOS for internal devices so the lowest number that will be seen by our program is 5. The reserved handles are:

0	keyboard input	CON:
1	screen output	CON:
2	error output (screen)	
3	auxiliary device	AUX:
4	printer	PRN:

The 32-bit file pointer that results from the file open request keeps track of the number of bytes read by the application program from the file buffers. When the file is first opened, the file pointer sits at Zero, indicating that no bytes have been read into the application program.

With the pointer identifying the next byte to be read or written from/to the buffer, Function 3Fh will read from the file and Function 40h will write to the file. In either case, the number of bytes to be read/written is carried in the CX register (maximum 64K bytes). After the Read or Write, the file pointer is automatically incremented by the CX value. A separate function (AH = 42h) is available to modify the pointer if the need should arise.

The conversion from sectors on the disk to individual bytes is performed in the "DOS buffer" (also known as the "disk transfer area"). This is a section of normal RAM fairly low in memory. The size of this area is set in multiples of 512 bytes by the BUFFERS command in the CONFIG.SYS file when the computer is first turned on.

```
Files=30
Buffers=20
```

The buffer's purpose is to improve the transfer efficiency between the application program and the disk surface. The BIOS code is responsible for moving new sectors between the disk and this buffer area as the application program requests Reads and Writes.

This buffer area will end up being a bit of a problem when file sharing is discussed so keep it in mind.

The following is a sample program that uses DOS functions to open a file and then display its first 256 bytes on the screen:

```
; ----------------------------------------------------------------------
; Read 256 bytes from a file and display on screen.
; ----------------------------------------------------------------------
        CODE    SEGMENT
        ASSUME CS:CODE, DS:CODE, ES:CODE, SS:CODE
        ORG 100h

START:  jmp  begin

fname:  db  "A:TESTFILE.TXT",00h ; disk drive and file name
storage: db  100h dup (00)
```

```
message:   db    "Here are the contents of the file...",0Dh,0Ah
lmess      equ   $-message
begin:     mov   bx,01              ; 01 = handle of display
           mov   cx,lmess           ; number of bytes
           mov   dx,OFFSET message  ; starting address
           mov   ah,40h             ; write to screen
           int   21h
           mov   dx,offset fname    ; point to file name
           mov   ax,3D00h           ; open file for read
           int   21h                ; ax returns file handle
           mov   bx,ax              ; bx = file handle
           mov   cx,100h            ; read 100h bytes
           mov   dx,offset storage  ; point to local buffer
           mov   ah,3Fh             ; read from file
           int   21h
           mov   bx,1               ; 1 = handle of stdio
           mov   cx,100h            ; 256 bytes
           mov   ah,40h             ; display
           int   21h
           mov   ax,4C00h           ; quit
           int   21h
CODE ENDS
END START
```

What changes are required if the file is on a mapped network drive instead of a local drive? Nothing, other than the obvious change to the line specifying the file's location:

```
fname:     db    "J:\JUNK\TESTFILE.TXT",00h
```

The Interrupt 21h request will be intercepted by the NetWare shell (NETx.COM). The shell will recognize the J: drive as a network drive and repackage the request as a network packet. No special network programming is needed, although, as explained in later chapters, many functions certainly are available.

Byte Order

The order in which bytes are held within 16- and 32-bit values creates problems for programmers because there are two conflicting entities: the microprocessor and the network.

In this book, all programs are written for 80x86 processors. This processor naturally holds 16- and 32-bit values with the least significant byte coming first (lowest address) in memory. This is commonly referred to as "Little Endian" order. All compilers and assemblers for 80x86 processors will take a number such as 0x1234 in the source code and flip it into 34h 12h in the executable code. In contrast, assemblers and compilers for the Macintosh 680x0 family of processors do not flip bytes because that processor is inherently "Big Endian" and wants the most significant byte first in its executable code.

Byte order can also present problems in a network. As indicated in the previous chapter, some fields in various network headers want 16-bit values in Hi-Lo order, while other fields must be in Lo-Hi order. Only a careful study of documents will explain which is needed. If Lo-Hi order is required and the programmer is compiling on an Intel type of processor, no further steps are needed. The programmer writes the number in Hi-Lo order in the source code, and the compiler will flip it. However, if another field requires Hi-Lo order, the number either has to be entered in flipped (Lo-Hi) order in the source code (documentation will be difficult to read as a result) or a routine included to do the flipping.

SOFTWARE ON A NETWORK

A supervisor must consider several things when trying to determine if a program will "run on a network." Almost any program can be stored on a server and then downloaded to a workstation, where it is executed. That part is rarely a problem. The next potential problem is with data storage and printing. Local drives and printers generally work correctly. However, if network drives and printers are used, the redirector must be able to intercept these requests and pass them back to the server. The final and biggest problem occurs when two users wish to share the same data file. This will be covered later.

The following pieces of code were taken from a popular spreadsheet program written for single-machine operation. They show five different DOS function requests to do things with disk files. The example is presented here so that we can see why a program written for non-network use can also use data files stored on network drives. The trick, of course, is that somehow the server subdirectories have to be MAPped into a DOS drive letter.

```
mov   ax,3D00h        ; function number 3Dh
mov   dx,si
mov   bx,es
mov   ds,bx           ; ds:dx = address of file name
int   21h             ; open file
mov   [1234h],ax      ; save file handle
......
mov   al,02           ; pointer will be set from EOF
mov   bx,[1234h]      ; file handle
sub   cx,cx
sub   dx,dx           ; cx,dx = 32-bit offset = 00
mov   ah,42h          ; function 42h
int   21h             ; set file pointer
......
mov   cx,00F0h        ; number of bytes to read
mov   bx,[1234h]      ; file handle
lea   dx,[4320h]      ; buffer address
mov   ah,3Fh          ; function 3Fh
int   21h             ; read from file
......
```

```
pop   cx                  ; number of bytes
mov   bx,[1234h]          ; file handle
mov   dx,[4320h]          ; buffer address
mov   ah,40h              ; function 40h
int   21h                 ; write to file
......
mov   bx,[1234h]          ; file handle
mov   ah,3Eh              ; function 3Eh
int   21h                 ; close file
```

Keep these portions of code in mind as we now examine the portion of network software used by Novell on each of the workstations. Part of this software redirects standard INT 21h requests.

Novell's Workstation Software

NetWare adds two files to each workstation (see Figure 2.14). One is the "shell" and is the NET3.COM, NET4.COM, or NET5.COM file that matches the DOS major

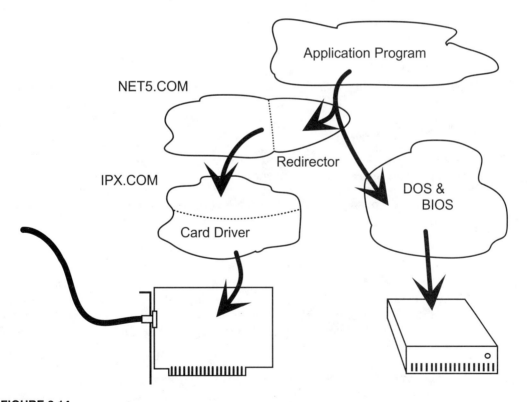

FIGURE 2.14
NetWare on a workstation. It consists of two Novell files running along with the operating system files (DOS).

version used on the individual workstation. This file includes the redirecting operation and modifications to DOS operations to make them suitable for networks.

The other file is IPX.COM. It performs the basic packaging and routable
addressing function for the network. The file includes a driver that matches the specific network card used. The network software contains many copies of the
IPX.COM file, each on a separate floppy and in an incomplete form. The installer
selects the one that matches the network card being used—Ethernet, ARCnet,
etc.—and links it with a common portion of code to make a complete file. Both files
stay resident when loaded.

The shell performs the following functions:

- Resets the interrupt vectors for INT 17h, 20h, and 21h so that application
  program requests to DOS can be processed
- Resets the interrupt vectors for the interrupt controller chip so that
  interrupts from the network card can be processed
- Monitors DOS requests for disk drives and printers and then passes
  selected requests through to the server
- Provides alternate code for processing some of the DOS functions
- Holds a list of network-to-DOS-drive mappings
- Buffers some network information

Here is a portion of the code that is run when the shell is first loaded. It saves the
old INT 21h interrupt vector and then replaces it with a new one. The new vector will
point to code within the shell program. This is only one of several vectors replaced.

```
cli                                    ; disable interrupts
mov   ax,0000
mov   es,ax                            ; Extra Segment = 0000
mov   safe_place,es:[0084h]            ; save old vector offset
mov   safe_place+2,es:[0086h]          ; save old vector segment
mov   es:[0084h],new_offset            ; install new offset
mov   es:[0086h],cs                    ; install new segment
sti                                    ; enable interrupts
......
```

Now think back to the portions of the spreadsheet program. After the vectors
have been altered, the normal DOS code will no longer respond, at least not initially. The shell program has redirected any INT 21h Function requests to new code
within the shell. A portion of this follows. The DOS function number will be in the
AH register as this code begins. (Notice the continuation of the address label
"new_offset".)

```
new_offset:      mov   bl,ah
                 mov   bh,00
                 shl   bx,01                 ; multiply by two
                 jmp   cs:table_locn[bx]     ; jump indexed
                 ......
```

The jump instruction will use one of the many entries in the following table. There is one entry for each of the DOS functions: 00 to 68h. Each entry is a 16-bit offset value within the shell program. The specific one is at an address given by (table_locn +2*ah). If, for example, the application program had requested DOS Function 3Dh, the portion of the shell program at CS:9ABCh would handle the call. The jump would effectively become JMP NEAR 9ABCh.

```
table_locn:     dw     1234h     ; Function 00 - terminate process
                dw     2345h     ;            01 - character input
                dw     3456h     ;            02 - character output
                dw     4567h     ;            03 - auxiliary input
                dw     5678h     ;            04 - auxiliary output
                dw     6789h     ;            05 - printer output
                ....
                ....
                dw     9ABCh     ;            3D - open file
                dw     9BCDh     ;            3E - close file
                dw     9CDEh     ;            3F - read from file
                ....
                dw     0BCDEh    ;            68 - commit file
```

The next portion of the code that responds to the file open request must parse (cut into pieces) the null terminated ASCII string that gives the full path and file name, i.e.,

```
H:\WORDPRO\HERMAN\JUNK3.ABC
```

The code is looking for the drive name. If it is a local drive (H: likely won't be), the shell simply passes the request on to the normal DOS code. The shell saved the address of the normal DOS code in a location we called "safe_place". If, instead, the request is for a network drive, the shell builds a packet that says, "User Herman wishes to open a file called WORDPRO\HERMAN\JUNK.ABC; can he?" The actual request doesn't look like this. Instead it is sent as a NetWare Core Protocol (NCP) message that is only a few bytes long. More of this packet will be discussed in Chapter 10.

The server may accept or reject the request depending on the user and directory rights. In either case, an appropriate reply will be sent back to the workstation shell—again, via NCP. The shell, in turn, would pass this response back to the user program.

DATA PACKETS

On all media-sharing networks, there is an upper limit to the amount of data that can be handled in one packet. Ethernet, for example, has an upper limit of 1500 bytes. What happens if the application program asks for something larger? Using DOS Function 3Fh, the application could ask for as much as 64K bytes—one Intel segment.

The difference is handled by the code within the shell program. NetWare is set to handle packets of 512 data bytes. If the application program has requested 10K bytes from the server, the shell will break this down into many requests of 512 bytes each. As these are received from the server, the shell will piece them back together in buffers. This means that the server and shell also need to communicate about the piece numbers and to confirm that all parts have been received and in sequence. This is handled inside the shell, working in cooperation with the "unreliable" IPX transportation system.

The shell won't return control to the requesting program until the correct number of bytes have been received. The application program, therefore, has no idea that the data came in smaller packets. It simply reads its requested bytes from a buffer.

The lower file IPX.COM has no knowledge of what is happening up in the shell. It simply looks after the packaging of whatever it is given.

FILE SHARING

How can two or more users share one file? A few years ago this was a real problem, and different network vendors all had their own solutions. DOS 3.1 added file-sharing and locking functions so that now the operation has been standardized. But please remember, not all applications were written for multiusers. The majority of wordprocessors and spreadsheets are sold so that, for each legal copy, one user can work on one project. If two users, either by making an illegal copy of the application program or by purchasing another copy, try to work on the same data file, a disaster could happen. The first person to save his or her work may have it overwritten when the second person later saves the file with the same name.

Having provided this warning, how do two users share one file? There are several mechanisms, one of which is part of DOS. If the application program was designed for it, the program will likely use DOS Function 3Dh (INT 21h with AH = 3Dh). For non-shared applications, the eight bits in the AL register are usually left as Zeros. For shared data files, these eight bits determine the "sharing mode." Three of these indicate, to whoever happens to get to the file first, what type of access he or she wishes—Read Only, Write Only, or Read and Write. Three other bits indicate what privileges the first user to open the file is going to allow others as they request subsequent opens (see Figure 2.15). Most newer wordprocessors use the "sharing mode" and lock the file after the first open. Other users can still read the file but cannot save it under its original name. This is one reason why software will be marked as "Requires DOS 3.1" on the box.

Other file-sharing mechanisms interact directly with NetWare, but these methods, while excellent, only work on NetWare LANs.

At this point some readers may be thinking that they are immediately going to modify several bytes in their favorite spreadsheet or database program and have a multiuser version. Unfortunately, it doesn't work that easily. If the sharing mode allows subsequent users to open the file for Writes, their Writes will destroy previous users' or vice versa.

RECORD LOCKING

There is a more exotic sharing possibility. Total locking of a file is acceptable for wordprocessing and spreadsheets, but not with a database. A database can be very large and may have many separate operators entering, modifying, or erasing data.

FIGURE 2.15
File sharing using DOS Function 3Dh. When INT 21h is executed, AH = 3Dh and the AL register will have a bit pattern selected from this diagram.

AL = | 0 | N | N | N | 0 | F | F | F |

First Open   0 0 0   Read only from file
(FFF)   0 0 1   Write only to file
               0 1 0   Read and write

Next Open   0 0 0   Old DOS compatibility
(NNN)   0 0 1   Deny any further opens
               0 1 0   Allow reads only
               0 1 1   Allow writes only
               1 0 0   Allow reads and/or writes

Fortunately, they tend to work on individual "records," and there is little interaction from one record to the next. Sharing between multiple users is possible only if the records of interest are locked by an individual.

A multiuser application program will attempt to lock the bytes using DOS INT 21h, Function 5Ch (only available since DOS 3.1). Most databases designed for multiusers will perform record locks—in some cases automatically.

WHERE IS THE BUFFER?

Now we have to backtrack a bit. Earlier in this chapter, we described the movement of data from a disk into an application program's data area. When DOS "opens" a file, it must read one full sector from a disk at a minimum. This goes into a DOS buffer area, and the application program's requests are filled from that buffer. In normal single-user programming, this isn't a problem. However, with multiple users operating on the same data file, it is. If any two users on the network are buffering overlapping portions of the same file, even though they are only using a few bytes, it will be impossible to keep a properly updated copy. Therefore, all good network operating systems will keep an eye out for this DOS function. Files opened with Function 3Dh that allow additional opens will be buffered only at the server. The individual users will be sent only the number of bytes they have requested and then that range of bytes will be marked as "locked." Function 3Dh requests that deny any further opens can safely be buffered at the workstation.

HARD DISKS

A frequent standard of comparison for network throughput is the stand-alone computer's hard disk. This will also be of interest because the network hard disk suffers the same limitations.

We will assume that the sector interleave is always set to 1:1. Seek times for locating the sectors are not included. Therefore, these are maximum figures and assume the host has plenty of horsepower to keep ahead of the drive.

MFM coding, 17 sectors per track, 512 data bytes per sector, 1:1 interleave, 3600 rpm

$$512 \div 17 \div 3600 \div \frac{1}{60} = 522 \text{ kilobytes/sec}$$

The same disk using Run Length Limited (RLL) coding will have 25 sectors per track. This will raise the data rate to 768 kilobytes/sec.

As discussed in Chapter 1, some typical real-life through-the-cable figures using NetWare, a medium network load, and various cards are:

10 megabits/sec Ethernet	400–525 kilobytes/sec
4 megabits/sec Token Ring	150–250 kilobytes/sec
2.5 megabits/sec ARCnet	100–225 kilobytes/sec

SUMMARY

In this chapter, we have examined the personal computer and found that:

- Four internal areas may have to be accessed by network cards—main memory, I/O memory, interrupt request pins, and DMA request pins.
- Interrupt system responds to hardware and software interrupts in the same way by using an interrupt number to select a starting address for new code (a vector) out of the interrupt table.
- Most application software programs don't include code for directly controlling keyboards, disks, etc. Instead, they rely on routines supplied by the memory resident portion of DOS and BIOS.
- The interface to these routines is through the microprocessor's interrupt table, held in main memory RAM.
- These DOS requests can be intercepted simply by changing four bytes at the appropriate location in the interrupt table.
- Application programs designed for shared access to data files must include extra code to lock either the total file or small portions of it.

Chapter 3

Cables, Wires, and Fibers

Cabling is a vital part of any network. It affects overall reliability and throughput and plays a very important role in securing a network against snooping. However, it definitely adds to a network's total cost, especially when installation rates are included.

In this chapter, we are going to get a little technical. We will examine the waveforms carried on these cables and how the properties of a cable can affect transmission. Learning these details will enable the purchaser or installer to be more informed and, ultimately, to create a better network.

WAVEFORMS AND CLOCKING

When a stream of bits moves from the network cable into the receiver portion of a network card, some sort of timing signal must be present. The card obviously must be able to distinguish a 0 from a 1, but it must also be able to separate a 1 from a following 1, and so on. It just isn't good enough to know that data is coming in at, say, one million bits per second (**BPS**)—there must also be some way to define bit position.

All LAN transmissions carry timing signals with them. These are part of the data encoding method used by each network card. Figures 3.1 and 3.2 show some generic ways in which a clock reference can be included.

The initial stream of data moving around inside a computer looks like the Non-Return-to-Zero (NRZ) waveform. It doesn't carry its clock with it. This is acceptable because the timing signal can be carried reliably on separate wires for the short distances on the main circuit board.

The remaining four waveforms all include clock signals. They use up a wider range of frequencies, but on a dedicated LAN cable, this isn't a big problem. In fact, there is a benefit to this bandwidth change. If we look at Figure 3.3 carefully, we see that the basic NRZ waveform has strong components at very low frequencies. None of the others do. The resulting upward shift in the frequency components avoids a common cable problem where lower frequencies travel slower than higher frequencies. On a long cable, waveshapes would distort as a result. This delay characteristic of cables will be described later in this chapter.

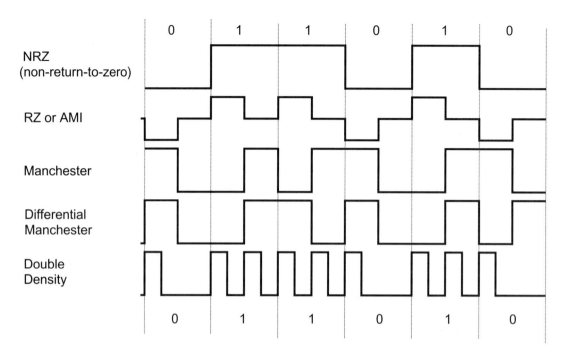

FIGURE 3.1
Four commonly used data waveforms. With the exception of NRZ, all are self clocking.

How do these waveforms apply to real network products? Manchester encoding is used by Ethernet. Something like RZ is used by ARCnet, and Differential Manchester is used by IBM's Token Ring.

Next we will see how the clock and data are separated in a receiver.

Phase Locked Loops

Buried in the integrated circuits of all popular network boards is a Phase Locked Loop (PLL) circuit (see Figure 3.4). Its purpose is to keep an oscillator, or clock circuit, running at the exact frequency of the bit-rate on the cable. This reference signal defines the time location of each received bit.

The PLL oscillator must "lock" onto the exact frequency and phase of the incoming data. Simply picking an average is not good enough because a short noise "hit" could make the average meaningless. The PLL must select and hold the exact frequency used during the good parts. It must ignore any noisy parts. The design can be difficult—as some 16 megabytes/sec Token Ring designers discovered. The three components of any PLL are described as follows.

Phase Comparator

The key component of the PLL circuit is a Phase Comparator. It has two input and one output terminals. Using the two inputs, it compares the difference between what

FIGURE 3.2
Each waveform has its own format for carrying the 0 and 1 data bits. Only an NRZ waveform matches 0, 1 with Lo, Hi.

TYPE	ENCODING	SELF CLOCKING
NRZ		No
	0 = Lo Voltage	
	1 = Hi Voltage	
RZ or AMI		Yes
	0 = Negative Pulse	
	1 = Positive Pulse	
Manchester		Yes
	At center of time slot....	
	0 = Change to Lo	
	1 = Change to Hi	
Differential Manchester		Yes
	At start of time slot....	
	0 = Change from previous	
	1 = No change from previous	

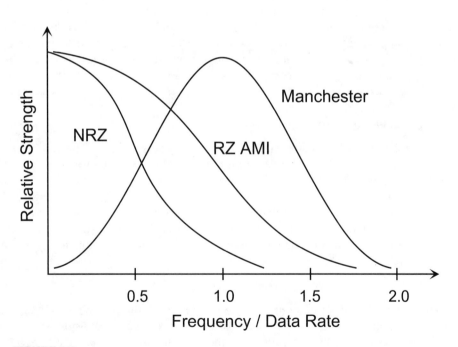

FIGURE 3.3
Frequency spectra of various data encoding techniques when they are carrying random data.

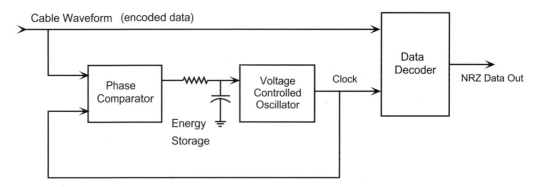

FIGURE 3.4
Phase Locked Loop (PLL) used to synchronize an oscillator to the incoming encoded data.

a local oscillator/clock is doing and what the incoming signal is doing. It changes an output control voltage in step with the input difference. When the two inputs are exactly in step, the output will hold some constant voltage. This voltage is used, in turn, to adjust the oscillator frequency.

PLL Oscillator Circuit

The PLL oscillator circuit is unlike other clock circuits in that a **dc** control voltage at its input can gently nudge its frequency up or down. This type of oscillator is often referred to as a Voltage Controlled Oscillator (VCO). It is designed to oscillate at approximately the correct frequency needed for the specific network, e.g., 10 MHz for Ethernet. The control voltage from the phase comparator then moves this to the exact frequency. If phase corrections are necessary, the frequency is temporarily increased or decreased, until the phases match, and then returned to the exact frequency.

Low-Pass Filter

The third PLL component is an energy storage circuit. This might also be called a time constant or Low-Pass Filter circuit. It is placed between the phase comparator and the oscillator. The circuit typically consists of one or two resistors and the actual energy storage component, which is a capacitor. The storage feature allows incoming data waveforms to skip timing signals every once in a while and still keep the local clock synchronized. We will see in the chapter on IBM's Token Ring that some of these "missing" time references are intentional and explain why they are used.

Noise

If a significant amount of noise contaminates the incoming data signal, errors may occur. There are two reasons for this. (1) The Hi/Lo decision will be more difficult because amplitudes are fluctuating. (2) The timing decision, controlled by the PLL, becomes more difficult because the reference edges in the signal will be moving (jittering) back and forth in time.

Most noise problems can be traced back to cable problems. The cables may be the wrong type, poorly installed, excessively long, badly placed, or have corroding connectors. Cable problems can affect network throughput because the network handles errors by attempting a retransmission, which adds time.

WIRING

All electrical wiring obeys a common set of rules—transmission line theory. Unfortunately, this theory carries some fairly heavy mathematics with it. Therefore, designers look for calculation shortcuts and "rules-of-thumb" whenever possible.

Not all wiring situations need to be treated as transmission lines. It all depends on the length of the wires relative to the frequencies being carried and the importance of what is being carried. Following are some examples:

1. Local power lines may be long, but they carry very low frequencies—50 or 60 Hz. The exact voltages and waveshapes aren't of any great concern, and gaps of even a fraction of a second are often tolerated. These lines are rarely installed with any great concern for transmission line theory (power line runs of several hundred miles are a different story).
2. Television cables are also long but carry very high frequencies. The information content is of great importance (debatable with some TV shows); therefore, TV cable installers are very careful to treat their cables as transmission lines.
3. Stereo speaker cables are of medium importance. Some acoustical aficionados claim to hear a difference when proper "transmission line" cabling is purchased. Most hear only the tinkle of wasted dollars. Large-diameter, low-**resistance** wire is all that is important here.

LAN lines must always be considered as transmission lines and carefully installed. These lines carry reasonably high frequencies (several MHz), are relatively long, and transmit very important information. Fortunately we can avoid the math calculations, but we must follow some rules when working with LANs.

Wires and High Frequencies

Four electrical phenomena are associated with signals moving down a pair of wires—energy losses, magnetic fields, electric fields, and transmission time. These apply to all cable types: short, long, twisted pair, shielded, unshielded, and coaxial cable.

Energy Losses

Energy is lost as a signal moves along any cable. There are three causes.

1. *Heating.* This most serious loss occurs when **current** flows through any resistance. This may be referred to as an I^2R loss because of the formula used to calculate power loss (Power = Current^2 × Resistance). Even the

best quality copper wire has some resistance, which creates losses. The longer the cables, the greater the loss. The heating itself is very minor. Of most concern to the network installer is the decrease in signal strength and the relative increases in noise level.

2. *Radiation.* The signal just takes off into thin air just like a wave from a radio antenna. This happens because the cable wave really is a radio wave and an antenna is simply a piece of wire sticking into free space. The amount of energy lost to radiation is usually fairly minor, but it can represent another problem. These signals can be picked up from a distance, creating a potential security leak because someone could monitor your network traffic. Similarly, if your signal can get out, other signals, such as noise from heavy electrical motors, can get in. This will interfere with your own packets and may generate network errors.

3. *Insulation.* Lower quality (and cheaper) insulation surrounding the copper slowly loses its insulation ability as frequencies climb. This loss of insulation between the two wires causes a very slight short circuit. Since insulation also deteriorates from weathering and exposure to moisture, cables must be protected from adverse elements.

Magnetic Fields

Our second phenomenon is that current traveling along any wire creates a magnetic field around that wire (see Figure 3.5). This property gives the wire an **inductance** along its length. There is nothing wrong with inductance and magnetic fields; in fact, they are absolutely necessary. However, the field extends some distance and may overlap other wires or objects that are nearby. Through magnetic coupling, signals can be transferred, which leads to crosstalk and noise. Shielding and twisting helps to reduce this coupling.

Electric Fields

The third phenomenon is that a voltage between two wires will create an electric field around the wires. This field also stores energy and may overlap other wires and nearby objects. This property creates a **capacitance** between wire pairs. As with magnetic fields, there is nothing wrong with electric fields and capacitance. However, they do represent a second mechanism to couple signal energy between two cables. Again, shielding and twisting helps.

Transmission Time

The fourth cabling phenomenon is that any signal traveling along a wire pair will take a very definite amount of time to travel the full length. The longer the wires, the greater the traveling time.

This time element ends up complicating the discussion of electric and magnetic fields and their associated capacitance and inductance components. It also means that transmission line calculations aren't handled like any other circuit. This leads to "transmission line" formulas, but we aren't going to get involved with them.

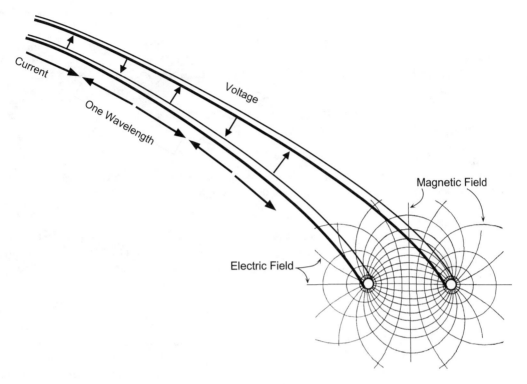

FIGURE 3.5
Electric and magnetic fields surrounding a pair of wires.

The traveling time prevents us from lumping all of the inductance of the entire cable into one equivalent component. The same is true for the capacitance and the resistance. Instead, the time element forces us to consider the components in smaller "unit" sections. The length of a unit isn't too important as long as it is considerably less than one wavelength because there will be little time difference over the unit distance. We are less concerned with actual values of inductance and capacitance within the unit length than with their ratio. This ratio will not be length dependent (see Figure 3.6).

Length

For short-length wiring, the first three phenomena are all we have to worry about. We aren't into the unique transmission line part yet. When needed, technicians and engineers can use relatively simple formulas to see how much signal will come out the other end of a pair of short wires.

Length, however, is relative. It depends on the highest frequency being carried on the cable. The important distinction in separating long wires from short is wavelength.

$$\text{Wavelength (meters)} = \frac{300}{\text{Frequency (MHz)}}$$

Equivalent circuit for a small
fraction of a wavelength

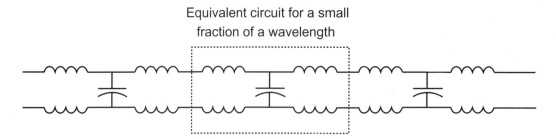

FIGURE 3.6
Distributed equivalent circuit of a transmission line. The segments must be chosen so
their length is much shorter than an electrical cycle or wavelength.

As an example, the wavelength at 10 MHz would be 30 meters (98 feet). When
wires are longer than about 5% of a wavelength, they should be handled as transmission lines. Beyond this point, transmission time becomes significant.

ELECTRO-MAGNETIC FIELD

On examining Figure 3.5, we notice that the electric and magnetic fields always cross
at right angles. This crossing creates a very special phenomenon called an Electro-
Magnetic (E/M) field. Radio waves and light waves are both electro-magnetic waves
but with different frequencies. The E/M field is a flow of energy that can either stay
with the wires or leave them and travel through free space. The field will stay within
the cable as long as it is either fully shielded or undisturbed by sharp bends or
nearby metallic objects.

It is interesting to make an analogy with water flowing in pipes. Wires, as we
have been describing them, have to occur in pairs. All of the electrons going down
the one wire must come back the other. This might make it appear that nothing is
left to "squirt" out the end. However, neither current nor voltage, by themselves,
represent a flow of energy. The voltage between the wires and the current through
the wires create the electro-magnetic field. It is this field that travels down the cable
and carries the energy the same as water travels down a hose, in one direction only.
The E/M field can squirt out the end.

If we look again at Figure 3.5, we will notice that the electric field and the magnetic field switch direction at the same points. This is important. If one switched and
the other didn't, the energy carried by the electro-magnetic field would reverse.
However, since they both switch at the same time they continue to support the field
going in a constant direction. Hence, water can flow down pipes, and electro-magnetic energy can flow down wire pairs.

Insulation

The strongest part of the electro-magnetic field is concentrated between the two
conductors. In most commercial cables, this area is full of insulation. Thus, many of

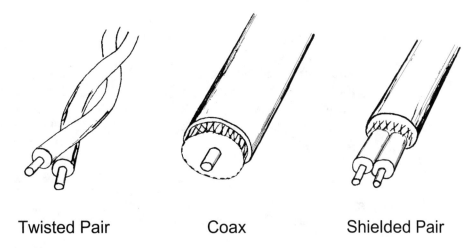

Twisted Pair   Coax   Shielded Pair

FIGURE 3.7
End views of three typical transmission lines showing different types of insulation
between and around the conductors.

the characteristics of a cable depend on the type of insulation between the wires (see
Figure 3.7). This will be apparent to users of hand-held network cable fault testers,
devices that measure the distance to a break or pinch. A cable type has to be entered
before accurate measurements can be made.

The most important property of insulation is its dielectric constant (k). This is a
dimensionless (no units) value that compares the dielectric properties of the material with that of free (empty) space. This number describes how hard it is to set up an
electric field inside the material. A value of 2, for example, means that for a given
voltage between two wires, the electric field will only be half as strong in that material as it would have been in free space. In other words, it is twice as hard to set up a
particular electric field in that insulation as it is in free space. Dielectric constant
affects only the electric field, not the magnetic field.

Velocity

The velocity of the electro-magnetic signal in all cables is also dependent on this
insulation and will have a corresponding effect on the signal wavelength. The exact
speed depends on a few other items including wire resistance, but dielectric constant
is the dominant factor. The larger the value of k, the slower the signal travels. The
relation between velocity and dielectric constant is:

$$\text{Velocity} = \frac{300 \times 10^6}{\sqrt{k}} \text{ (meters/sec)}$$

where k is the dielectric constant of the insulation (k is simply a ratio and has no units).

Some typical constants and resulting cable velocities are given in Figure 3.8.
Notice that the value of k for free space is 1.000 and the resulting speed is that of

MATERIAL	DIELECTRIC CONSTANT(k)	VELOCITY(m/s)
vacuum	1.0000	300.0×10^6
air	1.0006	299.9×10^6
Teflon	2.1	207.0×10^6
polyethylene	2.4	194.0×10^6
polystyrene	2.5	190.0×10^6
PVC	3.3	165.0×10^6
nylon	4.9	136.0×10^6

FIGURE 3.8
Dielectric constants and velocity of electro-magnetic waves for typical insulating materials.

light. All "real cables" have signal velocities somewhat below the speed of light with 60–75% being a common range.

Why do we care about velocity? It certainly doesn't affect the waiting time for information to be loaded from a server. After all, 1000 meters of polyethylene cable, for example, would add a delay of only about five microseconds to any packet—not enough even to be noticed, even after 1000 packets. The network timing and the maximum size of the network, however, are affected, as we shall see.

Losses on Long Wires

What causes a signal to become weaker as it travels down long wires? We already know that current flowing through any resistance creates a heating loss. Now we will add a complication.

At very, very low frequencies, charge carriers (electrons) will spread themselves evenly over the cross-section of a wire. Magnetic fields will be stronger near the center of the wire, but that doesn't bother electrons flowing in one steady direction. However, as frequency increases, these carriers will be changing their direction more frequently. By moving away from the center of the wire, they can move more easily, but less of the wire is available for conduction. The wire's effective resistance will increase as a result. This phenomenon is called the "skin effect" (see Figure 3.9).

The resulting change of a wire's resistance with frequency for several gauges (diameters) is shown in Figure 3.10. At low frequencies, the curve is flat at the direct current (dc) resistance value. At higher frequencies, the resistance climbs in proportion to the square root of the frequency. Larger diameter wire still has the lower resistance, but the change also starts earlier.

How do these losses affect the velocity of waves traveling on a cable? Figure 3.11 shows how velocity changes over a wide range of frequencies for a typical coaxial cable. It shows that cable velocity is somewhat slower and changeable at low frequencies and rises to a more consistent value at higher frequencies. This higher value will match that listed in Figure 3.8.

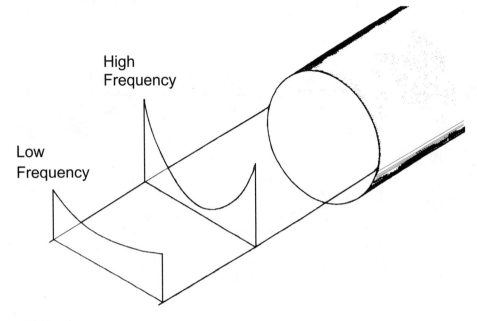

FIGURE 3.9
High-frequency skin effect causes charge carriers to move closer to the edge of wires.
The effective thickness of this layer is the skin depth.

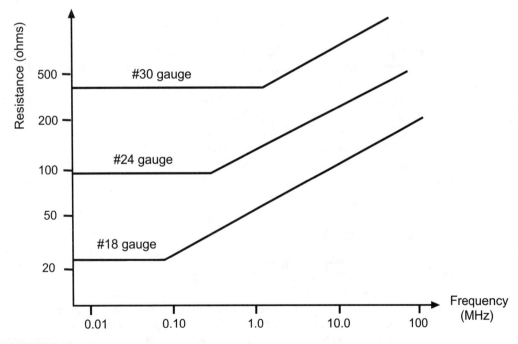

FIGURE 3.10
Resistance variation with frequency for a range of wire gauges.

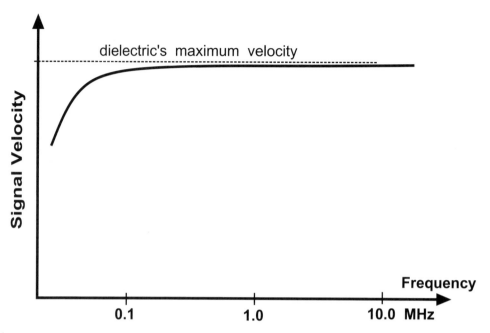

FIGURE 3.11
Variations in signal velocity on thin coaxial cable.

The reason for the changing value at the lower frequencies is somewhat complex, but it involves the relative rates at which resistance and inductive and capacitive **reactance** change with frequency. At lower frequencies, the wire resistance dominates. At higher frequencies, the wire inductance dominates. The calculations, although not too horrible, won't be shown here.

This variation in velocity can have a serious consequence. Network signals span a wide range of frequencies. If part of the range falls on the lower part of the curve, that part will travel more slowly down the cable. At the far end of the cable, the waveform will be distorted, and errors will likely occur.

To avoid the problem, all modern network designs have moved their range of frequencies high enough to avoid the low-frequency portion. This is a side benefit of the Manchester and other forms of clock encoding.

Characteristic Impedance

Characteristic impedance is an electrical property of every pair of wires. It is based completely on the cable's physical characteristics (diameters, spacing, and insulation) and has nothing to do with what is connected at either end.

The word "impedance" may suggest something to do with difficulty of movement. In this instance, it means nothing of the sort. A good analogy for characteristic impedance would be to liken it to the customs and languages of different countries in the world. No country's language or customs are any better than any others; they are simply different. Being disrespectful of a country's customs can land you in trouble, and ignoring a cable's characteristic impedance can result in the same thing.

Characteristic impedance is measured in ohms, but it has nothing to do with energy losses—it just happens to work out to the same units. Impedance is simply the ratio of the voltages and currents on the line. With 50 ohm Ethernet cable, for example, a current of 10 mA at some point on the cable would automatically result in a voltage between the wires at the same point of 0.5 volts. On a 75 ohm cable carrying the same energy (an arbitrary five milliwatts), the current would drop to 8.2 mA, and the voltage would increase to 0.61 volts.

In technical descriptions of cables, the characteristic impedance is given the symbol Z_0.

Here is a fictional demonstration that a cable possesses its own impedance. You may have used, or seen others use, a multimeter that can measure the dc resistance of light bulbs, fuses, and other electrical things. If you touch this meter to one end of a very long pair of wires, it will read the characteristic impedance but just for a brief moment. With a pair of wires, open at the far end, logic says that no current will flow because the wires aren't touching each other. However, current actually will flow for a very short time, just long enough for energy to travel to the far end and return, and then it stops. The initial burst of energy has been used to "charge" the line.

The current that flows during this short interval will depend completely on the cable characteristics. Cable energy travels at a limited speed (albeit very fast) and cannot see the open circuit that lies ahead.

The only fictional part of what we have just described is that neither your eye nor a meter pointer would be able to react fast enough to read what is happening. An ordinary analog or digital multimeter just doesn't work. However, it is possible to build reasonably simple circuits to perform a "pulse" measurement of impedance, and this feature is often built into handheld cable testers.

Now that we know what characteristic impedance is, what determines it? We already know that it depends on the physical properties of the cable—wire diameters and spacing. The dielectric constant of the insulation also plays an important role. Two calculations are shown in Figure 3.12. One is suitable for unshielded twisted pair and the other for coaxial cable.

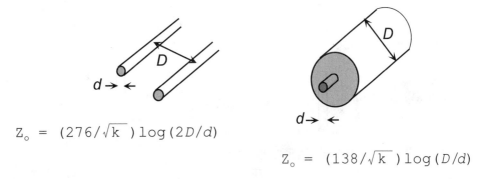

$$Z_0 = (276/\sqrt{k})\log(2D/d)$$

$$Z_0 = (138/\sqrt{k})\log(D/d)$$

FIGURE 3.12

Characteristic impedance of parallel-wire and coaxial lines can be calculated when the physical dimensions and dielectric constant (*k*) are known.

COAXIAL CABLES

Figure 3.13 compiles some of the characteristics of the more common coaxial cables used with local area networks. The RG numbering system refers to cable types that have been approved for use by the US Department of Defense. Most manufacturers use these numbers as generic names and supply numerous variations with their own specific product numbers.

For ARCnet and IBM 3270 terminals, a relatively high (for coaxial) cable impedance of 93 ohms is used. This could have been obtained through the use of a thin center conductor. However, this would be undesirable since the resistive/heating losses would be higher and the cable more fragile. Another solution is to lower the dielectric constant of the insulation, but most solid plastics offer little variation. Open air could be used but it isn't very good at providing mechanical support for the center conductor.

The compromise is shown in Figure 3.14. This is RG-62A/U cable. The combination of a solid outer ring of insulation and an inner spiral plastic strip provides good mechanical positioning and strength while reducing the average amount of polyethylene and increasing the air content. The average dielectric constant is now reduced, and the signal velocity increases to 84% of the speed of light. This, as we shall see, has an important effect on the maximum size of an ARCnet network.

REFERENCE NUMBER	IMPEDANCE (ohms)	OUTER DIAMETER	10 MHz LOSS*	CABLE** VELOCITY
RG-8A/U Solid Polyethylene	52	10.3 mm	1.87 dB	66%
RG-8/U Cellular Polyethylene	50	10.3 mm	1.10 dB	78%
RG-58A/U Solid Polyethylene	50	4.95 mm	4.95 dB	66%
RG-59B/U Solid Polyethylene	75	6.15 mm	3.30 dB	66%
RG-62A/U Polyethylene/Air	93	6.15 mm	2.33 dB	84%

* Loss per 100 ft at 10 MHz.
** Velocity relative to speed of light.

FIGURE 3.13
Popular coaxial cables.

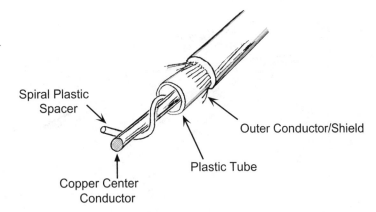

FIGURE 3.14
RG-62A/U coaxial cable uses a combination of air and polyethylene to obtain a relatively high characteristic impedance and high signal velocity.

Spiral Plastic Spacer

Outer Conductor/Shield

Plastic Tube

Copper Center Conductor

Losses and Bandwidth

When standard cables are used, the manufacturer will often have charts available that describe the cable losses for different lengths and different frequencies. A typical example is shown in Figure 3.15. For coaxial cables such as those included in the graph, a small portion of the loss may be due to signal leakage out through the shield. Another small portion will be due to losses in the dielectric insulating material. But the main loss comes from the skin-effect resistance of the relatively thin center conductor. The outer conductor has much more surface area, and its resistive losses will be negligible in comparison.

The center conductor losses can be reduced by increasing the diameter of the wire. However, this would cause a change in the characteristic impedance of the cable unless the outer conductor diameter were increased proportionately. Therefore, for the same impedance, thicker cable generally loses less signal than thinner cable. For the same outer diameter, high impedance cable has less loss than low impedance cable. Even though the center wire is thinner, its series resistance doesn't increase as much as the load resistance. Using the same diameter inner wire, a coaxial cable will have less loss than a twisted pair cable.

You might notice that the loss increases with the square root of the frequency. This is exactly the same rate that the resistance of the center conductor increases due to skin effect. In other words, this really is the dominant loss.

Network adapter cards are designed to handle these losses. They are allocated a "loss budget." They can also handle the increasing loss (loss tilt) at higher frequencies by including internal frequency compensation. These compensations assume that the correct cables and lengths are used. It is always best to follow the manufacturer's recommendations.

TERMINATIONS AND REFLECTIONS

We have described how voltages and currents support an electro-magnetic field which moves along a two-conductor cable. The field is normally a one-way device

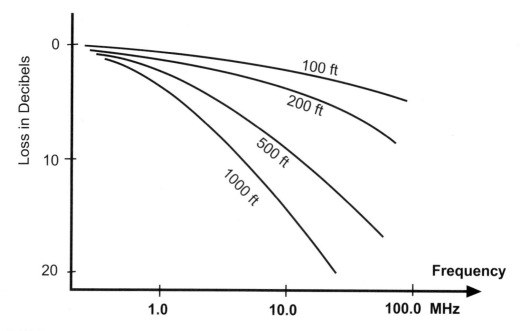

FIGURE 3.15
Overall signal loss for a thin coaxial cable depends on frequency and length.

carrying energy from the input to the output. However, when the energy reaches the cable end, there could be a problem.

Energy moving down the cable only knows what is happening in its immediate area—it cannot see ahead. Its voltages and currents will have the same ratio as the characteristic impedance. However, when the signal reaches the end of the line where the load is connected, it might see a sudden shift in its environment. If the load resistance happens to be exactly the same as the characteristic impedance, the signal moves into the load, and the energy is completely used up. However, if the load doesn't exactly match, some of the signal must turn back toward the source. The amount that turns back depends on how badly the characteristic impedance and load are "mismatched" (see Figure 3.16).

The reflected voltage may also undergo an immediate polarity shift just as it changes direction. If the load resistance is lower than the cable impedance, a complete inversion (180° phase shift) occurs. If the load is higher, no shift occurs.

The reflected pulse from any mismatch heads back toward the source. At that point, if the source is properly matched to the cable, the energy will be absorbed. For the low energies used on LANs, no damage will be done by this returning energy. If the source resistance doesn't match, there will be a second reflection, and a weak "echo" will head back toward the load. It will, in turn, create a reflection of its own. Because of losses on the line, the strength of this continually bouncing echo will grow weaker and weaker.

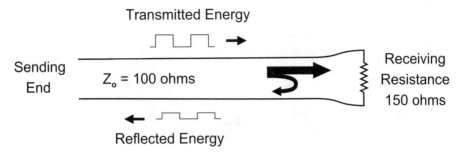

FIGURE 3.16
Pulses traveling along a transmission line and reflecting off a mismatched load.

Loss of energy isn't the only problem with mismatches. Of greater importance are the echoes bouncing back and forth. Because they arrive at unpredictable times, they distort the good waveform and can cause errors. A good analogy is trying to listen to a voice announcement over loudspeakers in a very large factory or warehouse. The multiple echoes make it almost impossible to distinguish the words.

A final point concerning mismatches. They don't always happen at the cable ends. With older telephone wiring, it is not unusual to find a second pair of wires spliced halfway along an existing pair. At the junction, the impedance drops to one-half and will cause line reflections if used for LANs. Trying to track down problems when using existing wiring could cost as much in time and money as if new wire were used. Reflections can also be caused by anything that disturbs the fields that surround the cable—staples, sharp bends, bulky splices, etc.

PULSE TESTING

Pulses can be used for testing transmission lines. Watching the input voltage waveform of a line as a series of very narrow, low repetition-rate pulses are sent in will help locate any breaks or abrupt impedance changes. Faults will cause signal reflections back to the input. The relative size of the reflections will represent the severity of the problem. The polarity will distinguish between shorts and opens.

The time delay between the main pulse going into the line and any echo coming back will represent the round-trip distance to the fault. Once the cable velocity, which depends on insulation type, is known, this time delay can be translated into exact distances.

A commercial instrument manufactured for this purpose is known generically as a "time delay reflectometer" (see Figure 3.17). A full test requires a video display (oscilloscope or LCD panel). A simpler test instrument uses a numeric readout to display only distance values.

If a fast oscilloscope (bandwidth > 100 MHz) is available, reasonable reflection measurements can be made. Any source of narrow pulses with a fast rise time can be used as long as the output impedance matches that of the cable. Generating narrow

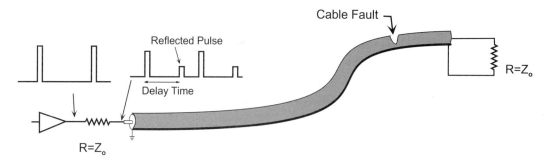

FIGURE 3.17
Time domain reflectometer.

pulses is not too difficult using logic gates. It is best to disconnect adapter cards before testing although many commercial units don't require this.

RADIATION AND PICKUP

All transmission lines radiate a small portion of their signal out to the outside world and pick up some noise from it. Some transmission lines are better than others. Although the FCC has limits on how much stray signal can be radiated, a more serious problem could result from radiation. If your network carries sensitive documents or drawings, a security problem could be posed if an unscrupulous individual picks up this radiation from outside your building.

Stray signal pickup (the reverse direction) could lead to errors in packets being carried. Generally these errors will be detected, but the packets have to be retransmitted, creating loads on the network. Token networks may be periodically forced into reconfigurations if certain errors occur, greatly slowing network throughput.

Shielding cables is the obvious, but not the only, solution. Coaxial cables are inherently shielded, but this isn't one hundred percent effective. Thick cable Ethernet (Chapter 5) uses a double shielding. Twisted pair is not inherently self shielded but shielding can be added for an extra cost—producing shielded twisted pair (**STP**). The ultimate protection against radiation and pickup is optical fiber.

Balanced Wiring

Without shielding, twisted pair must rely on maintaining a balanced condition for its fields. This includes watching the spacing between the cable and adjacent objects.

Figure 3.18 describes two variations on "parallel wire" transmission lines. In the first case, one conductor is connected to ground. The impedance (ac resistance) from each individual wire to ground is therefore not equal, making it an unbalanced transmission line.

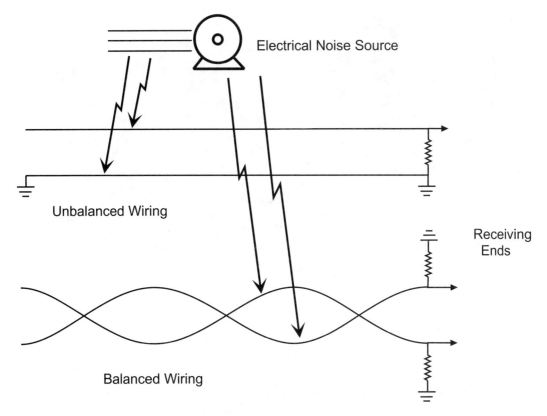

FIGURE 3.18
Balanced transmission lines try to pick up identical noise on each wire. The difference
between the two should then be zero.

As stray signals pass by the two wires, the ungrounded one is more likely to pick
up signals from the "air" than the grounded one because of its higher impedance to
ground. The result will be a difference between the two wires that will be unwanted
and will interfere with the normal signal.

The second case reduces the unwanted pickup drastically. The balanced pair
tries carefully to maintain an equal impedance to ground for each wire. This way
both wires should pick up the same amount of noise so there would be no net difference between them. The important information is being carried as a voltage difference between the wires, and any common voltage between the wires and ground is
ignored (common-mode rejection).

The subscriber loops that carry telephone signals to homes use a balanced pair
to minimize noise pickup. The 300 ohm "twin-lead" for television antennas is also a
balanced pair. Twisted pair Ethernet uses a balanced pair (actually two pair).

The term "twisted pair" refers to the twisting together of the wires partly to
keep them together for constant impedance but also to ensure that both wires get an
equal chance to pick up unwanted noise for optimum balanced operation.

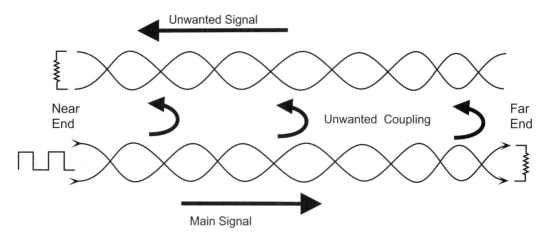

FIGURE 3.19
Near End Crosstalk.

Crosstalk

When several unshielded wire pairs are close together for long cable runs, there will be some transfer of energy from one to the other. Careful attention to twists and separation help to minimize this, but some will always sneak across. The unwanted coupling is called "crosstalk" and is caused by the overlapping of electric and magnetic fields.

An odd thing happens on the second wire. Most of the transferred energy flows in the reverse direction to what it traveled on the source pair. It heads back in the direction of the original signal. The unwanted signal is, therefore, stronger at the sending end of the cable than at the receiving end. For some reason, this end has become known as the "near end" as opposed to the "far end" and so the ratio of transmitted-to-unwanted-received energy at that end is known as Near End Crosstalk (see Figure 3.19). Since everything seems to need an acronym, you may see this listed as NEXT.

Near End Crosstalk is often measured in decibels. The higher the number, the better. For example, a value of 40 dB means that the signal picked up on the second pair is 40 dB weaker than on the original pair. This 40 dB represents one percent of the original voltage level (see end of this chapter).

CABLE TYPES

When IBM introduced their Token Ring network, they defined specific wire types that could be used. These became known as IBM cable type numbers. However, a second numbering system, adapted by the Electronics Industry Association (EIA) and others, defines five categories of twisted pair so be careful to distinguish between the two numbering systems.

The IBM cables in the following list are all for the Token Ring network. The older broadband network uses 75 ohm cable-television cable, RG-59B/U, described in Figure 3.13.

IBM Type 1	Two twisted pair using solid wire, shielded, 150 ohms.
IBM Type 2	Four unshielded pair for voice-grade telephone plus two shielded pair for data.
IBM Type 3	Four unshielded solid twisted pair. About the same as normal telephone cable, 100 ohms.
IBM Type 5	Two optical fibers.
IBM Type 6	Shielded with two twisted pair using stranded wire for increased flexibility.
IBM Type 8	Shielded twisted pair with a "flat" form factor for under carpet runs.
IBM Type 9	Plenum cable. Two shielded twisted pair with flame retardant coating.

Now we look at the five EIA twisted pair cable categories. The major difference between these categories is in insulation quality and attention to detail. This detail doesn't just make the cable look "nice." It controls the spacing between wires for uniform impedance over a wide range of frequencies. It controls twists per foot and separation between adjacent pairs for low radiation, noise pickup, and crosstalk. With the exception of Category 1, all wires are typically #24 AWG solid copper, and each pair will have a characteristic impedance of 100 ohms.

Category 1	Basic twisted pair for telephone use. Not recommended for data.
Category 2	Similar to IBM Type 3. Certified for data transmission to 4 megabits/sec. Typical cable loss is 8 dB per 1000 ft at a frequency of 1 MHz.
Category 3	At least three twists per foot. Certified for data transmission to 10 megabits/sec. If there are more pairs in the same jacket, they must not have the same number of twists per foot. This reduces inter-pair crosstalk. Typical cable loss is 30 dB per 1000 ft at 10 MHz and 40 dB at 16 MHz.
Category 4	The same as category 3 but certified to 16 megabits/sec. Typical cable loss is 27 dB per 1000 ft at 16 MHz and 31 dB at 20 MHz.
Category 5	The next best thing to fiber optic cables. Certified to 100 megabits/sec. Typical cable loss is 32 dB per 1000 ft at 25 MHz and 67 dB at 100 MHz.

Coaxial versus Twisted Pair

If coaxial cable and shielding are so great, why aren't they used everywhere? The answer is strictly in what the consumer wants. Although coaxial cables and shielded twisted pair are more expensive, when labor costs are added, the cost of the material becomes insignificant. The main reason that these cables are not used more is because they are bulkier and less flexible. A quick (and unfair) consumer test would be to ask people to make one connection with Thick Ethernet's half-inch coax and type-N screw connectors. Then ask them to make a connection with unshielded twisted pair and an RJ-45 "phone connector." The phone connector is much easier to use. The choice will have nothing to do with signal quality. The future seems to be unshielded twisted pair.

Fire Safety

One final comment on wires in general. If an office building catches fire, the flames spread above false ceilings and up vertical shafts built for pipes and wires. Any wiring for these areas must, therefore, meet local building code specifications for flammability, etc. For these applications, plenum cable that has teflon jackets is normally required. Flame retardant cable is somewhat more expensive, but so is a fire.

Some Cabling Tips

- Don't leave wiring around where it is constantly flexed and stepped on.
- Keep lengths to a minimum, but don't stretch wire tight.
- Don't place wiring close to known sources of electrical noise—motors and controllers, fluorescent lights, and radio transmitters.
- Install cabling carefully. Solid wire that has been "nicked" will eventually snap when flexed.
- Keep it dry. Moisture leads to corrosion.
- Use the best quality connectors available even though they are expensive. A very common problem is a corroded, broken, or loose connector.
- Use the correct connector for your wire type. Solid and stranded wire generally require different connectors.
- The twists in twisted pair serve a purpose. Don't untwist more than about one inch when making a connection.
- Use the best tools for stripping, inserting, crimping, etc.
- Make certain you have a detailed drawing of all cabling and the location of any out-of-the-way splices, junctions, connectors, etc.

WIRELESS LANS

Wireless LANs are the best choice for situations where cable runs are difficult. The wireless LANs can radiate the signal either as a radio wave or as an infrared optical signal. However, if network security is a concern, forget the wireless idea immedi-

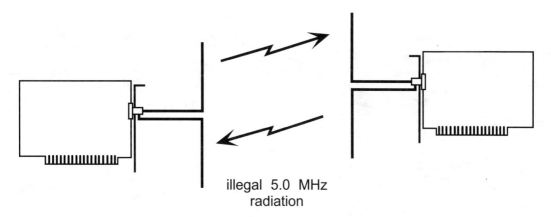

illegal 5.0 MHz
radiation

FIGURE 3.20
A LAN cable is severed and the conductors separated to form a transmitting antenna and
a receiving antenna. Don't try this with your LAN!

ately. Another concern may be possible health problems associated with long-term exposure to radio frequencies.

Figure 3.20 illustrates how simple the idea of a wireless LAN can be—at least in theory. The cable between two network cards has been cut and the conductors stripped back as shown. The cables now form transmitting and receiving antennas. This may also help to illustrate that the energy on the cable is already an electromagnetic wave and not just a bunch of voltages and currents. It also shows how easily a wave could accidentally radiate.

Although everything is theoretically correct, there are a few problems with the idea suggested in Figure 3.20. First, the card doing the receiving is probably expecting signals larger than a volt or so. Radiated signals, since they tend to fan out in all directions, weaken rapidly. For any distance, the signal level will be down to the millivolt or even microvolt level. Therefore, a wireless LAN will need special amplifiers at the receiving end.

The other problem is legal and involves being nice to your neighbors. Using ARCnet as an example, its frequencies cover a span of several MHz centered at 5.0 MHz. If you radiate this from an antenna, it will interfere with legal users of the "short-wave" radio spectrum—you are not licensed to transmit. The exact frequency of 5.000 MHz is used by station WWV, a time standard broadcast. Wireless LANs, therefore, need approved radio frequencies.

OPTICAL FIBERS

For some installations, thin optical fibers provide benefits over coaxial and other wire-based cables. These benefits show up when great distances are involved or if cable runs must pass by extremely noisy electrical equipment. Optical fibers may also be beneficial when data security is important. The fibers are difficult to tap into without being discovered, and they do not radiate any of their internal signals.

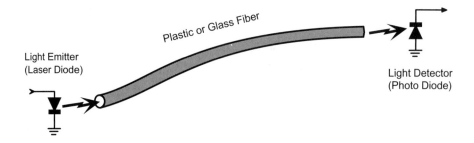

FIGURE 3.21
Optical fiber path.

A high-speed variation (100 megabits/sec) on ARCnet and the new Fiber Distributed Data Interface (FDDI) both take advantage of the higher data rates possible with fiber.

More traditional LAN technologies also offer fiber replacements for copper cables. They offer increased reliability in a noisy environment but no improvement in overall network size or data rate. Although fibers have much lower signal losses, cable runs can be lengthened only if timing limits won't be exceeded. If error rates due to cable problems are already low, the addition of fibers will change nothing.

Optical Link

A fiber link is shown in Figure 3.21. Light from a source enters one end, bounces along from side to side, and emerges at the other end to be picked up by a light detector.

Fibers

The fiber itself is generally made of high purity silica although some plastics are showing possibilities. The variation in losses at different wavelengths (colors) for silica glass fibers is shown in Figure 3.22. In general, fiber losses increase with optical frequency. The effect is due to Rayleigh scattering and is a diffraction caused by the molecular structure of the glass fiber. This increases inversely with the fourth power of the optical wavelength. In addition, there is an abrupt increase in losses between 900 and 1000 nanometers. This is an atomic resonance absorption by the glass material. The results leave two low-loss "valleys" for communication. The first is centered at 850 nm and the second at 1300 nm. Both are in the infrared region and lower in frequency (longer in wavelength) than visible light. The longer (1300 nm) of the two wavelengths usually has slightly lower losses and wider bandwidth.

Optical systems are not without their limitations. Depending on the diameter (and cost) of the fiber used, several different bounce angles can exist that will move the signal to the far end. The steeper angle results in a longer total path and signals moving this way will arrive later than smaller angle signals. Over great distances this "modal dispersion" will result in pulse smearing at the far end.

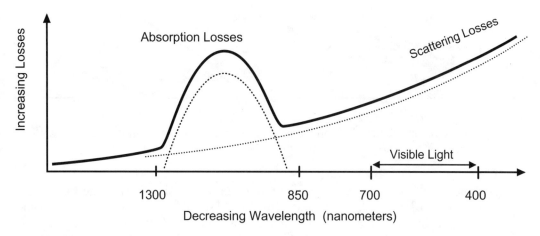

FIGURE 3.22
Typical losses of an optical fiber.

Larger diameter fibers are least expensive and have a uniform optical cross-section. An outer layer (cladding) of either glass or optical plastic is added with a lower refractive index (see Figure 3.23). The optical rays see this as a mirror and bounce back and forth down the tube. These fibers are called multimode fibers because many different bounce angles are unfortunately possible (see Figures 3.24 and 3.25).

Very thin, single-mode fibers eliminate the problem but are more expensive and also require a narrow spectral width laser source rather than a less expensive light-emitting diode (LED). Smaller diameter cables are generally made with a curved change in refractive index across their cross-section and an outside glass cladding. The optical rays follow a more curved path and fewer paths are possible—thanks in part to the smaller diameters.

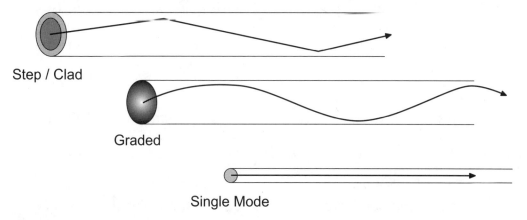

FIGURE 3.23
Refractive index across the diameter of the fiber may change abruptly or gradually.

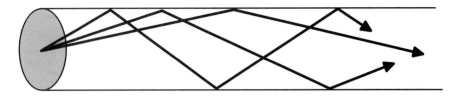

FIGURE 3.24
Larger diameter fibers will unfortunately support several different paths. Over long distances, this will cause a smearing of the input pulse width.

Optical fibers can easily carry information in two directions at the same time, just as copper cables can. Separating the input signal from the output at the same end and squeezing both a light source and a light detector into the narrow acceptance angle of a fiber is difficult, but not impossible. Many fiber optic systems use one fiber for transmission and a separate one for reception. Since the FDDI system is a ring, it inherently uses separate fibers.

Light Sources

Two types of light sources for a fiber are available. The least expensive is a normal light-emitting diode (LED). For data rates to about 10 megabits/sec, they are quite adequate. Beyond this they suffer from excessive spectral width. This means that the

DIAMETER (Core/Clad)	CORE TYPE	ATTENUATION (1-km length)	BANDWIDTH
5-10 micron	Single Mode	0.8 dB/km	>1000 MHz
50/125 micron	Graded Index	3.0-4.0 dB/km	>400 MHz
62.5/125 micron	Graded Index	3.75-6.0 dB/km	160 MHz
85/125 micron	Graded Index	5.0 dB/km	200 MHz
100/140 micron	Graded Index	5.0-6.0 dB/km	20-100 MHz
200/380 micron (polymer clad silica)	Step Index	8.0 dB/km	10 MHz

Attenuation and bandwidth are measured at 850-nm wavelength

FIGURE 3.25
Common optical fibers with typical diameters and loss characteristics.

light output of an LED isn't a single color (single frequency) but rather a narrow band of colors. When the light is changed in amplitude (amplitude modulation) at a fast rate, side colors (sidebands) are generated. At very high data rates, the side-bands merge with the original color band of the LED and cannot be separated. At 100 megabits/sec, the normal LED is useless.

At 100 megabits/sec, a laser diode is required, similar to those in compact disk players. A laser diode is very similar to a normal LED but has two parallel, polished surfaces and operates at a higher current level. The advantage is a narrower spectral width that can support higher modulation rates. The power output can also be higher.

> **Caution:** Fiber optic light levels are generally low but are extremely con-centrated. There is a slight chance of damage to your eyes if you hold the end of a fiber close to your eyeball. In any case, the optical wavelengths are too long to be seen so don't take the chance.

APPENDIX: DECIBELS

Measurements of cable losses in decibels (dB) are common because losses from multiple causes can be easily totaled.

Two formulas are used for calculating decibels depending on whether you are calculating power ratios or voltage ratios.

$$\text{Decibels} = 10 \times \log \frac{P_{out}}{P_{in}} = 20 \times \log \frac{V_{out}}{V_{in}}$$

–40.0 dB	99.99% power loss, voltage drops to 1%
–30.0 dB	99.9% power loss, voltage drops to 3.2%
–20.0 dB	99% power loss, voltage drops to 10%
–10.0 dB	90% power loss, voltage drops to 32%
–3.0 dB	50% power loss, voltage drops to 71%
–2.0 dB	37% power loss, voltage drops to 79%
–1.0 dB	21% power loss, voltage drops to 89%
0 dB	no gain or loss
+1.0 dB	26% power increase, voltage increases by 12%
+2.0 dB	58% power increase, voltage increases by 26%
+3.0 dB	100% power increase, voltage increases by 41%

Example: With a particular cable, the input signal is 2.0 volts, and the output is 0.5 volts. The ratio of output to input would be

$$\text{Decibels} = 20 \times \log \frac{0.5}{2.0} = -12.04 \text{ dB}$$

Chapter 4

ARCnet

ARCnet is a simple but effective network that was developed by Datapoint Corporation in 1977. The name is an abbreviation of "Attached Resource Computer network."

ARCnet has been extremely popular and, even with the original 2.5 megabits/sec design, is capable of reasonably good performance. A faster, 20 megabits/sec design called ARCnet Plus is now available. Although not having the highest data rate, ARCnet cards and connector hubs are low in cost, which gives ARCnet an excellent price–performance ratio. ARCnet does not have a finished **IEEE** (Institute of Electrical and Electronic Engineers) standard at the time of this writing, but one is being worked on.

THE ARCNET SYSTEM

We will describe the original ARCnet system first and then later in the chapter add details of the newer, but compatible 20 megabits/sec design.

A full ARCnet system can connect 255 machines spread over a maximum diameter of 20,000 feet (see Figure 4.1). Several cabling options are available, but the original and still most common is the coaxial cable star.

In a star system, each station is connected to the end of a 93 ohm coaxial cable. A collection of active (amplifier) and passive (resistor) "hubs" are used to connect these cables into a straggly-looking distributed star.

Data flows over the network at 2.5 megabits per second in packets that hold up to 508 data bytes. The passing of a special token packet from station to station determines the order in which stations get their chance to transmit.

ADAPTER CARD NUMBER

As with any network, each ARCnet adapter card must have a unique identification number. Most networks now use 48-bit serial numbers, which are preloaded during manufacturing and are generally unchangeable by the user. ARCnet uses only an eight-bit number, which must be set by the installer. At the time each card is being inserted into its host machine, a number between one and 255 is chosen and entered

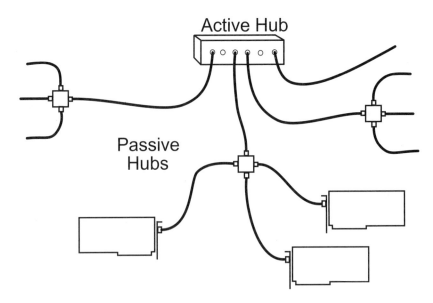

FIGURE 4.1
ARCnet can connect as many as 255 machines in a distributed star covering up to 20,000 feet.

via either DIP (Dual In-line Pin package) switch or software included with the card. No machine is given the number zero; it has a special meaning. The number must be different for each machine in the network, but no particular number or sequence is required. This becomes the workstation identification number and determines the station's position in the token-passing order.

ARCnet's star cabling essentially connects all its cards in parallel. Each station hears every transmission but pays attention only to those addressed to it. Although physically in parallel, ARCnet operates as a logical ring. Just as the tennis ball previously described could be used to control a business meeting, a token must be received by each individual station before it can transmit. The station's ID number determines the token-passing order. It is always passed from the lower toward the higher numbered station. The very highest numbered station passes it back to the lowest, thus completing the logical ring.

RECONFIGURATION

The logical ring is established through an initial network configuration procedure (see Figure 4.2). This process is automatic and does not require the user to perform any action.

Every workstation knows its own adapter card number. Starting with the highest numbered card, each will investigate, in turn, to see who the "next" numbered machine is. Each will sequentially send test messages to the numbers above their

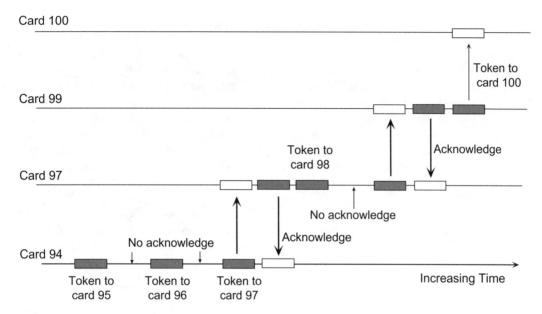

FIGURE 4.2
Network reconfiguration consists of a series of attempts to pass the token to the machine
that is next higher in number.

own to see who answers. The first response identifies the next higher numbered
machine. The short packet used as an "Invitation to Transmit" (ITT) token goes to
this next machine.

When another station is turned on or off, an abbreviated version of the reconfiguration operation takes place. Network operation is disrupted only for a few tens
of milliseconds during a reconfiguration.

SENDING A PACKET

When the reconfiguration is complete, the token circulates from machine to
machine asking each in turn if it would like to send something. This is the station's
"invitation to transmit." With nothing to send, the token passes from one machine
to the next in about 35 microseconds.

As each machine acquires the token, it will have the choice of either sending
data to any one machine, broadcasting a message to all machines, or simply passing
the token to the next station. This routine is followed when transmitting information
to a specific station:

1. A short "free buffer enquiry" (FBE) packet is sent asking the intended des-
    tination if it is ready and able to receive. If that machine recently accepted
    packets from other stations and had not processed them yet, it would reply

with a negative acknowledgment (NAK). If it is able to receive, a positive acknowledgment (ACK) is made, and the information packet is sent.

2. If the packet is correctly received, a positive acknowledgment is sent. Even if there is still more information to be sent, the token must now be passed to the next station in the logical ring. It must wait to send the rest of its message until the token returns.

3. When the originating station receives the ACK, it immediately passes the token to the next higher station. However, if there is an error in the received packet, the remote station will not acknowledge packet reception. In this case, an internal timer of 74 microseconds eventually expires, and the token will still be passed.

Figure 4.3 shows the sequence in which tokens and messages are passed. In this example, station 115 wishes to send a message to station 32. In preparation, it moves all the necessary information into a buffer on the network card and then tells the card

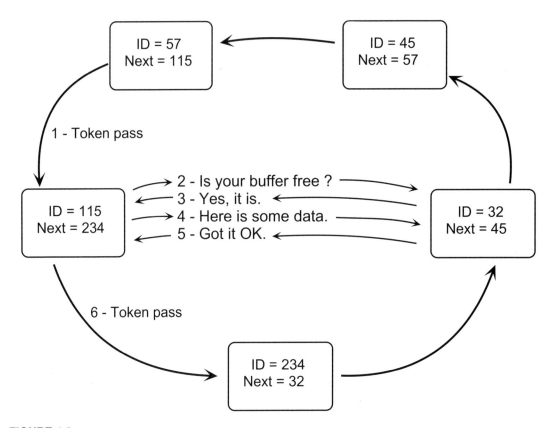

FIGURE 4.3
Each station passes the token to the next higher number that exists. The station holding the token can send one data packet to another station. The sending of this one packet involves an exchange of four messages in total.

to transmit. The controller understands the command but must wait for a token to arrive. When it receives the token from 57, it begins the transmit sequence. First, 115 sends a short packet to 32 asking, "Is your buffer free?" This means, "If I were to send you some information right now, do you have enough shelf space?" Station 32 returns a positive acknowledgment, and 115 sends the packet. Again, 32 acknowledges. Station 115 has now completed its turn and sends the token to 234, its "next" station.

Each station will receive the token within a predictable time limit and thereby get a chance to transmit (see Figure 4.4). The minimum time for a token to circulate is about 35 microseconds per station multiplied by the number of active stations. This assumes there is nothing to transmit. However, if all stations want to send something and their recipients are able to receive, the maximum time rises to about 2.3 milliseconds per station times the number of machines. The typical waiting time for another token is closer to the minimum than the maximum value.

True ARCnet allows only one packet to be transmitted each time the token is received. Some board manufacturers have modified this rule for server cards and allow several packets to be sent each time a single token is received. The justification is that in each pass around the ring, several workstations may have sent requests to the server; when the server finally gets the token, it may have several responses to make.

The predictable upper time limit makes ARCnet, and any other token network, "deterministic." This means there is an absolute maximum waiting time and a guaranteed minimum throughput for any one station. CSMA networks, such as Ethernet, operate on statistically probable delays, not absolute delays. This feature of token-

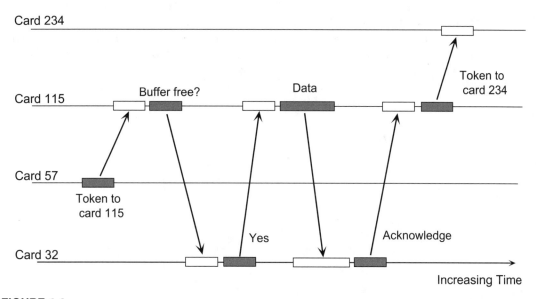

FIGURE 4.4
Time sequence diagram for the passing of packets. Time interval increases from left to right.

passing networks has to be put into perspective, though. An absolute guarantee on throughput isn't of any great advantage to humans, but it is very important for process control systems where various factory control functions absolutely must happen within a certain time limit.

CABLE WAVEFORM

With 2.5 megabits/sec ARCnet, each bit has a 400 nanosecond (ns) time slot. (The same time slot is also used in the newer 20 megabits/sec version.) A data "One" travels over the network as a dual polarity pulse (dipulse) in the first half of the time slot, followed by a flat line in the remaining half. These dipulses resemble a single cycle of a 5 MHz sinewave. The short space that follows allows the pulse to die down and also provides a contrast with the first half of the time interval for clock synchronization purposes.

A data "Zero" is simply a continuous zero voltage line for the full 400 ns time slot.

The One pulses reach peak voltages of plus and minus 10 volts—significantly larger than most other networks. As a result, ARCnet has excellent noise immunity when used with good quality coaxial cable (see Figure 4.5). The frequency spectrum is shown in Figure 4.6. However, if extra long cables or passive hubs are used, a fair bit of this amplitude advantage is lost.

The dipulse should begin with a positive half cycle immediately followed by a negative half cycle. Assuming the card is correctly built, this should not change—as long as coaxial cables are used. With the obvious difference between the center wire and the outside shield, it would be very difficult to accidentally reverse the two. However, ARCnet is also available in a twisted pair version. In that case, it is relatively easy to accidentally interchange two wires. Many of the twisted pair hubs have an indicator light to warn of pulse reversal.

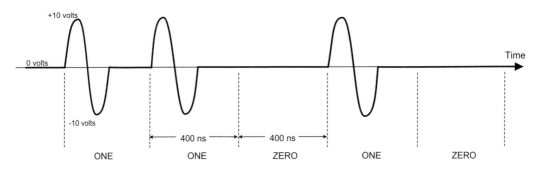

FIGURE 4.5
ARCnet One and Zero voltages carried on 93-ohm coaxial cable.

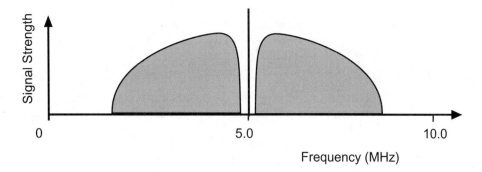

FIGURE 4.6
Frequency spectrum of an ARCnet cable waveform.

One Byte

Each byte of data requires 11 time slots of 400 nanoseconds each on the cable. The first three bits are always the same—each character begins with two Ones and then a Zero bit. These serve as periodic checks for the receiver's bit and byte clock synchronization. The eight data bits then follow with the least significant bit first (see Figure 4.7). The next 11-bit character grouping follows immediately after the first with no extra delay. The data stream might therefore be described as "isochronous" because bit timing is uniform and continuous through all bits of the packet.

It is true that only eight data bits are being carried for every 11 time slots, but the extra three bits are important. In addition to clock timing, they form a sort of "start-bit" to provide byte synchronization at the receiver. If we wanted to calculate the true "data" rate without including these three synchronizing bits, it would be closer to

$$\frac{2.5 \text{ megabits/sec} \times 8}{11} = 1.82 \text{ megabits/sec}$$

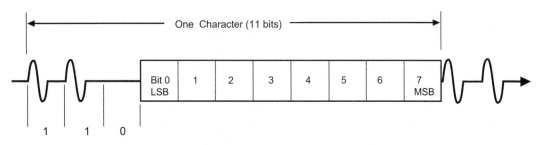

FIGURE 4.7
ARCnet eight-bit byte (or character) transmission. The grouping always starts with two Ones and then a Zero.

The header and trailer portions of the packet aren't included in this value, but they don't have as great an effect.

SIX DIFFERENT PACKETS

In order to be transmitted, the characters must be placed in a packet. Packets come in six flavors. Four of these are control packets, and two are used for data.

- short data packet (1–253 data bytes)
- long data packet (257–508 data bytes)
- invitation to transmit (ITT, the token)
- free buffer inquiry (FBE)
- positive acknowledgment (ACK)
- negative acknowledgment (NAK)

A seventh transmission is used for a network reconfiguration. It is quite different from the control and data packets and is only needed when a machine leaves or joins the network. We will explain that later.

Each of the six packets begin with what is referred to as an "alert burst." This consists of six Ones in a row. Its purpose could be described as alerting the receiver that something is coming but, in more technical terms, it is synchronizing the Phase Locked Loop (PLL) in the receiving card. This is the reference oscillator that separates out the 11 individual bits within each character grouping. This oscillator is "bit" synchronized. The two Ones at the beginning of each data byte are periodic checks for this oscillator to make sure it is still in step for the next byte. The change from the two Ones to the Zero provides character synchronization.

The four control packets are intentionally kept short because they are heavily used. This helps reduce the overhead traffic and increase data throughput.

The packet shown in Figure 4.8 is the invitation to transmit packet. This is the packet that is passed as the token. After the alert burst, it contains a single 04 hex character (ASCII "End Of Transmission" character) and two copies of the station

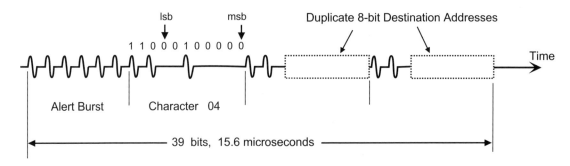

FIGURE 4.8
Invitation to transmit packet or "token."

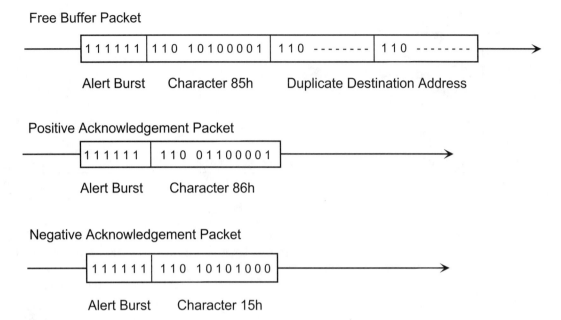

Free Buffer Packet

| 1 1 1 1 1 1 | 1 1 0 1 0 1 0 0 0 0 1 | 1 1 0 - - - - - - - - | 1 1 0 - - - - - - - - |

    Alert Burst   Character 85h   Duplicate Destination Address

Positive Acknowledgement Packet

| 1 1 1 1 1 1 | 1 1 0 0 1 1 0 0 0 0 1 |

    Alert Burst   Character 86h

Negative Acknowledgement Packet

| 1 1 1 1 1 1 | 1 1 0 1 0 1 0 1 0 0 0 |

    Alert Burst   Character 15h

FIGURE 4.9
The remaining three control packets. Each consists of the six-bit "alert burst" for clock synchronization and one or three 11-bit characters.

address where it is being sent. The address duplication helps to ensure that the right station knows it has the token. The source station doesn't include its identification number because it isn't needed and would only add to the length. Once a station has received and acknowledged this token, it is free to transmit a data packet (long or short) to a station of its choice.

The other three control packets are shown in Figure 4.9. Notice that the positive (ACK) and negative (NAK) acknowledgment packets have neither source nor destination addresses. Because of the orderly timing in the ARCnet system, the station with the token will know that any ACK or NAK refers to its previous "is your buffer free?" or data transmission.

The first character after the alert burst uniquely defines the type of packet. For the free buffer enquiry, it is the extended ASCII ENQuiry (85 hex). For the positive acknowledgment, it is the ASCII ACKnowledgment (86 hex) character. For the negative acknowledgment, the ASCII NAK (15 hex) is used.

TWO DATA PACKETS

The data packets are a bit more complex and are obviously longer. These packets will vary in overall length to suit the amount of data being carried.

The "short" data packet can carry from one to 253 bytes. The "long" packet carries 257 to 508 bytes. The obvious "hole" between short and long packets will be

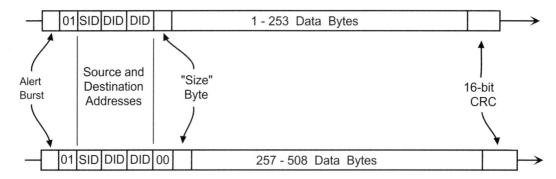

FIGURE 4.10
Short and long data packets as viewed on the cable.

explained shortly. Both packets start with the alert burst and the hex character 01 (ASCII "start of header"). The eight-bit source address and then a duplicate eight-bit destination address follow. Remember that each byte also has the 110 synchronizing pattern added to it.

The only structural difference between the two different-sized packets occurs next. If this is to be a short packet, this next byte is the eight-bit complement of the number of data bytes being carried (256-N). As an example, if 200 bytes are to be sent, the "size" byte will be 56 (hex 38). The 200 bytes of data will (on the cable) immediately follow the size byte.

For a long packet, the "size" consists of two bytes, the first of which is Zero and the second is the eight-bit complement of the number of characters over 256 (i.e., 512-N). For example, 400 bytes would require a second "size" byte of 112 (hex 70). Again, on the cable, the data portion follows the two size bytes.

Each packet finishes with a 16-bit Cyclic Redundancy Code (**CRC**) remainder. This is calculated by the controller chip using the 17-bit polynomial

$$x^{16} + x^{15} + x^2 + 1$$

Figure 4.10 shows how the two packets would appear on the cable. Be careful! The programmer assembles the information for these packets in memory in a slightly different fashion so don't confuse the cable packet with the buffer memory pattern.

BROADCAST MESSAGES

ARCnet cards allow packets to be sent either to specific stations or as a **broadcast** to all stations. Since only the specific station transmissions are acknowledged, broadcasts are considered to be a less reliable transmission mechanism. Broadcasts are useful, however. A typical application might be for a warning message from the server to all users, for example,

The server will be shut down in five minutes. Finish and save your work NOW!!!

ARCnet sends its all-station broadcasts as a regular data packet to station Zero. This is why zero cannot be assigned to any individual station. Every workstation can, therefore, receive packets for two addresses—station Zero plus its own unique ID. The controller chip can be programmed to ignore these broadcasts, but that could be dangerous as important warnings could be missed. Broadcast messages are not acknowledged because too many stations would have to respond; there is no mechanism to include the source address in the acknowledge packet or to control the acknowledge order.

NETWORK RECONFIGURATION

The assumption so far has been that all stations are up and running. However, if one station is shut off when the token is passed to it, there will be a long silence. ARCnet controller chips are designed to handle this. All controllers on the network constantly watch for quiet gaps that exceed 78 microseconds—the reason for this specific time will be explained shortly. As soon as a controller sees this time pass in silence, it knows something is wrong. Each controller starts an additional time delay equal to 146 microseconds multiplied by the difference between its own ID and the maximum ID of 255, i.e., $146 \times (255 - ID)$ microseconds. As an example, station 121 would wait about 19.5 milliseconds. Higher numbered stations would wait less time.

The highest numbered controller card will reach its time limit first. If there is still no activity on the cable, this controller starts looking for its "next" higher numbered neighbor. It sends an "invitation to transmit" token with the destination address initially set to its own ID number. No response will be obtained because it is initially "talking to itself." When no response is obtained within 75 microseconds, the token ID number is incremented and the attempt repeated. The process continues until, finally, a station answers with an ACK packet. The initiating station now knows whom its "next" address is. Meanwhile, the other stations see some activity and forget about their time delays.

This "next" station now has the token and starts its search for a live number above it. The procedure continues until the logical ring is again established. The procedure sounds lengthy but actually takes less than 61 milliseconds depending on the number of live stations.

There is a very slight advantage to setting one network card to a high ID number—e.g., 255. During a reconfiguration, this card will time out early and get the roll call started. This saves a whopping 37 milliseconds every morning. Except for this, there are *no* advantages to selecting any particular adapter number.

Once started, the reconfiguration time depends inversely on the number of active cards involved. A small network of five machines will spend 250 time slots of 75 microseconds each waiting for returns from nonexistent IDs and five shorter time periods, depending on cable length, getting proper acknowledgments (see Figure 4.11). In any case, reconfigurations shouldn't be happening frequently. If they are, the cause should be located— cable problems, card failure, or tampering.

A new station trying to join a network will cause a similar reconfiguration. Because none of the other stations know that the newcomer exists, it won't get any tokens passed to it. After 840 milliseconds, it will get angry and jam the network

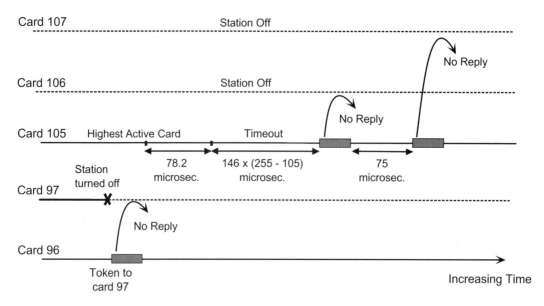

FIGURE 4.11
Network reconfiguration after one machine is turned off. Station 105 is the highest numbered station.

with a reconfiguration burst. This will consist of eight Ones and a Zero repeated 765 times (see Figure 4.12). As this lasts longer than any other type of transmission, it destroys the token passing and terminates all other transmitting. Once this long pattern ends, a silent period will follow. As before, the highest numbered station will eventually recognize the silence and start its search for the "next" station. The new station will then be inserted in the token-passing order.

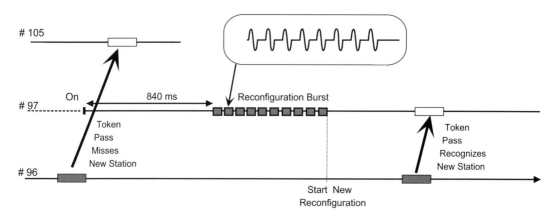

FIGURE 4.12
Reconfiguration jamming burst from a new station wanting to join the network.

THE NETWORK CARD

From a programmer's point of view, the operation of the ARCnet card appears quite simple. It is, in fact, the simplest network card with which to work. For this reason and because of its low cost (under $100 in most cases), ARCnet cards make a wonderful starting point for someone wanting to experiment.

This apparent simplicity is due mainly to the efficiency of the controller chip. Once the chip has the needed information, it performs all of the token reception, passing, message sending, receiving, and acknowledging by itself. It will interrupt the personal computer only when necessary, such as when a packet is received or something goes wrong.

The two main components of an ARCnet card are the COM 9026 controller (or equivalent) and a 2K byte RAM chip. The controller appears as only three or four registers to the programmer. Figure 4.13 includes the transmitter, receiver, and timers, but the programmer can't get at them—the chip controls the operation of these items.

The RAM buffer typically appears in the host computer's main memory map in the D000h segment. The three other registers typically appear in the I/O block of memory at 2E0h and 2E1h as indicated. Locations 2E2h to 2E7h are normally reserved (i.e.,

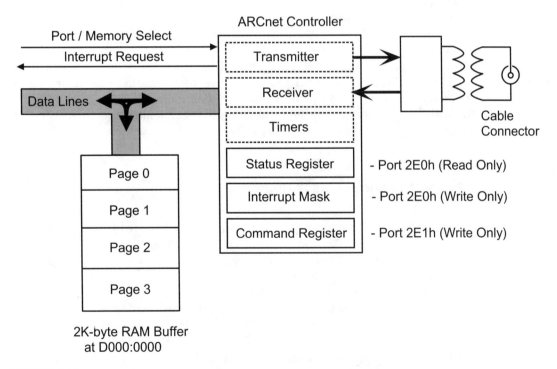

FIGURE 4.13

This is what the host computer and a programmer think an ARCnet adapter card looks like. The host can only access the buffer RAM plus three registers in the controller chip. The remaining items are shown for completeness.

unused). Any I/O Read or Write from/to address 2E8h will cause most adapter cards to perform a full reset.

Early ARCnet boards were provided with DIP switches to reposition these addresses if they conflicted with other installed boards. More recent boards are configured via software after installation and hold their settings in small Electrically Erasable Read Only Memory (EEROM) chips.

The 2K bytes of RAM are used by the controller as four blocks of 512 bytes each. This is large enough to hold four long packets. Two of these blocks hold packets for the transmitter, and the other two are available for the receiver. The programmer can select which are used for transmit and which for receive. With the proper host interface logic, one packet can be in the process of being transmitted by the 9026 controller while the next one is being loaded by the host. Similarly, on the receiver side, the host can be processing one packet at the same time that another is being received. This is normally referred to as "double buffering."

The hardware design of this dual access system can have significant effects on the throughput of the card. This is one enhancement area of high-performance ARCnet cards.

The four RAM areas are known as pages 0, 1, 2, and 3 to the controller; the programmer must bear this in mind when issuing commands to the controller. However, when moving packets in and out of the buffer RAM, the programmer sees the block as a continuous 2K bytes of host memory.

Inside the COM 9026, the programmer only has access to three registers: the Command, Status, and Interrupt Mask Registers. The Command and Interrupt Mask registers are Write Only. The Status Register is Read Only. Commands are sent to the Command Register to initiate packet transmission, enable and disable the receiver, etc. As events happen on the network, various bits in the Status Register will change from time to time. These bits may cause interrupts back to the host depending on individual mask bits in the Interrupt Mask Register.

Status and Interrupt Mask Registers

The 9026 controller makes individual status bits go Hi as packets are acknowledged or the transmitter becomes available. As shown in Figure 4.14, four of these bits could cause interrupts. Corresponding bits in the Mask Register can be used to suppress three of these, if desired, by placing a Zero in the proper position. When and if an interrupt is passed on, the host processor will know only that the adapter card caused it but not why. The application program would, therefore, immediately read the status bits to determine the cause of the interruption.

The individual status bits are:

Bit 7   RI   Receiver Inhibited. Indicates that a packet has just been received and placed in the buffer. The receiver is now inhibited from receiving any more packets until an ENABLE RECEIVER command is issued.

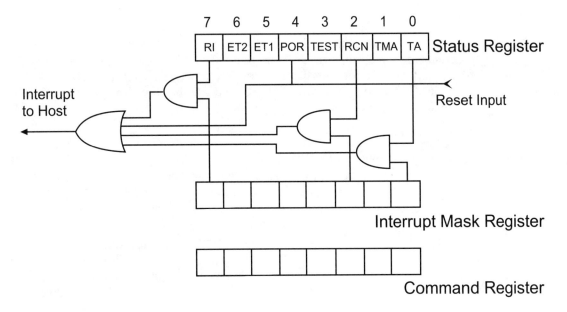

FIGURE 4.14
Three 9026 controller registers and the interrupt logic.

Bits 5 and 6		Concern time delay options read directly from the ET1 and ET2 pins on the controller chip.
Bit 4	POR	Power On Reset. Will be Hi immediately after power is applied to the chip. This always generates an interrupt which cannot be masked. It is cleared with a CLEAR FLAGS command.
Bit 3	TEST	Will normally be Zero. Used only during chip production.
Bit 2	RECON	Reconfigure. Indicates that the receiver has not seen any line activity for more than 78 microseconds and is starting into a reconfiguration procedure. The CLEAR FLAGS command will clear this bit.
Bit 1	TMA	Transmit Acknowledge. The packet that was just sent has been acknowledged as properly received (the TA bit should also be checked). Remember that broadcast messages are not acknowledged.
Bit 0	TA	Transmitter Available. Indicates that the previous transmission has completed and the transmitter is now available for further use.

The RI, POR, RECON, or TA bits are capable of interrupting the host. All except the Power On (POR) bit can be masked.

Command Register

There are six major commands that can be sent to the Command Register by the programmer. Some will have variations that indicate which RAM page (nn = 00, 01, 10, 11) is to be used for a particular operation, which status bits (r = RECON, p = POR) in the controller are to be cleared, and whether broadcast messages will be accepted (b = 1) or not (b = 0).

Binary Command	Operation
00000001	CANCEL a pending transmit command. If a transmission is already under way, it continues to completion. The TA (transmitter available) bit will be Set (One) after the next token is received.
00000010	DISABLE RECEIVER. If a packet is currently being received, the controller continues. Tokens can still be received and acknowledged, but responses to "BUFFER AVAILABLE?" from other stations will be negative. The RI status bit will be Set after the next token is received.
000nn011	ENABLE TRANSMIT. The next time a token is received, a packet will be transmitted from page "nn." TA and TMA (Transmitter Acknowledge) bits are initially cleared. After the transmission, the TA bit will be One, and the TMA bit should be One if the packet is acknowledged.
b00nn100	ENABLE RECEIVER. Enables the receiver and directs incoming packets to RAM page "nn." This will Clear (Zero) the RI bit. If "b" is also One, broadcast messages will be accepted as well.
000rp100	CLEAR selected bits in the Status Register. If "r" is One, the RECON bit is cleared. If "p" is One, the POR bit is cleared.
0000c101	DEFINE CONFIGURATION. Tells the controller the size of its buffer. A "c" = One indicates a 2K buffer, and so both short and long packets can be sent. A "c" = Zero indicates a 1K buffer (rarely used).

Power On

When power is first applied to the chip, it sets the bits in the Status Register as shown in Figure 4.15. All bits in the Mask Register will be cleared so that only the Power On reset can cause an interrupt.

The controller chip reads the eight-bit network identification (NID) number that was set via EEPROM or DIP switch at the time of card installation. Two bytes are then written to the beginning of page 00 of the RAM buffer. The first is an arbitrary D1-hex. The second is the card's ID value.

FIGURE 4.15
Status Register bits at Power
On.

7	6	5	4	3	2	1	0
1	-	-	1	0	0	0	1

RI ET2 ET1 POR TEST RCN TMA TA

Extended Time bits ET1 & ET2 depend on board jumpers

Now Bit 4 (POR) of the Status Register is allowed to interrupt the host processor. The host, if it wishes, can check the first two bytes of the buffer and thereby find its station number. It should assume the number is valid only if the D1h pattern is present.

At the same time, the controller will start a reconfiguration burst (see Figure 4.12) onto the network cabling to indicate that the workstation wants to join the network. The network will be disrupted for a few tens of milliseconds, and then a new token-passing order will be established that includes the new station.

Transmit and Receive Buffers

The byte pattern of a packet in the buffer is somewhat similar to the sequence shown for the cable waveform, but there are three important differences.

1. In the buffer, the destination address is only entered once; the controller adds the duplicate during transmission.
2. The CRC is left off; it is calculated during transmission by the controller. Even during reception, the incoming CRC is calculated by the COM 9026 and then stripped before writing to the buffer.
3. The data is pushed toward the end of the buffer, and the bytes in front are left as garbage (they are not transmitted). The "size" bytes are now important as they indicate where the data in the buffer begins (see Figure 4.16).

Size Byte

The value of the "size" byte within the buffer requires a little more explanation. The controller chips at both the send and receive ends use this value when they are moving bytes to and from the RAM buffer. It is also included in the packet.

When told to send, the controller starts to move bytes from the RAM buffer into the transmitter (see Figure 4.16). When it gets to the third byte, it will know if this is to be a short or long packet. If short, the third byte will be non-Zero and so is used as the "size" byte. The controller moves its internal address counter up to this "size" value and then continues to read bytes from the higher location in the buffer. If size = 1Eh, the controller would skip up to address 1Eh within the page after reading the first three bytes. The 27 bytes (decimal 30 minus the first three bytes) of garbage from some previous operation would, therefore, be skipped. The packet

BYTE	CONTENT		BYTE	CONTENT
00	Source ID		00	Source ID
01	Destination ID		01	Destination ID
02	Size (256-N)		02	00
			03	Size (512-N)
03				
04	Garbage		04	
...			05	Garbage
...			...	
...			...	
			...	
256-N			512-N	
...	N		...	
...	Data		...	N
...	Bytes		...	Data
255			...	Bytes
			...	
			511	

FIGURE 4.16
Byte order of a short and long packet in the RAM buffer. N represents the number of data bytes. Data bytes are pushed to the end of each buffer area, and any preceding unused bytes are left as is. The "size" byte actually indicates the starting byte number (address) of the data within the buffer.

would be sent out onto the cable with 226 data bytes plus the alert burst, the five-byte header, and the Cyclic Redundancy Code (CRC).

At the receiver, the first few bytes are moved into the buffer, and the size byte is used to increment the buffer address. The pattern in the receive buffer will, therefore, look the same as the one in the other station's transmit buffer. The padding characters are not important as they are not transmitted. However, the programmer must be careful because this means that a few bytes from an old, longer packet could remain in the buffer after a shorter packet is received.

The values for "size" are shown in Figure 4.17. For either packet, this byte must never be made 00. ARCnet has three sizes of data that cannot be handled directly: 254, 255, and 256 bytes. The driver must place these sizes in a larger packet and add a few padding bytes.

PROGRAM EXAMPLES

The following two assembly language programs form a simple one-way messaging system using ARCnet cards. The sender types a short message at one machine and,

DATA SIZE	"Size" BYTE	PACKET TYPE
1	255	Short
2	254	Short
3	253	Short
. .	. . .	Short
. . .	. .	Short
252	4	Short
253	3	Short

254	These sizes are not used and
255	must be bypassed by higher
256	layers using extra "padding" bytes.

DATA SIZE	"Size" BYTE	PACKET TYPE
257	255	Long
258	254	Long
. . .	. . .	Long
. . .	. .	Long
506	6	Long
507	5	Long
508	4	Long

FIGURE 4.17
Values for "size" byte for various amounts of data. This byte must never be set to Zero, or the transmission will abort.

on completion, it will appear at the other machine. The enterprising reader may wish to combine the two programs into one that can be run on both machines. The result would be a two-way messaging system.

Both programs are intended to be run as .COM files. You will have to use the DOS EXE2BIN program to convert it from an .EXE file to a .COM file after assembly and linking.

```
EXE2BIN SENDARC.EXE SENDARC.COM
```

Transmit Program

In this sending program, the operator will be asked to type a few lines of text, and these will be sent to another station. Before assembling this program, the correct card address for the destination (dest_id) station must be entered. The source address is read by the program.

```
;******************** SENDARC.ASM ********************
; Sends a message from one ARCnet card to another.
; Fill in the "dest_id" value before assembling.
; J.K. Hardy                 April 26, 1994
;*****************************************************
;
```

```
CODE        SEGMENT
assume  cs:code, ds:code
        org  100h
start:      jmp  begin

sour_id:    db   00               ; your card ID goes here
dest_id:    db   00               ; who is the message for?
            db   00               ; indicates long packet
p_size:     db   04h              ; assume a full 508 bytes
buffer      db   508d dup (00)    ; the message

prompt:     db   "Type your message, 6 lines max."
            db   0Dh,0Ah,"Terminate with a RETURN"
            db   0Dh,0Ah
lmess       equ  $-prompt
; ------------------------ place prompt on screen
begin:      mov  bx,01
            mov  cx,lmess
            mov  dx,OFFSET prompt
            mov  ah,40h
            int  21h
; --------------------- read message from keyboard
            mov  cx,508d          ; maximum 508 characters
            mov  di,OFFSET buffer
kbd:        mov  ah,01
            int  21h              ; read one character
            cmp  al,0Dh           ; was it a RETURN?
            je   done
            mov  [di],al          ; put character in buffer
            inc  di
            loop kbd              ; dec cx and jump if not 0
; ---------- read station ID & move message into page 00
done:       cld
            mov  ax,cs            ; source is DS:SI
            mov  ds,ax
            mov  si,OFFSET sour_id
            mov  ax,0D000h        ; destination is ES:DI
            mov  es,ax
            mov  di,OFFSET 0000
            mov  al,es:[01]       ; read this station's ID
            mov  sour_id,al
            mov  cx,0200h         ; move 512 bytes
            rep  movsb            ; move a bunch of bytes
; ------------------------ configure and send message
            mov  dx,02E1h         ; point to Command Register
            mov  al,1Eh           ; clear flags
            out  dx,al
            mov  al,0Dh        ; define config'n = 2K buffer
            out  dx,al
            mov  al,03h        ; enable transmit from page 00
```

```
            out  dx,al
;  ------------------------ terminate
            mov  ax,4C00h    ; DOS terminate
            int  21h
CODE ENDS
END START
```

Program Description

This is an absolute minimum program that will build a packet and send it. It assumes that 508 bytes of meaningful data are always being sent and that a long packet is being used regardless of the amount actually typed in. It also makes no attempt to shift the message to the end of the buffer and set the size byte. As a result, packets will often be sent carrying rubbish and wasting cable time. There is plenty of room here for student enhancements.

Before assembling the program, remember to add in the single-byte dest_id value for the second adapter card involved.

When it begins, the program uses DOS Function 40h to place a suitable message on the screen telling the user what to do—"Type your message. . . ." It then moves into a loop to read characters from the keyboard into the buffer area. As it reads each character, it watches for the ENTER key (0Dh) to be pressed. When it is, the loop terminates. The loop will always terminate when 508 characters have been entered. Program execution then moves to the point labeled "done:".

The next section begins by setting up segment and offset registers in preparation for a movement of 512 bytes. After the registers are set, the adapter card address is read from location D000:0000, which should be the beginning of RAM on the buffer card. The card number only appears at this location immediately after a Power On or a card reset—any OUT to 2E8h. The program then moves 512 bytes starting with the source and destination addresses, the two "size" bytes, and includes the 508 bytes in the buffer. The destination for the move is page 0 of the adapter card RAM.

Once the adapter RAM is loaded, three commands are sent to the controller chip Command Register. The first clears any flags. The second defines the on-board RAM size. The third sends the packet as a long packet from page 0. The program then immediately terminates.

Receiver Program

This is the companion program to SENDARC. It is run on the receiving station and should be started first. The program waits for an incoming packet and then displays the message contained in it. However, if a packet isn't received, the receiving machine will loop continuously and may "hang." How would you correct that?

```
;***************** READARC.ASM *****************************
; Waits for an incoming ARCnet packet and then displays it.
; J.K. Hardy                          April 26, 1994
;**********************************************************
;
```

```
CODE    SEGMENT
assume cs:code, ds:code
org 100h
start:    jmp  begin

signon    db    "We are waiting for a message",0Dh,0Ah,"$"

; ------------------------- display sign-on message
begin:    push cs
          pop  ds
          mov  dx,offset signon ; ds:dx points to string
          mov  ah,09
          int  21h
;------------------------- initialize card
          mov  dx,2E1h          ; point to Command Register
          mov  al,00001101b
          out  dx,al            ; define config'n = 2K buffer
          mov  al,00011110b
          out  dx,al            ; clear flags
          mov  al,00011100b
          out  dx,al            ; enable receiver to page 3
;------------------------- wait for packet
          dec  dx               ; point to Status Register
not_yet:  in   al,dx
          and  al,10000000b     ; select RI bit
          jne  not_yet
;------------------------- display message
          mov  bx,01            ; handle of screen
          mov  ax,0D000h        ; card buffer address
          mov  ds,ax
          mov  cx,508d          ; number of characters
          mov  dx,3*512+4       ; ds:dx points to page 3,
                                ; skip first four bytes.
          mov  ah,40h           ; display the message
          int  21h
;------------------------- terminate
          mov  ax,4C00h
          int  21h
CODE ENDS
END START
```

Program Description

The program begins by placing a message on the screen, "We are waiting. . . ." It then sends three commands to the controller chip Command Register. The first defines the RAM configuration. The second clears any flag bits. The third turns on the receiver and tells it to put any incoming messages in RAM page 3.

The program then moves into what could be an endless loop. It keeps reading the RI bit—the most significant bit of the Status Register. When this bit is set, we assume a packet has been received. We then read 508 bytes from adapter RAM page 3. The first four bytes are skipped because they will be the two addresses and the two size bytes. Although they might be interesting to see, they might show as weird control characters on the screen unless converted to ASCII.

Multi-Station Communication

The previous example required a different program at each end, and the transmission path was only one way. The following program, written in C, can be run at multiple stations to form a two-way communication system. The packets are arbitrarily limited to the shorter size (253 data bytes) but, within that limit, use variable length for greatest network efficiency.

The program assumes the card is located at address D000:0000 in the PC. Long (32-bit) pointers are used to define the card location, and so the appropriate memory model must be used with your C compiler. For example, using Microsoft Quick-C, the compile command is

```
qcl /AL  arc_chat.c
```

A message up to 253 characters can be typed into a local buffer. It is then sent to a selected ARCnet address by pressing Ctrl-T. While you are typing, any incoming message will cause the machine to beep. To display this message, use Ctrl-D. The program is terminated with Ctrl-Q.

```c
/* --------- ARC_CHAT.C --------------------------------------- *
 * ARCnet two-way messaging system.                             *
 * short packets only 1 - 253 characters                        *
 *    J.K. Hardy   April 7, 1994                                *
 * ------------------------------------------------------------ */
#include <stdio.h>

typedef unsigned char BYTE;

BYTE send_it();
void receive_it();
void display_it();

struct Short_Buffer{
   BYTE source_id;
   BYTE dest_id;
   BYTE size;
   BYTE data[253];
}Send;
BYTE who_from;
BYTE buffer[254];

void main()
   {
```

```
char key;
BYTE s_address, i = 0;
outp(0x2E8,0x00);                 // card reset
printf("\033[2J");                // clear the screen
printf("Ctrl-T= Transmit, Ctrl-D= Display, Ctrl-Q= Quit\n");
printf("What is the HEX address of this machine's card....");
scanf("%x",&s_address);
Send.source_id = s_address;
printf("Type a message for another ARCnet station ....\n\n");

outp(0x2E0, 0x00);        // suppress all interrupts
outp(0x2E1, 0x1E);        // clear flags
outp(0x2E1, 0x0D);        // define configuration
outp(0x2E1, 0x1C);        // enable receiver to page 3

while(1)
{
  receive_it();
  key = getche();
  switch (key) {
    case 0x14:            // Ctrl-T
        i=send_it(i);
        break;
    case 0x04:            // Ctrl-D
        display_it();
        break;
    case 0x11:            // Ctrl-Q
        printf("-------- All done, good bye ! ------- \n");
        exit(0);
        break;
    default:
        if (i < 253){
          Send.data[i] = key;
          i++;
          if (key == 0x0D) {  // if ENTER pressed
            printf("\n");
            Send.data[i] = 0x0A;
            i++;
          }
        } else
          printf("\n You have reached the 253 char limit\n");
    break; }              /* end case */
  }                       /* end while */
}                         /* end main */

// ----------------------------------
BYTE send_it(BYTE count)
```

```
  {
    int j = 253;
    BYTE d_address;
    BYTE *card, *t_buff;                    // two pointers
    printf("\nWhat is the HEX address of the destination card ");
    scanf("%x", &d_address);
    Send.dest_id = d_address;
    Send.size = 256 - count;
    printf("\n %d characters are now being sent. \n",count);

    while ( count < 0xFF) {// move to end of transmit buffer
       Send.data[j] = Send.data[count];
       count--;      j--;
    }
    card = (BYTE *)0xD0000000;// move 256 bytes to card
    t_buff = &Send.source_id;
    for (j=0; j<256; j++){
      *card = *t_buff;
      card++;   t_buff++;
    }
    outp(0x2E1, 0x03);                      // transmit command
    return count=0;
}

// ------------------------------
void receive_it()
{
  BYTE size, j;
  BYTE *card, *r_buff;
  card = (Byte *)0xD0000600;
  r_buff = buffer;
  if( inp(0x2E0) & 0x80) {
     printf("\007");                        // beep!
     who_from = *card;
     card = card + *(card+2);
     for(card; card < (Byte *)0xD0000700; card++){
        *r_buff = *card;
        r_buff++;
     }
     *r_buff = 0x00;                         // zero termination for
                   string
  }
  outp(0x2E1, 0x1C);                         // clear receiver
}
// -------------------------
void display_it()
```

```
{
  printf("This is a message from ... %X \n\n", who_from);
  printf("%s\n", buffer);
}
```

Program Description

ARC_CHAT.C prints instruction messages on the screen and asks the user for the address of the local card. It then turns on the receiver and moves into a loop. The loop continuously checks the receiver and waits for a key to be pressed. Most of the key presses will be characters for the message to be sent. The program keeps track of the number of characters using the variable *i*. As characters are typed, they are stored in the data portion of the Short_Buffer starting at the beginning.

When Ctrl-T is pressed for a send, the function "send_it" is run. This asks for the destination card address, calculates the ARCnet "size" byte, and shifts the characters to the end of the buffer. The packet is now in the correct form and is moved into the adapter RAM. Finally, the Transmit command is given, and the packet is sent.

When the receiver is checked, the program will beep if a message has been received. The packet is immediately moved into a "buffer," the receiver is reset, and the program returns to reading keystrokes. The message is only displayed when Ctrl-D is pressed. If the user waits too long, a second message could override the first.

ARCNET SCHEMATIC

The first part of an ARCnet card schematic is shown in Figure 4.18. This portion contains the COM 9026 network controller and the packet buffer RAM.

The inner bus of the card contains eight wires of multiplexed address and data information. The host, the network controller, and the packet RAM must each connect to this bus. Of course, only one of these devices would act as the source and one as the destination at a time.

The controller is the definite owner of the multiplexed bus. When the host wishes to talk to the ARCnet card, it must first decide whether it wishes to talk to the controller chip itself or to the RAM buffer. If the controller's internal registers are to be read or written, it then makes the appropriate "request" of the controller chip via IOREQ. For buffer Reads or Writes, the MEMREQ pin is used. Using its WAIT line, the controller forces the host to hold its present address and data line values while the controller multiplexes three bytes: Lower Address, Upper Address, and Data. This asynchronous access into the card by the host could take from 0.8 up to 2.0 microseconds to complete, depending on what the 9026 controller chip was doing at the time of the request.

The actual design of this interface is left for hardware engineers, but this area can have significant effects on the throughput of the card. Older designs could only achieve data rates of 100 kilobytes/sec. Recent improvements to the hardware inter-

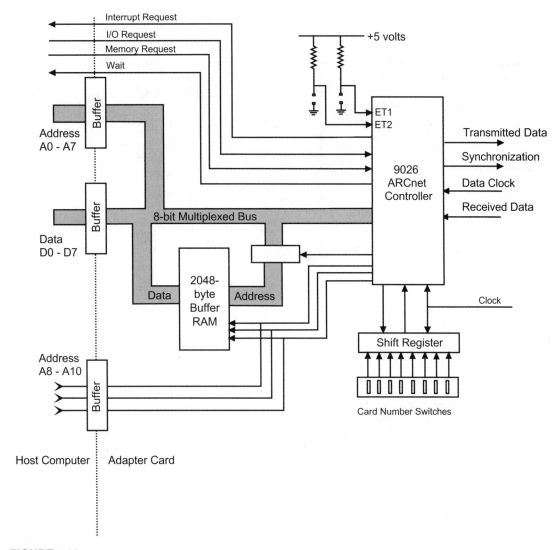

FIGURE 4.18
Schematic.

face and the use of a 16-bit interface to the host rather than an eight-bit one have more than doubled the throughput.

Although the basic operation of an ARCnet network hasn't changed much over the years, the cards have. In general, the more expensive cards will result in better performance. Corresponding improvements in driver software have raised the overall throughput to about 225 kilobytes/sec. At 11 bits per transmitted byte, this works out to just under 2.5 megabits/sec, which is ARCnet's design limit.

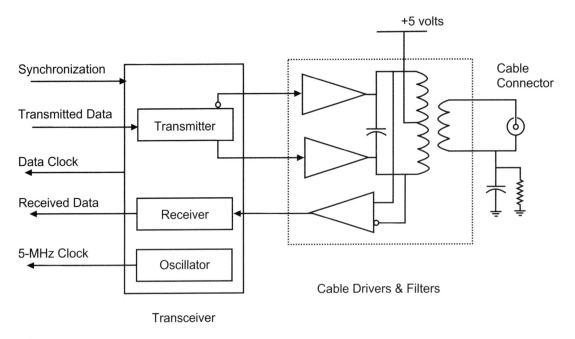

FIGURE 4.19
The remaining half of an ARCnet card consists of a transceiver chip and a hybrid filter circuit.

NETWORK TRANSCEIVER

The 93-ohm coaxial cable interface for ARCnet is shown in Figure 4.19. The chip shown here has several tasks. It acts as a combination transmitter and receiver and also generates several reference frequencies used by the rest of the board. The final interface to the cable is made with a hybrid circuit containing a **transformer**, filter, and some amplifiers. The same hybrid circuit is also used in the active hubs.

The two transmit amplifiers turn on alternately to transmit the positive and negative half cycles of the dipulse. The transformer and other filters control the rounding into a sinewave. The actual filtering is often more elaborate than that shown. The receiver amplifier adjusts its gain to compensate for losses in long or short cables and passive hubs.

LIGHTS

ARCnet cards generally are equipped with two light-emitting diodes on their back panel. One, generally green, glows constantly to indicate some activity on the cable. If no cable responses are being received, it flashes intermittently. This could indicate a broken cable or no other machine turned on. The other LED, typically red, indicates computer interface bus activity. Each time it flashes, some data is being moved between the host and the adapter. Together, the two lights form a simple and very effective troubleshooting tool.

ARCNET STAR CABLING SYSTEM

ARCnet can be cabled in either a star or a bus system. The cable can be either coaxial or unshielded twisted pair (**UTP**). Each of these require a matching network card. The original and still the most common installation is the distributed star based on 93-ohm coaxial cable. The reason for its continued existence is improvements in the central hub. The trend in networks is toward a central management system. A star network with individual stations connecting directly to a hub is the easiest to troubleshoot and manage.

The star configuration is made up of stations, cables, and active and passive hubs.

Passive Hubs

Passive hubs are used to interconnect up to four coaxial cables. Inside the hub, they simply contain four equal value resistors. These resistors split the energy coming in on one connector and divide it equally among the remaining three. The resistor values are selected to make any input appear as a 93-ohm load even though three cables are "paralleled" on the other connectors. The power loss from any input to any one output is 9.5 dB. This means that input signals that cycle between peak voltages of plus and minus 10 volts will be reduced to plus and minus 3.3 volts at each of the outputs. Because of this high "insertion loss" of passive hubs, any cable connected to one must be kept short (30 meters maximum) to limit additional losses (see Figure 4.20).

If only three cables are to be connected, it would be an easy task to design and build a special hub (three 31-ohm resistors and a sardine can—washed out, please!). The insertion loss would now be reduced to 6.0 dB and so the connecting cables could be slightly longer if necessary. Normally, however, an installer would simply use a four-port hub and place a 93-ohm terminating resistor on the unused connector to maintain correct input impedances.

Passive hubs, however, tend to defeat the idea of central station management. If three stations are connected through a passive hub into one port of an active hub and one should fail, all three would have to be cut off by the managing software.

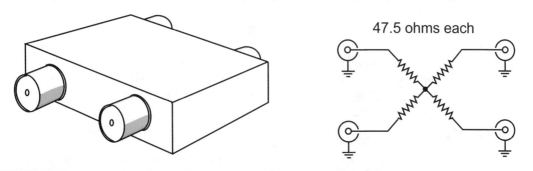

47.5 ohms each

FIGURE 4.20
The ARCnet passive hub comes only in a four-port version. The loss between any two connectors is 9.5 dB.

Active Hubs

Active hubs typically have four or eight connectors. Unlike passive hubs, they can receive weak signals on one connector and repeat this as full-strength signals on all remaining connectors. Much longer cables can, therefore, be used.

Each connector uses the same network filter module as is used on the ARCnet cards themselves. The module separates the cable signal into individual transmit and receive lines. The active hub then interconnects these transmit and receive lines with a logic circuit. Since an ARCnet system will only allow one station to transmit at a time, this logic simply performs a direction control function. It turns the transmitter off for the receiving connector and the receivers off on the remaining connectors for as long as the input lasts. In this way, a single direction amplifier is formed with no feedback problems. The hub receives on one connector and repeats everything out the remaining connectors (see Figure 4.21).

Active hubs that include central management capability would add the equivalent of a miniature workstation complete with ARCnet cable address. The hub would then be able to send status messages to a remote monitoring station and receive and process commands from that station. If another machine connected to that hub is misbehaving, a message could be received by the hub processor to cut it off.

STAR CABLE RULES

When the star network cabling is being assembled, some basic rules must be followed. These assure that the signal will be strong enough at each station and that the traveling time limits are not exceeded. Here are the rules:

1. There must be only one path between any two stations.
2. A machine may connect to either a passive hub or an active hub.
3. Any cable to a passive hub cannot exceed 30 meters (100 feet) whether it be from an active hub or a station.
4. The cable length from an active hub to a machine or another active hub cannot exceed 650 meters (2000 feet).
5. Passive hubs cannot be connected to each other. There would be too much signal loss.
6. Unused passive hub connectors must be terminated with a 93-ohm resistor. Unused active hub terminals don't matter because of the isolation the amplifier provides.
7. No two stations can be more than 6500 meters (20,000 feet) apart unless the time delay pins on every circuit card are altered (a rare situation).

Cable Timing

One of the cabling rules states that the maximum distance between any two stations cannot exceed 6500 meters (about 4 miles). This distance has an important effect on the system's operation. With RG-62A/U cable at 5.0 MHz, the velocity of propagation is 240×10^6 meters per second, 80% of the speed of light.

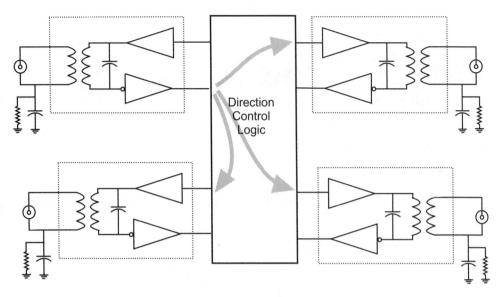

FIGURE 4.21
ARCnet four-port active hub. The signal is received on one input at a time, amplified, and transmitted out the remaining three.

If we take a simple extreme with one station at each end of a 6500 meter cable, some timing calculations can be made. When station A sends a token to station B, it will expect a reply within 74.7 microseconds. If it doesn't see any activity by this time, it will panic and start a network reconfiguration.

With 6500 meters of cabling and several repeaters and active hubs, the token will arrive at the far end in approximately 30 microseconds. The far end ARCnet card will take approximately 12 microseconds to process the token and send an acknowledgment. Again, a traveling time of 30 microseconds is required to get back to the machine at the near end of the cable. The elapsed time is now 72 microseconds (30 + 12 + 30). The maximum allowed time of 74.7 microseconds provides a small margin of safety. However, making a "small" increase in cable lengths beyond this limit can spell disaster.

If it does become necessary to work over greater distances, the time-out value can be changed with jumpers on the ET1 and ET2 pins of the COM 9026. All cards in any one system must have the same time-out setting.

ET1	ET2	Maximum Response Time
1	1	74.7 microseconds
1	0	283.4
0	1	561.8
0	0	1118.6

The 6500 meters of coaxial cable would satisfy the time delay requirement, but it would have high losses. The cable would, therefore, have to be broken into segments with maximum lengths of 650 meters each and two-terminal amplifiers added between segments. From a cost and maintenance point of view, such a long run would benefit from the lower losses of fiber optic cable. ARCnet cards are available in a fiber optic version or, for a single long run, fiber optic extender sets are available.

ARCNET VARIATIONS

Coaxial Cable Bus

A standard ARCnet card, such as the one previously described, represents a 93-ohm load to any cable. If two cards are connected at one end of a cable without using a passive hub, a cable mismatch would occur (46.5-ohm load on a 93-ohm cable). The reflected energy would cause an increase in errors, the number of retransmitted packets would increase, and the network would slow down.

However, ARCnet cards can also be purchased as "high impedance" cards, allowing the configuration shown in Figure 4.22 to be created. As many as eight high impedance cards can now be paralleled on a single 300-meter (1000-foot) section of cable. If a person doesn't look closely, this installation could accidentally look like an Ethernet system (thin Ethernet uses a smaller diameter 50-ohm cable; see Chapter 5). The network still requires proper termination so either a 93-ohm load or a low impedance card is required at the end of the cable.

The advantage of this configuration is lower cost because neither active nor passive hubs are needed. The disadvantage is decreased reliability. Since the cable is common to all stations, a failure in the wiring or the connectors (not unusual) will shut

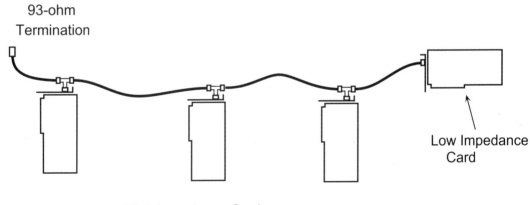

93-ohm
Termination

Low Impedance
Card

High Impedance Cards

FIGURE 4.22
High impedance cards can be paralleled on the same cable, but the cable still requires
93-ohm terminations.

down the whole network, not just the one station. Finding the fault will also prove difficult without the troubleshooting lights normally provided on the active hubs.

ARCnet Plus

Although adapter card designs were constantly improving, very few changes were made to the basic operation of ARCnet. Other adapter designs, such as Ethernet and Token Ring, rapidly surpassed it. They offered longer packets and higher data rates.

By 1992, the very overdue changes to ARCnet finally appeared. ARCnet Plus offers longer packets—up to 4096 bytes. The source and destination addressing was made IEEE-compatible and uses 48 bits instead of eight. Any one network can now have a maximum of 2047 stations. The data rate was increased to 20 megabits/sec. All of this was done while retaining compatibility with older cards (see Figure 4.23).

At a minimum, if the server and any one workstation are provided with the new cards, all communications between the two will occur at the higher data rate. Communications between the server and all older cards will drop back to the slower rate. Any active hubs between the high-speed cards must be replaced.

The cable waveform still uses 5.0 MHz sinewaves, but these now vary in amplitude. Where the original ARCnet transmitted a One with a single-amplitude 5 MHz sinewave (200 ns) that was always followed by a 200-ns silence, ARCnet Plus transmits independent sinewaves in both 200-ns time slots.

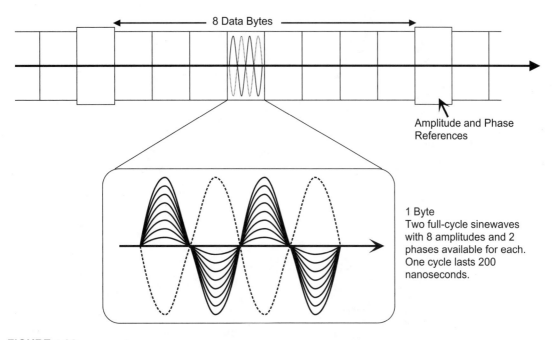

FIGURE 4.23
The 20 megabits/sec ARCnet Plus retains much of the original design but uses it more efficiently.

To increase the data rate by a factor of eight, ARCnet Plus allows eight different amplitudes (to a maximum of 12 volts) and two different phases of sinewaves in each of the 200-ns time slots. This results in 16 possible combinations (four bits) every 200-ns or eight bits in the 400-ns space that used to carry only one bit.

In addition, a calibration pattern is sent once every eight bytes instead of using three bits at the beginning of every byte. This consumes only 16% of the 20 megabits/sec throughput capability instead of the 27% in the older system. The pattern is an amplitude and phase reference for the following eight bytes. Because of cable losses, it is impossible to have an absolute reference. For example, a single sinewave with peak amplitudes of + and –12 volts might represent 1111 at the sending end of the cable, but several hundred feet down the line, this could be reduced to + and –6 volts. The receiving card must still read this as a 1111 pattern.

REFERENCES

1. SL90C65 ARCNET Controller/Transceiver Data Sheet. Silicom Ltd., Israel.

2. COM 9026 Local Area Network Controller Data Sheet. Standard Microsystems Corp., Hauppauge, New York.

Chapter 5

Ethernet

Ethernet is a CSMA/CD network—a significantly different animal from a token-passing system. When workstations don't have any messages to send, the connecting cable system stays totally quiet. When one decides to transmit, it doesn't wait for an invitation but simply goes ahead.

Ethernet is a product with quite a history. Its initial development was carried out by Xerox in Palo Alto, California, in 1972. Xerox then joined forces with Digital Equipment Corporation (DEC) and Intel to produce Ethernet 1.0 as a viable commercial product. The result is sometimes referred to as DIX Ethernet because of the three collaborators. A minor revision in 1982 created Ethernet version 2.0. The IEEE local area network committee then wrote and adopted the IEEE 802.3 standard for Ethernet. In 1989, the standard was amended to include a twisted pair version—likely the most popular of all network adapter cards.

VARIATIONS

All true Ethernet variations use baseband transmission with a 10 megabits/sec data rate. Each station "contends" for the use of the ETHER (the connecting cables) using Carrier Sense Multiple Access with Collision Detection (CSMA/CD). The stations do not have to transmit in any prearranged order so the overhead of a token-passing system is eliminated.

The original, and still common, cable system is a linear bus that uses a fairly large diameter coaxial cable. This is often referred to as Thick Cable Ethernet (see Figure 5.1).

Although offering very high performance, the original design with external transceivers is relatively expensive for personal computer use. Three cabling modifications have, therefore, been created in more recent years to reduce the costs. The general term "Ethernet" (with a capital letter) is used to refer to three of the four.

All four variations are described under IEEE's 802.3 revised standard using the following codes.

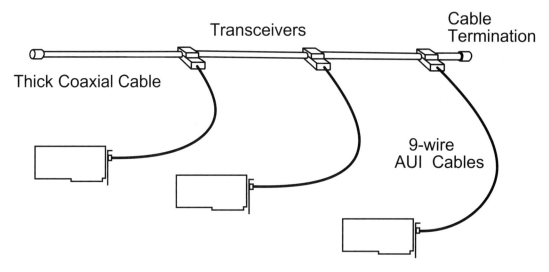

FIGURE 5.1
Original Thick Cable Ethernet separates the cable transceiver from the network card.

10Base5	Thick Cable Ethernet	500 meter bus
10Base2	Thin Cable Ethernet	185 meter bus
1Base5	Twisted pair StarLAN	500 meter diam. star
10BaseT	Twisted pair Ethernet	100 meter diam. star

THICK CABLE ETHERNET—10BASE5

As originally viewed by DEC, Intel, and Xerox (DIX Ethernet), the transceiver (transmitter and receiver) is external to the computer and mounted directly on the central cable. A 15-wire cable leads to the adapter card inside the computer (see Figure 5.2). Called an Attachment Unit Interface (**AUI**) drop cable, it can extend up to 50 meters between the workstation and the transceiver.

The transceiver performs the actual tasks of transmitting, receiving, and checking for collisions. It is clamped directly on the cable and makes electrical connection to it with a "vampire tap" which "bites" into the shield and center conductor. The cable itself is a rather large diameter (0.405-inch) double shielded coaxial—Belden 9880 with a foam polyethylene dielectric. It is fairly stiff and is occasionally referred to as "frozen yellow garden hose." Cable splices, terminations, and connections to inter-segment amplifiers use a large, threaded type-N connector which is specifically for use on double-shielded lines.

A maximum of 100 stations can be placed on any one cable segment, and they have to be spaced a minimum of 2.5 meters apart. This spacing was selected to minimize the accumulation of multiple cable reflections off the taps, which would cause errors. The cable is usually marked with this spacing to make tap installation easier. Each cable segment can extend to a maximum of 500 meters.

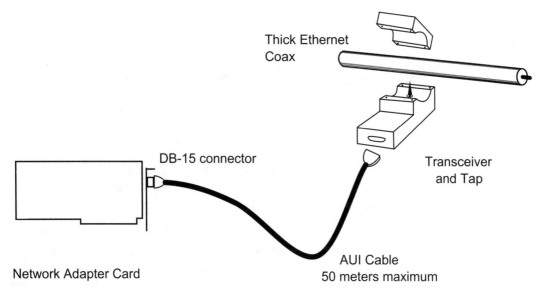

FIGURE 5.2
Transceivers for Thick Cable Ethernet mount directly on the cable and connect to the controller card with a 15-wire AUI drop cable.

For greater distances, as many as five segments can be interconnected using linear (amplitude information is important) two-way amplifiers between segments. The maximum network length is, therefore, 2500 meters. By connecting multiple stations to some of the transceivers, a maximum of 1024 stations can be placed on the total network. To grow beyond either the station count limit or the distance limit (and for several other reasons), we add **bridges** or **routers** (see Chapter 14).

Thin Cable Ethernet—10Base2

The original DIX physical arrangement with its separate components is too elaborate for widespread PC use. A variation, introduced by 3Com Corporation, follows all the Ethernet functional specifications but moves the transceiver onto the controller board inside the PC. The data rate stays at the original 10 megabits/sec.

The results are still very compatible with the original design. They should be—the founder of 3Com Corporation was also the original designer of Ethernet when he was at Xerox—Robert M. Metcalfe (along with David R. Boggs). Metcalfe left 3Com in 1990.

The larger diameter Ethernet cable is now replaced with a lower cost, more flexible thin cable (0.2-inch diameter) RG-58A/U. The separate taps and type-N connectors are replaced with BNC-T connectors right at the back of the PC (see Figure 5.3). Individual stations can now be connected as close as 0.5 meters.

The overall advantage is a reduction in cost, but this is obtained at the expense of a reduction in network size. A segment is now reduced to 185 meters compared with 500 meters for the thicker cable. Only 30 stations can be placed on any one seg-

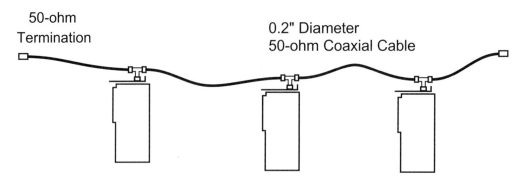

FIGURE 5.3
Single-card Ethernet uses thin cable and BNC-T connectors.

ment compared to 100 on the thicker cable. The length restriction is partly due to slightly higher cable loss and partly to slightly lower signal velocity on the thinner cable. As with the thicker cable, as many as five segments can be interconnected with repeaters for an overall maximum of 925 meters. Thin Cable Ethernet is also affectionately known as "cheapernet" for obvious reasons.

Thin cable cards are usually manufactured with the DB-15 AUI connector included. This allows them to be used on thick cable systems at a later time if desired. However, the separate transceiver and interconnecting AUI drop cable would then have to be purchased.

StarLAN—1Base5

A major variation on Ethernet (but not called Ethernet) uses a much lower data rate of 1 megabits/sec (see Figure 5.4). However, this allows standard telephone wiring to be used—an attractive choice for those with wiring already in place. This variation is AT&T's early StarLAN network. Up to ten stations can be "daisy chained" and then connected into a central wiring concentrator. By lowering the number connected on any one arm of the star to four, the overall radius can reach 250 meters.

The days of 1 megabit/sec StarLAN are now passing, and it has been replaced with a fully Ethernet-compatible 10 megabits/sec StarLAN.

Twisted Pair Ethernet—10BaseT

The final variation of Ethernet is similar to StarLAN in that an unshielded twisted pair (UTP) is used in a star network (See Figure 5.5). The data rate, however, climbs back up to the original 10 megabits/sec. The length of any one arm of the star is now reduced (officially) to 100 meters, but most manufacturers find they can easily exceed this.

This Ethernet variation was developed recently—while IBM's Token Ring was penetrating the LAN market. One of Token Ring's features is its ability to monitor the "health" of each network adapter and its associated cable and to cut them out of the picture should a failure occur. This is a great benefit when networks grow in size and

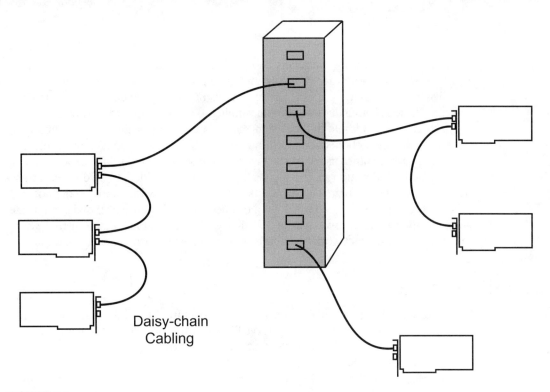

Daisy-chain
Cabling

FIGURE 5.4
1Base5 StarLAN is a 1 megabits/sec variation on Ethernet using twisted pair telephone
wiring and a bus/star configuration.

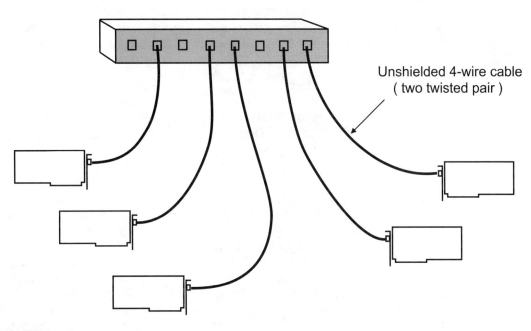

Unshielded 4-wire cable
(two twisted pair)

FIGURE 5.5
Twisted pair 10BaseT Ethernet.

cables start disappearing into walls and ceilings. Troubleshooting can be difficult in this case, and a network can stay down for a long time until the fault is located.

Twisted pair Ethernet retains all the benefits of the original design and adds a central concentrator with a dedicated cable running to each workstation. Continuous testing of this cable is inherent in the design, and panel lights indicate normal or abnormal operation. Should a connection fail or misbehave, it can be disconnected via software, without disturbing other users. In most cases, the disconnection is automatic.

The dedicated station cable contains two pairs of unshielded, twisted wires: a transmit pair and a receive pair. The two wires of each pair are twisted independent of each other to reduce crosstalk and maintain a balanced state. Because of the high data rate, good quality, EIA Category 3 wiring designed for 10BaseT should be installed. Existing telephone cabling might work for short distances but isn't worth taking a chance on.

IBM'S OTHER NETWORKS

We should briefly mention the two networks developed by IBM that are distantly related to Ethernet. These are the IBM PC Network Broadband and PC Network Baseband. Both are 2.0 megabits/sec CSMA/CD networks.

The broadband version is the older of the two, predating the Token Ring product by several years. It uses 75-ohm cable and cable television components to interconnect up to 72 computers in a 300-meter radius. The layout and frequencies were illustrated back in Chapter 1.

The baseband version is slightly newer. It was created by simply removing the radio frequency (RF) transmitters and receivers from the adapter cards and substituting twisted pair drivers instead. The layout now resembles that of StarLAN shown in Figure 5.4, but the data rate stays the same 2 megabits/sec as its broadband twin. A maximum of 80 PCs can now be connected within a 120-meter (400-foot) radius.

CSMA/CD

All versions and variations of Ethernet gain access to the shared cable using the "first-come–first-served" CSMA/CD method. This has already been described in Chapter 1, but let us look at the procedure again.

When a station wishes to transmit a packet, it must first listen to see if anyone else is transmitting (carrier sense). If no cable activity is sensed, transmission can begin. If there is some activity, the station will have to wait until it is complete and then defer an extra 9.6 microseconds before continuing. This extra gap ensures that all stations can distinguish the end of one packet from the beginning of the next.

Even after starting a transmission, the station continues to listen. There is a possibility that remote stations, further down the cable, will have sensed the "quiet" cable and started their own transmissions. Collisions would then result. This situation can arise because of the cable propagation delay, which, for a full 2500-meter network, is 25.6 microseconds end-to-end. This delay means that two stations at the extreme ends of the cable are 25.6 μsec "out of touch" with each other—like a distant star that may have exploded thousands of years ago, but the light hasn't reached us yet.

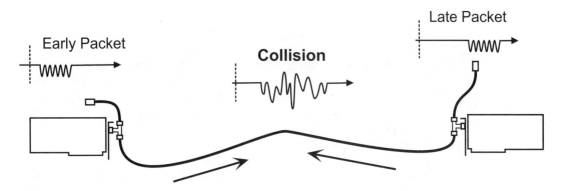

FIGURE 5.6
Packet collisions can occur when two widely separated stations start transmitting—
unaware, because of line propagation times, that the other has started.

Collisions are anticipated, and there is a definite procedure for handling them. Should one occur, there will be either a sudden change in the average cable voltage or a loss of the carrier. When either is sensed, all stations, including the two transmitting, will immediately cease sending. To ensure that all stations are aware of the conflict, the sensing stations will all transmit a short "jamming" burst (128 bits) and then shut up. This will be something like the boss starting to scream when too many people are talking at once. The "jam" is part of the Ethernet "collision consensus enforcement procedure."

Collisions due to cable propagation delay will only occur near the beginning of each packet in what is called the "collision window"—the first 51.2 microseconds. If a station at one end started a transmission 25.6 μs after a station 2500 meters away, it would sense a collision almost immediately. However, the first station wouldn't detect the collision until an extra 25.6 μs had elapsed. By this time, it would have been transmitting for 51.2 microseconds.

Figure 5.6 shows the results of two stations starting to send at about the same time.

Truncated Binary Exponential Back-off Algorithm

When a collision is sensed, all stations must stop transmitting and then wait. Eventually they will try again, and by this time, some additional stations might need to transmit. On the second attempt, collisions could reoccur. In fact, on each succeeding attempt, there might be a greater chance of collision as more and more stations get desperate. A CSMA/CD system, therefore, needs some form of orderly retry procedures for use after collisions. Within Ethernet, this procedure is called the "Truncated Binary Exponential Back-off Algorithm." It sounds awesome, but it is totally implemented by the network controller chip on the circuit board. The programmer never gets involved—at least not until things go totally wrong. Here is how it works:

1. When any packet collision is detected, the transmitting stations continue to transmit an extra 16 bytes of Ones (this is the jamming signal) and will then cease to transmit. This extra transmit time ensures that all stations recog-

nize that a collision has occurred. The stations involved will each wait (back off) a random length of time before trying again. This random wait tries to prevent all the retries occurring at once and is determined as follows.

2. Because all stations monitor the channel before they transmit, collisions will likely occur only near the beginning of a packet. This "collision window," as we have already explained, is a function of the round-trip propagation time on the cable. The retransmit delay after a collision was, therefore, designed to be multiples of this 51.2 μsec collision window time.

3. On the first retry after a collision, each station wishing to transmit will randomly decide either to send immediately (after the 9.6 μsec gap) or wait one collision window (51.2 μsec) and then send. With luck, only two stations were involved, and they will pick different times so no collision will occur. However, there is a good chance (50% if two stations are involved) that they will wait the same delay and then collide again.

4. The number of successive collisions is being recorded by each station, and they will realize that more drastic action is now needed. Before transmitting a third time (second retry), a random delay of 0, 1, 2, or 3 windows will be waited. Now there is only a 25% chance of any two stations waiting the same delay.

5. Should a third retry be necessary, the time delay will randomly be 0–7 window times (0–358.4 μsec), then 0–15, 0–31, 0–63 . . . 0–1023 window times. The last six retries will stay in the 0–1023 range until the maximum of 15 retries is reached.

6. If 16 collisions (15 retries) in a row are detected, the transmitter gives up, and higher levels of software must decide what to do. This is the only point where the programmer becomes involved.

This algorithm should fairly arbitrate a maximum of 1024 competing stations should they all try to send at once—which, although unlikely, could occur from time to time.

Once a successful transmission is made, all stations set their collision counters back to zero in preparation for the next packet.

This likely sounds like a real mess. Could it possibly work? Extensive tests have been run with a large number of stations competing for the cable. The technique allows the cable to carry good packets better than 95% of the time. In other words, if packets could be perfectly fitted onto the cable with only the minimum gap, the throughput would only be a few percent higher. This is not bad for what looks like a rather chaotic system! Remember that, in comparison, any token-passing system uses a small amount of time just for passing tokens around.

CABLE ENCODING

Manchester encoding is used to combine Ethernet's data and clock signals. IBM's Token Ring network, to be described in Chapter 6, uses a variation on this known as Differential Manchester.

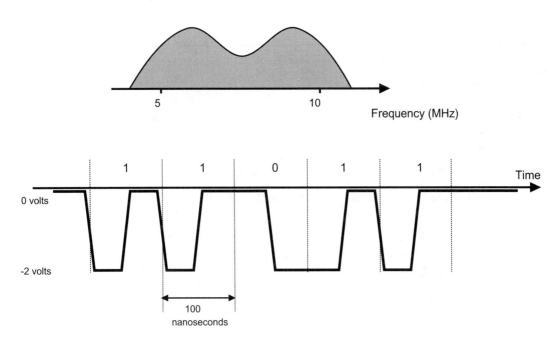

FIGURE 5.7
Manchester encoding of data and the resulting frequency spectrum.

At 10 megabits/sec, each data bit occupies a 100-nanosecond time slot. Manchester encoding, on the coaxial cable versions of Ethernet, uses a "square" wave with rounded edges. When no stations are transmitting, the center conductor sits at zero volts. A data value of Zero is indicated when the center conductor moves from Hi (0 volt) to Lo (–2.05 volts) in the middle of a time slot. A data One requires the opposite transition—Lo to Hi, again in the middle of the time slot. Transitions at the edge are whatever is necessary to prepare for the next data bit.

It is interesting (Network Trivia Time) that negative voltages on the cable were initially selected because NPN transistors (bipolar transistors are available in two polarities) were noticeably faster than PNP at the time (see Figure 5.7).

Ethernet is a baseband system. It doesn't use a separate radio frequency (RF) carrier. However, the specification does frequently refer to the "carrier." In this case, it means the periodic transitions within the data slots. They are important for clock recovery and also in the collision and end-of-packet sensing systems.

THE PACKET

All information is sent in variable length packets made up as shown in Figure 5.8. Like ARCnet and normal serial port communications, the least significant bit of each byte is transmitted first. This is only of interest to someone monitoring the cable waveform. Of wider interest, the most significant byte of each field in the header enters the cable first. Order in the data portion is not defined.

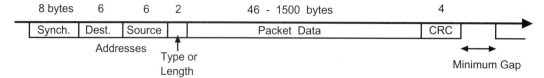

FIGURE 5.8
The Ethernet packet can handle from 46 to 1500 bytes of data. All bytes in the packet are transmitted least significant bit first.

Synchronizing Pattern (Preamble)

Ethernet's preamble contains 64 bits of alternating Ones and Zeros ending with two Ones. This alternating 1010 pattern synchronizes the phase locked loop (PLL) bit clock at the receiver. By ending the pattern with the final two Ones, the receiver can also synchronize a byte clock. The 802.3 standard redefines the header as a seven-byte (56-bit) preamble followed by a one-byte Start of Frame Delimiter (SFD). The words change; the pattern remains the same.

> 1010101010101010101010101010101010101010 . . . 10101011

The 64-bit size may seem rather long. It was chosen to ensure that enough remained to synchronize clocks after passing through all repeaters. Since repeaters, like all Ethernet receivers, are triggered by the presence of the carrier, the first few bits may be lost.

Source and Destination Addresses

Both address fields in the header are six bytes long (48 bits). Of these bits, 46 refer to adapter serial numbers and define the source and destination adapter. Beyond this, the first bit (the least significant bit of the most significant byte) of the destination address indicates the number of stations that will receive the message. If this bit is Zero, the message is intended for a single station. If it is One, the frame is being **multicast** to several stations. A variation on this sets all destination address bits to One to indicate an all-station broadcast.

The source address follows the destination address. Its first bit stays Zero. For IEEE compatibility, the second bit of each address may be used to indicate local (Zero) or global (One) administration of the addresses. This is further explained in Chapter 6.

The 802.3 standard also permits shorter 16-bit addresses, but this option is rarely used in practice.

Type/Length Field

This is a 16-bit value with its most significant byte transmitted first. The field can have two different meanings. In the Ethernet 2 definition, this field indicates the "type" of encapsulation used in the data portion. Novell places 0600h here to indicate Xerox XNS (Novell IPX) packets whereas TCP/IP places 0800h in this field to indicate IP packets.

The 802.3 specification, however, instead of type, defines this field as the "length" of data. Since the longest Ethernet packet contains only 1500 bytes, the highest number in the length field will be 05DCh. Type numbers are always selected to be larger than this so higher software layers shouldn't have a problem deciding whether type or length is being used.

A packet may still need a type field. Therefore, with the 802.3 Ethernet header, the type field can move into a Sub-Network Access Protocol (SNAP) header added by software after the adapter card header. The SNAP header, if used, will be placed immediately after the 802.2 LLC header. To the adapter card, this is simply added data passed down from higher layers.

Frame Data

Each frame can carry from 46 to 1500 bytes. There are no limitations on bit patterns, but they must be complete bytes. The minimum overall packet size of 76 bytes (46 data bytes) ensures that valid packets can be distinguished from collision fragments called "runt packets." This minimum was determined from the round-trip propagation time on the longest cable. When less than 46 bytes are to be carried, the programmer must arrange for padding bytes (any value) to be added after the data. The length field, if used, in the header indicates the amount of true data and doesn't include the amount of padding. Most adapter drivers look after this padding operation.

CRC Polynomial

To guard against errors during transmission, each packet carries a 32-bit Cyclic Redundancy Check (CRC) code at its end. This is generated inside the adapter card using the following 33-bit polynomial:

$$x^{32}+x^{26}+x^{23}+x^{22}+x^{16}+x^{12}+x^{11}+x^{10}+x^8+x^7+x^5+x^4+x^2+x+1$$

All of the packet from the destination address through to the last byte of data is divided by this polynomial. The 32-bit remainder is then added to the end of the packet as the CRC. At the receiver, a similar division is performed on the incoming packet and the results compared with the incoming CRC. If there is a discrepancy, upper software layers at the receiver are notified. Ethernet cards, by themselves, do not transmit positive or negative acknowledgments.

Inter-Packet Gap

A minimum gap of 9.6 microseconds must be left between the end of one packet and the beginning of the next. This ensures that a receiver recognizes the terminating CRC on one packet and the starting synchronizing pattern of the next. There is no special mark to indicate the end of one packet. Receivers sense the loss of carrier (no data transitions) and use that instead.

ADAPTER CARD SERIAL NUMBERS

Each adapter card that is manufactured carries a unique 48-bit serial number loaded into a Read-Only-Memory (ROM) chip. In most, but not all, cases, this is used as the station address. Address substitutions can be made by software and is done for testing purposes; these may even be required by some protocols— DECnet, in particular.

The serial number is unique for any Ethernet board produced by any manufacturer, and it should also be unique within all IEEE-controlled products—Ethernet, Token Ring, FDDI, ARCnet Plus. The addresses can have 2^{46} (two bits are reserved) different values, which is an awful lot of addresses. The intent is that this would make the interconnection of multiple networks much easier.

In the assignment of numbers, a particular value in the most significant three bytes is assigned to an individual manufacturer. They can then assign whatever numbers they want within the remaining three bytes. This means one board manufacturer could produce about 16 million boards before having to ask for a new number. It also means that manufacturers' boards are easily identified during protocol analysis. Some manufacturers' codes, in hexadecimal, are:

00000C	Cisco
000093	Proteon
0000C0	Western Digital/Standard MicroSystems
00DD00	Ungermann-Bass

COAXIAL TRANSCEIVER CIRCUITRY

The two coaxial versions of Ethernet use a common transceiver circuit design. They differ only in the physical location. The twisted pair transceiver is different and will be explained in a following section.

The actual connection to the coaxial cable occurs in the transceiver section. To eliminate possible interference from ground loop currents, no part of the transceiver or the main cable should be grounded. If a ground is absolutely necessary, it is made to the cable at only a single point on the whole system. Used for this purpose are 50-ohm cable terminating resistors with an extra ground lead. Much of the design of the transceiver interface to the card in the PC revolves around preserving this floating connection.

When sending, the transmitter acts as a current source pulsing between about 4 and 80 milliamps at the 10 megabits/sec data rate. As the current enters the cable, half will travel toward one end and half toward the other. The current is, therefore, working with a 25-ohm load resistance. The resulting voltage on the cable will swing between approximately –0.10 and –2.0 volts and will have a dc (average voltage) component of –1.05 volts.

All stations monitor the average of this dc cable voltage. Its value is very important. If it is approximately zero, no one is transmitting. When one station is transmitting, the average voltage should fall to about –1.05 volts. If it is more negative than about –1.5 volts, more than one station is likely transmitting, and a collision has occurred. Current, rather than voltage, driving is the key to the collision detection system, but it means that cable impedances, terminations, and ground loop currents must be carefully controlled.

All connections back to the rest of the adapter card circuitry are made through small transformers. These can only handle high-frequency signals in the vicinity of 10 MHz and will not pass dc or 60 Hz power line frequencies. Four transformers are required: one each for transmit, receive, collision signaling, and power (see Figure 5.9).

When a transceiver detects a collision on the cable, it turns on a small 10 MHz oscillator that sends a signal through the transformer and collision pair to the attached station. The adapter then knows to stop or defer any transmissions and follow the rules of the back-off algorithm previously discussed. Because it is vital, the transceiver keeps testing this collision detector system. Each time, after the local station has finished sending a packet, the transceiver will create a fake collision internally (not on the cable); this should result in a short burst of 10-MHz signal back through the collision pair. This is called the "heartbeat" signal. It should appear 1.1

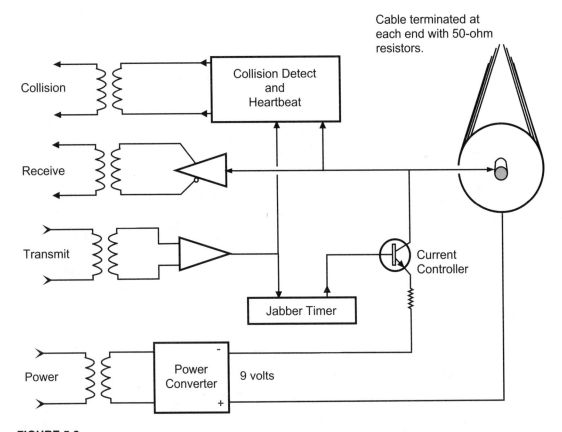

FIGURE 5.9
Coaxial Ethernet transceiver includes the transmitter, receiver, and collision detector circuits. This circuit is the same for both the separate "thick" and the onboard "thin" transceivers.

microseconds after the transmission finishes and last only 1.0 microseconds. This heartbeat is safely within the interframe gap and doesn't interfere with successive transmissions from other local stations.

If you are purchasing separate transceivers for thick Ethernet installation, be very careful of this heartbeat timing. Some transceivers use a different timing because the older Ethernet specification differs from the 802.3 specification. If cable segment repeaters are built up from transceivers, their heartbeat must be disabled.

The transceiver has one more task. Each time a local transmission begins, the transceiver starts an internal "jabber timer." A normal packet shouldn't be any longer than about 1.3 milliseconds. If the transmission continues beyond 20 milliseconds, something is terribly wrong. The transmitter will be immediately cut off, and a long "collision burst" will be sent back through the collision pair. It will take the network interface card (**NIC**) at least one-half second to find out what went wrong and recover. In the interim, it is out of action.

The power for all this transceiver circuitry must itself be fed through another isolation transformer. This is normally accomplished with a high-frequency oscillator on the main portion of the circuit board which feeds the primary of the transformer. Within the transceiver, the secondary voltage is rectified, filtered, and regulated to –9.0 volts.

If the transceiver is a separate unit, an Attachment Unit Interface (AUI) cable with 15-pin D-connectors is required (see Figure 5.10). The maximum length of this cable is 50 meters. Signals on this cable will travel along 20 or 22 AWG twisted pairs acting as 78-ohm transmission lines. The circuit boards at each end will include terminating resistors for this impedance. With the exception of the power supply pair, the voltages carried by this balanced wire interface are typically ±0.75 volts.

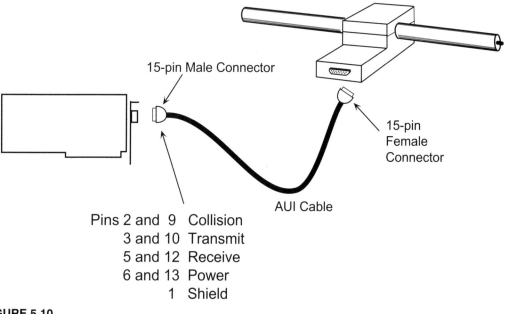

15-pin Male Connector

15-pin Female Connector

AUI Cable

Pins 2 and 9 Collision
3 and 10 Transmit
5 and 12 Receive
6 and 13 Power
1 Shield

FIGURE 5.10
AUI cable for separate Ethernet transceiver.

TWISTED PAIR ETHERNET

Like 10Base5, the transceiver for UTP Ethernet is built into the workstation's adapter card. However, the transceiver for twisted pair Ethernet shows some variations from the other transceivers. The big difference revolves around the change in cables.

All other versions of Ethernet use a common, shielded cable for both transmit and receive. 10BaseT, in contrast, uses one pair of wires for transmit and a separate pair for receive. The transmitter and receiver portions of the card now connect into their respective wire pairs through individual transformers rather than the direct current drive of the other transceiver. As a result, there are no dc voltages on the cables, and collisions must be detected by carrier signal alone. The transformers do remove the necessity for the floating power supply shown in Figure 5.9, and transmitter and receiver can now run directly from the computer's supply voltages. The result is simplified circuitry and reduced cost.

The other difference is also mandated by the cables. Since they are unshielded, the designers had to be very "environmentally friendly." This means being careful of the transmitted waveshape on the wires. If transmitted waves have sharp edges, harmonics (multiples) of the Ethernet frequencies could be radiated out into the surrounding area. These could interfere with radios, TVs, etc. However, if the shape can be kept closer to that of an ideal sinewave, the problem is greatly reduced (not eliminated). The transmit pair of 10BaseT, therefore, has a fairly elaborate filter to improve waveshape and match the approximately 100-ohm impedance of the twisted pair cable (see Figure 5.11).

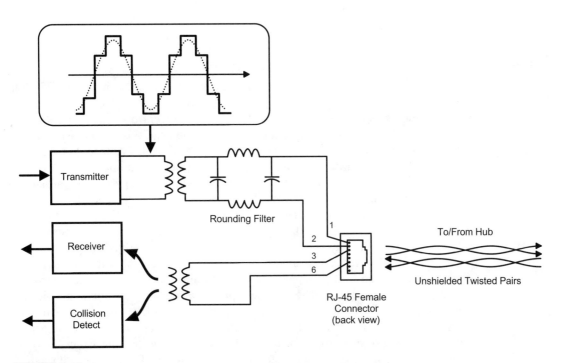

FIGURE 5.11
Transceiver portion of 10BaseT Ethernet adapter cards. The output waveform is built in steps and then filtered.

The wiring concentrator now plays an active role in checking the connection and detecting collisions. Single-polarity Link Integrity Pulses, also known as "I'm alive" pulses, are sent by adapter and concentrator if nothing else has been transmitted for the last 16 milliseconds. The receiving end of each pair watches for periodic activity and, if nothing has been received for more than 100 milliseconds, the port will be "failed." Both adapter and concentrator will, however, continue to send periodic link test pulses. A failed device will be removed from this state after either four consecutive link test pulses or a data packet is received.

In addition, because the Link Integrity Pulses are only one polarity, the adapter on the other end of the cable can check the polarity of its wiring and, if necessary, automatically reverse polarities to compensate for a wiring problem.

10BaseT adapter cards usually have four visible LEDs on their mounting bracket to assist with troubleshooting. The polarity and link integrity lights should be on constantly. The other two will flash as data is transmitted or received. Note, however, that a flashing receive light doesn't necessarily mean a packet is coming in for this station. Even with a concentrator, Ethernet still "broadcasts" to all stations.

The four lights and their usual colors are:

1	Green	Receive wire polarity is OK
2	Green	Link Integrity Pulses are being received OK
3	Yellow	Transmitting
4	Green	Receiving

CABLE TESTS

The collision detection mechanism on coaxial cable depends heavily on the 25-ohm dc resistance looking into the cable. Poor quality connections on the central cable can easily raise this resistance above 25 ohms. With current drive, this would cause an increase in the average voltage, and stations would read this as a collision. Also, 60-Hz ground currents along the cable could contribute to this voltage. For this reason, the cable must be isolated at all taps and only grounded at one point. Insulated coverings over any exposed metal of cable splices and terminators are recommended to prevent their accidentally touching other sources of ground current.

Ground resistance can be checked by temporarily removing the one cable ground (if you have one) and then measuring the resistance between the outside metal of the cable and any nearby metal that may be grounded: outlet ground pins, water pipes, etc. The resistance should be greater than a few thousand ohms. If not, try disconnecting the BNC connector at each station until the resistance jumps up. Again, the only ground should be the one separate wire from a terminating resistor.

Another simple test for an erratically operating Ethernet coaxial system is to measure the dc resistance of the cable and its two terminations. With all machines shut off, the measurement can be made by disconnecting the thin Ethernet BNC connector at one machine. The resistance looking into the T should be between 24 and 26 ohms. Using an analog meter (the only "real" kind) and gently wiggling the cable at various points along its length will often show up intermittent problems, usually at a connector.

PACKET RECEPTION

Each Ethernet receiver includes a "squelch" circuit that keeps small amplitude noise out. This circuit monitors the average dc voltage on the cable to see when a station is transmitting. As indicated, a cable voltage of about –1.05 indicates that a single transmission is in progress. As the average voltage moves down (negative voltages) toward this value, the receiver is turned on.

All stations monitor all packets at least to the end of the destination address. At that point, a station will have determined if the packet is of interest or not. The receiving station continues if:

- The destination address exactly matches this station address (first bit Lo). This will be a unique packet for this station.
- The destination address indicates a "broadcast" to all stations (all bits Hi).
- The destination address indicates a "multicast" to a group of which the receiving station is a member (first bit Hi).
- The receiving station has been set to the "promiscuous" mode. In this mode, the station monitors all packets from all stations—handy for network diagnostics.

If the packet is to be received, it is moved into a RAM buffer on the circuit board. Then, if the CRC and a few other error checks are valid, the host computer is notified that a packet has been received, usually via an interrupt.

NATIONAL SEMICONDUCTOR CHIP SET

Many Ethernet card manufacturers use a set of three integrated circuits produced by National Semiconductor (see Figure 5.12). (The IBM Broadband and Baseband CSMA networks initially used an Intel chip set.) The National Semiconductor chips look after all of the protocol implementation, the Manchester encoding and decoding, and the actual interface to the cable. The only other major chip needed is an 8K, or greater, RAM chip used as a packet buffer. A small ROM is also used to hold the card's network address.

The 8390 Network Interface Controller (NIC) is the heart of this chip set. In the following pages we will attempt to describe some of this chip's features. However, this is a very elaborate chip. For a detailed study, obtain National's data sheets on the DP8390 Network Interface Controller.

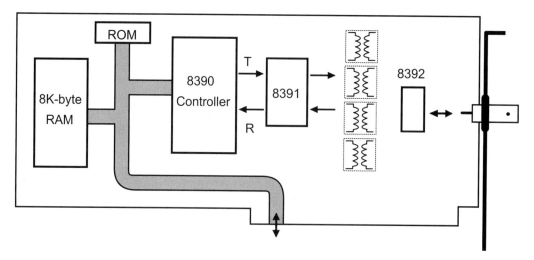

FIGURE 5.12
Three integrated circuits from National Semiconductor Corporation plus an 8K RAM chip
form the major portion of an Ethernet board. The card address is held in a small ROM chip.

8390 Network Interface Controller (NIC)

This 48-pin chip is responsible for the Ethernet protocol and for movement of information to and from the buffer RAM. Its operations include:

- moving data between NIC and the adapter's RAM buffer
- moving data between the host and the adapter buffer
- retransmitting packets if collisions occur
- interpreting commands from the host
- notifying the workstation of incoming packets or errors
- serializing and deserializing (transmit and receive)
- generating and checking CRCs
- recognizing station, multicast, and broadcast addresses
- recognizing and tallying (counting) various errors
- performing diagnostic tests including loopback.

8391 Serial Network Interface (SNI)

The SNI chip is smaller with only 24 pins. Its functions are:

- adding the 10-MHz clock to the transmitted data using Manchester encoding
- extracting a 10-MHz receive clock from the incoming waveform using a phase locked loop
- turning the 10-MHz "collision signal" from the cable interface into a Hi/Lo logic signal for the NIC.

8392 Coaxial Transceiver Interface (CTI)

The CTI chip is used only in coaxial versions of Ethernet. It is the smallest of the three chips with only 16 pins. It must be isolated from the rest of the card with small transformers and must receive its power through an isolated supply. The CTI requires supply voltages of 0 and –9 volts. Its functions are:

- converting transmit voltages from the SNI chip into current levels on the coaxial cable
- squelching and receiving incoming transmissions from the cable
- detecting collisions on the cable and signaling the network controller; also periodically tested with a "heartbeat" circuit
- monitoring packet lengths and turning the local transmitter off if lengths become excessive. This involves a "jabber timer."

ETHERNET PROGRAM MODEL

To the programmer, the National Semiconductor interface consists of registers within the NIC plus memory within the card's RAM chip. This sounds very similar to the ARCnet interface, but there are some major differences. First, the ARCnet programming model showed only three registers. The Ethernet model has 81 registers, which are squeezed, via paging, into only 16 bytes of I/O space.

The big difference is in the programmer's access to the onboard RAM and the small address ROM of the card. The National Semiconductor chip set is very versatile in this respect. Two techniques are provided.

If the board manufacturer so chooses, the RAM and PROM can be placed within the main memory map of the PC—in which case, they typically use up about 8–16K bytes. The other possibility is to have all RAM and ROM accessed through a single I/O port location. The advantage is that the complete card now requires a total of only 32 bytes of the host computer's resources—these are all in the I/O block with nothing in the main memory space. (Theoretically only 17 bytes would be needed, but I/O memory is usually decoded 16 bytes at a time and so 32 bytes are used up.)

As an example, the 3Com Etherlink II board uses the National set of integrated circuits (although somewhat modified) and allows the user to select either interface by moving jumpers on the circuit board (see Figure 5.13). One jumper selects the placement of the NIC registers. These are always accessed within the I/O block, but their address can be moved around to avoid conflicts with other cards. Another jumper selects the PROM and RAM interface. This can be placed at any one of four different locations within the host's main memory map, or it can be switched to the single I/O access point located just after the NIC registers (see Figure 5.14). In the latter case, the NIC's "remote" DMA system must be used (example to follow).

FIGURE 5.13
Interface options available for
the 3Com Etherlink II board.
The options are selected by
moving two jumpers around.
The registers will always be
someplace in the I/O block of
ports. The RAM and ROM
can be accessed either at
several locations within the
host's main memory or via a
single I/O port.

Register Locations

250 - 25Fh
260 - 26Fh
2A0 - 2AFh
2E0 - 2EFh
300 - 30Fh
310 - 31Fh
330 - 33Fh
350 - 35Fh

in I/O block

ROM and RAM Locations

C800:0000h   in main memory
CC00:0000h   in main memory
D800:0000h   in main memory
DC00:0000h   in main memory
-or-
offset 10h   in I/O block

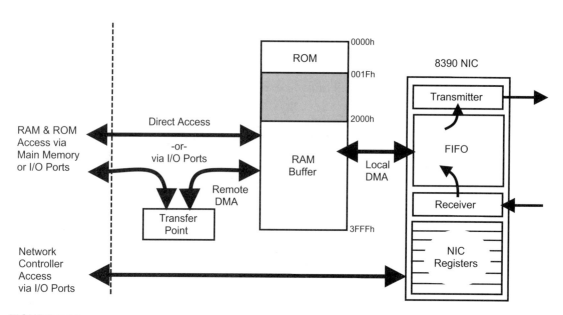

FIGURE 5.14
Programmer's model of an Ethernet card based on the National Semiconductor chip set.
RAM and ROM access can be through either main memory locations or a single I/O loca-
tion. The method is controlled by jumper blocks before the card is installed.

HOST AND NIC DMA

In Chapter 2 of this book, we briefly examined the DMA system of the PC itself—the host DMA. With a typical Ethernet card added to the PC, we could be discussing as many as three separate DMA systems depending on the jumper positions selected on the card. The variations are illustrated in Figure 5.15. In all cases, the NIC's local DMA is used for the movement of transmit and receive packets between the buffer RAM and the 16-byte FIFO. The remaining DMA usage is optional.

Although the following descriptions are for Ethernet, these DMA systems are common to other adapter types, too. The three access choices are:

1. *Buffer in main memory map.* The NIC's local DMA is used to move packets between transmitter/receiver FIFO and the adapter buffer. Moves between the host and the adapter's buffer use host processor MOV instructions.
2. *Host DMA to I/O block.* The NIC's "remote" DMA must be used to move data between the I/O transfer point and the adapter's 8K buffer. The programmer uses two registers that control buffer addresses and quantity to be moved. Movement to and from the transfer point uses the host computer's DMA. Three DMA systems are involved.
3. *Buffer within I/O block.* Again, a transfer point is used, but in this case, it has a definite address in the block of I/O ports (typically offset 10h from the adapter's base address). The movement between main memory and this transfer address uses IN and OUT instructions.

1 - Buffer in Main Memory

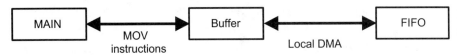

2 - Buffer in I/O Block, Host DMA Used

3 - Buffer in I/O Block, Host DMA Not Used

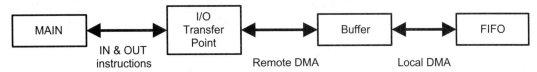

FIGURE 5.15
Ethernet cards can provide up to three options for moving data between the host's main memory and the 8K adapter buffer.

NIC REGISTERS

The NIC registers are always located within the I/O block of ports. There are 81 different registers in total, and they are spread across three different "pages" of 16 bytes each (see Figure 5.16). Two bits within the Command Register determine which page of registers is to be used for subsequent Reads and Writes. The command register itself is common to all pages. The most frequently used registers are placed in page zero for faster access.

Some of the registers are Read Only and others Write Only. Some that are both Read and Write will have the Read function on one page and the Write function on another. Although this will seem strange, the placement was chosen to keep the most frequently needed functions on page zero. The other two pages will be heavily used only at initialization time.

Command Register

The command register is located at the first address (offset zero) on each page. This is necessary simply because it contains the page control bits. Before issuing a command, the programmer would normally have to load several other registers first and then use the command register to initiate the desired action. The individual bits of this register are shown in Figure 5.17.

PS1, PS0	Determines the page setting for the remaining 15 addresses. Only three of the four possible pages are used. There is no fourth page.
RD2, RD1, RD0	Controls the operation of the remote (buffer to host) DMA. Other DMA registers would have to be loaded before these commands were issued. The three most useful operations are:

        0 0 1   move information from buffer to host

        0 1 0   move information from host to buffer

        0 1 1   move complete packet from buffer to host and update a number of registers.

TXP	Transmit Packet. Initiates the transmission of a packet via local DMA into the FIFO of the transmitter.
STA	Start. Takes the NIC out of the reset mode.
STP	Stop. Places the NIC in the reset mode (this mode will be indicated by a bit in the Interrupt Status Register). The chip will automatically be in the reset mode when power is first applied.

Interrupt Registers

There are two registers directly involved in interrupts. One indicates where the interrupt is coming from—Interrupt Status Register (ISR). The other contains masking bits so that individual sources can be suppressed—Interrupt Mask Register (IMR).

Address	PAGE 0 PS1 = 0, PS0 = 0		PAGE 1 PS1 = 0, PS0 = 1		PAGE 2 PS1 = 1, PS0 = 0	
	Read	Write	Read	Write	Read	Write
300h	Command	Command	Command	Command	Command	Command
301h	Current Local DMA Address 0	Page Start Register	Physical Address 0	Physical Address 0	Page Start Register	Current Local DMA Address 0
302h	Current Local DMA Address 1	Page Stop Register	Physical Address 1	Physical Address 1	Page Stop Register	Current Local DMA Address 1
303h	Boundary Pointer	Boundary Pointer	Physical Address 2	Physical Address 2	Remote Next Packet Pointer	Remote Next Packet Pointer
304h	Transmit Status	Transmit Page Start	Physical Address 3	Physical Address 3	Transmit Page Start Address	——
305h	Number of Collisions	Transmit Byte Count 0	Physical Address 4	Physical Address 4	Local Next Packet Pointer	Local Next Packet Pointer
306h	FIFO	Transmit Byte Count 1	Physical Address 5	Physical Address 5	Address Counter Upper	Address Counter Upper
307h	Interrupt Status	Interrupt Status	Current Page	Current Page	Address Counter Lower	Address Counter Lower
308h	Current Remote DMA Address 0	Remote Start Address 0	Multicast Address 0	Multicast Address 0	——	——
309h	Current Remote DMA Address 1	Remote Start Address 1	Multicast Address 1	Multicast Address 1	——	——
30Ah	——	Remote Byte Count 0	Multicast Address 2	Multicast Address 2	——	——
30Bh	——	Remote Byte Count 1	Multicast Address 3	Multicast Address 3	——	——
30Ch	Receive Status	Receive Configuration	Multicast Address 4	Multicast Address 4	Receive Configuration	——
30Dh	Frame Alignment Error Counter	Transmit Configuration	Multicast Address 5	Multicast Address 5	Transmit Configuration	——
30Eh	CRC Error Counter	Data Configuration	Multicast Address 6	Multicast Address 6	Data Configuration	——
30Fh	Missed Packet Counter	Interrupt Mask	Multicast Address 7	Multicast Address 7	Interrupt Mask	——

FIGURE 5.16
National Semiconductor Ethernet I/O block memory map. The offset addresses are relative to the starting point of whichever I/O block is selected with jumpers, i.e., 300–31Fh. The desired register page is selected with two bits in the Command Register.

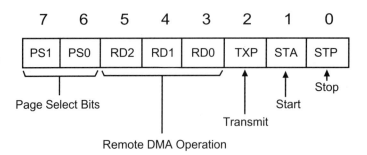

FIGURE 5.17
NIC Command Register appears at offset zero on each page. It can be both read from and written to.

Interrupts can come from any one of seven different places within the NIC controller (see Figure 5.18). Many of these bits also appear in the receive or transmit status registers. They can be read at either location but only cleared through the ISR location. An interrupt will be generated when one of the unmasked ISR bits goes Hi. The interrupt is cleared by writing a One back to the same bit position. The most significant bit (7-RST) doesn't generate an interrupt; it only indicates whether the controller is in its RESET state or not. Interrupts are masked (suppressed) by writing Zero into the corresponding position of the IMR.

RST   Reset. Indicates that the NIC is in the reset state. This does not generate an interrupt.

RDC   Remote DMA Complete. This bit will be One when the remote DMA has completed its movement of all bytes.

CNT   Counter Overflow. Indicates that one of three error "tally" counters (frame alignment, CRC, frames lost) has reached a count of 128.

OVW   Overwrite. Incoming data cannot be moved into a buffer.

TXE   Transmit Error. Either too many collisions (more than 16) have occurred, or the transmit FIFO has run out of bytes to send.

RXE   Receive Error. Something is wrong with the packet just received.

PTX   Packet was transmitted without errors.

PRX   Packet has been received without errors.

Transmit Status Register

This register is cleared at the beginning of each transmission. When the packet has been sent or transmission is aborted, these bits can be read to see what happened (see Figure 5.19).

OWC   Out of Window Collision (beyond $51.2\,\mu s$).

CDH   No heartbeat detected after transmission.

FU   FIFO ran out of data (underrun).

CRS   Carrier lost during transmission.

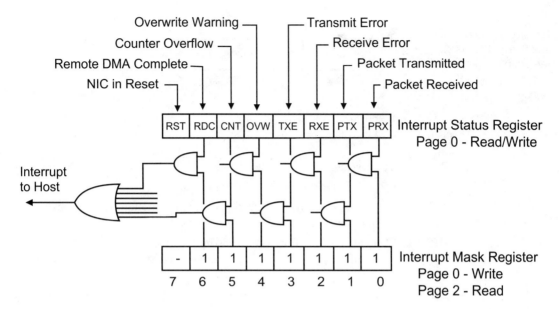

FIGURE 5.18
The Interrupt Status Register (ISR) contains seven bits that could interrupt the host if the corresponding bit in the Interrupt Mask Register (IMR) is enabled. After an interrupt, the ISR register would have to be examined to determine the cause. Interrupts are cleared by writing a One into the corresponding bit position.

ABT   Transmission aborted from excessive collisions.
COL   At least one collision occurred.
DFR   Transmission completed without deferring.
PTX   Packet transmitted without error.

Receive Status

This register is located within the I/O block the same as all other registers (see Figure 5.20). However, its contents change every time a new packet appears on the cable even if that packet isn't destined for the local station. A copy of this register is

FIGURE 5.19
Transmit status register located on page 0. Some of these bits will generate interrupts via the interrupt status register.

7	6	5	4	3	2	1	0
OWC	CDH	FU	CRS	ABT	COL	DFR	PTX

FIGURE 5.20
Receive status register. An
identical pattern is stored in
the adapters buffer after each
successful receive.

7	6	5	4	3	2	1	0
DFR	DIS	PHY	MPA	FO	FAE	CRC	PRX

also saved in the buffer RAM when each packet is correctly received by this station. This is the copy that will be more useful.

DFR — Deferring.

DIS — Receiver Disabled.

PHY — Zero indicates the received packet was uniquely sent to this station. One indicates a multicast or broadcast.

MPA — Missed Packet. For some reason, the packet didn't get moved into the buffer, probably because there was no space in the buffer.

FO — FIFO Overrun. Not enough buffer space.

FAE — Frame Alignment Error. Packets must contain whole bytes, and this bit indicates that the current packet didn't. Increments FAE tally counter.

CRC — CRC Error. Increments CRC tally counter.

PRX — Packet Received Intact.

SAMPLE PROGRAM—READ ADAPTER NUMBER

The following program is an example of using both the host DMA and the NIC's remote DMA to read the adapter's buffer memory. The focus here is on adapter initialization and DMA procedures and using them to read the adapter address from its ROM. There are shorter methods of reading addresses if that is all that is required.

This reading of the card address is a necessary first step in many programs. Back in Figure 5.16 we saw a space on page 1 of the NIC registers for the station address. This must be loaded by the programmer. The following program could be easily adapted to perform the job.

The program reads 32 bytes from addresses 0000–001Fh in the ROM. The example assumes that the card has been placed in I/O space 300–30Fh and that the ROM/RAM interface is not in main memory but was selected instead as I/O port access (single-byte transfer point) using the host DMA.

You should recall from Chapter 2 that the DMA channel on the host computer moved information between the main memory and a single I/O port. In the general situation, this port doesn't need to have a known address. It is activated by the appropriate DMA acknowledge line from the host. On most Ethernet cards, however, the transfer point will have a specific I/O address. If, for example, the NIC registers are set to 300–30Fh, the transfer point will be at I/O address 310h. Having a specific location now allows the programmer to choose between the host DMA

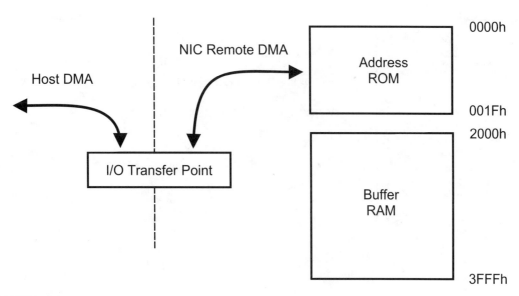

FIGURE 5.21
Both the host DMA and the NIC remote DMA are involved in this example.

method or the loopable IN/OUT method. As we have said, this example (and only this example) will use the host's DMA (see Figure 5.21).

The program begins by initializing the controller chip. The code for this is in a separate file shown later.

The NIC remote DMA is then provided with a 16-bit "Remote Start Address" and a 16-bit "Remote Byte Count," both on register page 0. The host's DMA channel 1 is then programmed with the full 20-bit address of the main memory destination (not segment:offset values) and the same byte count (actually one less). Both DMA systems are started in the single-byte transfer mode. The NIC Remote DMA reads one byte from the buffer and places it in the transfer point. Hardware on the adapter card senses this write and makes a host DMA request on channel 1. The host then DMAs the single byte from the transfer point into the desired place in memory (called "contents" in this example). The sequence is repeated until all bytes are moved. The 32 bytes are then converted into hex ASCII and displayed (see Figure 5.22).

At the time of the transfer, no code is running. The host microprocessor is momentarily halted until the transfer is complete.

```
; ------------------ ETHER_AD.ASM ----------------------------------
; Reads card address from PROM using NIC remote DMA
;       and PC's DMA channel 1.
; Displays in ASCII.
; -----------------------------------------------------------------
CODE            SEGMENT
assume  cs:code, ds:code
            extrn Initialize: near
```

FIGURE 5.22
The results of running the
Ethernet address program.

```
C:\> ADDRESS

Here are the PROM contents in hex ...

    XX XX XX XX XX XX XX XX

    XX XX XX XX XX XX XX XX
```

```
            org  100h
start:      jmp  begin

contents    db       32 dup (00),'$'
prompt      db       "Here are the PROM contents in hex...."
            db       0Dh,0Ah,'$'

display     db       96 dup (2Eh), 0Dh,0Ah,'$'

table       db       30h, 31h, 32h, 33h, 34h, 35h, 36h, 37h
            db       38h, 39h, 41h, 42h, 43h, 44h, 45h, 46h

; ------------------------ initialize NIC -------------------------------
            call _INITIALIZE
; -------------------------send prompt to screen ------------------------
begin:      push  cs
            pop   ds
            mov   dx,OFFSET prompt
            mov   ah,09h
            int   21h
; --------------calculate host 20-bit address ------------------------
            mov   ax,cs        ; get segment value
            mov   cl,04
            rol   ax,cl
            push  ax
            and   al,0Fh       ; top 4 bits of 20-bit address
            out   83h,al       ; into DMA page register
            pop   ax
            and   ax,0FFF0h
            add   ax,OFFSET contents
; ----------------------- load 8237 ------------------------------------
            out   0Ch,al       ; clear byte flip-flop
            out   02,al        ; load Lo address
```

```
            mov     al,ah
            out     02,al       ; load Hi address
            mov     al,32d
            out     03,al       ; load Lo count
            mov     al,00
            out     03,al       ; load Hi count
;------------------------load NIC remote DMA ------------------------------
            mov     dx,308h
            mov     al,00
            out     dx,al       ; Remote DMA Start Lo
            inc     dx
            out     dx,al       ; Remote DMA Start Hi
            mov     ax,32d      ; size of PROM
            inc     dx
            out     dx,al       ; Remote Byte Count Lo
            mov     al,00
            inc     dx
            out     dx,al       ; Remote Byte Count Hi
            mov     al,55h   ; 8237 mode = single step, read, ch-1
            out     0Bh,al
            mov     al,01       ; unmask 8237 ch-1
            out     0Ah,al      ; host DMA is now ready
            mov     al,0Ah      ; NIC remote DMA read command
            mov     dx,300h
            out     dx,al
;
; ** The two DMA systems are running now *********************
; ****** They are transferring one byte at a time ***********
; ***************************** Now they are finished *****
;
;
; ----------------------convert 32 bytes into ASCII -----------------------
            mov     bx,OFFSET table
            mov     cx,32d
            mov     si,OFFSET contents
            mov     di,OFFSET display
next:       mov     al,[si]
            shr     al,1
            shr     al,1
            shr     al,1
            shr     al,1
            xlat            ; convert most signif. 4 bits
            mov     [di],al ; to ASCII
            inc     di
            mov     al,[si]
            and     al,0Fh
            xlat            ; convert lower 4 bits
            mov     [di],al
            inc     di
            inc     di      ; leave a blank
```

```
                inc     si
                loop    next
; ----------------------------display results -----------------
                mov     dx,OFFSET display
                mov     ah,09h
                int     21h
; ---------------------------terminate -------------------------
                mov     ax,4C00h            ; DOS terminate
                int     21h
CODE ENDS
END START
```

The next section of code is the initialization module that must be included with some of the programs in this chapter. It is separately compiled and then linked with each program.

A number of buffer management registers are mentioned here that have not been discussed yet. They are not essential for this first example but will be used when programs to send and receive data are presented. They are, therefore, included as part of the general initializing procedure.

```
; -----------INITIALIZE.ASM --------------------------------------------
; Initialization procedure for National Semiconductor
;          Ethernet controller chip.
; ----------------------------------------------------------------------
.MODEL SMALL
.CODE
        PUBLIC  _INITIALIZE

_INITIALIZE PROC
                mov     al,21h          ; page 0, stop mode
                mov     dx,300h
                out     dx,al           ; command register
; Configure NIC for 8-bit operations & set FIFO threshold ------
                mov     al,58h
                mov     dx,30Eh
                out     dx,al           ; data configuration register
; Clear 16-bit remote byte count -------------------------------
                mov     dx,30Ah
                xor     al,al
                out     dx,al           ; remote byte count Lo
                inc     dx
                out     dx,al           ; remote byte count Hi
; Initialize receive configuration -----------------------------
                mov     al,00
                mov     dx,30Ch
                out     dx,al           ; receive configuration register
; Place NIC in temporary loopback (test) mode ------------------
                mov     al,02           ; temporary loopback mode
                mov     dx,30Dh
                out     dx,al           ; transmit configuration reg.
```

```
; Set starting address of receive buffer to 2600h -----------------
        mov     al,26h
        mov     dx,301h
        out     dx,al           ; receive page start register
; Set end of receive buffer address to 3FFFh ------------------------
        mov     al,40h
        inc     dx              ; dx = 302h
        out     dx,al           ; receive page stop register
; Set "next page to be read by host" to 2600h ------------------------
        mov     al,26h
        inc     dx              ; dx = 303h
        out     dx,al           ; boundary register
; Clear all interrupts ----------------------------------------------
        mov     al,0FFh
        mov     dx,307h
        out     dx,al           ; interrupt status register
; Mask all interrupts. We will poll instead --------------------------
        mov     al,00h
        mov     dx,30Fh
        out     dx,al           ; interrupt mask register
; Switch to page 1 --------------------------------------------------
        mov     al,61h          ; page 1, stop mode
        mov     dx,300h
        out     dx,al           ; command register
; Set next address available for incoming packet to 2700h ------
        mov     al,27h
        mov     dx,307h
        out     dx,al           ; current page register
; Return to register page 0 ----------------------------------------
        mov     al,21h          ; page 0, stop mode
        mov     dx,300h
        out     dx,al           ; command register
; Start NIC ---------------------------------------------------------
        mov     al,22h          ; page 0, run mode
        mov     dx,300h
        out     dx,al           ; command register
; Configure transmitter for normal operation (no loopback) -----
        mov     al,00
        mov     dx,30Dh
        out     dx,al           ; transmit config. register
        ret
_INITIALIZE ENDP
        END
```

3COM ADAPTER ADDRESS

The previous example was presented to demonstrate the general techniques of transferring data using a dual DMA system. The application selected happened to be the reading of the network address ROM.

If the 3Com Etherlink II adapter is being used (Card 3C503) and the network address is to be read, then the following short C program will do the job. 3Com uses the National chip set on this model board but has added a gate array chip to perform many functions. Part of its task is to replace the normal DMA of the National Semiconductor chip. The result is improved and more consistent performance.

These extra functions are controlled by a set of 16 one-byte registers located 0x400 higher in the I/O block than the selected base for the NIC registers. Within this group, bits 3 and 2 of the new "control register" (at byte offset 06h) determine what is seen in the 16 bytes of the normal base address.

For the following values of bits 3 and 2 in the control register, you will see

00	National's NIC registers
01	address ROM bytes 0–15
10	address ROM bytes 16–31
11	reserved

The following program forces bits 3 and 2 of the control register to 01 and then reads the six address bytes from what would normally be the range used by the NIC registers. Before terminating, it puts the bits back the way they were. The initialization procedure is not used with this program.

```
/* -------------------------------------------------------------- *
 * Read Network Address Directly from 3Com  *
 * Etherlink II card - model number 3C503   *
 * --------------------------------------------------------------*/
  #include <stdio.h>
  #define BASE   0x300
  main()
  {
    int i, value, original;
    printf("Address, in hex, is...");
    original = inp(BASE+0x406);       // save original
    outp(BASE+0x406, original | 0x04 & 0xF7);
    for (i=0; i<6; i++)  {
       value = inp( BASE + i );
       printf("%02X", value & 0xFF);
    }
    outp(BASE+0x406,original);        // restore
    printf("\n");
  }
```

ADAPTER BUFFER

A number of registers inside the National NIC are involved with managing the buffer RAM on the adapter. You will have already seen these registers if you followed through the initialization procedure. We need to discuss them now before we get into any send and receive programs (see Figure 5.23).

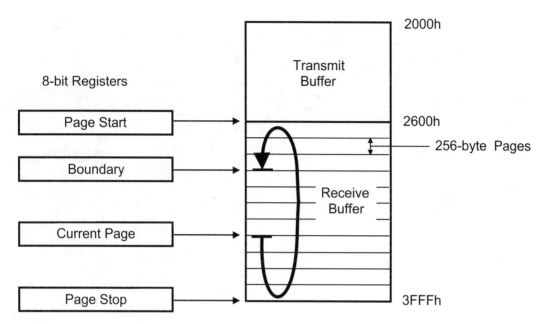

FIGURE 5.23
The adapter buffer RAM is split into a transmit portion and a receive portion. The receive portion operates as a circular buffer. The NIC registers handle buffer RAM in pages of 256 bytes each.

The NIC uses a 16-bit address bus to control its buffer RAM. A few of the registers involved will hold all 16 address bits, but the majority will hold only the most significant eight bits. With these shorter registers, the NIC is working with RAM one "page" at a time. Each page will be 256 bytes. (Don't confuse these RAM pages with the register pages discussed earlier.)

The available RAM is broken into two portions: one for transmit and the other for receive. It doesn't matter which is placed first. The receive portion is identified with two eight-bit page registers. The Page Start register identifies the most significant eight bits of the receive area start address, and the Page Stop register identifies the ending address (it is actually set to the page that is one byte higher than the ending address).

Between these limits, the buffer operates as a circular queue for received packets and is usually large enough to hold several packets at one time. The Current Page register indicates the next available page within the queue, and the Boundary register indicates the starting page of packets that have not yet been read by the host. RAM is used in 256-byte increments so a received packet of 300 bytes will consume two full pages.

Received packets are moved into the buffer with the local DMA. When a new packet reception begins, the local DMA addressing system moves down four bytes below the Current Page pointer. This leaves a hole that will be filled later if the reception is error free. The local DMA system keeps filling the buffer until it hits the Page Stop limit. It then continues at the Page Start value, thereby forming a circular queue.

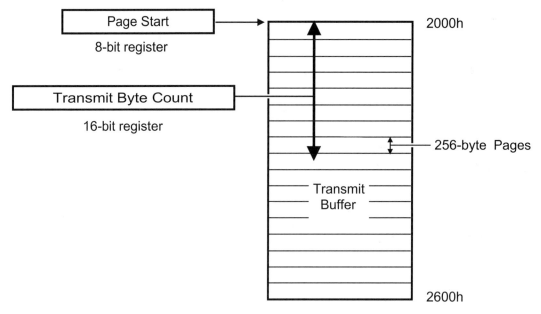

FIGURE 5.24
Data to be transmitted is placed in the buffer, and two registers are initialized before the transmit command is given.

As it fills the buffer, it will stop before it reaches the Boundary pointer value. This prevents previous packets that have not been read by the host from being overwritten by new packets. If the new packet has not been fully received when the Boundary is reached, an error occurs, and the packet is rejected. If the packet is received correctly (valid CRC, etc.) the four-byte hole at the start of the packet is filled in.

RECEIVE STATUS	8 bits
NEXT PAGE AFTER THIS PACKET	8 bits
LENGTH OF PACKET	16 bits

The Current Page register is then set to the next available free page.

If an error occurs during the reception, all register values are automatically returned to their previous values, and the buffer space is recovered.

The transmit portion of the buffer is much simpler. It is not used as a circular queue, requires only two registers, and is described in the next section (see Figure 5.24).

PACKET TRANSMIT

This example uses the NIC's remote DMA and 80x86 IN and OUT instructions.

A packet to be transmitted is assembled someplace in the adapter buffer area, starting on a page boundary. The eight-bit Transmit Page Start Address register is set to this starting point. The total number of bytes including addresses, data, and any necessary padding is loaded into the 16-bit Transmit Byte Count register, and the transmit command is given.

Destination Address (6 bytes)

Source Address (6 bytes)

Length (2 bytes)

Data (46–1500 bytes)

Padding if needed

The NIC starts transmitting the 64-bit synchronizing preamble while it moves the data, using its local DMA channel, in bursts of several bytes at a time, into its internal 16-byte FIFO (First byte In is the First one Out) memory. When the preamble is completed, the addresses and then the data provided are transmitted in turn. The bits within each byte are sent least significant first. When the FIFO needs more bytes, it will automatically get them from the buffer using the NIC's local DMA. As these bytes are being sent, the NIC continuously calculates the 32-bit CRC. When the last bit of data is sent, the CRC "remainder" is added to the end of the data stream, and the transmission ends.

The following send program will ask for the source and destination addresses and save these in the host buffer. Then the user can type a message of up to 1500 characters. To transmit, press Ctrl-T. Another message can then be sent if desired or the program terminated with Ctrl-C.

```
/* --------------------------------------------------------------------- *
 * SEND PROGRAM FOR generic Ethernet card                               *
 * Card buffer is accessed via an I/O port and remote DMA               *
 * NIC Register is in I/O block starting at 300h                        *
 * J.K. Hardy August 19, 1994                                           *
 * ---------------------------------------------------------------------*/
#include <stdio.h>
#define    Base        0x300
#define    CmdReg      Base
#define    TrPgStReg   Base + 0x04

extern void INITIALIZE();       // external assembly routine

typedef unsigned char Byte;

struct Buffer{              // Transmit buffer structure
   Byte destination[6];
   Byte source[6];
   int  size;
   Byte data[1500];
}Send;
```

```
main()
  {
   void Get_Address();
   Byte Send_Frame();

   char key;
   int size = 0;
   Byte result;

   INITIALIZE();          // initialize the NIC
   printf("\033[2J");        // clear the screen using ansi.sys
   printf("What is the address of this machine's card?\n");
   Get_Address( Send.source);
   printf("What is the address of the destination machine?\n");
   Get_Address( Send.destination);

   printf("\nType your message. ");
   printf("Press Ctrl-T when you are ready to send it. \n\n");

   while(1)    {
      key = getche();
      if (key == 0x14) {          // Ctrl-T for Transmit
         result = Send_Frame(size);
         size = 0;
      }
      else if (size < 1500) {
         Send.data[size] = key;
         size++;
         if (key == 0x0D) {
            printf("\n");
            Send.data[size] = 0x0A;
            size++;
         }
      }
      else
         printf("\n You have reached the 1500 char limit\n");
   }                         // end while
  }                          // end main

/* ----------------------------------------------------------------- *
 * Read 12 characters from keyboard and pack into 6 bytes *
 * ----------------------------------------------------------------- */
void Get_Address(Byte *ptr)
{
  int input, j;
  printf("Enter 12 hex characters  ");
  for (j=0; j<12; j++){
     input = getche();
     if (input > 0x40){
        input = input + 9; }
```

```
        if(j%2 == 0)            // even inputs shifted left
            *ptr = input << 4;
        else{                   // odd inputs ORed with even
            *ptr = *ptr | (input & 0x0F);
            ptr++;
        }
    }
    printf("     Thank You\n\n");
    return;
}


// ------------------------------------------
Byte Send_Frame(int count)
{
    int j, copy;
    char *buffer;

    buffer = Send.destination;
    copy = count;
    Send.size = copy << 8;      // swap upper and lower bytes
    copy = count;               // of data count.
    Send.size = Send.size | (copy >> 8);
    if (count < 46){
        count = 46;             // if padding is needed
    }
    printf("\ncount = %u", count);
// -----------Move into adapter buffer using remote DMA
    outpw(0x308, 0x2000);       // Remote Start Address
    outpw(0x30A, count+14);     // Remote Byte Count
    outp(CmdReg, 0x12);         // Start remote DMA
    for (j = 0; j < count+14; j++){
        outp(0x310, *buffer++);  // Feed the transfer point
    }
// -------------------------------- Transmit from buffer
    outp(TrPgStReg, 0x20);      // Transmit page start = 0x2000
    outpw(0x305, count+14);     // Transmit byte count
    outp(0x307, 0xFF);          // reset a bunch of ISR bits
    outp(0x300, 0x26);          // start the transmit
    printf(",   Frame sent.\n");
    return(inp(0x304));         // return transmit status
}
```

REFERENCES

1. *DP839EB Ethernet Evaluation Kit.* National Semiconductor Corporation, Santa Clara, California

2. *EtherLink II Adapter Technical Reference Manual.* 3Com Corporation, Santa Clara, California

■ Chapter 6

Token Ring (IEEE 802.5)

IBM introduced their Token Ring network in October 1985. It was the company's second entry into the local area network market and a major improvement over the older 2.0 megabits/sec broadband network.

The data rate of the 1985 version was 4.0 megabits/sec. In 1989, a second version was introduced that moved this up to 16.0 megabits/sec. Newer adapters are capable of both data rates.

Token Ring will connect a maximum of 260 stations in one ring and permits multiple rings to be interconnected to include more stations and span greater distances (see Figure 6.1). Packets or frames can reach a maximum length of 4500 bytes on the 4 megabits/sec ring and a huge 18,000 bytes on the 16 megabits/sec ring. These are upper limits. In practice, most frames are shorter—constrained by upper software layers.

Since the first token network examined was ARCnet, a comparison should be made between ARCnet and Token Ring. Both networks pass a token around a logical ring to determine the order of transmission; that is about the end of the similarities. The data rates, of course, are different (2.5 versus 4.0 megabits/sec), but there is much more. ARCnet is physically a star with all stations effectively in parallel. All stations hear every transmission, but, if it isn't for them, they don't respond. In contrast, IBM's Token Ring places each station in series. At the media level, when one adapter hears a transmission from the previous station, it must then repeat that same packet to the following station.

The major differences, however, involve the higher complexity of both the Token Ring card and the ring protocol in general. Most of these differences are the result of a design performed eight years later than that of ARCnet (1977). One of the greatest added features is that of ring management. Adapter cards perform a continual test of both themselves and the ring. They can either remove themselves, or be removed, if something is wrong.

151

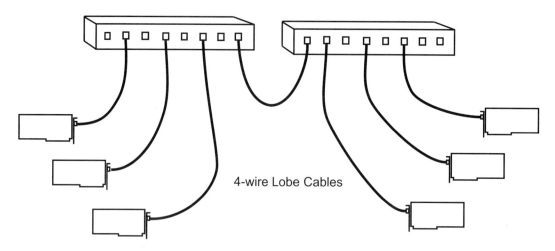

FIGURE 6.1
IBM's Token Ring Network.

PHYSICAL RING

The Token Ring is physically a ring of 150-ohm, shielded, twisted pair wire. Each card has a pair of input connections and a pair of output connections all in one nine-pin connector. Segments of wiring run from the output of one card to the input of the following one to form a chain. The output of the last card connects back to the input of the first, and so a ring is formed. Token and data frames pass into each station in sequence, where they are examined, regenerated, and then sent on to the next station. Since each station acts as an amplifier and only one card will be at the other end of any segment of wire, no external active or passive hubs are needed.

Twisted pair wiring between any two stations can stretch about 200 meters. Through multiple stations and optional repeaters and fiber optic cables, the circumference of the ring can extend to about 2 kilometers (ARCnet's diameter can reach 6.5 km).

Unshielded wiring options are also available but initially only for the 4.0 megabits/sec ring. However, the maximum number of stations is now reduced to 72, and the permissible length between stations drops. The possibility of errors also increases because of the lack of shielding.

It would theoretically be possible to run wiring directly from one station to the next without using wiring concentrators—after all, it is a physical ring. Separate connectors on the adapters would then be required for the input cable from the previous station and the output cable for the next station.

Although simple, this arrangement would pose a definite problem. If any station were to be shut off or physically removed, the network would fail because the ring would then not be complete. Of course, the network supervisor could run around and plug the two ends of the cables together for each machine that wasn't being used—but some supervisors have better things to do with their time.

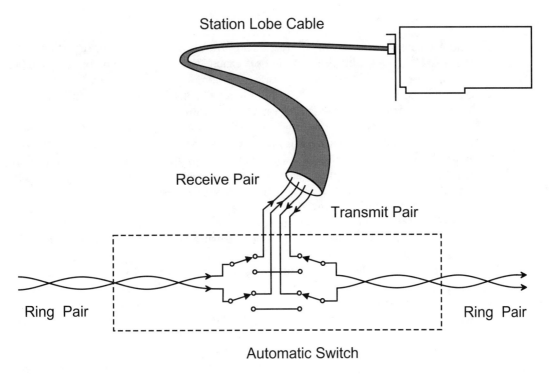

FIGURE 6.2
Instead of direct wiring, the ring is confined to connector boxes (MAUs) and then extended to the machine through lobe cabling.

Therefore, instead of a simple ring that physically involves the workstations, the main ring of wire is moved back to "connector boxes." Four-wire lobe cables extend the incoming and the outgoing signal from these boxes to the actual stations. Inside these connector boxes, or Multi-Station Access Unit (**MAU**) as they are more properly called, relay contacts bridge the four wires of each lobe cable when a corresponding station is off or not connected. When a machine is turned on, it causes this bypass relay to open. The circumference of the ring is then extended to include the lobe cabling, and the station is inserted into the ring (see Figure 6.2).

The end result is that each computer connects to a central box through its lobe cable, and the overall appearance now looks more like the star shape of ARCnet. The electrical layout, however, is quite different. If you were to follow the twisted pair in and out of the MAUs, the lobe cables, and the stations, you would find the "ring."

This star arrangement has another purpose. It is central to the idea of network management and fault detection and isolation. As we saw with the 10BaseT option for Ethernet, a central, intelligent box allows misbehaving nodes to be cut off.

Now we will look at the ring's inner details, starting with the clock encoding and then covering the structure of the packets.

WAVEFORMS AND VOLTAGES

The 4 megabits/sec version of Token Ring transmits one bit of information every 0.25 μs. The 16 megabits/sec version uses exactly the same encoding but uses a 0.063 μs time slot instead. To combine both clock and data information, Differential Manchester encoding is used. We have already seen that Ethernet uses Manchester (not Differential Manchester) encoding on a coaxial cable.

There is a reason for the differences. When installing coaxial cable, it is easy to identify the center connector and the outer shield and to keep them separate. With twisted pair, however, the two wires could easily be interchanged. Much of the wiring may be done in tight or dark places where wire colors aren't visible. Differential Manchester encoding is not polarity sensitive and so was chosen to avoid strict requirements of wire polarity. The installer, of course, should still strive to maintain correct polarity and colors as an aid to troubleshooting.

The voltages that carry the data are measured as a differential value between the two wires (this is a second use of the word "differential" and is not related to "Differential Manchester"). If the waveform on one wire is viewed relative to the cable shield, it alternates between zero and 1.5 volts. The other wire will show the same swing in voltage levels but with the opposite phase. In other words, the second wire voltage will be Lo when the first wire is Hi, and vice versa. The voltage between the two wires, which is the part that counts, will alternate between +1.5 and –1.5 volts (3 volts peak-to-peak).

To include the clock or timing signal, both a data Zero and a data One have a transition, in one direction or the other, at the middle of the 0.25 μs time cell. To distinguish the data, a Zero will have an additional transition at the beginning of its time cell, but a One will not (see Figure 6.3).

In addition to carrying data values of Zero and One, there are two specific coding violations called "J" and "K." These ensure that portions of tokens and frames are easy to recognize with no chance that user data could generate the same pattern.

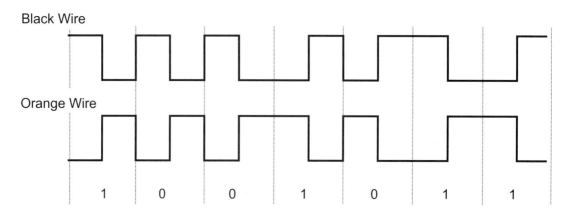

FIGURE 6.3
Differential Manchester encoding changes voltage level in the middle of both a Zero and a One data cell. A Zero will also have a change at the beginning.

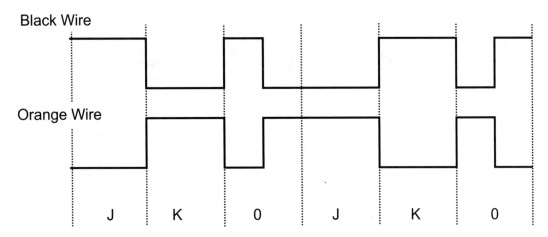

Black Wire

Orange Wire

J   K   0   J   K   0

FIGURE 6.4
J and K coding violations serve as unique identifiers within a transmitted frame.

(A similar technique is also used within the sector coding of a computer's hard disk.) A J variation leaves out the transition both at the beginning and the middle. The K variation has a single transition at the beginning but not the middle (see Figure 6.4).

Ring wiring can, therefore, indicate four unique conditions in any 0.25 μs time slot—Zero, One, J, or K.

RING OPERATION

In a basic ring, each bit occupies a 0.25 μs time slot on the 4 megabits/sec ring. Most bits have a transition in the middle because of the clock encoding. Therefore, two consecutive voltage levels on the cable represent one data bit. Each half (0.125 μs) portion of the Differential Manchester waveform is called a **baud**. The data rate is, therefore, 4.0 megabits/sec, and the baud rate is 8.0 megabits/sec.

In a simplified view, each station appears to be a five-stage shift register. Each register stage holds a baud, or half a data bit, and represents a time delay of 0.125 μs. The five-stage shift register in any one station would then represent a delay of 0.625 μs. In addition to shift register delays, the wiring has its own delay with every 50 meters or so adding another 0.25 μs (one data bit) delay. Because the stations are all in series, this delay is cumulative. These delays are all important, but even more is required.

One of the stations on the ring adds in two additional delays. One of these comes from an "elastic buffer" whose function will be described shortly. The other delay is from a "latency buffer" of 24 data bits (a 48-stage register). This just happens to be the size of the ring token—the "tennis ball" that tells each station when it can transmit. The purpose of the latency buffer is simply to make sure that the token can fit on even the smallest network.

The station with these two extra delays is called the "active monitor" (see Figure 6.5). All network cards are exactly the same so any station can perform this duty.

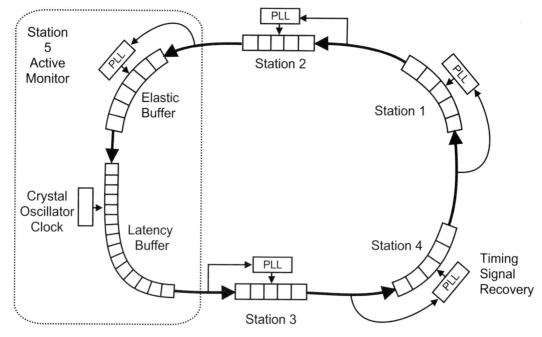

FIGURE 6.5
One ring station acts as an Active Monitor. It uses its own quartz oscillator to set the ring data rate. Other stations follow as closely as possible. The elastic buffer absorbs momentary phase differences between incoming and outgoing signals.

The selection of the active monitor is performed at ring start-up time and will be described shortly.

The ring always carries something. If no data is flowing for a moment, each station sends binary Zeros to its "downstream" neighbor. Zeros have two transitions per data bit, and so the ring "idles" with a continuous 4.0 MHz square wave. Since the ring is always being clocked, frames do not require synchronizing patterns at their beginning as does, for example, Ethernet.

Elastic Buffer

The active monitor provides a second delay. It uses a quartz crystal to determine its transmitting data rate. All other stations (now referred to as "standby monitors") use a phase locked loop (PLL) oscillator to follow the incoming data and extract a clock or timing signal from it. Because of slight hesitations within each station and possible physical movement of the cable, the instantaneous frequency and phase will occasionally shift very slightly. Each station's PLL must follow the accumulated shifts of all stations before it. The station before the active monitor has the most difficult job.

When the frames arrive back at the active monitor, there will likely be a net phase difference between what is being sent out and what is coming in. Moreover,

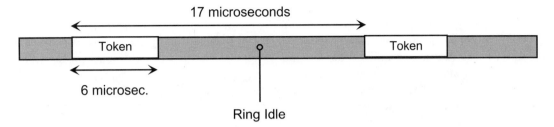

FIGURE 6.6
On a ten-station network with 600 meters of wiring, a freely circulating token would
appear every 17 μs. If any station "claims" the token and then sends a data frame, the
delay will be longer.

this could change with time due to momentary jitters in the other stations. The
active monitor therefore clocks the data in using a PLL plus a 0–12 stage (baud)
"elastic" buffer.[1] This absorbs the dynamic changes in phase. The buffer normally
operates as a six-stage register but can expand or contract six half-bits in either
direction to absorb momentary differences.

On even a small network of two machines, the total delay will never drop below
the 24-bit minimum even for an instant. Larger networks will accumulate a total
delay of 24 data bits from the latency buffer of the active monitor, a nominal 3 bits
in the elastic buffer, 2.5 bits in each machine, and various wiring delays (approximately 0.5 μs per 100 meters). A ten-station network with 600 meters of wiring
would have a total ring delay of about 17 μs (see Figure 6.6).

TOKEN OPERATION

When no data is flowing on the network, a simple three-byte token circulates, working its way through each adapter in sequence. When a station wishes to send, it must
wait for this token to enter its network board. If this is a free token, the station now
has permission to transmit a frame. It first sets an internal bit in its adapter to
remember that it has the token and then releases its prepared data frame.

This frame will proceed around the ring, passing in and out of each station.
Most stations will simply examine the destination address near the beginning of the
packet, find that the message is not for them, and pass it on. The intended recipient
will recognize the address, copy the packet into its network board memory, check for
errors, and then change two bits near the end of the packet to indicate "address recognized" and "message received." The full packet, along with the two changed bits,
continues around the ring until it returns to the original sending station.

---

[1]A few years ago, some manufacturers were having clock stability problems with 16 megabits/sec rings.
The problem showed up when the number of stations in one ring grew beyond about 50. The PLL at
some stations would occasionally lose track of the incoming data rate, and the ring would have to be
reset. The problem underlined the difficulty of designing stable PLLs as the data rate increases.

Sometime after the sending station has sent the first 24 bits, the head of its own frame will have circulated back into its receiver. It has been expecting this and will not repeat the frame back onto the ring. It confirms that the frame is its own when the destination address arrives and "swallows" the packet. As the last of the frame enters the originating station, it will examine the two bits near the end, which should indicate that the message was successfully received. Higher layers of software will be notified of this success (or lack of it). Then, after a short delay, the three-byte token is released for use by the next station.

There is a time limit for any one station to use the ring. A starting delimiter, either in a token or frame, must pass by each ring station within any ten-millisecond period. Therefore, any one station has a maximum of ten milliseconds between placing the starting delimiter of a data frame on the ring and the starting delimiter of a free token. On a small ring, this could allow data frames to reach a maximum of 4500 bytes. On very large rings, this may have to be reduced somewhat as the total ring latency (accumulated delay) increases.

Token Frame

The 24 bits that make up the token are shown in Figure 6.7. The J and K bits are the encoding violations described back in Figure 6.4. They ensure that a receiving station recognizes the starting and ending of the token and the data frames. PLL circuits within each workstation are designed to survive this momentary loss of clock information. Within the access control field, the fourth bit (the Token bit) will be Zero to identify this as a token. (One would normally think that a bit marked as "token" should be set, not cleared, to indicate a token frame. But then who said computers had to be logical?)

The first three bits, "ppp," indicate the priority of the token. This is a feature added to allow a station with an urgent message to override the normal sequence. The "m" bit is used only by the active monitor, and the three "rrr" bits are part of the token priority reservation system.

The End Delimiter byte also includes J and K coding violations to uniquely identify it. The very last bit, marked as "e," is always sent as a Zero. If any adapter

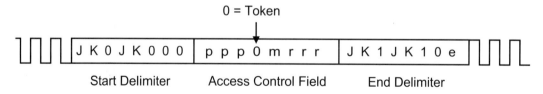

FIGURE 6.7
The three-byte token. The Zero in the middle of the Access Control field identifies this as a token. The most significant bit (J) of the Start Delimiter is the first bit to enter the ring. Lowercase values are variables .

senses an error, it will set this bit to alert other stations. This will be more significant in a data packet than a token since the token has no CRC for error detection.

Data Frame

The Token Ring data frame (or packet) is divided into a number of individual control areas. The data itself can vary in length from one up to 4500 bytes. On the 16 megabits/sec ring using newer chips, this can increase to 18,000 bytes. This upper limit is imposed by the 10 ms ring timing limit already mentioned.

The data frame is shown in Figure 6.8. It uses the same Start and End delimiters, with their unique coding violations, as the token does. This is the basic frame—there are changes yet to come. There are several "types" of data frames, with the word "data" being used in a very broad sense. In particular, there will be extra control bytes added at the beginning of what is labeled as the "information" section to perform various functions yet to be described. These will vary with the frame "type."

- START DELIMITER. The same unique one-byte pattern used in the token. It indicates the switch from the continuous ring idle clocking to the start of a token or data frame.

  J K 0 J K 0 0 0

- ACCESS CONTROL byte. Contains three priority bits, a token bit, a monitor bit, and three reservation bits. In all data frames, the "token" bit will be One (yes, this is illogical). Reservation bits allow stations to request that the next token be issued at a higher level of priority. This will be granted by the station that is presently transmitting a frame. The Monitor bit is used by the active monitor to prevent a high-priority token from circulating forever.

  p p p 1 m r r r

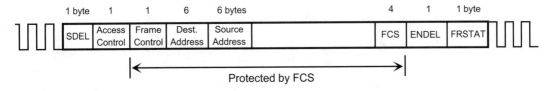

FIGURE 6.8
Token Ring data frame. All bytes are sent most significant bit first, which is the reverse of ARCnet and Ethernet.

- FRAME CONTROL byte. Uses its first two bits to indicate the "type" of the rest of the frame.[2] A 00 indicates a MAC frame; 01 indicates a user data frame (sometimes called an LLC frame). The last four bits carry an "attention" code that is only used if the frame is a MAC frame.

  f f 0 0 a a a a

- ADDRESSES. Consist of 48 bits (six bytes) for both the destination and the source. The multicast, broadcast, and local/universal variations are the same as for Ethernet; however, there is a twist on which end of the byte is used.
- INFORMATION bytes. Transmitted data is carried most significant bit first. In the 4 megabits/sec network, there can be a maximum of 4500 data bytes. There are no restrictions on byte content.
- FRAME CHECK. A 32-bit CRC remainder. It covers all bytes starting with the frame control byte (FC) and continuing to the end of the frame check sequence (**FCS**) itself. The transmitted FCS is the Ones complement of the remainder obtained after dividing all these bytes by the polynomial:

$$x^{32}+x^{26}+x^{23}+x^{22}+x^{16}+x^{12}+x^{11}+x^{10}+x^{8}+x^{7}+x^{5}+x^{4}+x^{2}+x+1$$

- END DELIMITER (one byte). A unique ending pattern that also indicates "Intermediate Frame" (i) which is rarely used and "Error detected" (e). The "e" bit can be set by any ring station that senses an error—most likely an FCS that doesn't match the rest of the data. The End Delimiter byte itself is outside the protection of the FCS.

  J K 1 J K 1 i e

- FRAME STATUS (one byte). a = address recognized; c = frame copied. When a receiving station recognizes its own address, it will set the "a" bit to One. If it copies the packet into its buffer, it will also set the "c" bit. When the message loops back to the originating station, it will know that the destination station is both alive and has copied the message. These two bits are duplicated because the Frame Status byte is outside the protection of the FCS. (This is intentional because the receiving station won't have the time to calculate a new FCS after changing the two bits. Besides, it had to check the existing FCS to see if the packet was worth copying.)

  a c 0 0 a c 0 0

[2]Caution: IBM and several chip manufacturers, in much of their Token Ring documentation, call the Zero bit the most significant bit of a byte or word. This is the opposite of what the rest of the industry normally uses and conflicts with what we have been using throughout this book. For consistency, we will continue to call Zero the least significant bit of a word or byte.

Transmission Abort

If, for any reason, a sending station decides to abort its transmission, it will send a Start Delimiter immediately followed by an End Delimiter. Other stations will recognize the sequence and simply ignore it.

RING PRIORITY

With ARCnet, the token is always passed, in sequence, to each and every station on the network. If one station happens to have a very urgent message, it will still have to wait its turn. Token Ring can use the three priority bits and the three reservation bits in the Access Control (AC) field to alter the ring sequence and give an urgent message priority. This is most important in ring maintenance frames but could be used by any software. This is how it works.

As an information packet from some other station passes a station impatiently waiting with an urgent message, the waiting station can increase the value of the reservation bits in the AC field. Nothing else happens just at that instant, and the frame proceeds as usual. When the original sender of this frame receives it back, it will release a token—again, as is normal. However, it will first copy the three reservation bits into the priority bit positions (see Figure 6.9).

Other stations downstream from that station will see the high-priority level and simply pass the token on—even if they had wanted to send information (low-priority info). The station with the urgent message will, therefore, probably get its chance sooner. If no other station on the ring was waiting to transmit, nothing has been gained, but the demanding (impatient) station didn't know that. After a full circle of the priority message, the demanding station releases a high-priority token and the original station that made the priority switch moves it back to the previous priority level.

The active monitor is also watching this process and, with the monitor bit, can detect a high-priority token that is circulating too long. The first time a high-priority token passes by, it will set the "m" bit. If it sees the same priority appear again with the monitor bit set, it knows something is wrong. It will purge the ring and release a new token.

FIGURE 6.9
Priority reservation (rrr) bits set by an impatient station are copied into the priority (ppp) position by the station releasing the token.

Access Control Field

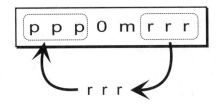

ADDRESSES

Token Ring was designed from the very beginning to handle message transfers through multiple rings. If a frame is destined for a different ring than the one in which it originated, it will carry an additional Routing Information field of 2–18 bytes immediately after the source address. For our initial descriptions, we will assume the frames are contained within the one ring and this extra field will not be present. It will be discussed later in Chapter 14.

Each network circuit board holds a permanent 48-bit card serial number burned into a small ROM chip. The numbers are IEEE-controlled and will always be unique even if cards are purchased from different manufacturers. In fact, they should be unique even across hardware types, i.e., Ethernet, FDDI, and Token Ring. Unless overridden by outside software, this serial number is used as the station's address.

The space for both the source and destination addresses within the frames is also 48 bits. Of these, 46 are used for actual addresses, and the two most significant bits of each field are used to resolve variations on the destination. Some of these variations will require the extra source routing bytes just mentioned.

The IEEE definition of 48-bit LAN addresses indicates that the first address bit placed on the cable determines the individual or group feature. With Ethernet, this will be the least significant bit of the most significant byte. With Token Ring, this will be the most significant bit of the most significant byte.

Universal versus Local Administration of Addresses

If the "burned-in" serial number from the card is used, it is guaranteed to be unique as we have already indicated. However, some network commands will allow or possibly even require a substitute address for as long as the station remains turned on.

This temporary address possibility raises the issue of who controls the new address selected. If the interconnected rings belong within a small group of offices, one individual with a list of the existing card addresses could easily suggest several thousand alternatives. The fact that one happens to be duplicated in the company across the street is of no importance since the respective rings are not connected. The addresses are, therefore, being locally administered.

In a different situation, machines may be part of a worldwide network. In this case, the addresses will always have to be globally administered. That service is currently provided by the IEEE.

Source Address

The lower 46 bits of the source address within each frame will be either the adapter's serial number or its substituted value. The most significant bit indicates whether extra source routing information is included later in the frame or not. The next bit position indicates, if set, that the remaining 46 bits of the address are "universally administered"—meaning that they are guaranteed unique in the entire world.

Destination Address

The destination address can indicate several more variations. First, the frame may be destined for either one specific station, a group of stations, or all stations. Then, the address may be within the local ring or it may be in another, connected ring. Finally, if it is in another ring, the address and path may be known either by the sending station or by the bridge station to the other network. The situation becomes more complicated if the stations are part of a multicompany national network. However, two extra bits within the frame's destination address plus two in the source address space can answer the destination questions (see Figure 6.10).

Single Station

If D47 is Zero, the destination is a specific single-station address. The lower 46 bits will be some unique card number. D46 will indicate whether that address is locally or globally administered.

```
┌──────────────────────────────────────────────────────┐
│ D47  D46  D45 . . . . . . . .   D31 . . . . . . . . . . . . . . . . . . . . . . . D0 │
└──────────────────────────────────────────────────────┘
```

D47   0 = Address is an individual station
        1 = Address is a group address

D46   0 = Locally administered
        1 = Globally administered

If D47 indicates a group address...

D31   0 = Functional address indicator
        1 = Normal group address

```
┌──────────────────────────────────────────────────────┐
│ S47  S46  S45 . . . . . . . . . . . . . . . . . . . . . . . . . . . . . . . . . . S0 │
└──────────────────────────────────────────────────────┘
```

S47   0 = No routing information included
        1 = Routing information is included

S46   0 = Locally administered
        1 = Globally administered

FIGURE 6.10
The 48-bit destination and source addresses. The two most significant bits of each have special meanings. A middle bit of the destination address will have a special meaning if it is a group address.

Group Addresses

If D47, D46, and D31 of the destination address are all set to One, the frame is for a group of stations. The lower 31 bits of the destination address will contain a pattern indicating the group. The method is usually controlled by higher layers, but it is common to "hash" each station address into a single-bit position (the pattern won't be unique). Messages can, therefore, be sent to several stations at once by setting several bits.

Broadcast

If both D47 and D46 are Hi and the lower 32 bits are also Hi, this indicates a broadcast to all stations on this ring.

C000 0000 FFFF FFFF

Function Group

This is a set of addresses known to all stations. If stations have to communicate with the "Ring Parameter Server," for example, they simply use the address of that function rather than trying to figure out which physical machine that function resides on (usually a server machine). In the 48-bit destination address, D47 and D46 will be Hi, and D31 will be Zero. The lower 31 bits indicate the functional group.

Some reserved functional addresses are:

Active Monitor	C000 0000 0000 0001
Ring Parameter Server	C000 0000 0000 0002
Ring Error Monitor	C000 0000 0000 0008
Configuration Report Server	C000 0000 0000 0010
NetBIOS	C000 0000 0000 0080
Bridge	C000 0000 0000 0100
Lan Manager	C000 0000 0000 2000

MEDIUM ACCESS CONTROL (MAC) FRAMES

We have already said that there are two types of "data" frames that can circulate on the network. One is generated by higher layers of software and usually contains application data or network commands. These are referred to as LLC frames or Non-MAC frames. The other frame type is initiated by the card itself and rarely requires the involvement of higher software. These are for housekeeping operations, and the resulting frames are MAC frames. Let's look at MAC frames in more detail (see Figure 6.11).

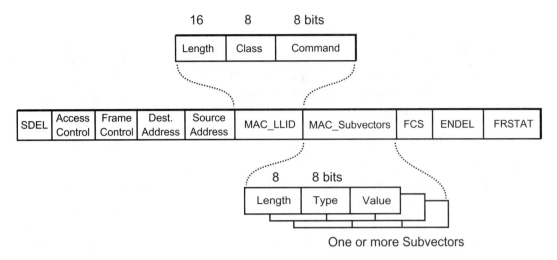

FIGURE 6.11
MAC Frame Format. The first two bits of the Frame Control field will be Zero.

The third byte of every Token Ring data frame is the Frame Control field. The first two bits of this field indicate who is placing data in the "information" portion of the frame. A 01 indicates that higher levels, LLC and above, are responsible. A 00 indicates that the MAC, in other words the card itself, is responsible. The cards are talking to themselves in this case. This is also where the active monitor plays its biggest role.

$$\text{Frame Control} = \boxed{\text{f f 0 0 a a a a}}$$
$$\text{f f} = \text{frame type:} \quad 0\ 0 = \text{MAC frame}$$
$$0\ 1 = \text{higher layer frame}$$

Attention codes (a a a a) are used only by MAC frames. They indicate that some MAC frames are very important, and any non-zero value indicates they should be copied into a small 40-byte "express buffer" at the receiver in the event that the normal buffers are full. Some MAC frames may also require the attention of higher software layers.

The information portion of a MAC frame always consists of vectors and subvectors. The use of the word "vector" in these cases tends to be somewhat confusing because vectors are often thought of as addresses. If you wish, simply substitute the word "component" for "vector."

The component list begins with a four-byte MAC frame Length and Identification (MAC_LLID) field that is broken into three parts—LENGTH, CLASS, and COMMAND—each described below. This same field is also called the MAC Major Vector. It may be followed by several subvectors. Each subvector has the same general form as the major vector but with some size differences.

Major Vector

LENGTH. 16 bits. Indicates the overall length of the information portion of the MAC frame including the Major Vector (Major component) with its length field and any subvectors (subcomponents).

CLASS. 4 bits for the destination followed by 4 bits for the source.

    0000 = ring station
    0100 = configuration report server
    0101 = ring parameter server
    0110 = ring error monitor

COMMAND. 8 bits as shown in the following.

Subvectors

Each consists of 1 LENGTH byte + 1 TYPE byte + 2 or more bytes of subvector information.

MAC COMMANDS

Some of the MAC commands will be referred to in the following sections. However, there are too many details needed to fully describe each one. Many use subvectors, which further complicates their description. About 25 commands are defined in total. Some of the more common are:

Command Byte	Function
00h	Response to a MAC command
02h	Beacon
03h	Claim Token
04h	Ring Purge
05h	Active Monitor Present
06h	Standby Monitor Present
07h	Duplicate Address Test
08h	Lobe Media Test
0Bh	Remove Ring Station
0Dh	Initialize Ring Station
0Fh	Request Ring Station State
20h	Request Initialization
29h	Report Soft Error

Three of the MAC frames are used only in unusual situations, and they don't wait for a token before being sent. These "immediate" frames are Beacon, Claim Token, and Ring Purge. The Active Monitor Present MAC frame will make a token reservation at the highest-priority level (seven) and then wait for the token before sending. All other MAC frames reserve a token with a priority level of three. MAC responses are all level zero, the normal level used by other data frames.

Active Monitor Present and Neighbor Notification

Every seven seconds, the active monitor will send an "Active Monitor Present" MAC frame (command = 05h). The access priority within the Access Control (AC) byte will be set to seven to ensure that it passes. It is used to check the integrity of the ring, inform other stations that there is an active monitor, and initiate the periodic neighbor address notification process.

This MAC frame is sent as an all-station broadcast with the card address of the active monitor in the source field. The first standby monitor (all other stations are standby monitors) will copy the source address and thereby know the address of its nearest upstream neighbor. It then sets the "a" (address recognized) and "c" (frame copied) bits in the frame status field. Each following (downstream) station will know from these bits that the source address has been copied and so does not represent its own upstream neighbor. They let the frame pass without alteration.

After a 20 ms delay, each station will originate a Standby Monitor Present MAC frame with its own address as the source and the "a" and "c" bits cleared. Its nearest downstream neighbor will recognize these two cleared bits and copy the source address as that of its own upstream neighbor. The process continues until all stations know the address of the station ahead of them. This is needed for part of the fault detection and isolation (station removal) process.

Beacon Frame

A beacon frame is sent by any station that detects a serious error. This would likely be a hardware error as detected by the receiver portion of the station's card. The beaconing process consists of MAC frames sent immediately without waiting for tokens. The frame is repeated every 20 ms and includes the local station address and that of its nearest upstream neighbor. After the upstream neighbor receives about eight of these frames, it realizes that something could be wrong with its own sending circuitry. It, therefore, removes itself from the ring and conducts a full internal test including loop-back transmissions through the lobe cable. If everything appears correct, it will activate the MAU bridging relay and rejoin the ring. If the upstream neighbor reappears, the beaconing station performs the same self test.

If a "ring error monitor" function has been included at higher levels elsewhere on the ring, it will be monitoring this process and will note the addresses of the two stations involved. If the problem persists, one or both stations will be told, via MAC frame, to remove itself from the ring.

Ring Purge Frame

The ring purge is sent "immediately" by the active monitor when it thinks the ring is not working properly. The monitor does not wait for a token to arrive because one may never appear. The frame is addressed to all stations on this ring. If this MAC frame circulates correctly back to the active monitor, it assumes the network is now operating correctly and sends an "Active Monitor Present" frame.

Token Claiming Procedure

The token claiming procedure is how the ring stations decide who will be the active monitor. The process can be initiated at any time by several error conditions. Each participating station sends Claim Token frames spaced every 20 ms for about one second. Each initiating station will use its own card number as the source address and makes the destination an all-station broadcast. In a worst-case situation, every ring station could be transmitting these frames.

As these MAC frames circulate, each station examines the source address. If the address is less than its own card number, it stays in the fight. If it is greater, it drops out of the competition, removes its latency buffer if it was turned on, and then behaves as a normal, repeating station. Within a short while, all lower-numbered stations will have dropped out, leaving only one as the active monitor. This will be the highest-numbered station that was allowed to participate.

At installation time, an adapter card can be set so it will never become an active monitor.

Two samples of MAC frames are given in Figure 6.12. Both destinations are broadcasts (C000FFFFFFFFh) and come from the same source (48000A001234h). The information field contains 18 bytes (0012h) consisting of a major vector and two subvectors. The first subvector is six bytes long and contains the subvector type 0Bh, indicating a physical drop number. The second subvector is eight bytes long and contains the subvector type 02h, which provides the address of the upstream neighbor.

(1) Active Monitor Present (Command = 05h)
```
0000    10 05 C0 00 FF FF FF FF    48 00 0A 00 12 34 00 12
0010    00 05 06 0B 00 00 00 00    08 02 40 00 00 00 12 45
```

(2) Ring Purge (Command = 04h)
```
0000    10 04 C0 00 FF FF FF FF    48 00 0A 00 12 34 00 12
0010    00 04 06 0B 00 00 00 00    08 02 40 00 00 00 12 45
```

SDEL	Access Control	Frame Control	Dest. Address	Source Address	MAC_LLID	MAC_Subvectors	FCS	ENDEL	FRSTAT
1	1	6	6	4		14 bytes			

FIGURE 6.12
Two examples of MAC frames. The code samples start with the AC field and end just before the FCS field.

PARTIAL SCHEMATIC

The wiring pictorial shown in Figure 6.13 is a simplified view of the output portion of a Token Ring Network card. Transformers are used at both the send and receive pair to couple the signal into and out of the ring. Current to activate the MAU relay comes from the phantom voltage pins of the driver integrated circuit (IC). The secondary of the sending transformer is split to allow this current to pass from the pins, through the low resistance of the windings, and into the orange and black "send" wires. At the higher frequency of the ring data, the capacitor across this split will appear as a short circuit, and the data will be sent "between" the orange and black pair of wires. Each send wire, therefore, carries identical dc currents for the relay but opposite **ac** signals for the data.

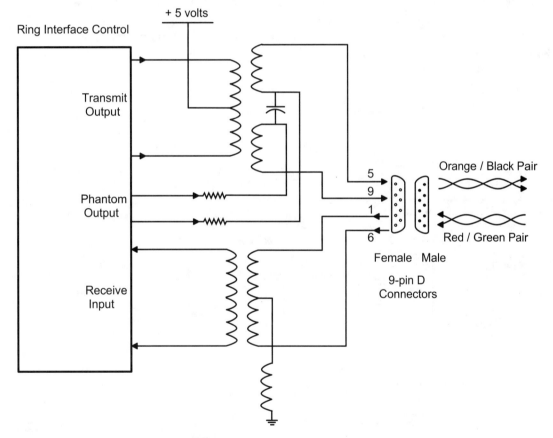

FIGURE 6.13

Schematic diagram of the ring interface. All signals pass to and from the ring via small transformers. A dc current of approximately one milliamp also flows out each transmit wire and back, to ground, through the corresponding receive wire of the same card. Data goes out the transmit pair of one card and into the receive pair of the next.

At the receiving end, the input side of the transformer is grounded in the middle. The relay activation currents from the phantom drive on the same card pass to ground here—as long as all external wiring is intact. The ring data from the upstream station passes from primary to secondary of this transformer and into the integrated circuit. Numerous protection diodes are included to absorb any damaging transient voltages that may be picked up on the long ring cabling.

The rest of the adapter is shown as a block diagram in Figure 6.14. This consists of two main chips in later model adapter cards but could be considerably more in earlier models.

The Ring Interface IC performs only a few functions. It converts to and from the balanced wiring of the ring and runs a phase locked loop to extract the data

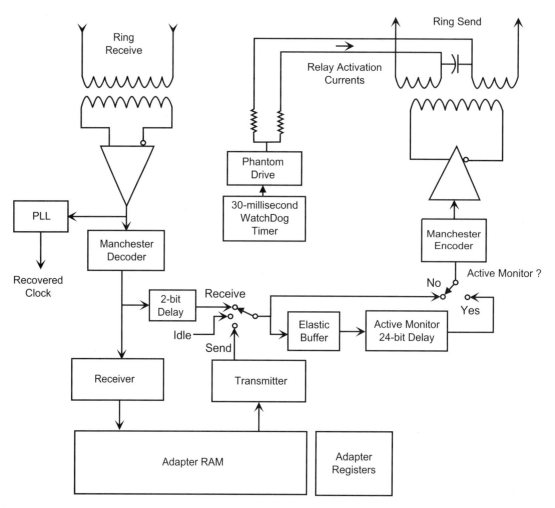

FIGURE 6.14
Adapter block diagram. This is a continuation of the schematic diagram in Figure 6.13.

clocking signal for the adapter card. If this card is not acting as an active monitor, that clock is used for both transmit and receive timing. If it is the active monitor, the clock is used only for the receive operation, and a quartz-crystal-controlled clock is used for transmit.

The Ring Interface chip also includes a "watch dog" timer. This is "kicked" every 20 or 30 milliseconds by the dedicated microprocessor on the adapter card. If this periodic pulse is missing, the timer will assume that the card has failed and, within 30 milliseconds, the phantom drive voltage will be removed. The MAU relay should then bypass the station with the failed card.

The loop between receive and send appears in the next chip. If this is the active monitor, the elastic buffer and the 24-bit delay are switched in. Otherwise, the only delay is two data bits used to balance other delays in internal processing. This two-bit value, plus a few small delays in the ring interface circuit, produce the five-baud delay described back in Figure 6.5.

The transmitted output from the card can come from one of three sources. It can be a repeat of incoming ring data, a continuous idle pattern of data Zeros, or serial data from the adapter RAM. The continuous idle is used while a sending station is waiting for its own frame to enter its receiver.

A dedicated microprocessor controls these two electronic switches and many more functions. Later in this chapter we will see that this local processor executes a large amount of onboard code. When a programmer is interfacing with the adapter, it is mainly this code that is involved.

The initial "triggering" of this code is through several adapter registers whose functions change with adapter manufacturer.

MULTI-STATION ACCESS UNIT

The Multi-Station Access Unit (MAU), shown in Figure 6.15, is used to connect up to eight workstations into a ring. If only a single MAU is used, the ring exists totally within the box. Multiple boxes (30 maximum) can be interconnected to form larger networks. The purpose of the MAU is to break open the ring and insert a new station after it has performed a self test on its card. By doing this, a disconnected or off workstation does not disrupt the operation of the loop.

The MAU and one end of the lobe cable use identical (hermaphroditic) connectors shown in Figure 6.16. When the connectors are apart, two small shorting bars inside each form a return loop from the transmit pair back to the receive pair. A user can, therefore, test a workstation's card and cable before it is physically plugged into the MAU.

Upon physical insertion, these shorting bars inside the connectors move out of the way and expose the internal wiring of the MAU and cable. This physical action, however, is not what inserts a working station into the ring. At power-on, each card tests itself and its cable to see if everything is operational. It then switches the Phantom Voltage pins on, and this results in a dc current of about one milliamp up each wire of the transmit pair and back down a corresponding wire of its own receive pair. This is the current that triggers the switching of the relay inside the MAU from

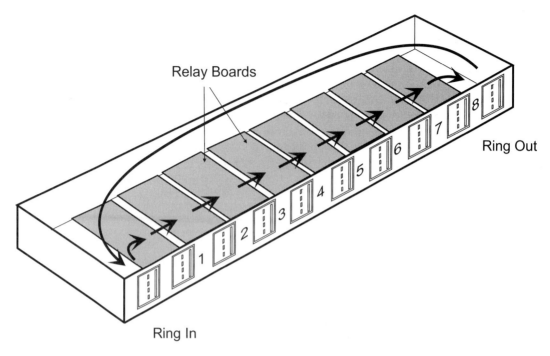

FIGURE 6.15
8228 Multi-Station Access Unit uses internal relays to break the network ring and insert an operating workstation. Early versions were passive devices with no internal amplifiers and performed only a switching function.

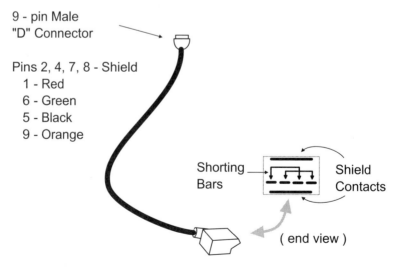

FIGURE 6.16
Token Ring lobe cable and connectors.

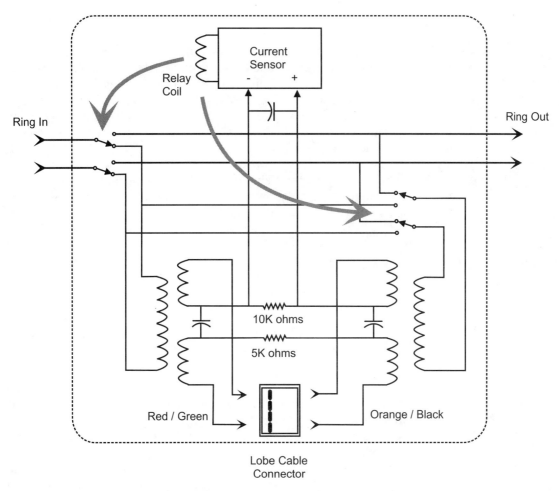

FIGURE 6.17
Individual circuitry for each lobe connection inside the MAU. In older units the circuit is self powered.

bypass mode to insert mode. The circuitry for one lobe connector inside the MAU is shown in Figure 6.17. This circuit is repeated eight times inside each MAU.

Each four-wire lobe cable is connected into the MAU with small transformers to separate the dc control currents from the Manchester data. The only dc path is out the transmit pair and back into the receive pair of the same station. The Manchester signal cannot follow this same path because of the high value series resistors and the low parallel reactance of the capacitors at the operating frequency of the ring (the data itself has no low-frequency component). Instead, the data passes through from one winding to the other and heads for its downstream neighbor. So we have two paths: one for the dc current and one for the data. The ring signal, on its route from one card, through the MAU and into the next card will pass through a total of four transformers.

In the original MAU design, the relay circuitry was completely powered by this current. No extra connection to ac outlets was required. More recently, it is common to add indicator lamps and internal processing for network management. Newer MAU designs have an ac power cord that must be plugged into a wall outlet.

When the dc insertion current is first activated, a circuit at each lobe measures the current through one set of wires (red-orange) and determines if it is within the correct limits. If it is, the relay is switched from the bypass state to the workstation insert position and then back. The dc resistance of this path within the MAU should be between 4300 and 5500 ohms.

Bypass relays in the original design are magnetically held in either the "inserted" or "bypassed" condition. They only need a short burst of energy to switch their state. This energy is provided by a large-value storage capacitor beside each relay. The capacitor is slowly charged (a few seconds) from the workstation's dc current. Relay switching is, therefore, delayed a few seconds after the current is activated until the charging is complete.

The internal MAU circuitry is mounted on foam rubber pads to reduce bumps. During shipping (or earthquakes), the relay contacts could be jostled into a different position. Original MAUs were, therefore, shipped with an "alignment tool" to charge the internal capacitor and pull each relay into the bypass position. Normally this procedure is only needed at the time the equipment is being assembled. However, if at any time there is doubt about the relay state, the tool can be used again. It is inserted into each of the eight connectors in turn and held for about five seconds. Within that time, the capacitor should have reached full charge and the relay will have "clicked."

The components inside the tool are very simple and are shown in Figure 6.18. If the original tool is lost, a replacement can be easily built with a nine-volt battery, a 1500-ohm resistor, and a nine-pin female "D" connector (pin 9 positive and pin 1 negative). You don't even need the light-emitting diode. This replacement would be connected to the workstation end of a spare lobe cable and the MAU end of the cable slowly moved through the eight connectors. Don't leave this gadget connected for long because the lobe cable, once removed, provides a short circuit that will slowly drain the battery. The original tool does not have these shorting bars.

FIGURE 6.18
Relay alignment tool for older
Multi-Station Access Units.

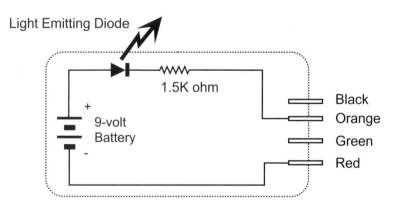

Power On and Insertion

Here are the approximate steps taken by an adapter as its host computer is turned on and the card gets inserted into the ring:

1. At initial power on, the adapter will run its own "bring-up" diagnostics. The MAU relay will be initially closed, wrapping the transmit pair back to the receive pair. The adapter sends a quantity of Lobe Media MAC frames out through the cable and back to its own receiver.
2. System software will monitor a register on the adapter to determine the success of this test. If this is OK, the adapter is initialized for transmission.
3. A higher protocol will issue the ADAPTER OPEN command. This will switch the MAU relay and insert the adapter into the ring. Within a few seconds, an Active Monitor Present frame should appear from the network. If not, the station will start a monitor contention process.
4. The adapter waits for a token and sends several MAC frames around the ring addressed to itself. If another station copies this frame, the new station will see the "Copied" bit set and know there is a problem—its address is not unique. In this case, it closes the relay and removes itself from the network.
5. Within a few seconds, the active monitor should be conducting a ring poll. This procedure is normally repeated every seven seconds and requires that each station send its six-byte address to its downstream neighbor.
6. The adapter may request a number of parameters from the Ring Parameter Server if it exists. The request is made with a MAC frame carrying a 20h command, REQUEST INITIALIZATION. The RPS will respond with a MAC command 0Dh, INITIALIZE RING STATION, and any necessary values.

The adapter is now on the network. Elapsed time is about 20 seconds.

PROGRAMMING MODELS

Direct programmer interface to a Token Ring card is not an easy task. There are several major variations of Token Ring cards being produced, and, in any case, the interface is fairly complex. The adapter cards execute a lot of internal software, and the programmer will be interfacing partly with registers and partly with this software. The two major cards are those produced by IBM and those produced around two generations of chips from Texas Instruments.

Examining the command and status registers will show the variety of operations that can be performed (commands) and what types of problems are anticipated (status).

Texas Instruments

One programming model for a Token Ring card is shown in Figure 6.19. This would be typical of most adapters built around either the original or the newer Texas Instruments chip sets. (IBM's Token Ring adapter for the RT-PC used the older TI

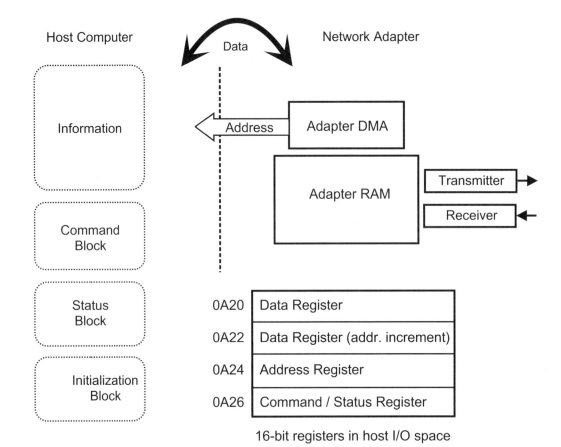

FIGURE 6.19
Programming model for Token Ring adapters based on TI chip sets. The host system does not have direct access to adapter RAM and must do so via data and address registers and an onboard DMA.

set and has an interface identical to what we are about to describe.) This interface is completely contained within 16 bytes of the personal computer's I/O block of ports. In a sense, it is similar to one of the Ethernet options available with the National Semiconductor chip set described in the previous chapter.

The adapter contains two DMA systems (no relation to the host DMA). One system is used to access all internal memory locations. The other onboard system can access host memory. Although the adapters do contain RAM for buffers, as shown in Figure 6.20, the programmer does not deal with it directly. All information is assembled in the host's own RAM, and the adapter becomes responsible for pulling it into its own RAM using its DMA.

To move information into the adapter RAM, the program running on the host would first place a starting address in the adapter's address register. Then it would

Most Significant Bit   Least Significant Bit
▼   ▼

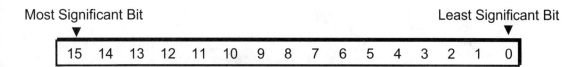

| 15 | 14 | 13 | 12 | 11 | 10 | 9 | 8 | 7 | 6 | 5 | 4 | 3 | 2 | 1 | 0 |

Read - Status   **Write - Command**

15 Interrupt Status   Interrupt Adapter
14 Reset Status   Reset Adapter
13 Status Block Available?   Clear System Status Block
12 Execute Status   Execute
11 Command Block Available?   Indicate Command Block Available
10 Receive Cancel Status   Cancel Current Receive
 9 Receive Valid Status   Receiver Cleared
 8 Transmit Valid Status   Transmitter Cleared
 7 Interrupt Status   Clear all Interrupts
 6 Initialize Status
 5 Test Status
 4 Error Found during Test
3 - 0 Interrupt Source Codes

FIGURE 6.20
Token Ring combined Command/Status register. Commands are written to the register,
but when the register is read, it contains status bits.

use a loop to feed bytes or words to the post increment data register. Each consecutive Write to this location would automatically increment the address by the correct amount. About the only information moved in this way is a 22-byte initialization block. Among other pieces of information, this block passes two host memory addresses to the adapter. These are the 24-bit linear addresses (not segment:offset) that the onboard DMA will use to locate Command and Status blocks used for all further communications (see Figure 6.21).

IBM Adapters

In another version (and as used more recently by IBM), much more of the adapter's functions are placed directly in the main memory map of the PC where they are accessible with a variety of the host's addressing modes. There are now only four registers in the I/O block, and these have a very different function from the model previously described (see Figure 6.22).

The programmer now has three separate memory and I/O location groups to worry about. First, there is the group of four registers in the I/O block. The functions of these will change slightly depending on whether the adapter is built for the Micro Channel bus or for the Industry Standard Architecture (ISA) or AT bus.

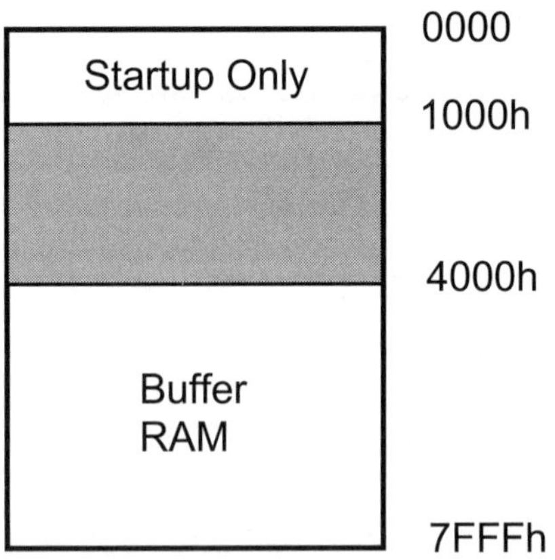

FIGURE 6.21
Adapter internal memory
diagram.

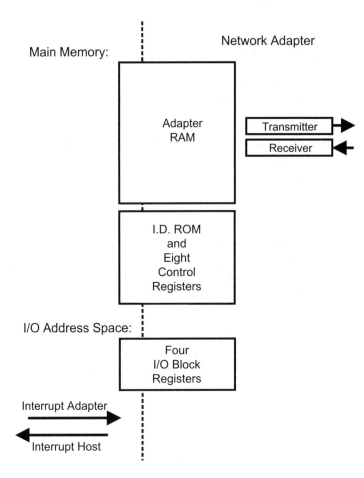

FIGURE 6.22
Programming model for IBM
Token Ring adapters not
based on the TI chip set.

IBM will allow two Token Ring adapters to coexist inside any one machine. For example, this is a requirement of a bridge between two rings. The first adapter is called the primary and the next, obviously, is called the secondary. The I/O ports used are:

Primary Adapter   0A20h–0A23h
Secondary Adapter   0A24h–0A27h

The main-memory segment location of the second group is determined by switches (physical or software) set at the time of adapter installation. A program can read these switches via one of the eight-bit registers in the I/O group. This second group contains eight 16-bit registers plus a small ROM for the adapter serial number, etc. There is also space for an optional BIOS ROM that is only used if the workstation doesn't use a local hard or floppy disk and must be self booting. This group can be placed at many different segment addresses but generally will be:

Primary Adapter   CC00
Secondary Adapter   DC00

The third and final group is the adapter's RAM buffer—usually 8K, 16K, 32K, or 64K bytes. It also is placed in main memory but at a segment address different from the ROM/register group. Its address is set by one of the registers in the previous group. Common locations are:

Shared RAM starts at   D800 (primary adapter)
                        D400 (secondary adapter)

Notice the sequence between the three groups. First, some switches are set on the adapter card before it is placed into the station. These are readable through an I/O port and determine the location in main memory of the ROM/register group. One of these registers is read to determine the location of the third group, the shared RAM.

Now let's look at the adapter card and each of these groups in more detail.

THE CARD

A look at the card must begin with the switches. These are shown in Figure 6.23. The first six switches (starting from the left) set the segment address of the ROM/register group. Normally, this would take eight bits, but the most significant bit, A-19, is assumed always to be One and the least significant bit, A-12, is assumed always to be Zero. A short program is shown later which reads the adapter's serial number and includes a reading and conversion of these six address bits.

The next two switches determine the IRQ interrupt to be used by the card to get the attention of the host. For an ISA bus adapter, 00 = IRQ-2, 01 = IRQ-3, 10 = IRQ-6, and 11 = IRQ-7. These last two combinations change to IRQ-10 and IRQ-11 on a Micro Channel bus adapter.

FIGURE 6.23
Configuration switch.

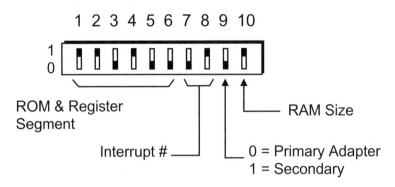

Switch nine determines whether this is a primary (0) or secondary (1) adapter. The last switch determines the size of buffer RAM on the card.

The four I/O block registers are shown in Figure 6.24. Their individual functions depend on whether they are being written to or read from. The addresses shown are for the primary adapter (with secondary adapter addresses in brackets).

- SET-UP 1 (port A20h). Provides the segment address for the register/ROM block and IRQ settings from the switches (see Figure 6.25). If this is a non-Micro Channel adapter, the A19 is assumed to be One.
- SET-UP 2 (port A22h). Set-up values used only by Micro Channel adapters. Defines the starting address of the shared RAM block.
- ADAPTER RESET (port A21h). Any value written to this location will place the adapter in the reset state.
- ADAPTER RELEASE (port A22h). Any value written to this location will remove the adapter from the reset state so that normal operations can begin with known starting conditions.

	READ	WRITE
0A20h (0a24h)	Set Up 1	---
0A21h (0A25h)	---	Put Adapter in RESET
0A22h (0A26h)	Set Up 2	Release from RESET
0A23h (0A27h)	---	Interrupt Enable

FIGURE 6.24
I/O block registers. Addresses in brackets are for the secondary adapter. Notice that the SetUp2 byte is only available on Micro Channel adapters.

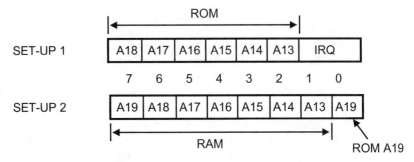

FIGURE 6.25
Individual bits read from SET-UP registers 1 and 2. SET-UP register 2 is only used on a Micro Channel adapter.

- INTERRUPT ENABLE (port A23h). Any value written to this location will enable the interrupt system of the adapter. The enabling and disabling of specific functions is done through two of the memory-mapped registers, ISRP and ISRA (see Figure 6.26).

Three of the memory-mapped registers can be accessed at four different offset addresses. The lowest address permits Read and Write. The next address allows

FIGURE 6.26
Memory-mapped 16-bit registers and ROM group. The segment address of this group is determined by physical switches on ISA bus cards.

1E00	RRR - RAM Relocation Register
1E02	WRBR - Write Region Base Register
1E04	WWOR - Write Window Open Register
1E06	WWCR - Write Window Close Register
1E08	ISRP - Host Interrupt & Status Register
1E0A	ISRA - Adapter Interrupt & Status Register
1E0C	TCR - Timer Control Register
1E0E	TVR - Timer Value Register
1E20	
1E30	AND / Reset Registers
1E40	OR / Set Registers
1F00	
1FFF	ID ROM (256 bytes)

Reads Only. The third will AND a new value with the existing contents. The highest address ORs a new value with the existing contents.

The two interrupt registers—ISRP and ISRA—plus the timer control register—TCR—can be accessed at their normal offset address or their normal address +20h or their normal address +40h.

At their normal addresses, all eight registers can be read and those that will allow Writes can be written to. For the three registers with the extra addresses, the +20h address performs an AND operation between the incoming Write and the existing content of the register. This would normally be used for clearing specific bits while leaving others unchanged. For example,

```
MOV AX,11111110b
MOV DS:[1E0Bh+20h],AX     ; clears bit Zero of ISRA odd
```

Using the +40h address instead causes an OR operation to be performed between the incoming data and the existing register contents. This would often be used to set specific bits while leaving others unchanged. For example,

```
MOV AX,00100000b
MOV DS:[1E0Bh+40h],AX     ; sets bit five of ISRA odd
```

SHARED RAM REGISTERS

Shared RAM on the adapter card can consist of 8, 16, 32, or 64K bytes of memory. Although Read–Write RAM is used for this memory, the host computer does not have Write access to all of it. Four 16-bit registers control the use of shared RAM. The RAM Relocation Register (RRR) determines both the starting offset of this memory and its size. The adapter has Read–Write access to the total shared RAM. The host can read any part of the RAM but can write only to two areas.

As shown in Figure 6.27, the lower portion of shared RAM is Read Only as far as the host is concerned. The first writable area for the host is defined by offsets in the two 16-bit registers, WWOR and WWCR. Immediately above this is another Read Only region. Then, starting at an address defined by the WRBR and extending to the highest available RAM location, the host again has Write access.

The following program will find out which segment the ROM and memory-mapped registers have been placed in and then read the 12-character serial number of the card. The ROM is typically a 256 × 4 bit device, which means that only one-half of each byte (the lower half) has any significance.

```
;  ************************************************
;   Read Token Ring Serial Number and Display It
;  ************************************************
;
CODE SEGMENT
     ASSUME cs:CODE, ds:CODE, es:CODE, ss:CODE
          org   100h

START:    jmp begin
```

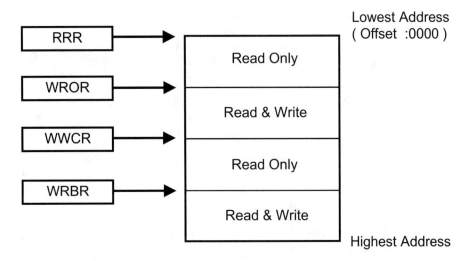

FIGURE 6.27
Shared RAM memory protection using the four RAM control registers. RAM is split into four groups of alternating Read–Write and Read Only areas, starting with Read Only.

```
display      db    "Primary Adapter Serial Number is "
serial_numb  db    12 dup (00),'$'
ROM_address  dw    0

; --------- read Set Up 1 -------------
begin:     push    ds
           mov     dx,0A20h    ; set primary adapter I/O address
           in      al,dx       ; read setup 1
           mov     cx,0FC01h
           and     ch,al       ; ch now contains six addr bits
           ror     cx,1        ; rotate right & move "1" into msb
           mov     ds,cx        ; ds = ROM segment address
           mov     ROM_address,ds  ; save it

; ------------ read 12 bytes from even ROM locations
           mov1    si,1F00h    ; offset of ROM in segment
           mov     di,OFFSET serial_numb
           mov     cx,0Ch      ; 12 bytes will be read
           cld
loop_1:    lodsb               ; al <-[ds:si++]
           inc     si          ; skip odd bytes
           and     al,0Fh      ; use only the lower four bits
           cmp     al,09h
           jbe     numeral
           add     al,07h      ; if > nine
numeral:   add     al,30h      ; convert to hex ascii
           stosb               ; al -> [es:di++]
           loop    loop_1
```

```
;  ------------------------------- display string at ds:dx
          pop     ds
          mov     dx,OFFSET display
          mov     ax,0900h
          int     21h

;  -------------------------------- terminate
          mov     ax,4C00h
          int     21h
CODE ENDS
     END START
```

ADAPTER PROGRAMMING

IBM's preferred interface to the adapter cards is through the adapter support software supplied with each card. This will be described, in limited detail, in the following chapter. In the remainder of this chapter, we will give a general description of the direct interface between the support software and the card.

Use of the term "direct" can be somewhat confusing. IBM has used the word "DIRECT" in parts of its interface commands both at the adapter level and through external drivers. Use the word with caution.

In any case, working "directly" with the card involves roughly similar techniques for both send and receive. Host-initiated commands start with the building of a small System Request Block (SRB) someplace in the adapter's shared RAM. Some commands will also require a separate block of data. This "someplace" will be within the Read–Write region controlled by the offset address in the 16-bit WRBR register. The size of the SRB will vary with the specific command but will be between 6 and 60 bytes long. The first byte of this block carries a specific command code.

A bit in the interrupt register (ISRA odd, bit 5) is then set to cause an interrupt to the card. The card will read the items in RAM and perform the requested operation. When finished, it will report back on the success or failure with a return code in the SRB and may also, depending on the command, leave a more detailed System Status Block (SSB).

For the reception of a frame, the adapter will create an Adapter Request Block (ARB) in its shared RAM and then interrupts the host using an IRQ request. The host will perform the necessary functions, issue a return code in the ARB, and might also complete an Adapter Status Block (ASB) so the adapter will know how things went (see Figure 6.28).

The preferred interface to the adapter card is through external drivers. However, the typical Token Ring adapter performs a lot of internal processing and can handle a wide range of commands "directly." These include commands for the transmission and reception of frames as well as control of Service Access Points (SAPs) for 802.2 LLC protocols.

A few of the adapter commands along with the command code that is placed in the first byte of the SRB follow. The dots or periods in the command names are sim-

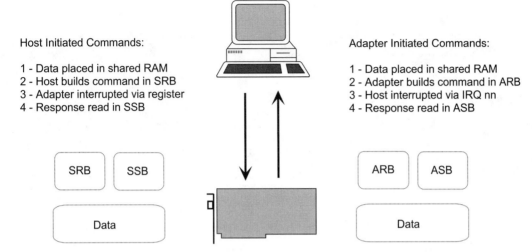

Host Initiated Commands:

1 - Data placed in shared RAM
2 - Host builds command in SRB
3 - Adapter interrupted via register
4 - Response read in SSB

Adapter Initiated Commands:

1 - Data placed in shared RAM
2 - Adapter builds command in ARB
3 - Host interrupted via IRQ nn
4 - Response read in ASB

SRB   SSB

ARB   ASB

Data

Data

FIGURE 6.28
Adapter to support software interface uses one command and one status block for each
direction of communication. These blocks, plus any associated data, are placed at specific locations in the adapter's buffer RAM.

ply spacers. This is the group of commands labeled in documentation as DIRECT,
but this word does not relate to our working "directly" with the card. In fact, the
same set of DIRECT commands are also available when working through the preferred software driver DXMC0MOD.SYS.

- 00 INTERRUPT. Forces an adapter interrupt and expects a 00 return
  code. Simply used to see if the adapter is alive.
- 03 OPEN.ADAPTER. The first command after a machine is turned on
  and used only once. The SRB will be unusually large for this initial command since it holds a complete description of the initial settings, node
  addresses, etc., that are being requested. This command may also start
  the current that opens the MAU relay, thus inserting the station into the
  ring.
- 04 CLOSE.ADAPTER. Terminate processing and remove the adapter
  from the ring.
- 01 MODIFY.OPEN.PARMS. Used to change any of the parameters that
  were originally set with the OPEN.ADAPTER command.
- 02 RESTORE.OPEN.PARMS. Used to restore specific parameters back
  to their original values.
- 06 SET.GROUP.ADDRESS. Makes the adapter part of a group for specific types of messages.
- 07 SET.FUNCTIONAL.ADDRESS. Alters the effective network
  address of the adapter.

- 08 READ.LOG. Returns 14 bytes of error counts, e.g., number of lost frames, number of frames not copied, etc.
- 20h INITIALIZE. Takes the adapter out of reset, performs a self test of the adapter and lobe cable.

REFERENCES

1. *IBM Local Area Network.* Technical Reference. IBM Corp. SC30-3383-2.

2. *IBM Token-Ring Network.* Architecture Reference. IBM Corp. SC30-3374-02.

3. *IBM RT PC Technical Reference for Token-Ring Network Adapter.* IBM Corp. SK2T-0291-1.

Chapter 7

802.2 Logical Link Control

We continue our discussion of Token Ring with a look at non-MAC frames and a programming interface for the adapter.

In IBM's preferred use of the Token Ring adapter, three files are involved, as shown in Figure 7.1. These provide two separate interfaces and implement the Logical Link Control (LLC) and NetBIOS protocols. In this chapter, we are most concerned with the operation of the LLC protocol and the Data Link Control (DLC) interface to it. The NetBIOS interface will be described in Chapter 9.

- DXMT0MOD.SYS contains the code for the NetBIOS interface and for what is often referred to as the NETBEUI protocol.
- DXMA0MOD.SYS is the LLC protocol code. It provides a Data Link interface for programmers.
- The DXMC0MOD.SYS file is an Interrupt Arbitrator. Its main task is to coordinate requests for the two different interfaces and for up to two adapter cards. Both interfaces use software interrupt 5Ch, hence the name. The DXMC0MOD.SYS file also performs a totally unrelated function—identifying the language (English, French, German, etc.) that will be used for error messages.

LLC IN PERSPECTIVE

Logical Link Control is a Data Link protocol that provides two data transportation services—one is connection oriented and the other connectionless.

Although a connection-oriented service may seem unusual at this low level, it parallels the older HDLC protocol used for many years by IBM at a data link level. When protocols such as IPX/SPX and TCP/IP are used with Token Ring or any other adapter boards, they have no need of connection-oriented services at this level. These protocols specialize in this at higher levels. Therefore, if the LLC support file were to be used, it would essentially be operating as an inefficient adapter driver that could only handle two boards and could not handle multiple higher layer

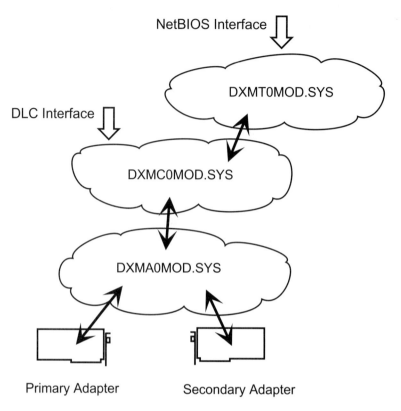

FIGURE 7.1
Three files make up the preferred interface to the Token Ring system.

protocols. Shortly after the introduction of the Token Ring, Novell used this approach until proper general-purpose drivers could be written. For these, see the techniques shown in Chapter 12 for NDIS, ODI, and Packet Drivers.

TOKEN RING FRAME

Let's go back, for a moment, to the Token Ring itself. In addition to the token, there are four basic types of frames that can move around the ring. The split is shown in Figure 7.2. We already know that the two most significant bits in the Frame Control field determine whether the frame is MAC (00) or non-MAC (01) and have spent some time looking at the structure of MAC frames.

$$\text{Frame Control} = \boxed{\text{F F 0 0 Z Z Z Z}}$$

F F = frame type: 0 0 = MAC frame
 0 1 = LLC frame

MAC and DIRECT FRAMES

SDEL	AC	FC	DEST	SOURCE	MAC or DIRECT Data

LLC FRAMES

SDEL	AC	FC	DEST	SOURCE	LLC Header	LLC Data

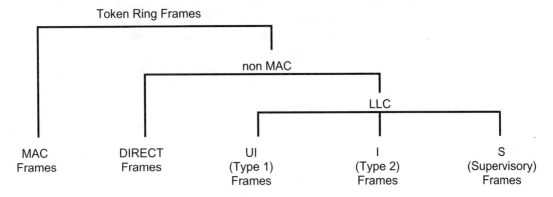

Token Ring Frames

non MAC

LLC

| MAC Frames | DIRECT Frames | UI (Type 1) Frames | I (Type 2) Frames | S (Supervisory) Frames |

FIGURE 7.2
Five basic types of Token Ring frames. The MAC/non-MAC distinction is made in the
Frame Control field. The remaining distinctions are made in an LLC header.

MAC frames were discussed in the previous chapter. In this chapter, we are
more concerned with non-MAC direct and LLC frames. These provide several
mechanisms for moving data and for controlling the movement of data.

MAC frames are generally sent between cards without input from higher layers
of software and are more concerned with fundamental network maintenance. Direct
and LLC frames are usually sent at the request of upper software layers.

NON-MAC FRAMES

Upper software layers send data using the non-MAC frames. Three of these frames
can carry data: Direct, Unnumbered (UI), or sequenced (I) frames. A fourth type,
Supervisory, is used only for control information.

Direct Frames

One possibility for sending data is with a Direct frame. This isn't really a separate
frame but rather an interfacing technique. Data for the frame is first assembled in

memory, and then a command called TRANSMIT.DIR.FRAME is used to send it. LLC software does not add a header, and only the data provided gets packaged into a Token Ring frame. This technique is used to access the Token Ring adapter for use on non-LLC networks. For example, an IPX-NCP structure could be created in memory and then sent to a Novell server via direct frames and Token Ring adapters.

LLC Frames

Within LLC, there are two mechanisms for sending messages. If we choose to transmit our data using UI-frames, we must assemble our own data in memory and use a command called TRANSMIT.UI.FRAME. The LLC software will then automatically add a three-byte header. UI-frames are connectionless/unreliable frames and do not carry sequence numbers.

For sequenced I-frames, we again provide only the data, and the interface software will add its header, only this time it is four bytes instead of three. The command changes to TRANSMIT.I.FRAME. I-frames carry sequence numbers between logical connections called link stations. This mode of operation adds overhead but does add reliability, especially for long data transfers involving multiple frames.

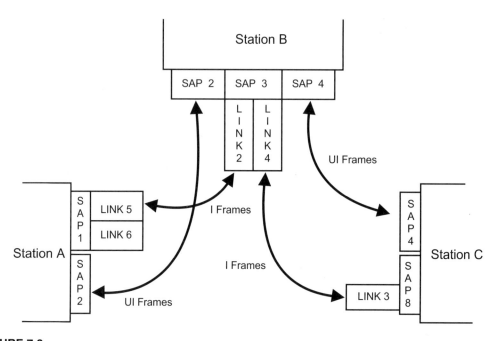

FIGURE 7.3
All LLC communications involve SAP numbers. I-frame communications also require "link station" numbers.

SAPS AND THE LLC HEADER

The details of the LLC header are shown in Figure 7.4. This header is placed immediately after the source address of the Token Ring header. Should source routing be used in a particular packet, that information is squeezed in just ahead of the LLC header.

The first two bytes of every LLC header are addresses within each station called Service Access Points (SAPs). DSAP is the SAP on the destination machine, and SSAP is the SAP on the source machine. SAPs are connecting points for upper level programs. If you have several application tasks running, each can have its own SAP. By selecting the correct DSAP, you can control which task at the far end picks up your data. Only a small number of SAPs would be in use at a time. Since each requires a buffer, a large number of SAPs wouldn't fit in the adapter's memory.

SAP numbers are usually given as eight-bit values, but only the upper six bits are used. Usable SAP numbers would, therefore, be 00, 04, 08, 0Ch, 10h, etc. There are a few reserved numbers. Some of these are IEEE controlled; others are user controlled but are "well known."

Destination SAP

The destination SAP (DSAP) resides on the remote machine. The eight-bit DSAP is made up as follows:

```
DSAP  7 6 5 4 3 2 1 0
     | D D D D D D U I/G |  ← Least Significant Bit
      D D D D D D = 6-bit Destination SAP number
      U           = User-defined SAP number if 0
                    IEEE-defined SAP number if 1
      I/G         = Individual SAP destination if 0
                    Group SAP destination if 1
```

The least significant bit of the DSAP indicates whether the SAP address is Individual or Group. If the bit is set to One for a group SAP, every frame sent to one member on that workstation will also be copied internally to other SAPs within the same group. Messages sent to the Global DSAP will be received by all SAPs.

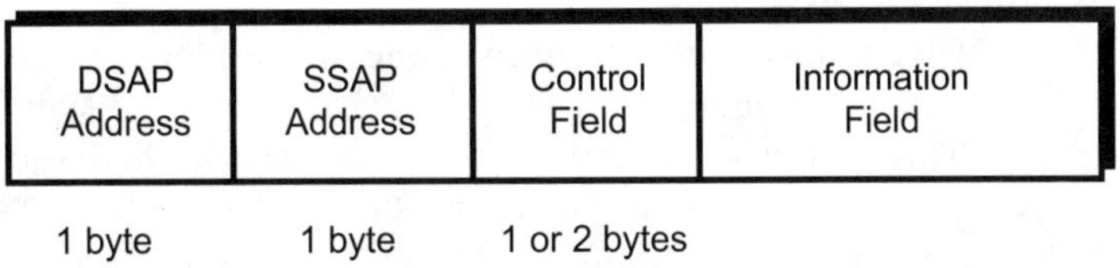

DSAP Address	SSAP Address	Control Field	Information Field
1 byte	1 byte	1 or 2 bytes	

FIGURE 7.4
LLC header is three bytes long for Type 1 (UI) frames and four bytes for Type 2 (I) frames and for Supervisory (S) frames. The differences are in the control field.

Source SAP

The eight-bit SSAP defines a connection point on the source machine. It is built as follows:

SSAP 7 6 5 4 3 2 1 0

| S | S | S | S | S | U | C/R | ← Least Significant End

The least significant bit of the Source SAP really has nothing to do with SAPs. It was just a handy place to put it. It indicates whether the following message is a command (least significant bit = 0) or a response (least significant bit = 1).

Some reserved SAPs, including U and I/G bits, are:

00	Null SAP for internal communication
02	Sublayer management
06	TCP/IP
42h	Spanning Tree
F0h	NetBIOS
F8h	Remote Program Load (RPL)
FEh	ISO network layer
FFh	Global DSAP

The Null SAP (00h) and Global SAP (FFh) are opened automatically and are immediately available for use on every station.

CONTROL FIELD

The LLC control field will be one or two bytes and may or may not be followed by data or information. It all depends on what type of LLC frame is indicated within the control field. Three types are possible. Two of these can carry user data.

Unnumbered Information

Unnumbered Information (UI) frames are used for a variety of control messages and also for the connectionless movement of user data. UI-frames do not require links to be set up.

If UI-frames are used, each frame is considered a separate unit. No sequence numbers are included, and no acknowledgments are sent back from the receiving end. This isn't as unreliable as it sounds because the basic Token Ring frame does have a good CRC and the receiving station does indicate "address recognized" and "copied" with bits in the frame trailer. Because they don't involve the overhead of extra frames, UI-frames have a higher efficiency than the next type. However, a complete UI-frame could be lost or delivered out of sequence, and LLC would never know it had happened. Unnumbered frames are also known as IEEE Type 1 frames and are generally referred to as connectionless.

The UI control field is one byte. It ends in a 11 to indicate a UI-frame.

Control Field = | M M M P/F M M 1 1 |

The five M-bits define the operation:

000 00	Connectionless data
111 00	Links TEST command or response
101 11	XID exchanges three bytes of identification or information
100 01	FRMR describes why a frame was rejected
011 00	UA response
011 11	SABME—Set Asynchronous Balanced Mode Extended
010 00	Disconnect Command
000 11	Disconnect Response

Information Frames

The operation of Sequenced Information frames is very similar to another IBM protocol—High Level Data Link Control (HDLC). Numbered Information (I) frames transfer sequentially numbered frames between links. These links must first be created and then later closed.

For transmission of a large file that will have to be split into smaller pieces (4K bytes or less per frame), there is an advantage to including sequence numbers and acknowledging frame reception by number. This greatly reduces the chance of missing a portion of the file or having two parts out of sequence. The chance of this happening on a single ring is very low but increases when bridged rings and congestion are involved.

Extra frame transmissions are now involved to open and close and maintain the "virtual" link needed for this type of transfer. I-frames are also known as IEEE Type 2 frames and are connection oriented.

I-frames use two control bytes. The first byte ends in a Zero to indicate an I-frame.

N(S)	ø	N(R)	P/F

N(S) is a frame sequence number (0–127) sent from source to destination and indicates the sequence number of this particular data frame. Once frame number 127 is sent, the count simply cycles back to 0, 1, 2, etc.

N(R) is a frame sequence number sent from the destination back to the source and indicates the next frame sequence number expected. At the same time, this also acknowledges that everything up to frame N(R)-1 was received correctly.

In a command frame (dictated by the least significant bit of SSAP = 0), the P/F bit means POLL? (Yes/No). In a response, the P/F bit means FINAL? (Yes/No).

Supervisory Frames

Supervisory (S) frames perform only control functions. No user data is carried by this frame type. Two control bytes are used in S-frames. The first byte ends in 01 to indicate an S-frame.

0 0 0 0 S S 0 1	N(R)	P/F

S S = Supervisory function bytes
0 0 = Receiver is ready and the next expected frame is N(R)
0 1 = Receiver is not ready and acknowledging frame N(R) – 1
1 0 = Request retransmission of sequenced frames starting at N(R)

IBM'S DLC INTERFACE

To use the Data Link interface, a programmer first creates a "command block" of necessary information and then issues a software interrupt (int 5Ch). If you have been flipping ahead through the pages, you might have noticed that the NetBIOS interface also uses a very similar command block and the identical 5Ch interrupt. The first byte of the block changes to distinguish NetBIOS from LLC interface requests.

Within the DLC interface, one group of commands is used mainly for the control of the adapter but also includes the transmission of frames which do not involve LLC headers. These are labeled Direct commands. The other set contains what IBM calls DLC commands that involve transmissions with LLC headers.

The basic command block (CCB) for any command is shown as:

Size (bytes)	Field
1	Adapter number (0 = primary, 1 = secondary)
1	Command (see following lists)
1	Return Code
1	Work Area
4	Optional Pointer to next CCB
4	Optional Pointer to a Post program
4	Pointer to a parameter table

The parameter table contains additional pieces of information needed for specific commands.

Direct Commands

The following is only a sample of the approximately 50 commands available.

In the descriptions there are references to "stations." These are not the PCs or workstations but rather the internal functions that can transmit and receive. Stations can be direct stations, SAP-nn stations, or Link-ss stations. Notice that the latter two will have specific numbers attached. In contrast, there is only one direct station.

The hexadecimal value in brackets is the command placed in the second byte of the command block. The periods between the words are simply artificial "spaces."

The first group contains both general commands for the control of the adapter and commands to send and receive "direct" messages.

DIR.INITIALIZE	(20h)	Performs a self-test of the adapter and initializes many values. Could take 12 seconds or more to complete.
DIR.OPEN.ADAPTER	(03h)	Sets initial values for node address and buffers and places the adapter on the ring. This command should be used immediately after DIR.INITIALIZE.
DIR.CLOSE.ADAPTER	(04h)	Terminates all communications with this adapter and removes it from the ring.
DIR.INTERRUPT	(00h)	Tests only to see if the adapter is actually alive.
DIR.READ.LOG	(08h)	Copies the adapter logs out to a buffer and then resets all event counters.
DIR.STATUS	(21h)	Reads information on addresses, SAPs, and links.
DIR.TIMER.SET	(22h)	Sets a timer to go off after some multiple of 491.5 milliseconds.
TRANSMIT.DIR.FRAME	(0Ah)	Sends a frame that has been constructed by the user to a remote "direct" station.
RECEIVE	(28h)	Prepares a specific station for reception of direct, SAP, or link station frames.

LLC Commands

This group contains additional commands needed for various types of LLC operations. Direct commands are still needed for many of the basic setup operations.

TRANSMIT.I.FRAME	(0Bh)	Transmits prepared information with sequence numbers to a specific link station.
TRANSMIT.UI.FRAME	(0Dh)	Transmits prepared information to a specific SAP.
TRANSMIT.TEST.COMMAND	(11h)	Causes a TEST command frame to be sent.
TRANSMIT.XID.COMMAND	(0Eh)	Causes an XID command frame to be sent.

DLC.OPEN.SAP	(15h)	Activates an individual or group SAP and reserves a number of link stations for it.
DLC.CLOSE.SAP	(16h)	Deactivates a SAP.
DLC.OPEN.STATION	(19h)	Allocates resources for a link station including timers and counts.
DLC.CLOSE.STATION	(1Ah)	Deactivates a link station.
DLC.CONNECT.STATION	(1Bh)	Initiates a link for the subsequent transfer of numbered data frames. For remote stations on other networks, routing information is involved in the initial transfer.
DLC.FLOW.CONTROL	(1Dh)	Controls data flow across a link by setting or resetting a "local busy" status.
DLC.STATISTICS	(1Eh)	Reads and optionally resets the DLC status logs for a given SAP.
DLC.RESET	(14h)	Aborts all LLC communications and closes one or all SAPs and their associated links.

COMMAND SEQUENCE

The following is a typical sequence of commands needed to get an adapter started in the morning, open a SAP, establish a link, and send some data. Later the link, SAP, and adapter have to be shut down.

```
DIR.INITIALIZE
DIR.OPEN.ADAPTER
RECEIVE
DLC.OPEN.SAP
RECEIVE
DLC.OPEN.STATION
RECEIVE
DLC.CONNECT.STATION
......
TRANSMIT.I.FRAME
......
DLC.CLOSE.STATION
DLC.CLOSE.SAP
DIR.CLOSE.ADAPTER
```

Based on this sequence, it should be obvious that a full programming example involving the opening of SAPs and link stations and transferring a file could be fairly

lengthy. What follows is an excerpt that does nothing more than open a SAP using
the command DLC.OPEN.SAP. This should provide a general idea of what is
involved in adapter programming through the Token Ring support software interface.

```
// --------------------------------------------------------------------
//  first a few definitions
// --------------------------------------------------------------------
#define DIR_INTERRUPT                   0x00
#define DIR_OPEN_ADAPTER                0x03
#define DIR_CLOSE_ADAPTER               0x04
#define TRANSMIT_DIR_FRAME              0x0A
#define DLC_OPEN_SAP                    0x15
#define DIR_INITIALIZE                  0x20
#define RECEIVE                         0x28


typedef unsigned char  BYTE;
typedef unsigned int   WORD;
typedef unsigned long  DWORD;
typedef unsigned char *ADDRESS;


// -----------------------------------------------------------------------
//   Definition of basic Command Control Block (CCB)
// -----------------------------------------------------------------------
typedef struct {
     BYTE     adapter;         // adapter number (0 or 1)
     BYTE     command;         // command
     BYTE     retcode;         // return code
     BYTE     work;            // adapter work area
     ADDRESS  nxt_CCB;         // pointer to next CCB
     ADDRESS  cmd_cplt;        // optional exit routine
     ADDRESS  parm_table;      // pointer to parameter table
  } CCB;


// -----------------------------------------------------------------------
//    Parameter table for DLC.OPEN.SAP
// -----------------------------------------------------------------------
typedef struct {
     WORD     station_id;      // SAP station id (returned)
     WORD     status;          // DLC status
     BYTE     timer_t1;        // T1 response timer
     BYTE     timer_t2;        // T2 acknowledge timer
     BYTE     timer_ti;        // Ti inactivity timer
     BYTE     maxout;          // max outstanding transmits
     BYTE     maxin;           // max outstanding receives
     BYTE     maxout_inc;      // maxout increment
     BYTE     max_retry;       // max retry
     BYTE     max_members;     // max SAPs in group SAP
     WORD     max_i_frame;     // largest i-frame info size
```

```
         BYTE     sap_value;        // SAP to be opened
         BYTE     options;          // SAP options
         BYTE     link_count;       // number of link stations
         BYTE     reserved[2];
         BYTE     group_count;      // length of group list
         ADDRESS  group_list;       // list of group SAP numbers
         ADDRESS  dlc_status_exit;  // I/O appendage exit
         WORD     dlc_buf_size;     // size of buffers in pool
         WORD     dlc_pool_len;     // length of pool buffer
         ADDRESS  dlc_pool_addr;    // pointer to buffer pool
       } SAP_PARAM;

   // -----------------------------------------------------------------------
   //      Open a Service Access Point
   // -----------------------------------------------------------------------
      ......
      ........
      printf( "We will try opening a SAP \n" );
      dlc_open_sap( &ccb_one, adapternum, SAP );
      // .....wait for completion.......
      if (ccb_one.retcode)
        printf("That didn't work right \n");
      else {
        printf("We have opened SAP %02Xh\n,SAP_PARAM.station_id");
      }
      .......
      .....

   // -----------------------------------------------------------------------
   //    Open a SAP and two link stations for the SAP.
   // -----------------------------------------------------------------------
   void dlc_open_sap (ccb_one, adapternum, sap)
      CCB *ccb_one;
      BYTE adapternum;
      BYTE sap;
      {
         static SAP_PARAM param_tabl;
         static BYTE sap_buffer_pool[4096];
         ccb_one->command    = DLC_OPEN_SAP;
         ccb_one->adapter    = adapternum;
         ccb_one->parm_table = (ADDRESS) &param_tabl;
         ccb_one->pointer    = ZEROADDRESS;
         ccb_one->cmd_cplt   = (ADDRESS) CCBCpltApp;
         memset(&param_tabl,0,sizeof(OPEN_SAP_PT));
         param_tabl.sap_value      = sap;
         param_tabl.station_count  = 2;
         param_tabl.options        = 0x04;        // Individual SAP
         param_tabl.dlc_pool_addr  = (ADDRESS) sap_buffer_pool;
         param_tabl.dlc_pool_len   = 256;
```

```
    param_tabl.dlc_status_exit = (ADDRESS) DlcStatApp;
    geninterrupt(0x5C);
    return;
}
```

REFERENCES

1. *IBM Local Area Network*, Technical Reference, IBM Corp. SC30-3383-2

2. IEEE 802.2 Specification

Chapter 8

Fiber Distributed Data Interface

In the never-ending quest for speed, optical fibers are an important component. Fibers have a much higher bandwidth capability and lower loss and are, therefore, capable of very long distance runs. Copper wire, in contrast, can only support high data rates over significantly shorter distances. Fiber is also immune to electrical noise.

The Fiber Distributed Data Interface (FDDI) is a very high-speed Token Ring network designed specifically to use optical fibers as the connecting media. The data rate is 100 megabits/sec, and the ring can support up to 500 nodes with as much as 2 km spacing between adjacent nodes. Thanks to the low losses of optical fibers, the overall circumference can reach 200 km (125 miles). The network will handle a mixture of normal data plus time-critical information such as digitized voice and video.

Because of the higher adapter and fiber costs, FDDI has initially been used only in **backbone** networks and for high-speed communications between host processors. However, as costs fall, FDDI-based networks could be as common as Ethernet.

DUAL RINGS

The basic operation of FDDI has much in common with the Token Ring. Since it is very difficult to tap into a fiber, as required with a bus topology, a ring was about the only choice. FDDI is a loop arrangement of stations with each station having an input fiber from the previous station and an output to the following one. The last station connects back to the first to complete a ring.

The simplest installation would be a single ring with all data circulating in one direction, just as the Token Ring does. However, designers wanted the highest possible reliability so two fibers could run in parallel. One would carry data clockwise, and the other would carry data in the opposite direction. The double fiber could provide double the throughput, 200 megabits/sec, but the greater advantage is improved reliability. It is, therefore, more common for the secondary fiber to be left "idle" and only used should the primary fail (see Figure 8.1).

If a break should occur at any one point, the stations on either side would perform a "wrap" from primary to secondary, and a ring would be recreated.

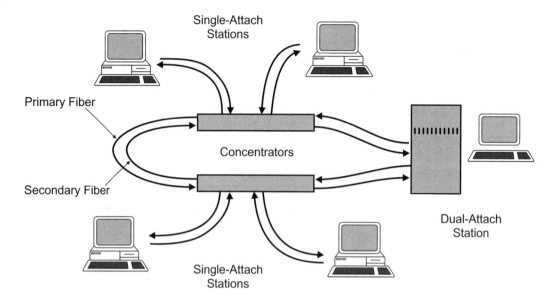

FIGURE 8.1
FDDI network with dual fiber optic cables.

STATION TYPES

FDDI defines two station types: single attach and dual attach. Class A or Dual Attach Stations (DAS) use a more expensive adapter card with two inputs and two outputs. Dual Attach Stations connect to both the primary and secondary fibers and have improved reliability and throughput. However, since the station connects directly in the ring, it would have to be left connected and turned on. The most common application for a dual attachment wouldn't be a station at all but rather a "wiring" concentrator similar to the Multistation Access Units of Token Ring.

DAS stations must be capable of forming a wrap connection from the primary fiber to the secondary one should an external fault occur. Incidentally, wrapping an optical signal with the power off is not an easy task. Therefore, the power to a dual attach station has to be reliable.

Most workstations, servers, and minicomputers would attach as a second type—class B or Single Attach Stations (SASs). Their adapters would have single input and output connections. As with the 802.5 Token Ring, they would rely on concentrators to connect into the dual ring and perform a bypass when they are not turned on.

One twist is to also use a dual attach card in a workstation or server that needs high reliability access to the ring. One input and output fiber pair could then be connected into one concentrator while the second pair could lead to a different concentrator. Under certain circumstances, this will improve reliability. The simultaneous attachment through dual concentrators is called "dual-homing."

A variation on the full fiber concentrator is to change the short runs between concentrator and workstation to copper wire instead of fiber. The attached adapter could then be a copper variation on FDDI which is lower in cost but, for limited distances, provides the same data rate. The concentrators themselves would still be interconnected with a dual fiber backbone and so retain the full data rate and low-loss benefits of fiber over long distances.

The concentrator could also convert into lower speed Ethernet or Token Ring for stations that don't need 100 megabits/sec data rates. Such a concentrator requires a considerable amount of buffer RAM to accommodate the speed differences.

FDDI STANDARDS

The FDDI specification was started back in 1984 and is still being worked on by ANSI subcommittee X3T9.5. Now known as FDDI-II, there are four main components to the specification. Some options are provided, but they all retain the 100 megabits/sec data rate while offering different distance/cost trade offs.

1. Physical Media Dependent (PMD) standard. Defines cable, connectors, transmitters, and receivers. Several choices are available:

    multimode 62.5 micron fiber for runs under 2 km
    single mode fiber with laser source for runs to 60 km
    copper twisted pair (not optical)
    low-cost 200 micron fiber

2. Physical Protocol (PHY) standard. Defines clock rate, encoding, and elastic buffer operation.
3. Media Access Control (MAC) standard. Defines the token protocol, addressing, and frame format.
4. Station Management (SMT) standard. Defines ring monitoring and management.

CLOCK ENCODING

All networks must combine a clock signal along with their data if they are to use synchronous transmissions. Ethernet and Token Ring use variations on Manchester coding. ARCnet uses little 5-MHz sine waves. Because of the already high FDDI data rate, designers needed a method that didn't push operating frequencies much higher. The solution is called 4B/5B Group Coded Encoding.

Each four bits of data is transmitted on the fiber as a five-bit "symbol" using an NRZI (Non-Return-to-Zero, Invert on Ones) waveform. The cable baud rate (the rate at which changes occur) is, therefore, 125 Mbaud, and the cable data rate is 100 megabits/sec.

For comparison, if either of the Manchester encoding techniques had been used, the fiber baud rate would have been 200 Mbaud per second. This wouldn't have bothered the fiber, but it would have made the optical transmitters and receivers more expensive.

With NRZI encoding, a One causes the light source at the fiber input to switch states—if it was off it turns on, and if it was on it turns off. A Zero in the NRZI code tells the light source to stay where it was—don't change. If it was off, it stays off, etc. Now how do we get the clock in there?

What if we just transmit each bit of data directly using the NRZI coding? Obviously, a long stream of Ones wouldn't be a problem. The light source will keep alternating between on and off, and the receiving station will see plenty of transitions and will easily synchronize a clock to the waveform. However, long sequences of Zeros would be a big problem. The light source would stay in one state, no changes would be received, and nothing would be synchronized.

The five-bit symbols solve the problem. Each symbol is selected to limit the maximum number of Zeros in succession to three. This also means that any random sequence of symbols must also limit the number of consecutive Zeros to three. The Zeros are "run length limited"—sound familiar?

4B/5B SYMBOLS

Figure 8.2 shows all 16 combinations of four data bits and the corresponding five-bit symbol. Notice that either within any five-bit symbol or by adding one symbol after another, there will never be more than three Zeros in sequence. Each bit in the symbol now controls the light source on/off switching using NRZI rules as shown in Figure 8.3.

The second part of Figure 8.2 describes control symbols. These never appear within the data portion of the frame. The locations are always under the control of the adapter card controller and will be in the header and trailer portion only. Also, a "J" symbol is always followed by a "K," and an "H" is never followed by an "R."

THE TOKEN

The FDDI token is shown in Figure 8.4. With Token Ring, the token is converted to a frame header by simply flipping a bit and then appending data. At the lower rates, this works well, but FDDI data rates are too high. The FDDI token is, therefore, handled differently. When passed to a station wishing to transmit, the token is absorbed and held. After verification, the station will begin to transmit its own frames. However, there could be a short delay, and until the frame is ready, the station transmits idles.

The token itself is only three bytes long, and two of these are nothing more than delimiters. The Start Delimiter is always a "J" followed by a "K" symbol that forms a unique start pattern. The key part of the token is the Frame Control (FC) byte. Its eight bits do not have individual meanings. Three patterns used in tokens (most significant bit is on the left) are:

0x00 0000	void frame
1000 0000	non-restricted token
1100 0000	restricted token

Two "T" or terminator symbols follow the frame control field and simply end the token. To keep it short, the token does not use a CRC field. A preamble of at

4B BINARY   HEX   5B SYMBOL
Data Symbols:

4B Binary	Hex	5B Symbol
0000	0	11110
0001	1	01001
0010	2	10100
0011	3	10101
0100	4	01010
0101	5	01011
0110	6	01110
0111	7	01111
1000	8	10010
1001	9	10011
1010	A	10110
1011	B	10111
1100	C	11010
1101	D	11011
1110	E	11100
1111	F	11101

Control Symbols:

Idle	11111	– in Preamble
J	11000	– in Start Delimiter
K	10001	– in Start Delimiter
H	00100	– Halt
R	00111	– Reset
S	11001	– Set
T	01101	– Terminator

FIGURE 8.2
4B/5B coding for FDDI uses five-bit symbols to carry four bits of data and include some timing information. The seven control symbols are never used within the data portion of a frame.

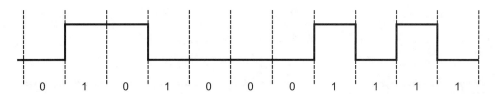

FIGURE 8.3
NRZI waveform used to encode symbols on the fiber.

FIGURE 8.4
FDDI three-byte token.

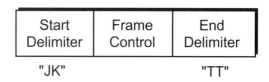

least 64 bits must appear in front of the token to ensure correct synchronization of the receiver's clock. Although the FDDI ring is always clocked (with "idle" symbols), this 64-bit requirement simply assures a minimum gap between the end of the last frame and the start of the token.

DATA FRAMES

The structure of a data frame is very similar to the IBM ring packet—that's one advantage of ISO standards. These frames could carry user data or be housekeeping MAC or management SMT frames. As with the token, a preamble is specified to ensure spacing. The frame fields are shown in Figure 8.5. Again, like Token Ring, the most significant bit of each byte is sent over the fiber first.

The fields within a MAC or data frame are:

PREAMBLE	At least eight bytes of idles (11111111). Used for initial synchronization of the receiver clock.
START DELIMITER	One byte. Indicates the start of a data or token frame. Contains the two unique symbols—"JK."
FRAME CONTROL	One byte. Distinguishes synchronous/asynchronous, MAC/LLC/SMT/void, address field size (16 or 48 bits).
ADDRESSES	Usually 48 bits but could have 16 bits. Within the destination address, the most significant bit (Bit 47) is transmitted first and indicates Individual or Group address. Bit 46 follows and indicates Universal or Local address administration. The most significant bit of the source address is used to remove a circulating frame from the ring when remaining bits of source address match My Address. The 16-bit addresses must be locally administered.

Start Delimiter	Frame Control	Destination Address	Source Address		Frame Check	End Delimiter	Frame Status
1	1	8	8		4	0.5	1.5 bytes

FIGURE 8.5
FDDI data frame structure.

DATA	Each frame can carry up to 4500 bytes of data.
FRAME CHECK	Four bytes. The CRC is calculated using the standard IEEE polynomial.
END DELIMITER	Transmitted as a single "T" symbol which indicates the end of the data and FCS.
FRAME STATUS	Contains 1.5 bytes or three symbols. The first is an "error" indicator and is transmitted initially as RESET. If any other station detects an error, this symbol is changed to SET. The second symbol indicates "address recognized" and the third and last symbol indicates "data copied." The originating station transmits both symbols as RESET (R). If everything goes correctly, the receiving station will change both to SET (S).

The frame control byte again contains few distinct bit positions. Instead, some of the patterns which could appear are:

0x00 0000	void frame
1L00 0001	
. . . .	range used for MAC frames
1L00 1111	
1L00 0010	MAC beacon frame
1L00 0011	MAC claim frame
0L00 0001	
. . . .	Station Management (SMT) frames
0L00 1111	
CL01 0000	
. . . .	LLC frames
CL01 0111	
0L01 0PPP	asynchronous priority transmission
1L01 0000	synchronous data frame

where:

C = Class (0 = asynchronous, 1 = synchronous)
L = address field length (0 = 48 bits, 1 = 16 bits)
PPP = priority

Two types of bad frames could appear. A "stripped" frame is one that was partially generated or repeated by a node. However, before the End Delimiter appears, the byte sequence changes to idles.

A second frame error is called a "lost" frame. This is one whose symbol stream is corrupted so that a symbol encountered after the Start Delimiter results in a non-data, non–End Delimiter symbol.

S-FRAMES AND A-FRAMES

Before starting into the ring protocol description, we need to understand another difference between other LANs and FDDI. Because of the higher data rate, the designers felt that users might want to include time-critical data on the fibers along with ordinary file transfers, etc. This time-critical stuff might be digitized real-time voice or video. The ring then requires a priority system that is different from that built into the 4 and 16 megabits/sec Token Ring. (Asynchronous priority still exists.)

FDDI, therefore, allows the transmission of two categories of frames: S-frames and A-frames. S-frames are synchronous frames that must be transmitted within a time limit. During ring initialization, some stations will have indicated a need to handle synchronous frames. Later, when those stations receive a token, they will always have time to transmit an S-frame but will have a time limit in which to do it.

The second frame type is the A-frame or asynchronous data frame that can tolerate a longer and less predictable delay. Most file transfers will move as asynchronous or A-frames. When a token is received, a station may or may not be able to send asynchronous data depending on how long it has been since it last saw a starting delimiter in a token. We will return to these frames after we look at ring operation.

Ring Protocol

Being a token network, each station must wait until it receives the token before it can send. Once acquired, each station has a time allotment and can use it to send one long packet or several short ones.

Like Token Ring, the destination station accepts the frame and then marks it as "address recognized" and "data copied" and lets it continue around the ring. The originating station is then responsible for removing it from the ring when it completes the roundtrip. Then a new token is generated. On very long rings or with short data packets, an "early token" can be released—similar to the 16 megabits/sec Token Ring.

The FDDI protocol is based on a "timed token rotation" system. This requires several timers and registers at each station.

1. *Token Rotation Timer (TRT)*. This measures the time since the last token was received. If this timer exceeds a particular value (yet to be described), ring recovery action (initialization) will be required.
2. *Target Token Rotation Time (TTRT)*. This is a register-held value that is common to all stations. It is an agreed-upon value for the *average* amount of time that it should take a token to rotate. From rotation to rotation, the timing could be more than this value or less, but it should hold this average.
3. *Token Holding Timer (THT)*. This timer in each station starts after the token is received and any priority synchronous frames have been transmitted. It

controls the time remaining for asynchronous frames. Once it has decremented to Zero, a new token must be released. If the station runs out of data sooner, it releases the token earlier. The value for THT changes with each rotation and will depend on how early or late the token is relative to TTRT.

4. *Absolute Maximum Time.* This register simply holds a value equal to twice TTRT. When a token arrives later than this value, the ring must restart.

Ring Initialization

When an FDDI ring starts operation, all stations must initially agree on a TTRT value. A typical value is eight milliseconds but could be higher if the ring has many stations and if many want to handle synchronous data.

An initial "bid frame" is placed on the ring, and each station will inspect a suggested time value held in the data portion of the frame. If it wants a shorter time, a station will insert its suggested value and its own address. Otherwise, it simply forwards the bid frame unchanged. After another full rotation of the ring, the station with the shortest bid will have won. If two or more stations had made the same timing suggestion, the station with the highest address wins.

The winning station then sends a frame that makes one full circulation of the ring without any attempts at any station using it. Its purpose is like the winner of the checkered flag at an automobile race. All stations know that the bidding is complete and copy the time value into their TTRT registers. After this initial rotation, the ring is operational, and the token can be captured.

The average time that each station sees the token should be TTRT, but the timing could climb to an absolute maximum of twice TTRT. As mentioned, a typical value for TTRT is eight milliseconds, which is about enough time for 20 stations to each send a 4000-byte packet on each rotation.

The timed token rotation system is based on the assumption that rotation time has a linear relationship with the ring load. If the token reappears earlier than TTRT, a station knows the load is light. It, therefore, has time to send synchronous data, if it has any, and then asynchronous data. The token holding timer begins running when the asynchronous transmission begins (see Figure 8.6).

If the token comes back later than the TTRT value, the load is heavier, and only synchronous data can be sent.

The protocol guarantees that an average synchronous response time does not exceed TTRT and the maximum synchronous response time never exceeds twice the TTRT. Any excess capacity is available for asynchronous traffic.

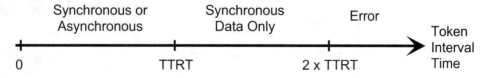

FIGURE 8.6
Time between two successive tokens, as measured by TRT, determines the type and amount of data that can be sent.

ELASTIC BUFFERS

An elastic buffer is required to prevent data loss due to the frequency difference between the PLL-controlled bit clock in the receiver and the quartz-crystal-controlled clock used for the transmitter. With FDDI, elastic buffers are included at each station—not just the one "active monitor" station as used in Token Ring. By distributing this function, each machine now only has to worry about accommodating jitters, phase, and frequency errors from the one previous station rather than all other stations. This buffer must be at least ten bits long.

The elastic buffer allows nodes to operate at slightly different (±0.005%) clock rates as specified by the standard. The buffer will either insert or delete idle symbols (to a maximum of three) to adjust timing. The associated loss of preamble symbols is handled by a smoothing filter. When the elastic buffer is "centered," it is capable of expanding or contracting a minimum of five bits in either direction. Assuming reasonable oscillator tolerances, this guarantees that the chips can handle frames up to 10,000 symbols (5000 bytes) in length without dropping any data bits. Frames longer than 10,000 symbols or clock frequencies out of tolerance can cause the buffer to overrun or underrun.

SMOOTHING FILTER

The smoothing filter prevents unconstrained preamble shrinkage (possibly as a result of elastic buffer actions) by effectively taking IDLE symbols from long preambles and inserting them into shorter preambles. The smoothing filter is typically a two-threshold unit. When the filter is active (it can be bypassed), it attempts to add

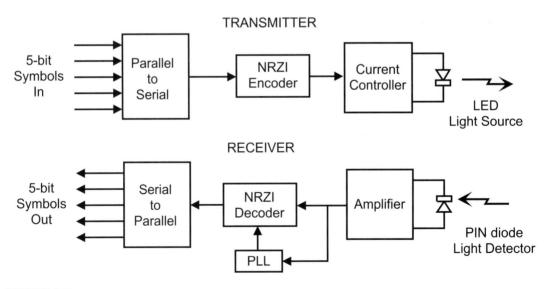

FIGURE 8.7
Simplified FDDI symbol transmitter and receiver.

preamble symbols (IDLE pairs) to any preamble whose length is two to four symbol pairs. If a preamble is five pairs long and the smoothing filter is not fully expanded, it adds one symbol pair to the preamble. A pair of IDLE symbols is inserted into preambles that are six pairs long if the filter is fully contracted. Preambles of length eight or greater cause the smoothing filter to contract, if necessary, shrinking the frame's preamble. A preamble less than seven symbol pairs in length is never shrunk. No action is taken on zero, one, or seven pairs in length.

The two smoothing states are IDLE and REPEAT. In the idle state, the filters output is IDLE regardless of the input. The filter enters repeat mode when it receives a "JK" pair and remains in this state until an IDLE symbol is received.

RING STATES

Again, like Token Ring, there are several states in which an FDDI ring can be—especially during initialization.

- CLAIM STATE—used to negotiate the operative time for token rotation and to determine which node will issue the token. The first four bytes following the source address of a MAC claim frame will represent this value. Each node bids, via claim frames, on network parameters such as THT and TTRT. The lowest bidder establishes the network parameters during the claim process.
- BEACONING—used to guarantee ring integrity by verifying the path of the ring. A beacon frame is sent by any station that detects a serious error. This would likely be a hardware error or a timer-expired operation. The beaconing process consists of MAC frames sent immediately without waiting for tokens. The frame is repeated every 20 ms and includes the local station address and that of its nearest upstream neighbor. The packets, of course, will have to circle the ring to reach this upstream neighbor, and this will expose any cabling or station faults. Once located, faulty stations will remove themselves, and cable breaks will be wrapped by the concentrators.

CONNECTORS

The standard connector for the optical cables holds two fibers—one for transmitting and one for receiving. Called a Fixed Shroud Duplex (FSD) connector, it recesses the fiber ends inside a hood or shroud for protection.

The same cables and connectors can be used for connecting either DAS concentrators onto the dual ring or SAS workstations to the concentrators. In the former case, one fiber transmits to the primary ring, and the other receives from the secondary ring as shown in Figure 8.8. For SAS stations, the transmit and receive are both for the primary ring, and the concentrator must switch to the secondary if needed.

To assist with initial network construction, connectors have interchangeable plastic keys. "A" and "B" keys indicate DAS connections to the dual ring. "M" and

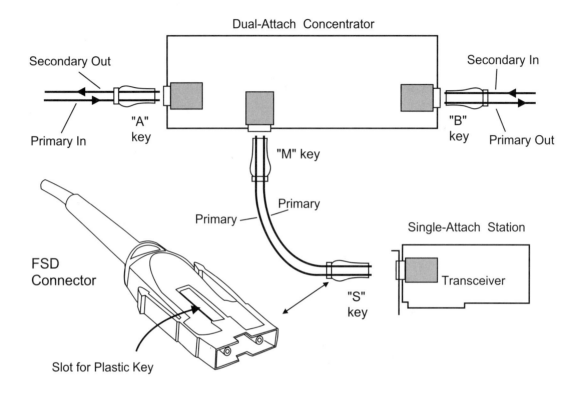

FIGURE 8.8
Fixed Shroud Duplex connectors are used both for Single and Dual Attach Stations but
have a different plastic key.

"S" connections are used for single attach workstations. In this case, the "M" (master) end is at the concentrator and the "S" (slave) end is at the workstation.

FDDI on Copper

The key item in the cost of an FDDI adapter board is the optical transceiver that converts electrical to optical signals and back. To reduce costs, but at the penalty of greatly reduced cable lengths, a variation on FDDI called Copper Distributed Data Interface (CDDI) has been implemented. CDDI uses a different modulation technique, called MLT-3, developed by Crescendo Communications. It reduces the baud rate and substitutes amplitude changes to retain the same 100 megabits/sec data rate.

REFERENCES

1. *FDDI Supernet Family Data Book.* Sunnyvale, CA: Advanced Micro Devices, 1992.

2. *T7351 FDDI Physical Layer Device Data Sheets.* Allentown, PA: AT&T Microelectronics, 1992.

Chapter 9

NetBIOS

This is the first of two chapters on standardized network programming interfaces. Writing to a standard interface is preferred to writing directly to the adapter card because any card can then be used.

APPLICATION PROGRAM INTERFACES

Many application programs running on a network could just as easily run on a single-user machine. Other than controlling the sharing and security of files (very important in itself), the network doesn't add anything very special. The services these programs require of a network do not extend beyond normal DOS functions. The workstation shell redirects these for server use.

In some cases, however, it may be desirable to write programs specifically for a network. Some of the attractions might be the organized sharing of a data file, a messaging system, or a meeting scheduler. Such programs would not run on DOS-only PCs because, in addition to some DOS functions, they would be relying on extra services provided by the network software (see Figure 9.1).

Having decided to write a network program, a programmer is faced with the choice of which network application program interface (API) to use. This chapter uses NetBIOS.

NetBIOS functions aren't as versatile as Novell's (there are only 20 of them), but they are available on a wide range of networks. The disadvantage of NetBIOS is lower speed. The biggest alternative is Novell's collection of NetWare APIs, which include NetBIOS as a subset (Chapter 10).

NETBIOS

When IBM released the documentation in 1984 for their broadband CSMA network, shown in Figure 1.11, they carefully documented how to use the software that was in the BIOS ROM of the network adapter cards. These interfacing rules rapidly

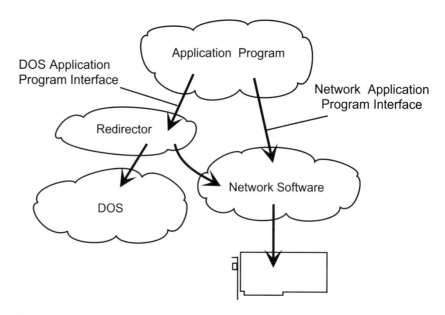

FIGURE 9.1
Network services can be used through both intercepted DOS calls and direct network calls.

became a de facto standard known as the Network BIOS interface (NetBIOS). This software was developed for IBM by Sytek, Inc. (now Hughes LAN Systems, Inc.). Early cards used an onboard 80188 microprocessor that executed the code. More recent cards omit the ROM code and rely on the host processor to execute disk-based code.

NetBIOS is a big step above the board-level programs that have been described in the previous four chapters. Programmers no longer have to worry about the type of network adapter board being used, the size of packets allowed, or proper receipt of the messages, nor do they have to worry about hexadecimal addresses of each station. These are just some of the extra services offered by NetBIOS. There are some disadvantages, of course—extra processing, network traffic increases, and, quite often, additional memory use.

NetBIOS vaguely fits into the OSI model as a horizontal line between the session and presentation levels. It is an "interface" specification, not a description of how the protocols work or how the packets are formed. On more recent IBM networks, NetBIOS is implemented by the NETBEUI protocol. On a UNIX network, NetBIOS, if used, rides on top of TCP/IP. In NetWare, it rides on IPX. In short, NetBIOS is not the key to connecting diverse computers and networks.

Figure 9.2 shows that NetBIOS is the core component of Microsoft and IBM networks. A separate file contains a redirector and the code to implement the Server Message Block (SMB) protocol. All network traffic is then passed through NetBIOS to a protocol handler—often referred to as the NETBEUI protocol handler.

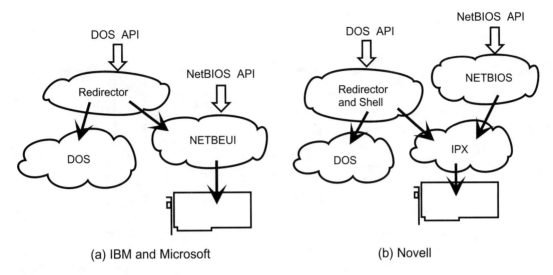

(a) IBM and Microsoft   (b) Novell

FIGURE 9.2
Variations in NetBIOS implementations.

Novell and other manufacturers use their own Shell program, which includes a redirector. All network traffic is passed through the IPX protocol layer. When Net-BIOS compatibility is required, the optional file is added. It also directs its traffic through the IPX layer. This separate program emulates the interface but not the NETBEUI protocol. In other words, you cannot have a Novell version of NETBIOS at one end of a cable and a Microsoft version at the other.

USING NETBIOS

An application programmer accesses the network through NetBIOS by performing three steps:

1. Information to be transferred is first assembled in a convenient RAM buffer someplace in the host's memory.
2. A 64-byte Network Control Block (NCB) of necessary information is assembled someplace else in the host's memory. The information buffer's address and size are included in this block (see Figure 9.3).
3. The NetBIOS program is asked to do its work. On 80 x 86 personal computers, this is accomplished by placing the address of the NCB in the processor's ES:BX register pair and issuing an INT 5Ch instruction. (Don't confuse this with DOS INT 21h, AH=5Ch, which controls file locking on a network.)

NetBIOS provides several alternative communication methods. The programmer must decide on one before the NCB can be constructed and the 5Ch interrupt issued. The main choice will be between datagrams and virtual circuits.

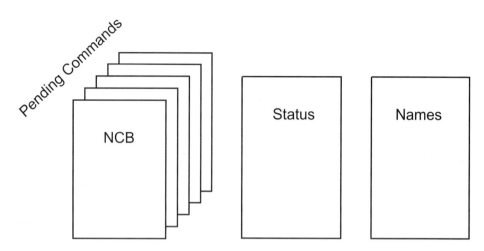

FIGURE 9.3
At each station, NetBIOS holds multiple command blocks, a name table, and status information.

Datagrams

A datagram is a very efficient means of sending short messages of up to 512 bytes. However, its receipt is not automatically acknowledged by the station to which it is sent. If a datagram is not received for some reason, the sender would not be notified. Datagrams are often used for "chatting," i.e., "Fred, pick me up a cup of coffee when you take your break!" Datagrams can also be used for more serious work if the programmer includes code to acknowledge receipt of messages and to retransmit after a certain delay if no acknowledgment is received.

Sessions and Virtual Circuits

The terms "session" and "virtual circuit" are closely related. The idea of a virtual circuit is a carryover from wide area data communications through the telephone network. It means that lower layers of software select the actual path and maintain it and the users send their messages through an error-free, prearranged channel. It could be compared to riding in a chauffeur-driven limousine through all toll gates and around traffic jams, right to your front door. When the programmer starts a new session, NetBIOS opens and maintains a virtual circuit.

Where datagrams are limited to 512 bytes, session commands can handle message or file transfers up to 64K bytes at a time. The network will, of course, have to break this into packets of various sizes, but that does not concern the programmer.

In addition to the increase in message size, the major benefit of sessions is their inherent reliability. Internal NetBIOS code spends a lot of time ensuring that messages are correctly received (see Figure 9.4). The programmer doesn't have to include acknowledgment and retransmission code in the application program. The disadvan-

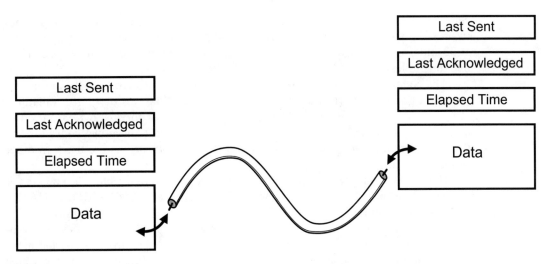

FIGURE 9.4
Virtual circuits use counters and timers to ensure complete message delivery.

tage is the extra demand in processing time and the extra network packets involved for acknowledgments and periodic testing of the virtual circuit.

NAMES

When NetBIOS is first started on each workstation, it automatically reads the network card, determines its serial number, and stores it in an internal "name table." This becomes one of the "names" that other stations can use to establish contact. NetBIOS also allows more normal names to be used.

To make life easier for users at other workstations, the local user can add several names such as "Wanda Smith," "Ms. Smith," "President," and "O Great One" to their table. If another station addresses a message to any of these names, it will be received. That is certainly simpler than sending a message to good old "0C FC 49 A7 CE 04." The underlying software will always use the absolute card address, but the user/programmer is shielded from it.

In addition to these unique, single-user names, any station can also have one or more group names such as "Accounting" or "Administration." When a message is sent to "Accounting," all the stations that are turned on and have that group name in their table will receive a copy of the message.

By default, each name table can hold 17 different names (see Figure 9.5). The first of these is the permanent card number—the "burned in ROM" address. A user can add 16 more. Each name space in the table uses 19 bytes—16 bytes for the name itself, one byte for a Name_Number, and one byte for a Name_Type. The remaining byte is simply a 00h terminator. Name number 01 will be the permanent serial number of the card padded "on the left" with bytes of 00h to fill the 16 bytes. The 16-

character unique and group names are "left-aligned" and padded on the right with the ASCII space character (20h). Unique and group names start at Name_Number = 02 and can go as high as 254, although only 16 added numbers can be used at any one time unless different parameters are selected at load time.

The Name_Type can be either the unique name (Name_Type = 04h) of one station, or a group name (Name_Type = 84h) of several stations that have something in common—i.e., Maintenance Department. Other codes for this byte are used to indicate that a name has been deleted or is about to be. (These two codes assume that only the single most significant bit and the three lower bits are used. In other words, the Name_Type byte has been masked with 87h.)

Here is what happens when a name is added to the internal table. The commands, as we shall see shortly, are ADD_NAME (unique name) and ADD_GROUP_NAME. Once the command is given, NetBIOS must do some checking first to ensure that no one else is using that as a unique name. The code that handles NetBIOS will repeatedly send out a general broadcast saying "Does anyone object to me using the name 'Wanda Smith' as a unique name?" All stations hearing the broadcast will then search their own name tables to see if they are using that name. If so, they send back an objection. If not, they say nothing. The originating station will repeat this broadcast several times (Novell default = 20 times) with a delay between each attempt (Novell default = 0.55 seconds). The Add_Name process can, therefore, be somewhat time consuming (about 11 seconds) but need only occur when a NetBIOS application program is initiated.

If successful, a one-byte Name_Number is returned as a reference number for future use of that name—similar to DOS file handles.

Users should tell others verbally what names they have chosen—these aren't passwords and should be publicly known. It is also worth noting that these names don't imply an e-mail operation. If a user's station is not turned on, the message isn't received. Messages are not stored for later forwarding.

16-byte NAME	NAME NUMBER	NAME TYPE	TERMINATOR
..........12FC56	01	Unique	00
Wanda Smith.....	02	Unique	00
President.......	03	Unique	00
O Great One.....	04	Unique	00
Administration..	05	Group	00
	06	Empty	00
	....	.....	...
	17	Empty	00

FIGURE 9.5
NetBIOS name table. The first name is the adapter card serial number. A maximum of 16 alphanumeric names can be added with up to 16 bytes in each.

Names are inherently case sensitive in most NetBIOS implementations. The wise programmer will store all names in capitals and then convert accordingly.

The name search method is a weak point of some versions of NetBIOS. Depending on the underlying protocol, when two or more networks are bridged together, some implementations will not search outside of the local group of machines. The result is that some machines may not get their messages or two machines with the same unique name, but in different groups, may interfere with each other.

WAIT VERSUS NO-WAIT

For most NetBIOS commands the programmer can select one of two possible command codes. One code (most significant bit of command byte = 0) tells NetBIOS to wait until it has fully completed its task before returning control to the calling program. The wait option is the easiest to use but, in some cases, can be dangerous. A computer will be locked up if it is waiting for something that never happens.

The other command code specifies a no-wait option (most significant bit of command = 1). After NetBIOS initiates a no-wait task, execution returns to the calling program. NetBIOS will continue to monitor things in the "background." The no-wait command can be further divided into two possibilities—with or without a "Post Address."

In the Network Control Block (NCB), there is a 32-bit value referred to as the Post Address. If this is set to all Zeros, the application program must periodically test (poll) a completion value (COMPL_CODE) in the NCB to see if the task has completed. The alternative is to place the address (Intel Segment:Offset) of some executable code in the Post Address location. When the NetBIOS event finally occurs, the normal code will be interrupted, and the code at this post address will begin. At the end of this Post routine, the programmer will have placed an IRET instruction, and execution will return to the place left off at in the normal code.

Figure 9.6 should help to clarify the three command options.

NETWORK CONTROL BLOCK

At any given moment, NetBIOS can have as many as 32 (the default value) commands in various stages of completion. Each command will need its own Network Control Block (see Figure 9.7). Once a command has begun, the NCB must not be disturbed until the command has fully completed. Each block requires 64 bytes of the host's memory and is organized as follows.

NCB Fields

The following description of the NCB fields are for their most common usages. However, the fields are not used in a consistent manner by every command. Any variations will be explained.

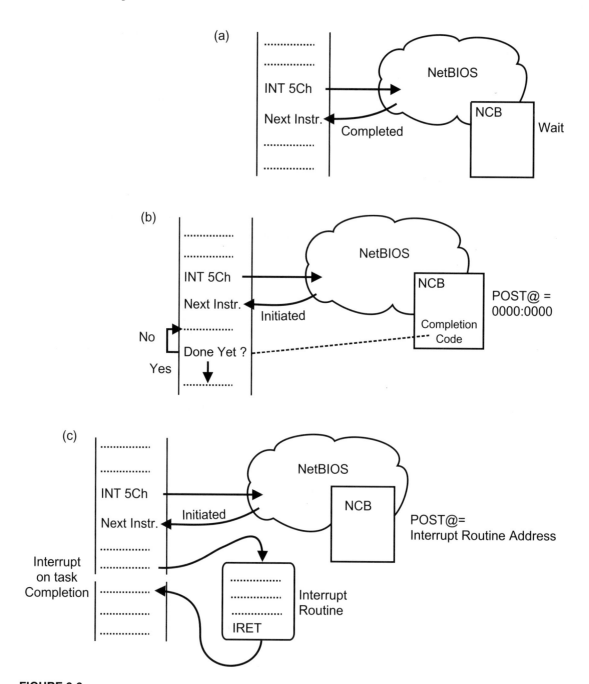

FIGURE 9.6
NetBIOS commands can complete in three different ways: (a) Wait, (b) No-Wait with Post
= 0000:0000, and (c) No-Wait with a Post Address.

FIELD NAME	SIZE	CONTENT
COMMAND	1 byte	Command Code
RET_CODE	1 byte	Return Code
SESS_NUMB	1 byte	Session Reference Number
NAME_NUMB	1 byte	Name Reference Number
BUFFER@	4 bytes	Offset:Segment
BUFF_LEN	2 bytes	Buffer Length
CALL_NAME	16 bytes	Destination Name
MY_NAME	1 byte	Local Name
RTO	1 byte	Receive Time Out
STO	1 byte	Send Time Out
POST@	4 bytes	Offset:Segment
ADAPT_NUMB	1 byte	One of two adapter cards
COMPL_CODE	1 byte	No-wait completion code
RESERVED	14 bytes	

FIGURE 9.7
The 64-byte Network Control Block used by each outstanding NetBIOS command.

COMMAND — Defines the NetBIOS operation to be performed. There are 20 possible commands that can be used on most networks. Most of these will also have a wait/no-wait option. The commands are described in detail in the following section.

RET_CODE — A one-byte value returned by NetBIOS. (Most implementations on the PC will also return an identical value in the processor's AL register.) For a wait command, this will be the full indication of the command's success or failure. However, if a no-wait command was selected, this will just be a preliminary code, and the final result will be returned in the COMPL_CODE field. In either case, 00h indicates "success," FFh indicates "still busy," and any other value indicates that something went wrong. The full range of return codes is described in a following section.

SESS_NUMB — A reference number returned by NetBIOS when a Session Call command is completed if sessions (virtual circuits) are being used. This number must then be used for all future Sends and Receives involving that "circuit." Session numbers are not used for Datagrams.

NAME_NUMB — A reference number between 2 and 254 returned by NetBIOS after an ADD_NAME or ADD_GROUP_NAME command is completed. This must be used in place of a local name for future Sends and Receives. The programmer can also use the value 255 to mean any local name.

BUFFER@ — The full address (Segment:Offset) of the beginning of the data being sent or the empty area for data being received.

BUFF_LEN	The number of bytes available in this buffer area.
CALL_NAME	The full name of a message destination. It could be one of the names in a local name table, which would mean that the station was talking to itself. More likely, it is a remote name that belongs to another machine.
MY_NAME	The name assigned to the local workstation by the user. After this name is added to the table, it is referred to by using the corresponding NAME_NUMB.
RTO (receive time out) STO (send time out)	Often given a value of Zero, indicating no time limit. Any other values used indicate the number of half-seconds to wait until a timeout error is generated. For example, RTO = 08 will terminate a receive command four seconds after it was started—even though data is still being received! Timeouts are most valuable with wait commands but should be used with care.
POST@	Used only in combination with a no-wait command and is optional. It is the full address (Segment:Offset) of some code that is executed when a no-wait command finally completes. If POST@ is set to Zero (0000:0000), the no-wait command simply returns to the existing code that was executing, and the application program will have to periodically test for completion.
ADAPT_NUMB	Network Adapter Card Number can only be 00 (primary adapter) or 01 (secondary adapter). This is intended for Token Ring systems and may not work on other physical networks.
COMPL_CODE	A value returned by NetBIOS to indicate the final status of no-wait commands. As with RET_CODE, 00h indicates successful completion, and FFh indicates that NetBIOS is still busy (or certain events haven't happened yet). The full set of codes is given after the following command section. When no-wait commands with POST@ set to 0000:0000 are used, this byte (not RET_CODE) should be tested for command completion.

Commands

The following is a list of the 20 NetBIOS commands generally used. Some implementations include more, but the extra ones are usually for something specific to that network. One-byte command codes are given for each, along with the fields in the NCB that must be filled. Remember, the fields sometimes hold values that don't really correspond to their names.

Certain assumptions are made for all of the commands:

1. NetBIOS will often support two network cards in the same machine. The following table assumes one card with ADAPT_NUMB = 00h (the primary adapter).
2. The POST@ address is assumed to be 0000:0000. If the no-wait option is selected, this field may have to be filled.
3. All commands will have a value for RET_CODE when they complete. Any additional returns are indicated.

General Commands

RESET   Resets the status of the local NetBIOS software—clears the name (except permanent card number) and session tables and alters the number of sessions and outstanding NCBs allowed.

COMMAND = 32h—wait
SESS_NUMB = maximum number of sessions (1–32)
NAME_NUMB = maximum number of outstanding NCBs (1–32)

CANCEL   Cancels the execution of a particular NCB. Normally used to cancel commands that were issued with a no-wait option.

COMMAND = 35h—wait
BUFFER@ = address of NCB to be canceled

ADAPTER STATUS   Returns the status of a local or remote adapter card plus the status of NetBIOS itself. On completion, the buffer will contain 60 bytes of information followed by 18 bytes for each name in the table (not including the permanent name). Returns BUFF_LEN as an updated value. Some of the values returned are very hardware specific. (See the NET_STAT.C example.)

COMMAND = 33h—wait, B3h—no-wait
BUFFER@ = address of buffer used for returned data
BUFF_LEN = requires a maximum of 348 bytes
CALL_NAME = any unique remote name

Name Support Commands

ADD NAME   Adds a unique name to the name table. Returns NAME_NUMB needed for all future references to that name.

COMMAND = 30h—wait, B0h—no-wait
MY_NAME = 16-byte name to be added

ADD GROUP NAME   Adds a group name to the name table. Other stations can also use the same name and become members of the group. Returns NAME_NUMB. Group names should only be used for datagrams.

COMMAND = 36h—wait, B6h—no-wait
MY_NAME = 16-byte name to be added

DELETE NAME   Deletes any name from the local table. All sessions involving this name must be finished before using this.

COMMAND = 31h—wait, B1h—no-wait
MY_NAME = name to be deleted

Session Commands

LISTEN   Accepts calls from other stations. Won't complete until a call comes in. Returns SESS_NUMB and CALL_NAME when completed. The STO and RTO timeout values are for subsequent Sends and Receives and have no effect on the Listen command itself.

COMMAND = 11h—wait, 91h—no-wait
CALL_NAME = can be a specific name or "*"
MY_NAME = the name on the listening station
RTO = number of 0.5 sec (optional)
STO = number of 0.5 sec (optional)

CALL   Opens a session with another station. The other station must have a Listen command outstanding which will then complete. Returns SESS_NUMB = 1–254. The STO and RTO timeout values are for subsequent Sends and Receives and have no effect on the Listen command itself.

COMMAND = 10h—wait, 90h—no-wait
CALL_NAME = query for the name being called
MY_NAME = the station's unique name
RTO = number of 0.5 sec. for receive (optional)
STO = number of 0.5 sec. for send (optional)

SEND   Sends a maximum of 65,535 bytes of data once a session has been opened. Any send timeout values (STOs) must have been previously set with Call or Listen.

COMMAND = 14h—wait, 94h—no-wait
SESS_NUMB = session number
BUFFER@ = full address of data buffer
BUFF_LEN = number of bytes to be sent

CHAIN SEND   Similar to a Send except that two separate buffers can be used with a maximum of 64K bytes in each. This means that 128K can be sent with one command.

COMMAND = 17h—wait, 97h—no-wait
SESS_NUMB = session number
BUFFER@ = full address of first buffer
BUFF_LEN = number of bytes in first buffer
CALL_NAME = second buffer length (2 bytes) + second buffer full
address (4 bytes)

RECEIVE   Receives data once a session has been opened. Returns BUFF_LEN to indicate number of bytes actually received. Any timeout values must have been previously set. Timeouts of Zero, however, could "hang" the workstation if no messages are received. If RET_CODE indicates the buffer is too small (06h), another Receive should immediately be sent.

COMMAND = 15h—wait, 95h—no-wait
SESS_NUMB = session number
BUFFER@ = full address of data buffer
BUFF_LEN = number of bytes must be large enough for incoming data

RECEIVE ANY   Similar to Receive but will receive from any station with which a session has been opened. Returns SESS_NUMB and BUFF_LEN. If FFh is used as the NAME_NUMB, the workstation will receive from any station that has a session for any of its local names.

COMMAND = 16h—wait, 96h—no-wait
BUFFER@ = full address of data buffer
BUFF_LEN = number of bytes must be large enough for incoming data
NAME_NUMB = local name numbers or FFh for "any"

SESSION STATUS   Returns the status of all sessions that were opened in the workstation's name or names. At least three bytes of general information plus 36 bytes for each session are returned. On completion, BUFF_LEN will indicate the total number of bytes returned.

COMMAND = 34h—wait, B4h—no-wait
BUFFER@ = buffer for returned information
BUFF_LEN = minimum (36 × number of sessions + 3) bytes
NAME_NUMB = can specify one name or use " * " for all local names

Buffer contents:

1 byte	number of sessions reported
1 byte	number of sessions with this name
1 byte	number of datagrams pending

And for each session:

1 byte	session number
1 byte	state of session:

01h = Listen pending

02h = Call pending

03h = Session established

04h = Hang Up pending

05h = Hang Up completed

06h = Session aborted

16 bytes	local name

16 bytes   remote name

1 byte   number of Receives outstanding

1 byte   number of Sends outstanding

SEND NO ACK   Same as Send but no acknowledgment is expected at the NetBIOS level. Intended for networks with acknowledgments at lower levels (ARCnet and Token Ring).

COMMAND = 71h—wait, F1h—no-wait

CHAIN SEND NO ACK   Same as Chain Send but no acknowledgment is expected at the NetBIOS level.

COMMAND = 72h—wait, F2h—no-wait

HANG UP   Terminate a session.

COMMAND = 12h—wait, 92h—no-wait
SESS_NUMB = session number to be terminated

Datagram Commands

SEND DATAGRAM   Sends a datagram to a unique or group name. If that name doesn't have a Receive Datagram outstanding, the message will be lost.

COMMAND = 20h—wait, A0h—no-wait
BUFFER@ = full address of the data buffer
BUFF_LEN = maximum 512 bytes
NAME_NUMB = a valid number of a local name
CALL_NAME = name being called

RECEIVE DATAGRAM   Prepares to accept datagrams (not broadcast datagrams) from any station. Command will complete when a datagram is actually received. Returns BUFF_LEN and CALL_NAME to indicate the size of the message and the source.

COMMAND = 21h—wait, A1h—no-wait
BUFFER@ = full address of the data buffer
BUFF_LEN = maximum 512 bytes
NAME_NUMB = one valid local name number or FFh for any local name

SEND BROADCAST DATAGRAM   Sends a datagram to every name that has a Receive Broadcast Datagram outstanding.

COMMAND = 22h—wait, A2h—no-wait
BUFFER@ = full address of the data buffer
BUFF_LEN = maximum 512 bytes
NAME_NUMB = a valid number of a local name

RECEIVE BROADCAST DATAGRAM   Prepares to accept broadcast datagrams. Returns BUFF_LEN and CALL_NAME to indicate the size of the message and the source.

COMMAND = 23h—wait, A3h—no-wait
BUFFER@ = full address of the data buffer
BUFF_LEN = maximum 512 bytes
NAME_NUMB = one valid local name or FFh for any local name

NetBIOS Return Codes

While NetBIOS is still working on an NCB-directed task, it will place the value FFh in both the RET_CODE and COMPL_CODE fields of the command block. As long as RET_CODE = FFh is present, the block should not be altered. When the task is finished or a problem is encountered, RET_CODE (or COMPL_CODE for no-wait commands) will be changed to one of the following:

00h	Command completed properly
01h	Wrong buffer length
03h	Invalid command code
05h	Command timed out
06h	Message incomplete, local buffer too small
08h	Illegal local session number
09h	No resource available
0Ah	Session closed
0Bh	Command canceled
0Dh	Name is already in name table
0Eh	Name table full
0Fh	The name you are deleting still has active sessions
11h	Already using maximum number of sessions
12h	Session can't be opened
13h	Illegal name number
14h	Remote name not found
15h	Local name not correct
16h	Another adapter is using that name
17h	Name has been deleted
18h	Session terminated abnormally (time out?)
19h	Name conflicts
1Ah	Incompatible remote device

21h	Interface busy
22h	Too many commands (NCBs) outstanding
23h	Invalid adapter card number in NCB
24h	Command completed while cancel was executing
26h	Trying to cancel an invalid command
FFh	Command is still in process

EXPERIMENTING

To experiment with NetBIOS in a Novell environment, the server machine does not have to be running, and the shell program is not needed. Obviously, any machines involved will need a network card and connecting cables. For resident software, the correct version of the IPX.COM file that matches the adapter card must be loaded, and then Novell's emulator NETBIOS.EXE is executed on each machine (see Figure 9.8).

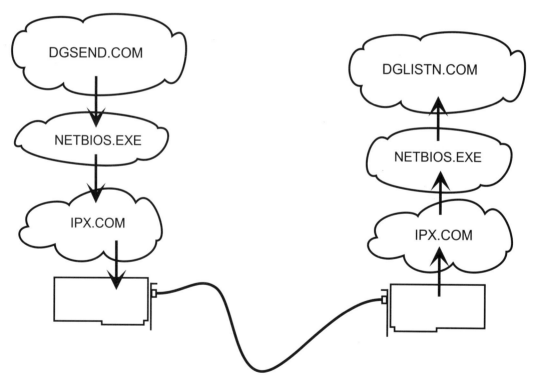

FIGURE 9.8
In a Novell environment, each machine must run the two "stay-resident" files—IPX.COM and NETBIOS.EXE, in that order. The DGSEND program is then run on one machine and the DGLISTN program on the other.

The programmer now has direct access to every machine—this is an example of peer-to-peer communications. All machines are equal, and the word "server" has no special meaning.

Some network card manufacturers also sell a NetBIOS emulator that works directly with their card without requiring a separate driver file. However, different NetBIOS implementations should not be mixed on one network. There are some inconsistencies between the implementations, but more importantly, the underlying transport mechanism and packet structure vary widely. Remember that NetBIOS is an interface, not a protocol.

DATAGRAM EXAMPLE

As an initial example of how NetBIOS commands are used, the following two programs are provided. Together, they form a one-way message system based on datagrams. The message length was arbitrarily fixed at 160 characters—two lines on most display monitors. The enterprising programmer could easily make this variable, up to the datagram maximum of 512 characters/bytes.

The two names are also fixed at assembly time. Again, the programs can be extended to include name entry at execution time, but that is a good excuse for moving into a higher-level language.

The receiving program uses a no-wait command and should be started first. The sending program uses a wait command with no time limit (which means that the system could "hang" if the message doesn't go through).

```
;  ************** DGSEND.ASM ********************************
;  This program sends a short message using a NETBIOS Datagram.
;  The source and destination names are fixed in the NCB.
;  **********************************************************
;
CODE            SEGMENT
       assume   cs:code, ds:code, ss:code, es:code
                org   100h
start:          jmp   begin
;  -------------------------------------------------------------
storage         db    160 dup (00)
prompt          db    " Type your message, 2 lines maximum . . ."
                db    0Dh,0Ah
                db    " Press RETURN only at the end.",0Dh,0Ah
lmess           equ   $-prompt
;  -------------------------------------- send prompt to screen
begin:          mov   bx,1
                mov   cx,lmess
                mov   dx,offset prompt
                mov   ah,40h
                int   21h
;  --------------------------------------------- NetBIOS Add Name
                push  cs
                pop   es
```

```
                        mov   bx,offset NCB   ; ES:BX points to NCB
                        mov   command,30h
                        int   5Ch
; ------------------------------------------ read message from keyboard
                        mov   cx,160            ; maximum 160 characters
                        mov   di,offset storage
kbd:                    mov   ah,1
                        int   21h               ; read a character & echo it
                        cmp   al,0Dh            ; is it a carriage return?
                        je    next
                        mov   [di],al
                        inc   di
                        loop  kbd
; ------------------------------------------ NetBIOS Send Datagram
next:                   mov   BUFFER@, offset storage
                        mov   BUFFER@+2,cs
                        mov   BUFF_LEN,160
                        mov   bx,offset NCB
                        mov   COMMAND,20h      ; send datagram, wait
                        int   5Ch
                        cmp   RET_CODE,00
                        je    quit
; --------------------------------------------------- Error and Terminate
error:                  mov   ah,09h
                        mov   dx,offset ERROR_MESS
                        int   21h
quit:                   mov   ax,4C00h
                        int   21h
; -------------------------------------------------------------------
; NETBIOS Network Control Block (NCB) - 64 bytes
NCB             equ   $
COMMAND         db    00
RET_CODE        db    00
SESS_NUMB       db    00
NAME_NUMB       db    00
BUFFER@         dw    0000              ; Offset
                dw    0000              ; Segment
BUFF_LEN        dw    0000
CALL_NAME       db    "Michael "        ; 16 byte dest. name
MY_NAME         db    "Jim "            ; 16 byte source name
RTO             db    00                ; No timeouts with
STO             db    00                ; datagrams
POST@           dw    0000              ; Offset
                dw    0000              ; Segment
ADAPT_NUMB      db    00
CMD_STAT        db    00
RESERVED        db    14 dup (0)
;-------------------------------------------------------------------------------
ERROR_MESS      db    0Dh, 0Ah, "Something went wrong !"
```

```
              db    0Dh, 0Ah, "$"
;----------------------------------------------------------------------
CODE ENDS
END START
```

The following Receive program should be started before the Send program. It tells NetBIOS to listen for a datagram and then returns immediately (no-wait) to perform other "useful" work, such as filling the screen with dots. When the message does come in, it is displayed, and the program terminates.

```
; ******************** DGLISTN.ASM **********************
; This will display a message received using a NETBIOS
; datagram. The no-wait option is used but without a
; post address.
; ********************************************************
;
CODE            SEGMENT
     assume  cs:code, ds:code, es:code
                org 100h
start:          jmp   begin
storage         db    160 dup (00)    ; two lines of characters
signon          db    "We are waiting for a DATAGRAM to appear"
                db    0Dh,0Ah
len_mess        equ   $-signon
; ----------------------------------- send signon to screen
begin:          mov   bx,1
                mov   cx,len_mess
                mov   dx,OFFSET signon
                mov   ah,40h
                int   21h
; -------------------------------------------- NetBIOS Add Name
                push  cs
                pop   es
                mov   bx, offset NCB       ; NCB is at ES:BX
                mov   COMMAND, 30h
                int   5Ch
; -------------------------------------- NetBIOS Receive Datagram
                mov   BUFFER@, offset storage
                mov   BUFFER@+2, cs
                mov   BUFF_LEN, 160
                mov   COMMAND,0A1h         ; receive - no-wait
                mov   bx, offset NCB
                int   5Ch
still:          mov   ax,0EF9h             ; display dots
                mov   bl,07                ; attribute
                int   10h
                mov   al,CMD_STAT          ; command complete?
                or    al,al
                jnz   still                ; still waiting
```

```
; ----------------------------------------------- display the message
                mov    bx,01
                mov    cx,160
                mov    dx,offset storage
                mov    ah,40h
                int    21h
; ----------------------------------------------------- Terminate
                mov    ax,4C00h
                int    21h
; -------------------------------------------------------------------------

; NETBIOS Network Control Block (NCB) - 64 bytes
NCB             equ    $
COMMAND         db     00
RET_CODE        db     00
SESS_NUMB       db     00
NAME_NUMB       db     0FFh              ; Receive for any local name
BUFFER@         dw     0000              ; Offset
                dw     0000              ; Segment
BUFF_LEN        dw     0000
CALL_NAME       db     16 dup (20h)        ; 16 spaces
MY_NAME         db     "Michael         "  ; 16 byte local name
RTO             db     00                ; No timeouts with
STO             db     00                ; datagrams
POST@           dw     0000              ; Offset
                dw     0000              ; Segment
ADAPT_NUMB      db     00
CMD_STAT        db     00
RESERVED        db     14 dup (0)
;-------------------------------------------------------------------------
CODE ENDS
END START
```

As an example of what NetBIOS looks like inside network packets, the information in Figure 9.9 was pulled from a transmission. It shows the information portion of the frame and ignores the transmission header (source, destination, etc.) and the trailing CRC. The network card happened to be ARCnet, and it was an all-station broadcast (destination 00). The first 30 bytes are part of NetWare's IPX packet structure and will be explained in Chapter 10.

NETBIOS STATUS

The following C program uses the ADAPTER_STATUS command (wait = 33h) to display 60 bytes of status information plus an extra 19 bytes for each name registered.

The program also provides the option of resetting NetBIOS. This is handy if, after continuously experimenting with it, the programmer needs to recover from, perhaps, a bad added name. Remember that the NetBIOS code and all of its values stay resident in memory. Names, for example, will continue to accumulate until the

```
        0  1  2  3  4  5  6  7     8  9  A  B  C  D  E  F
0000   FF FF 00 50 00 14 00 00    00 00 FF FF FF FF FF FF   ................
0010   04 55 00 00 00 00 00 00    00 00 00 0B 04 55 00 00   ................
0020   00 00 00 00 00 00 00 00    00 00 00 00 00 00 00 00   ................
0030   00 00 00 00 00 00 00 00    00 00 00 00 00 00 40 03   ..............
0040   53 54 41 54 49 4F 4E 5F    4F 4E 45 00 00 00 00 00   STATION_ONE.....
```

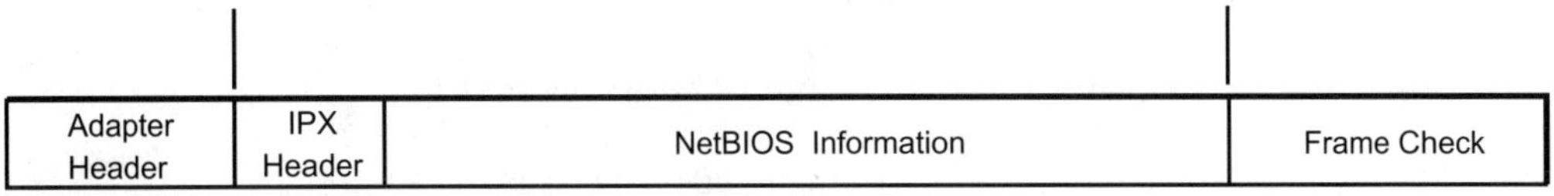

Adapter Header	IPX Header	NetBIOS Information	Frame Check

FIGURE 9.9

The NetBIOS ADD_NAME command from the previous program created an 80-byte packet with these contents. The first 30 bytes are a standard NetWare IPX header. The remaining bytes are part of NetBIOS.

limit (normally 16) is reached. At that point, some names will have to be deleted or the name table cleared.

The header file NETBYAS.H is required at compile time.

```c
/* ---------------- NET_STAT.C ------------------------------------
      NETBIOS Adapter Status and Reset program.
      Displays the first 60 status bytes in hex
      then a list of names, name number and name status.
                        J.K. Hardy    April 22, 1994
   -------------------------------------------------------------------- */
#include <stdio.h>
#include "netbyas.h"
Byte Get_Status();

Byte Reset_NetBIOS();
struct NCB Status_ncb;
char  buffer[512];                  /* status buffer */
char  far *buff_ptr = buffer;

/* --------------------------------------------------------------------- */
main()
{
    char  key;
    Byte  ret_code;
    int i, j, k, names;
    printf("\033[2J");              /* ANSI.SYS clear screen */
    printf("For this station \n");
    ret_code = Get_Status();
    if (ret_code != 0)  {
       printf("Something went wrong \n");
       exit(0);
    }
```

```
        printf("Buffer size is %u bytes\n Status (in hex) is:\n",
                                         Status_ncb.length);
        for (i=0; i < 60; i++)
           printf("%3X ", OxFF&buffer[i]);
        names = (Status_ncb.length - 60) / 18; /* how many names? */
        printf("There are %d names registered\n", names);
        printf("\n---------NAME--------- NUMB STATUS\n");
        for (j = 0; j < names; j++){
           for (k=0; k<16; k++)
              printf("%c", buffer[42+18*names+k]);
           printf("%d     %X\n", buffer[60+18*names-2],
                            buffer[60+18*names-1]&0x87);
        }
        printf("\nWould you like to reset NetBIOS? (Y/N)");
        key = getche();
        if (( key == 'y') || (key == 'Y'))
           Reset_NetBIOS();
     }

     /* ------------------------------------------------------------------- */
     Byte Get_Status()
      {
       struct SREGS SegRegs;
       union REGS InRegs, OutRegs;
       struct NCB far *NCBptr =  &Status_ncb;
       Status_ncb.command = 0x33;  /* Get Adapter Status - wait */
       Status_ncb.buffer =(char *) FP_OFF(buff_ptr);
       Status_ncb.buff_seg = FP_SEG(buff_ptr);
       Status_ncb.length = 512;
       strcpy(Status_ncb.call_name, "*");
       SegRegs.es = FP_SEG(NCBptr);
       InRegs.x.bx = FP_OFF(NCBptr);
       int86x(0x5C, &InRegs, &OutRegs, &SegRegs);
       return Status_ncb.retcode;
      }
     /* ------------------------------------------------------------------- */
     Byte Reset_NetBIOS()
     {
       struct SREGS SegRegs;
       union REGS InRegs, OutRegs;
       struct NCB far *NCBptr =  &Status_ncb;
       Status_ncb.command = 0x32;            /*   Reset with wait   */
       SegRegs.es = FP_SEG(NCBptr);
       InRegs.x.bx = FP_OFF(NCBptr);
       int86x(0x5C, &InRegs, &OutRegs, &SegRegs);
       return Status_ncb.retcode;
     }
```

Figure 9.10 is a sample output from the status program. Because of variations between NetBIOS implementations and to keep the example simple, no attempt was made to break the first 60 bytes into fields. For NetWare, a few of the fields in this block can be described as follows. With the exception of the permanent name, multi-byte values are in Intel reversed order (low byte followed by high byte) also known as "Little Endian."

- The first six bytes hold the permanent ARCnet card number (00000000000Bh). This is name number one.
- Offset 10 (009Fh in this example) is the length of time NetBIOS has been active in minutes. A NetBIOS Reset doesn't clear this.
- The four bytes starting at offset 20 count the number of frames sent by this station (00000034 hex in this example).
- The next four bytes count the number of frames received (00000083 hex).
- Offset 40 is a 16-bit count of the number of commands that can still be used (001Dh = 29).
- Offset 42 indicates the maximum number of commands that can be outstanding at any one time (0020h = 32).
- The last two bytes tell how many extra names are registered (0002).
- The 16-bit value before that indicates the number of session information bytes that can be carried in one frame (0200h = 512 bytes).

The numbering of added names starts at 2 when NetBIOS is first invoked. As names are entered, the numbering system increments until 254 is reached. The numbers then continue back at 2, 3, 4 etc., using whichever numbers are vacant.

The status byte will be 04h for unique names and 84h for group names. Other status values are possible, but these indicate names that are no longer active.

```
For this station:
 Buffer size is 96 bytes
 Status (in hex) is:
 00   0   0   0   0   B  40   0   1   0  9F   0   0   0   0   0   0   0   B   0
 34   0   0   0  83   0   0   0  DC   0   0   0   0   0   0   0   0   0   0   0
 1D   0  20   0  FF   0   0   0   0   0   0   0   A   0   A   0   0   2   2   0

There are 2 names registered:

    ------NAME------     NUMB    STATUS(hex)
    TERRIBLE_TESSIE       12         4
    WILD_WANDA            13         4

Would you like to reset NetBIOS? (Y/N) _
```

FIGURE 9.10
Output of NET_STAT.C. The first 60 bytes contain general status information. This is followed by 18 bytes for each name registered. The program concludes with a chance to reset NetBIOS.

HEADER FILE

The following header file is required for both of the C programs in this chapter. Its most important function is to define the structure of the NetBIOS control block. For completeness, it also includes definitions normally found in Microsoft's #include file "dos.h".

```
/* --------------- NETBYAS.H header file ------------------------- */
typedef unsigned char Byte;

struct NCB{
    Byte command;                 /* NetBIOS Command          */
    Byte retcode;                 /* return code              */
    Byte       lsn;               /* local session number     */
    Byte nam_numb;                /* name number              */
    char *buffer;                 /* buffer pointer           */
    unsigned  buff_seg;
    unsigned  length;             /* buffer length            */
    char call_name[16];
    char my_name[16];
    Byte rto;                     /* timeout values           */
    Byte sto;
    char *post_at;                /* post subroutine address  */
    unsigned  post_seg;
    Byte adapt_numb;              /* adapter number           */
    Byte compl_code;              /* final completion code    */
    char reserved[14];
  } ;

/* MICROSOFT (c) Macros to break "far" pointers
   into their segment and offset components */

  #define FP_SEG(fp)  (*((unsigned *)&(fp) + 1))
  #define FP_OFF(fp)  (*((unsigned *)&(fp)))

/* word registers */

  struct WORDREGS {
     unsigned int ax;
     unsigned int bx;
     unsigned int cx;
     unsigned int dx;
     unsigned int si;
     unsigned int di;
     unsigned int cflag;
     };

/* byte registers */
```

```
struct BYTEREGS {
    unsigned char al, ah;
    unsigned char bl, bh;
    unsigned char cl, ch;
    unsigned char dl, dh;
    };

union REGS {
    struct WORDREGS x;
    struct BYTEREGS h;
    };

/* segment registers */

struct SREGS {
    unsigned int es;
    unsigned int cs;
    unsigned int ss;
    unsigned int ds;
    };
```

DATAGRAM CHAT PROGRAM

The next C program continues with the messaging system begun in the earlier assembly programs. This is now a two-way messaging system, and the same file can be executed on each station.

```
/* ----------------------- NET_CHAT.C ---------------------------- *
   NETBIOS chat program ......
   uses Datagrams with a 512 byte limit.
   Copyright   J.K. Hardy   April 14, 1994
 * ----------------------------------------------------------------- */
#include <stdio.h>
#include "netbyas.h"

void  check_receive();
void  send_it();
void  receive_it();
void  display_it();
void  finish();
Byte  Add_Name();

struct NCB Rec_ncb;
struct NCB Send_ncb;
char  s_buffer[512] = "SEND BUFFER";
char  r_buffer[512] = "RECEIVE BUFFER";
char  far *s_buff_ptr = s_buffer;
char  far *r_buff_ptr = r_buffer;
```

```
/* ------------------------------------------------------------------------ */
main()
  {
  char  key;
  Byte  ret_code;
  int   i = 0;
  printf("\033[2J");                    /* clear the screen */
  printf("Ctrl-T = Transmit message, Ctrl-D = Display message,
                                      Ctrl-Q = Quit\n\n");
  ret_code = Add_Name();
  if (ret_code != 0) {
     printf("Something went wrong \n");
     exit(0);
  }
  receive_it();   /* set up receive NCB ...... */


  printf("Type a message for another station ....\n");

  while(1)
  {
    key = getche();
    switch (key) {
      case 0x14:          /* control-T */
         send_it(i);
         break;
      case 0x04:          /* control-D */
         display_it();
         break;
      case 0x11:          /* control-Q */
         finish();
         exit(0);
         break;
      default:
         if (i <512) {
           s_buffer[i] = key;
           i++;
           if (key == 0x0D) {
             printf("\n");
             s_buffer[i] = 0x0A;
             i++; }
         } else
           printf("\n 512 character limit has been reached\n");
         break;
    }              /* end case */
  }                /* end while */
}                  /* end main */


/* ------------------------------------------------------------------------ */
```

```c
Byte Add_Name()
 {
  char name[16];
  struct SREGS SegRegs;
  union REGS InRegs, OutRegs;
  struct NCB far *NCBptr = &Send_ncb;
  printf("What name will you use for this station ?");
  scanf("%s", name);
  printf("This will take about 12 seconds\n");
  strcpy(Send_ncb.my_name, name);
  Send_ncb.command = 0x30;  /* Add name, wait for completion */
  SegRegs.es = FP_SEG(NCBptr);
  InRegs.x.bx = FP_OFF(NCBptr);
  int86x(0x5C, &InRegs, &OutRegs, &SegRegs);
  return Send_ncb.retcode;
 }

/* ------------------------------------------------------------------------- */
void send_it(int count)
 {
  char dest_name[16];
  struct  SREGS SegRegs;
  union REGS InRegs, OutRegs;
  struct NCB far *NCBptr = &Send_ncb;

  printf("\nWho is this message for? ");
  scanf("%s", dest_name);
  strcpy(Send_ncb.call_name, dest_name);
  Send_ncb.command = 0x20;          /* Datagram Send   */
  Send_ncb.buffer = (char *) FP_OFF(s_buff_ptr);
  Send_ncb.buff_seg = FP_SEG(s_buff_ptr);
  Send_ncb.length = count;
  SegRegs.es = FP_SEG(NCBptr);
  InRegs.x.bx = FP_OFF(NCBptr);
  int86x(0x5C, &InRegs, &OutRegs, &SegRegs);
 }

/* ------------------------------------------------------------------------- */
void receive_it()
 {
  struct  SREGS SegRegs;
  union REGS InRegs, OutRegs;
  struct NCB far *NCBptr = &Rec_ncb;

  Rec_ncb.command = 0xA1;  /* Receive Datagram - no-wait   */
  Rec_ncb.buffer = (char *)FP_OFF(r_buff_ptr);
  Rec_ncb.buff_seg = FP_SEG(r_buff_ptr);
  Rec_ncb.nam_numb = 0xFF;    /* Receive from anyone */
  Rec_ncb.length = 511;
  SegRegs.es = FP_SEG(NCBptr);
```

```
        0  1  2  3  4  5  6  7    8  9  A  B  C  D  E  F
0000   FF FF 00 79 00 04 00 00   00 00 00 00 00 00 00 0A  ..............
0010   04 55 00 00 00 00 00 00   00 00 00 0B 04 55 00 0B  ..............
0020   42 52 45 4E 44 41 00 00   00 00 00 00 00 00 00 00  BRENDA..........
0030   41 4C 49 43 45 00 00 00   00 00 00 00 00 00 00 00  ALICE...........
0040   48 65 6C 6C 6F 20 41 6C   69 63 65 2C 20 54 68 69  Hello Alice, Thi
0050   73 20 69 73 20 61 20 74   65 73 74 20 6D 65 73 73  s is a test mess
0060   61 67 65 20 62 65 69 6E   67 20 73 65 6E 74 20 62  age being sent b
0070   79 20 42 72 65 6E 64 61   2E FF FF FF FF FF FF FF  y Brenda.
```

Adapter Header	IPX Header	NetBIOS Information	Frame Check

FIGURE 9.11
Message encapsulated inside a NetBIOS Datagram. The first 30 bytes are NetWare's
standard IPX header. The original message was 57 bytes long.

```
        InRegs.x.bx = FP_OFF(NCBptr);
        int86x(0x5C, &InRegs, &OutRegs, &SegRegs);
       }

   /* ----------------------------------------------------------------------- */
   void display_it()    /* test for received message and display */
     printf("Return code %X\n", Rec_ncb.compl_code);
     printf("This is the message ...  \n");
     printf("%s\n", r_buffer);
     receive_it();                    /* issue new receive block */
   }

   /* ----------------------------------------------------------------------- */
   void finish()
    {
     printf("\b All done, goodbye ");
        /* we should also close all NCBs */
    }
```

Figure 9.11 is another sample packet. This time it is a Datagram message sent
from the station named BRENDA to another station named ALICE.

COMMUNICATING VIA SESSIONS

The session messaging system is a much more elaborate way of communicating. This
is the "limousine" method where the driver worries about the traffic and we sip our
Perrier, secluded behind darkened windows. Once names have been established, the

user will request the opening of a virtual circuit using a CALL command, and the ensuing communications will flow over this as a session. Even without traffic, the underlying software will constantly check to see if the "circuit" is still open. Acknowledgments are made for all packets correctly received, and those with errors are retransmitted. A session may last several hours or just a few seconds. However, each session uses processing and network time even when useful information isn't being carried.

Messages can be up to 64K (twice this if the "chain" command is used) in length, but these obviously won't fit in any of the network packets. Internal Net-BIOS code, therefore, cuts the message into smaller chunks (see the session packet size value in the previous status example) and sews them back together at the other end. Each piece will have a sequence number so that missing packets or packets in the wrong order are readily detected. When a Session Send is completed with a Return Code (or COMPL_CODE, if no-wait command) of Zero, the user can be very confident that the full message was correctly received by the other station.

Any one station can be involved in multiple sessions at the same time, and several of these might even be with the same station—in fact you can have a session with yourself if you like.

Stations willing and able to participate must first use a LISTEN command. Several outstanding LISTEN commands would be better. Then the station wishing to initiate a session must issue a CALL command. By checking the "return_code" in the NCB, the callers will know if they were successful. A session can now be established, and, if successful, a session number will be returned in the NCB. Now multiple Send and Receive commands can be used to communicate. NetBIOS looks after all the details of packets and acknowledgments. When the user no longer needs the circuit, the session must be closed.

A typical example would involve the transfer of a huge file. The application program would open a session, send 64K bytes of the file at a time to NetBIOS, and, after the entire file has been sent, close the session. The advantage is the security and reliable sequencing of the transmissions.

NETBIOS CONFIGURATION

On a Novell network (as with most implementations), NetBIOS is configurable to a certain extent. At the time the IPX, NETx, and NETBIOS files are loaded into memory (in that order), they each look for another file called SHELL.CFG. This file is optional and, if used, is created with an ASCII editor. Each of the three executable files recognizes certain entries in the configuration file. The next chapter discusses the impact of SHELL.CFG on IPX.COM and NETx.COM. This section discusses the contents of interest to NETBIOS.EXE.

Lines are typed into the configuration file exactly as shown in the corner of Figure 9.12, i.e., "NETBIOS SESSIONS = 13 <enter>". If a line is left out, a default value is assumed. All of the timing values used in this file are measured in timer "ticks." Ticks are generated by timers on the PC's system board 18.21 times each second. Ticks, therefore, occur every 55 milliseconds.

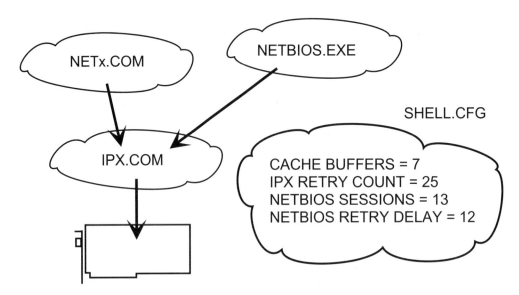

FIGURE 9.12
SHELL.CFG contains default overrides for the three main NetWare files on a workstation.
A simple example is shown.

NETBIOS SESSIONS = 4 to 100 (default 10)   Maximum number of sessions at any one time.

NETBIOS SEND BUFFERS = 4 to 20 (default 6)   Maximum number of send buffers available.

NETBIOS RECEIVE BUFFERS = 4 to 20 (default 6)   Maximum number of receive buffers available.

NETBIOS RETRY DELAY = (default 10)   Number of timer ticks (18.21 per second) between each retry during attempts to register a name or establish a session.

IPX RETRY COUNT = (default 20)   The number of times NetBIOS will try to establish a session or add a name. (This value is also used by other code, which is why it seems to have a different name.)

NETBIOS ABORT TIMEOUT = 0 to 65,000 (default 540)   The length of time in "ticks" that NetBIOS will wait without receiving any response from the other side during a session. When this time expires, the session will be automatically terminated. The default value works out to about 30 seconds.

NETBIOS VERIFY TIMEOUT = 0 to 65,000 (default 54)   The length of time in "ticks" that NetBIOS will wait between sending "I'm still alive packets" that keep the session open. This value must be adjusted with the ABORT TIMEOUT value in mind. The default value (54) works out to about three seconds.

NETBIOS LISTEN TIMEOUT = 0 to 65,000 (default 108)   If a NetBIOS session doesn't hear any kind of packet from the other side for this length of time (in "ticks"), it will send a request packet. The default delay is approximately six seconds and should be adjusted with the previous two values in mind.

REFERENCES

1. Haugdahl, J. Scott. *Inside NetBIOS,* 2nd ed. Minneapolis: Architecture Technology Corporation, 1988.

2. Schwaderer, W. David. *C Programmer's Guide to NetBIOS.* Indianapolis: Howard W. Sams & Company, 1988.

Chapter 10

Inside NetWare

In this chapter, we examine the inner workings of Novell's NetWare. We will cover briefly the server operations and then examine in more detail the programming interface available at the workstation. We will also discuss the structure of the packets that flow between workstation and server.

This chapter is essential for programmers who will use LAN analyzers that decode the NCP, SPX, and IPX protocols on a Novell network.

SERVER DISK OPERATIONS

The prime function of many servers is to be only a file server—a glorified warehouse. The speed of disk Reads and Writes is, therefore, crucial. Here are a few of the steps taken to improve this performance.

A starting point is a fast disk with low average access time. Server disks, although not operating under any of DOS's rules, still use the same selection of MFM, IDE, and SCSI controller interfaces as would a DOS machine. Information is still stored on the disk in sectors of 512 data bytes each. Each sector on the disk still has a head, cylinder, and sector number at the beginning to identify it and a CRC at the end to protect it.

The hard disk (now called a "volume" instead of drive C: or D:) has a minimum working size called an allocation block. One block is always a multiple of the 512-byte sector size and can be set at 4K, 8K, 16K, 32K, or 64K. The concept is the same as a DOS "cluster," but the number of choices is greater. A block is the minimum size read from or written to the disk. If a disk (volume) is set to an 8K block size, a file of 45 bytes and one of 7653 bytes would each use up 8K of disk space.

NetWare, rather than DOS, now controls what goes into each sector. The normal DOS directory structure and File Allocation Table changes considerably.

File Allocation Table

The File Allocation Table (FAT) is the key to locating what is on the disk. It forms one part of the file system. A FAT system can be good. The concept in a DOS environment has received much criticism—most of it unjustified. There is nothing wrong with the concept of a FAT, provided it is implemented efficiently.

As with DOS, the FAT table is a linked list of disk allocation blocks for each file. With a FAT-organized disk, a file does not have to occupy contiguous sectors. Although this could lead to some speed problems when a file is broken into many segments (fragmentation), it does avoid the problem of not enough unbroken space for a file even when enough sectors are available. Without a FAT, space can be reclaimed only after a very time-consuming shuffle of sectors to free up large spaces.

To describe how a FAT is used, we must start with all blocks on the disk being sequentially numbered. The directory, which is in an area separate from the FAT, will give the name and size of each file along with the block number for the beginning of the file. If the server needs that file, it will read the directory and the first block and then look in the FAT to find the block number for the next part. If the first part of the file is in block number 17, the server will read that block and then look at the 17th entry in the FAT table for a new block number, perhaps 25. The next part of the file will be in block 25. Again, after reading this block, the server will return to the FAT table and look at the 25th entry to find the next block. A special entry, such as FFFFh, will indicate that there are no more blocks and that the entire file has been read.

Novell sets each FAT entry at eight bytes. With DOS 5 and 6 on a hard disk, a FAT entry is only two bytes. Eight-byte entries allow massive server disks to be handled—up to 32,000 gigabytes (32 terabytes).

The server file system is well protected. A duplicate copy of the FAT is maintained on the disk and is kept up to date. In addition, because every disk Write is followed by a Read for verification purposes, the operating system immediately knows if there is a surface problem and can relocate a damaged block on the disk. Novell calls this a "Hot Fix."

The FAT is also fully buffered in server RAM to improve performance. This eliminates time wasted in moving the disk heads over to the FAT area of the disk between every block read. Moreover, an automatic "Turbo-FAT" feature provides added performance when larger files are involved. A Turbo-FAT table is automatically created in server RAM for each open file with more than 64 FAT entries that requires random access. From the supervisor's view, these files will show up with the "indexed" attribute when using the FLAG utility.

Directory

The file system also needs a directory table of file names. This, again, is similar to DOS but is much more elaborate. Like the FAT, duplicate copies of the directory table are held on the disk.

Each directory table entry uses 128 bytes. For comparison, a DOS directory entry on the local disks of a workstation is only 32 bytes. The total space used by the directory on each server disk changes in 4K chunks as required. DOS's directory size, in contrast, remains fixed. The SYS: volume starts with six blocks. Because of their shorter names, files for DOS workstations require only one directory entry on the server. Macintosh files require two entries.

The following is an example of the directory information held for just one file.

```
Short Name:                          README.TXT
Long Name:
Size:                                902 bytes
Last Updated:                 11-12-90 9:56a
Last Archived:                10-01-92 1:00a
Last Accessed:                10-02-92 3:15p
Created/Copied:               2-03-92 11:04a
Flags:                    [Rw--A--------------------]
Owner:                               SWILLIAMS
Inherited Rights:                  [SRWCEMFA]
Effective Rights:                  [SRWCEMFA]
```

One major difference between NetWare and DOS is in the handling of subdirectories. DOS places the list of all files for a given subdirectory in a separate file and records the subdirectory name, as another file, in the directory table. NetWare places all file names, regardless of subdirectory location, in the main table, which is allowed to grow. This improves reliability and performance because fewer disk accesses are required for subdirectory files.

Server RAM

NetWare holds two tables for a volume's directory in RAM. The first is a hash table containing an ordered combination of directory and file names. This table can be used to locate the starting block of a file (the FAT shows the rest of the file blocks) when the full name is known. The other table is similar but is divided into groups by directory so that wild card searches are more efficient (see Figure 10.1).

RAM must be sufficient to hold the following:

NetWare multitasking core and file manager

NLM executables (print server, etc.)

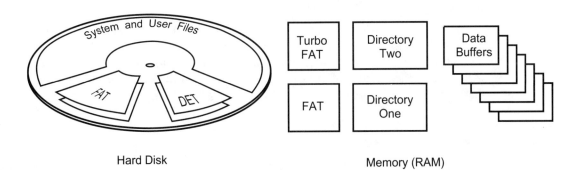

Hard Disk   Memory (RAM)

FIGURE 10.1
NetWare disk and RAM allocation.

The entire File Allocation Table

Part of each volume's directory table

A hash table of directory names

A large number of file caches

File Caching

On a workstation, the bulk of memory is used for application programs and their data. A relatively small amount of memory is set aside for disk caches. In contrast, on the server, only file and printer control software may be running. The bulk of RAM, often in tens of megabytes, holds cached portions of files that have been recently read from or are about to be written to the disk(s). With this extensive caching, disk Reads take priority over Writes, and Writes can be delayed until time is available. Performance improves as a result. However, a sudden loss of power is a bit more serious with extensive caching; some form of backup power is highly recommended.

Elevator Seeking

The mechanical parts of a hard disk's operation are the slowest—waiting for the disk Read/Write heads to move in or out to the proper cylinder and waiting for the disk to spin around to the proper sector. The natural tendency is to read and write sectors in the order in which client requests arrive—first come, first served. However, if the heads are passing over a sector that will be needed later, it is more efficient to read it at the time instead of later. The elevator analogy is good. An elevator stops at the floors in the order in which they appear, not in the order in which people pressed the buttons.

NetWare maintains two queues for disk requests. The first is for system requests, in the order received. These are then moved into a second queue in the order for servicing.

Read After Write Verification

After every disk Write, the same sector is read back. If this doesn't correspond to what is still in the Write buffer or if the CRC reads incorrectly, the sector is marked as bad. The sector is then rewritten to a new "hot fix" area, and the failure recorded. After a specific number of failures of this type, a warning is issued to replace the hard disk.

THE BINDERY

The bindery is a small database, built on the server disk, describing the resources and users available on the network. It is the basis for NetWare's security and accounting systems. The bindery database contains objects and properties of each object. Objects can be users, groups, or a print server, etc. Each of these names will have properties such as passwords, restrictions, rights, network addresses, etc.

Bindery security is independent of file security. Each component of the bindery has an eight-bit security byte associated with it. The higher four bits control Write access, and the lower four bits determine Read access. The meaning of the four-bit patterns is the same in the higher and lower half.

anyone	0000	even if not logged in
logged	0001	anyone logged in
object	0010	
supervisor	0011	
NetWare	0100	operating system only

For example, a bindery object with a security byte of 31h (0011 0001) can be seen by anyone currently logged into that server but can only be changed (written to) by the supervisor.

The bindery is maintained as three hidden files in the server's SYS:SYSTEM directory (two files with NetWare 2.x). The file names are NET$OBJ.SYS, NET$PROP.SYS, and NET$VAL.SYS. Information in the bindery can be accessed by application programs as long as they have the proper privileges.

There are 21 function calls available for working directly with bindery objects and properties. These deal with reading and altering each of the bindery items.

The bindery describes a user's rights on only one server. Starting with NetWare version 4.x, the bindery has been replaced by the multiserver NetWare Directory Services (NDS). This new feature makes it easier for users needing simultaneous access to several servers.

NETWARE PROGRAMMING

The total number of functions provided by Novell for both workstation and server use is massive. This section covers the basics, but programmers should investigate more complete descriptions before attempting any serious programming in this area. An excellent source for more information is Novell's *NetWare C Interface and System Calls*.

In a NetWare environment, programmers can write programs in two ways.

1. Programs to run on the workstation. These stations would probably be using DOS and running their processors in 80x86 Real Mode. If the program is badly written, it could crash the workstation but probably wouldn't (but it's not impossible) bother the rest of the network.
2. Programs to run on the server. DOS will not normally be available in this case, and the programs will run in 16-bit or 32-bit protected mode (NetWare 2.x and 3.x or 4.x respectively). Program errors here could easily disrupt the entire network and cause data to be lost or corrupted.

Server-based programs are called VAPs, Value Added Programs (NetWare 2.x), or NLMs, NetWare Loadable Modules (NetWare 3.x and 4.x). VAPs and NLMs are not covered in this book—not because they are difficult but because they can be dangerous unless very thoroughly tested. The following sections concentrate on programs that run on a workstation.

NetWare Protocols

In their implementation of the Xerox **Internet** protocol, Novell made some slight changes to XNS. The resulting layer 3 is called the Internetwork Packet eXchange (IPX). The IPX protocol is one of two functions within the IPX.COM file (or IPX-ODI.COM). The second protocol is called Sequenced Packet eXchange (SPX).

Figure 10.2 shows the conventional interconnection of the various workstation components. An alternative to this diagram appears in Chapter 12 where three multiprotocol interfaces to adapters are described.

The most important path through the illustration is the one from the shell, down through the IPX function, to the card. This is the path taken by all redirected DOS commands. SPX and NetBIOS play no part in this path.

Following is a review of the key components of a workstation.

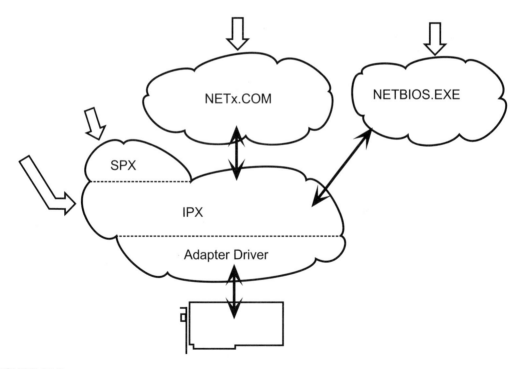

FIGURE 10.2
NetWare's workstation files provide a variety of programming interfaces for application software.

The Card—Controls the workstation's access to the shared cable system. A very wide range of cards is supported. Either Novell or the card manufacturer will provide a driver that is linked into the IPX.COM file at network installation time.

IPX—The basic packaging system. At this level, the software is only concerned with addresses and individual packet routing and does not arrange the packets in any particular order. The IPX function, by itself, is an "unreliable" transport mechanism.

SPX—Sequenced packet exchange adds a "reliable" protocol. It can handle file transfers larger than one packet and includes sequence numbers and a great deal of error checking. Available mainly for network programmers, it is roughly similar to NetBIOS session operations.

NetBIOS—This is only loaded if an application program specifically needs NetBIOS compatibility. It uses up another 20K of memory if loaded.

The Shell—This is the NET3, NET4, or NET5.COM file that contains the interceptor. Data for the network is broken into packet size chunks and marked with sequence numbers before being passed to IPX for transmission. The error checking and flow control are similar to SPX. The messages passed between the shell and the server follow the NetWare Core Protocol (NCP).

NetWare Interfaces

The workstation programmer has four possible ways of interfacing with these files and, through them, the network.

1. Through redirected DOS INT 21h functions AH = 00 to 70h.
2. Through Novell's extended INT 21h functions AH = B6h to F3h. (More than 150 functions available to access the "shell.")
3. Through direct CALLs to IPX and SPX. Note the use of "CALL" instead of INTERRUPT. (20 functions available.)
4. Through INT 5Ch to Novell's NetBIOS emulator. (20 functions available.)

SHELL PROGRAMMING

Shell programming describes the set of NetWare APIs that operate directly with the shell. The number of functions that are available is huge (roughly 160 and growing) and with it goes an embarrassing personal story.

When my NetWare API manuals first arrived, I randomly flipped through the functions, noting the wide variety available. At the end of the three manuals, I didn't remember seeing any shell mechanisms for reading and writing server-based files. I went through the manuals carefully a second time—a lengthy procedure. Sure enough—nothing. There were IPX and SPX Send and Receive functions but none at the file level.

Then, with appropriate words, like "stupid" and "%#!^#$," I realized that the shell functions augment those of DOS. DOS, of course, already has a variety of file-handling functions which continue to work, provided a mapped drive exists. Several shell functions are supplied to map drives.

Shell Interface Examples

This first example illustrates a very simple shell operation. Assuming a workstation is connected to a server, this program will read and display the adapter card number and then the server connection number. It does not cause any messages to be sent to or from the server and is safe to use. The shell itself will have already communicated with the server for these values. Two of the simpler NetWare extended INT 21h function calls are used.

The highest logical user connection number depends on the price of the Net-Ware package. The most expensive packages will handle 250 or 1000 users; the least expensive, only five. The number displayed by this program depends on how early you connected to the network this morning and changes from day to day, depending on the time of connection.

```
/* ------ STATION.C ---------------------------------------------- *
 * Displays the NetWare Server Logical                  *
 * Connection and 6-byte Adapter Card Number.           *
 * J.K. Hardy x15 December 14, 1994                     *
 * ----------------------------------------------------------------- */

#include <stdio.h>
#include <dos.h>

int    GetConnectNumb(void);
void   AdapterNumber(void);

main(void)
{
   int LogConn;              // NetWare logical connection number
   LogConn = GetConnectNumb();
   if ( LogConn == 0 )
     printf("Shell not connected to a server!\n");
   else {
       printf("NetWare logical connection is %d \n", LogConn);
       printf("Card serial number is ");
       AdapterNumber();
   }
}

// --------------------------------------------------------------------
int    GetConnectNumb(void)
{
   _AH = 0xDC;        // Get Connection Number function
```

```
    geninterrupt(0x21);
    return _AL;          // AL = ConnNumb if > zero
}

void  AdapterNumber(void)
{
    _AH = 0xEE;          // Get 6 byte Adapter Number
    geninterrupt(0x21);
    printf(" %04X%04X%04X hex\n", _CX, _BX, _AX);
}
```

To verify the logical connection number, users can type either of these NetWare commands: USERLIST or WHOAMI. To check the adapter number, they can add the line "WRITE P_STATION" to their login script and log in again. Users should always check with their supervisor first before modifying a script.

The previous program is written about the same as with any other DOS INT 21h function calls. No extra information was needed. However, most other NetWare function calls aren't this simple and require a table of information to be built before the function can be used.

Incidentally, modifying processor registers in the middle of a C program, as done here, is a dangerous procedure. A good debugging system should always be available.

This second example is very similar to the first program shown in Chapter 2. It simply displays the contents of a file. The difference is that the server drive mapping is now included inside the program.

```
// -------------- READFIL2.C ----------------------------------------------
// Creates a Mapped NetWare drive
// and then reads the server file TESTFILE.TXT
// from server directory SYS:TEST, using mapped drive J:
// -----------------------------------------------------------------------
#include <stdio.h>
#include <dos.h>

typedef unsigned char BYTE;
typedef unsigned int WORD;

struct HandleRequestBlock {
  WORD  BlockLength;                      // Structure length - 2
  BYTE  Function;
  BYTE  Handle;
  char  Drive;
  BYTE  PathLength;
  BYTE  Path[255];
} Request;

BYTE Reply[4] = { 2, 0, 0, 0, 0};
        // Length Lo, Length Hi, Handle, Rights

int MapDrive(char Drive);
```

```
main()
{
  FILE *fp;
  int c, result;
  result = MapDrive( 'J' );
  if (result == 0){
      printf( "We have mapped drive J: \n" );
      printf( "Directory Rights are %02X \n", Reply[3]);
      fp = fopen("J:TESTFILE.TXT", "rb");
      if (!fp)
          printf("File Open didn't work!\n");
      else do {
          c = getc(fp);
          putchar(c);
      } while (c != EOF);
      fclose (fp);
  }
  else {
      printf("Directory Access Denied\n");
      printf("Error code %02X\n", result);
  }
  return (1);
}

// ------------------------------------------------------------------------
int MapDrive(char Drive)
{
                              // Fill in the request block.
  strcpy(Request.Path, "SYS:TEST");
  Request.PathLength = strlen(Request.Path);
  Request.Drive = Drive ;
  Request.Handle = 0x00;  // a full path will be specified
  Request.Function = 0x12;
  Request.BlockLength = Request.PathLength + 4 ;
                              // Request a drive handle.
  _SI = FP_OFF((void far *)&Request);
  _DS = FP_SEG((void far *)&Request);
  _DI = FP_OFF((void far *)Reply);
  _ES = FP_SEG((void far *)Reply);
  _AH = 0xE2;
  geninterrupt(0x21);
  return _AL;
}
```

IPX PACKETS

IPX, as already explained, is Novell's fundamental packet packaging and delivery system. Like TCP/IP's IP protocol, it is routable, meaning that it carries enough

Shell Header	Shell Data

IPX Header	

Ethernet Header		Ethernet CRC

FIGURE 10.3
IPX header and "data" fit into the data portion of a lower-layer packet. The data portion of the IPX packet contains a header and data for one of the higher layers—SPX, NetBIOS, or the shell.

information to cross routers and bridges and move information into distant networks.

IPX packets can carry from 0 to 546 bytes of data, although recent versions of NetWare can extend this upper limit in some cases. To this data, IPX adds a 30-byte header. The total IPX packet is then placed inside the data portion of the adapter card's structure (see Figure 10.3). The size or length field of the adapter card header will indicate the total number of bytes including the 30 bytes for the IPX header.

Ethernet, Token Ring, and the newer ARCnet Plus will handle this size with ease. However, the 2.5 megabits/sec version of ARCnet will require two successive packets to carry IPX packets that are near the upper size limit. We will see shortly how ARCnet manages this.

IPX does not guarantee packet delivery. This is the task of software at higher layers—SPX, NetBIOS, or the shell. A programmer working with IPX directly must check for correct delivery. Although some adapter protocols such as ARCnet and Token Ring include an acknowledgment, the method used should be independent of lower-layer protocol variations.

IPX Header

The first 30 bytes that follow the adapter card header of all NetWare packets form an IPX header. Its structure is described below (see Figure 10.4). All of the multibyte values in this header will appear in high-byte followed by low-byte "Big Endian" order instead of the reversed "intel" order. Data within the information

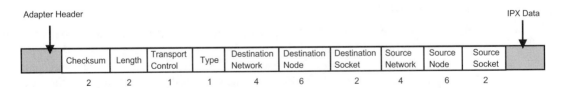

FIGURE 10.4
IPX header fields. Field sizes are given in bytes. Multibyte fields are sent high byte first, low byte last.

section, however, will be in whatever order it normally appears within the workstation application.

> *Checksum* (two bytes)—This is a relic from the XNS inheritance. It is not calculated on most modern networks and is simply set to 0xFFFF. The CRC feature of the adapter cards is used instead to check the integrity of the total packet. The checksum calculation, even if not performed, requires an even number of data bytes. A "garbage" or padding byte of any value is often needed at the end of the data to satisfy this requirement. The length field within the header indicates the true amount of data, and the padding byte would be discarded at the receiver.

A bit of trivia—if the checksum were to be calculated, it would cover all bytes of the IPX header and the data, plus the possible garbage byte. It would not include the two checksum bytes themselves. The calculation would start at the end of the packet and add words together using one's complement arithmetic. Before each successive 16-bit value is added, it is rotated left one bit for each word position from the packet end.

> *Length* (2 bytes, Hi-Lo order)—Indicates the number of bytes in the packet, including the 30 bytes of the IPX header and all of the data. The padding byte, if used, is not included in this count. The length value will be a minimum of 30 (header only) and a normal maximum of 576, although this is extended in some cases.

> *Transport Control* (one byte)—Will be Zero on a "local" network. When crossing into an adjacent network, the lower four bits, which form a "hop count," are incremented by the bridge. When the count passes 15, the packet is killed by the bridge on the assumption that no interconnection would stretch beyond 15 networks. The packet probably has started circulating back along paths it has already trod.

> *Packet Type* (one byte)—Indicates what is being carried inside the data portion of the IPX structure:

>> 04h indicates pure IPX, no inner headers
>> 05h indicates SPX (a series of packets)
>> 11h indicates shell information
>> 14h indicates NetBIOS information

Network Addresses

NetWare is designed to handle the interconnection of multiple networks. The next 24 bytes fully describe the destination and source of the packet using a three-part addressing system. Again, this is taken, under license, from the original Xerox Network System (XNS) specification. To continue with our description of the IPX header:

> *Network Address*—Four bytes are used for a network address. When NetWare is installed, the administrator chooses this number. If only two or three

networks are interconnected, any numbers can be randomly used. However, if a network is connecting to a large national network involving multiple businesses, some central authority must provide the network number.

Node Address—NetWare uses six bytes for a station address within any one network. This will be the card address. The 48-bit Ethernet address fits nicely into this size, while the 8-bit ARCnet address hides at the lower end with extra bytes padded with 00h.

One way to see the network adapter number is to add this line to a personal login script:

```
WRITE P_STATION
```

or use the previous program.

Socket Number—Used to separate higher-layer applications and protocols. NCP uses socket 0451h, and NetBIOS uses 0455h. RIP (a routing protocol) uses socket 0453h. SAP uses socket 0452h. Socket numbers are two bytes long and are carried high-byte first.

Figure 10.5 is an example of an Ethernet packet carrying information in an IPX format. This hex dump starts with the destination address of the Ethernet header. The information for this particular packet was generated by the program which follows. This example does not contain any shell information.

The network number is "C0 4B 47 61," and the socket used at both ends is an arbitrary 5678h. The overall message length including the 30 bytes of the IPX header is 73 bytes (0049h). Ethernet adapters add 14 bytes in front of this. Note that the size in the Ethernet header is an even number (004Ah) and is one byte larger than the IPX header size.

NetWare on ARCnet

Original ARCnet adapter cards (not ARCnet Plus) have a minor deficiency when used with NetWare. They can only carry a maximum of 508 bytes in their data portion, whereas NetWare could require up to 576 bytes.

```
        0  1  2  3  4  5  6  7    8  9  A  B  C  D  E  F
0000   00 00 C0 34 78 30 00 00   C0 C9 78 30 00 4A FF FF
0010   00 49 00 04 C0 4B 47 61   00 00 C0 34 78 30 56 78
0020   C0 4B 47 61 00 00 C0 C9   78 30 56 78  T  h  i  s
0030    i  s     a     t  e      s  t     m  e  s  s  a
0040    g  e     t  h  a  t      s  h  o  u  l  d     b
0050    e     r  e  c  e  i  v   e  d     a  t     y  o
0060    u  r  .. .. .. ..
```

FIGURE 10.5
Ethernet packet carrying an IPX header and data.

NetWare solves this problem by adding four bytes immediately after the adapter card header and before the IPX header. These bytes allow NetWare to cut a longer data packet into two parts and send them as Fragment 1 and then Fragment 2. Fragment 2 packets will not be required very often and will always be very short.

BYTE 0	Always FAh. Indicates ARCnet fragment header
BYTE 1	Indicates no more fragments (00) or one more (01)
BYTES 3 & 4	A 16-bit sequence number (Lo-Hi order)

NetWare on Ethernet

Ethernet, like ARCnet, is an older design and has accumulated some redefinitions and additions. These are not to accommodate deficiencies such as the packet length of ARCnet but rather to meet modern standards.

When NetWare is installed on an Ethernet system, four choices are available for the "frame type." These are shown in Figure 10.6. The variations center on the use of the type/length field and the addition of IEEE 802.2 fields.

Originally, the "Raw 802.3" header was the NetWare recommendation. Since April, 1993, however, Novell's recommendation is the "802.2 frame type." This is the

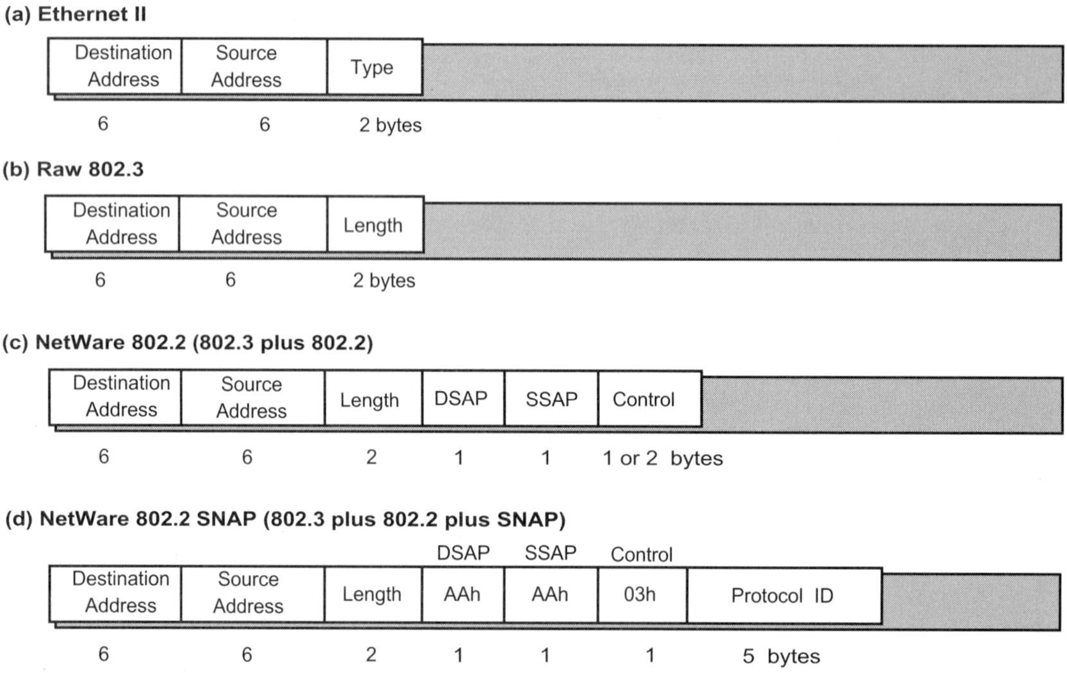

FIGURE 10.6
NetWare's four possible frame types for use on Ethernet systems. NetWare 802.2 frame is recommended.

standard adapter card header with the third field used as packet length and the three fields of the IEEE 802.2 specification added. This change allows NetWare to coexist with other protocols such as TCP/IP on the same machines and cables.

IPX FUNCTION PROGRAMMING

IPX (and SPX) packets can move between any two stations on the cable—they don't need a server. Thus, IPX is a peer communication system, and the server is simply another adapter card as far as IPX is concerned. However, the layers above IPX know what a server is.

To write some simple programs and experiment with IPX and SPX, the shell (NETx.COM) and a server aren't needed. The minimum requirement is cable, some adapter cards, and a properly linked IPX.COM file or its ODI equivalent (Chapter 12).

All IPX/SPX functions should be accessed by a direct CALL to a memory location inside the IPX.COM file. Note that this is quite different from the shell function calls that were previously shown. The user finds this address by using the DOS multiplex interrupt INT 2Fh with AX = 7A00h. If IPX is loaded, the interrupt will return with AL = FFh, and the ES and DI registers will hold the segment and offset address respectively for the IPX function call entry point. The functions can also be accessed with an INT 7Ah, but this reduces performance because of the extra stack operations required in any interrupt and return operation. Novell recommends the use of the call over the interrupt.

The functions are then accessed by the following:

```
mov bx,function_number
call far IPX_location
```

The following short program uses the DOS multiplexer function to locate the IPX entry point. Again, be very careful of inserting assembly language in the middle of a C program.

```
// ------------------ FIND_IPX.C ----------------------------------------
//      Find IPX Entry point
//                      J.K. Hardy    March 20, 1994
// ---------------------------------------------------------------------

#include <stdio.h>
#include <dos.h>
typedef unsigned char BYTE;
typedef unsigned int WORD;

main()
  {
  WORD   seg, off;
  BYTE   result;
```

```
printf("This program looks for the IPX/SPX entry point.\n");
asm {
  mov ax,0x7A00
  int 0x2F
}
result = _AL;
seg = _ES;
off = _DI;
printf("The multiplexer returned %02Xh\n", result);
printf("This return should be FFh to be valid\n");
printf("IPX/SPX Entry Address = %04X : %04X\n", seg, off);
}
```

Twelve IPX function calls are available to the programmer. The desired one is selected by placing a specific value in the BX register prior to the CALL. Of course, additional information is required, but this varies with the specific call.

BX = 00	Open Socket
01	Close Socket
02	Get Local Target
03	Send Packet
04	Listen for Packet
05	Schedule IPX Event
06	Cancel Event
07	Schedule Special Event
08	Get Interval Marker
09	Get Internetwork Address
0A	Relinquish Control
0B	Disconnect from Target
0C	used internally
0D	used internally
0E	used internally
0F	used internally

The references to "events" and "markers" mean that IPX has hooked into the personal computer's 55-millisecond timer "tick" system and is, therefore, aware of time. This allows low priority messages to be transmitted at some future time.

The Local Target function checks hardware addresses versus IPX addresses of stations with which the user intends to communicate. For this function call, the user supplies the network, node, and socket numbers for the other station. The function will return with an adapter address, which is usually the same as the node address if the destination is on the local network. For more distant stations, the returned address will be a router through which the remote station can be reached. The returned address can then be used in the "immediate" portion of the Event Control Block (described following). The function return also provides a rough estimate of the time (in "ticks") required to reach that station.

Event Control Block

Many IPX function calls require additional information that is passed to IPX in a memory structure called an Event Control Block (ECB). The idea is somewhat similar to a NetBIOS NCB. One of the differences is that no "command" is carried in the block. Instead, as already shown, the specific IPX function is selected by the value in the BX register at the time of the call. The same technique is used for SPX functions.

When a specific IPX or SPX command requires an ECB, the starting address of the structure is placed in the ES (segment) and SI (offset) registers before the call is made.

The minimum length of an ECB, using one fragment, is 42 bytes. Larger ECBs grow in steps of six bytes as more fragments are added. The ECB structure is as follows:

Link: offset	2 bytes	
segment	2 bytes	
ESR: offset	2 bytes	required
segment	2 bytes	
In Use flag	1 byte	
Completion Code	1 byte	
Socket Number	2 bytes	required
Workspace	16 bytes	
Immediate Address	6 bytes	required
Fragment Count	2 bytes	minimum one
Each fragment:		
buffer offset	2 bytes	
buffer segment	2 bytes	
buffer size	2 bytes	

For simple tasks, the Link Address is set to Zero. In other situations, it can be used to link a chain of ECBs together.

The ESR Address is also set to Zero for simple tasks. It could be the address of code which would be executed immediately after the current ECB task is completed.

The In-Use flag will hold a value in the range F8–FFh while the IPX code is still working on this ECB task. When completed, the In-Use byte will be set to 00h. At that time, a Completion Code will be available in the following byte. If everything went correctly, this code should be 00h.

Immediate Address is the adapter card address of the station or router on this local network to which a message is being sent (or received). If you are certain this address is local, it can be entered directly. Otherwise, the Get Local Target function call should be used.

The six-byte "fragment" information is simply a reference to a data buffer. These buffers hold the information to be transmitted or space for what will be received. Multiple buffers can be used, as implied by the term. For IPX Send operations, the first portion of this buffer will be the IPX header structure. This is illustrated in the following program example. Each buffer fragment is located with the segment and offset address and size value contained in the six bytes at the end of the ECB.

IPX Sample Program

This is the program that generated the IPX packet sample shown earlier. In keeping with our philosophy of minimum program length for ease of understanding, the IPX functions are accessed using the slower INT 7Ah mechanism. This approach allows ample room for experimentation and improvement.

```
// ------------- IPX_SEND.C -----------------------------------------
//  Send text messages using IPX.
//  Assumes both stations are on the same network.
//                          J.K. Hardy   May 24, 1994
// ------------------------------------------------------------------
#define SOCKET      0x7856      // socket number 5678 (hi-lo)
#include <stdio.h>
#include <dos.h>
#include <string.h>

typedef unsigned char BYTE;
typedef unsigned int WORD;

BYTE   Send_it();
BYTE   Open_Socket();
BYTE   Close_Socket();

struct ECB   {
    void      far *link_address;
    void      far *event_service_routine;
    BYTE      in_use_flag;
    BYTE      completion_code;
    WORD      socket;                    // hi-lo
    BYTE      IPX_workspace [4];
    BYTE      driver_workspace [12];
    BYTE      immediate_address [6];
    WORD      fragment_count;            // lo-hi
    WORD      ipx_offset;                // lo-hi
    WORD      ipx_segment;               // lo-hi
```

```
    WORD      length;  // length of IPX header + data, (lo-hi
                         order)
    } ecb;

struct  IPX    {
    WORD      checksum;
    WORD      length;  // filled automatically by IPX (hi-lo)
    BYTE      transport_control;
    BYTE      packet_type;
    BYTE      dest_network [4];
    BYTE      dest_node [6];
    WORD      dest_socket;              // bytes in hi-lo order
    BYTE      source_network [4];    // set by IPX
    BYTE      source_node [6];       // set by IPX
    WORD      source_socket;         // set by IPX
    BYTE      send_data [546];
    } ipx_data;

main()
  {
  char  key;
  BYTE  result;
  int   i = 0, loop = 1;
  BYTE DESTINATION[6] = {0, 0, 0xC0, 0x34, 0x78, 0x30};
  BYTE NETWORK[4]     = {0, 0, 0, 0};  // same network

  memmove(ecb.immediate_address, DESTINATION, 6);
  ecb.fragment_count = 0x0001;  // 1 fragment
  ecb.ipx_offset = FP_OFF((void far *)&ipx_data.checksum);
  ecb.ipx_segment = FP_SEG((void far *)&ipx_data.checksum);
  ecb.in_use_flag = 0xFF;

  ipx_data.checksum = 0xFFFF;   // not calculated
  ipx_data.transport_control = 0x00;
  ipx_data.packet_type = 0x04;  // type 04 is "IPX"
  memmove(ipx_data.dest_network, NETWORK, 4);
  memmove(ipx_data.dest_node, DESTINATION, 6);

  result = Open_Socket();
  if (result != 0x00) {
     printf("Cannot open a socket - Good Bye!\n");
     exit (0);
  } else {
     printf("OK - We have opened a socket.\n");
  }

  printf("Type a message of 546 characters or less.\n");
  printf(" It will be sent when you press Ctrl-T\n");
  printf("  Program terminates after one message.\n");
```

```
    while(loop) {
        key = getche();
        if (key == 0x14) {  // control-T
            result = Send_it(i);
            loop = 0; }
        else if (i < 546){
            ipx_data.send_data[i] = key;
            i++;
            if (key == 0x0D) {  // add LineFeed character
                printf("\n");
                ipx_data.send_data[i] = 0x0A;
                i++;
            }
        }
        else
            printf("\n You have reached the 546 character
                        limit\n");
    }                       // end while
    Close_Socket();  // not really needed but good insurance
    printf(".......All done.......\n");
}                       // end main

// -----------------------------------------------------------------
BYTE Send_it(int count)
 {
  ecb.length = 30 + count;
  _SI = (unsigned)&ecb;
  asm {
     push es; push ds; push bp
     push ds; pop es                 // es:si points to ECB
     mov bx,03    // IPX Send Packet function
     int 0x7A     // IPX Interrupt
     pop bp; pop ds; pop es
  }
  return (_AL);
 }

// -----------------------------------------------------------------
BYTE  Open_Socket()
{
  BYTE result;
  _BX = 00;       // IPX Open Socket function
  _AL = 00;       // socket will close on program termination
  _DX = SOCKET;   // a randomly selected socket
  geninterrupt(0x7A);
  ecb.socket = _DX;
  result = _AL;
  ipx_data.source_socket = ecb.socket;
  ipx_data.dest_socket = ecb.socket;
  return (result);
}
```

```
// --------------------------------------------------------------------------
BYTE Close_Socket()
{
  BYTE result;
  _BX = 01;    // IPX Close Socket function
  _DX = SOCKET;
  geninterrupt(0x7A);
  result = _AL;
  return (result);
}
```

SEQUENCED PACKET EXCHANGE (SPX)

SPX functions build on those available through IPX. The NetWare code that responds to these functions is still within the IPX.COM file so the same initial address search is required. These functions are solely for the use of the application programmer. Although not using SPX functions directly, the shell uses a header structure very similar to that of SPX. It then accesses IPX directly, which possibly improves the speed. Likewise, the NetBIOS emulator also works directly with IPX and bypasses SPX. With standard DOS applications redirected over the network, a true SPX packet is rarely seen.

The IPX layer of NetWare and the electronics of the network cards combine to provide the basic packet movement operation. They include full addressing and a CRC error check on the packet contents. However, if data files larger than one packet must be sent, these basic services are not sufficient—they are considered "unreliable." If two or more packets are needed for a file transfer, one of them could be lost, damaged, or arrive out of order. Remember that CRCs can only indicate that something went wrong within one packet; they cannot check the order of multiple packets or determine if a packet is missing.

SPX adds a connection-oriented, full duplex, reliable service. The operation is very similar to that described for NetBIOS in the previous chapter.

Now each packet carries a sequence number and its correct reception must be acknowledged (positive acknowledgment) by that number. Missing or damaged packets in the sequence would be retransmitted.

Before data begins to flow, a connection must be established with a handshake. Then data moves over the connection using a sliding window system to control acknowledgments and retransmissions.

Sliding Window

The SPX flow-control window operates at the frame or packet level to control the speed at which messages are received. It maintains three 16-bit pointers at each end (source and destination) of the data link. For comparison, UNIX's somewhat similar TCP protocol counts bytes and uses 32-bit counters. In Figure 10.7, one SPX pointer (A) indicates the dividing point between frames sent and not sent. Another (B) indicates the division between frames sent and acknowledged and those not acknowledged. The third pointer (C) is further down the stream of bytes and indicates the highest packet number that the remote receiver is prepared to handle at the time.

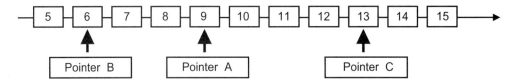

FIGURE 10.7
NetWare's sliding window used by SPX functions. NetWare counts packets, whereas TCP counts bytes.

SPX Header

SPX adds 12 more bytes to the end of the IPX header to bring the combined IPX + SPX total to 42 bytes (see Figure 10.8). The only change within the first 30 bytes is that the Packet Type is set to 05 to indicate SPX. The fields in the IPX header have already been discussed so we will concentrate on the seven new SPX fields. As with IPX, all multibyte values are sent high byte first.

> *Connection Control* (one byte)—Only the most significant four bits are used. They indicate
>
> > Bit-4 = end-of-message
> > Bit-5 = attention
> > Bit-6 = ACK required
> > Bit-7 = a system packet.
>
> *Datastream Type* (one byte)—Types 00-FDh are user defined, are ignored by SPX itself, and read only by higher protocols. Type FEh indicates an End-of-Connection, and FFh is an End-of-Connection acknowledge.
>
> *Source and Destination Connection IDs* (two bytes each)—Connection numbers used to multiplex/demultiplex messages passing through any one socket.
>
> *Sequence Number* (two bytes)—Each transmitted packet with a connection carries a sequence number starting at 0000 and incrementing on a per-packet basis.

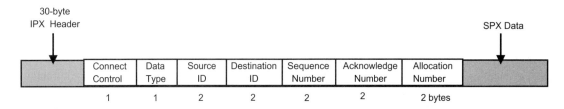

FIGURE 10.8
A full SPX header includes 30 bytes from IPX plus an extra 12 bytes for connection control and sequencing.

Acknowledge Number (two bytes)—This number is sent by the receiver back to the source. It indicates the next packet sequence number that is being expected at the destination. In effect, an acknowledge number of 500 indicates that all packets up to and including 499 were received correctly.

Allocation Number (two bytes)—Sent by the receiver back to the source. This represents a guess on the part of the receiver on the highest packet sequence number it can handle at the moment without overflowing local buffers. This is the flow control mechanism that tells the source to speed up or slow down.

SPX Program Interface

As with IPX functions, the programmer places a function number in the BX register and then calls SPX at the same address as was used for IPX—only the function numbers have changed. Depending on the function, an Event Control Block (ECB) may also be required. The ECB structure is the same as that illustrated earlier.

BX =	10h	Check SPX installation
	11h	Establish Connection
	12h	Listen for Connection
	13h	Terminate Connection
	14h	Abort Connection
	15h	Get Connection Status
	16h	Send Sequenced Packet
	17h	Listen for Sequenced Packet

NETWARE CORE PROTOCOL

NetWare Core Protocol (NCP) is Novell's own development. It is the "language" used by the shell (NETx.COM) to talk to the server about logins, user rights, file transfers, etc. It is the addition of this layer that turns the peer communication service of IPX into a hierarchical server/workstation environment (see Figure 10.9). An application pro-

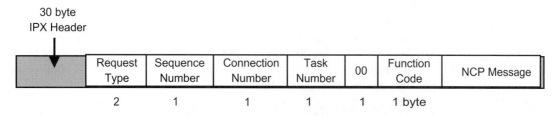

FIGURE 10.9
NCP adds a header immediately after the IPX header. The type number within IPX is set to 11h to indicate that an NCP message follows.

grammer does not use this protocol. For that reason, it is not well documented. Fortunately, protocol analyzers are available to interpret this and many other protocols.

The structure of the NCP message is

2 bytes	Request Type
1 byte	Sequence Number
1 byte	Connection Number
1 byte	Task Number
1 byte	Reserved, usually 00h
1 byte	Function Code
n bytes	information (may include subfunctions)

The two-byte Request Type can be

1111h	Create a Service Connection
2222h	File Service Request from Workstation
3333h	File Service Response from the Server
5555h	Destroy Service Connection
7777h	Packet Burst Protocol
9999h	Go Away, I'm Busy

The bulk of NCP messages will use request types 2222h and 3333h. A sample of each is shown in Figure 10.10. Service connections are created (1111h) at login and destroyed (5555h) at logout.

Packet Burst is a more recent addition. With it enabled, a workstation can make a single request for as much as 64K of data, and the server will send the appropriate number of data packets to complete the request. Without Packet Burst, virtually every 2222h request from the workstation would generate a 3333h reply from the server. The use of Packet Burst reduces both network traffic and server processing.

Sequence Number—This one-byte value starts at 01 and just keeps incrementing for each new request for one specific workstation. The server will reply with the same sequence, task, and connection number.

Connection Number—This is the same number that appears beside the user's name when the NetWare command USERLIST is given. It is a logical connection number that indicates when the user logs on each day. It will never be higher than the legal maximum number of users for the copy of NetWare purchased for the server.

Task Number—Because several programs may be running at the same time on a workstation, this number enables file requests to be kept separate. For most DOS applications, the task number remains at 01.

Function Code—There are well over 100 different messages that can be sent by NCP. The one-byte Function Code determines what the message is. If the

```
            0  1  2  3  4  5  6  7    8  9  A  B  C  D  E  F

REQUEST:
0000   00 00 C0 15 09 05 00 00   C0 50 0A 05 00 32 11 11
0010   FF FF 00 32 00 04 00 00   00 01 00 00 C0 15 09 05
0020   04 51 00 00 00 01 00 00   C0 50 0A 05 40 07 22 22
0030   3A 05 02 00 48 00 9E 00   FE 16 04 00 00 00 00 00
0040   04 00

RESPONSE:
0000   00 00 C0 50 0A 05 00 00   C0 15 09 05 04 38 11 11
0010   FF FF 04 28 00 11 00 00   00 01 00 00 C0 50 0A 05
0020   40 07 00 00 00 01 00 00   C0 15 09 05 04 51 33 33
0030   3A 05 00 00 00 00 04 00    I  t     w  a  s     t
0040    h  e     b  e  s  t       o  f     t  i  m  e  s
0050    .     I  t     w  a  s       t  h  e     w  o  r
0060    s  t     o  f
```

FIGURE 10.10
Sample hex dump of an NCP request to read bytes from an open file and then the reply.
Both examples include 802.3 headers with SSAP and DSAP set to 11h.

function code is set to 16h, it indicates a newer, extended series of functions. The subfunction number will be placed three bytes later in the header. Some NCP functions are

1. Single-Byte Function Codes

01h	Log Record
16h	Create a Subdirectory
21h	Negotiate Buffer Size
40h	Get File Size
42h	Close a File
44h	Delete a File
45h	Rename a File
48h	Read Bytes from a File
4Ch	Open a File
4Dh	Create a File

2. Some Extended Two-Byte Codes. These always use 16h in the function code position. The second number is the subfunction number.

16h, 1Bh	Scan Salvage Files
16h, 1Ch	Recover Salvageable Files
16h, 1Dh	Purge Salvageable Files

16h, 1Eh	Scan a Directory
16h, 1Fh	Get a Directory Entry
16h, 20h	Scan Volume User Disk Restrictions
16h, 21h	Add a User's Disk Space Restrictions
16h, 22h	Remove a User's Disk Space Restrictions
16h, 23h	Get a Directory's Disk Space Restrictions by Handle
16h, 24h	Set a Directory's Disk Space Restrictions by Handle
16h, 25h	Set Directory Entry Information
16h, 26h	Scan Extended Trustees for File or Directory
16h, 27h	Add Extended Trustee to Directory or File
16h, 28h	Scan a Directory Disk Space
16h, 29h	Get Object's Disk Usage and Restrictions on Volume
16h, 2Ah	Get My Effective Rights for a Directory Entry
16h, 2Bh	Remove Extended Trustee from Directory or File
16h, 2Ch	Get Volume Info

WORKSTATION CONFIGURATION

The previous chapter described the use of the SHELL.CFG file to alter default values within NetWare's NetBIOS emulator. As indicated, this file also holds values of interest to the NETx.COM and IPX.COM files. A partial list follows.

In this description, "tick" refers to the personal computer's 18.2 Hz interrupt that occurs approximately every 55 milliseconds.

IPX.COM Options

IPX PACKET SIZE LIMIT = (default determined by adapter driver)

Typically set to 1500 bytes for Ethernet. Token Ring can handle larger packets, but this consumes memory for added buffer space.

IPX SOCKETS = 1 to 50 (default 20)

Specifies the maximum number of sockets that can be open at any one time on any workstation.

IPX RETRY COUNT = (default 20)

Sets the number of times that NetBIOS, SPX, or the shell will attempt to resend a packet that wasn't correctly acknowledged. The default value, for example, causes an 11-second delay when a NetBIOS ADD-NAME command is issued. Increasing the retry count will increase this delay and generate more network traffic. However, it may be necessary in unreliable environments. IPX itself only performs individual retries when ordered to do so by higher layers.

SPX CONNECTIONS = (default 15)

> Specifies the maximum number of connections that can be used at any one time on any workstation.

SPX ABORT TIMEOUT = 1 to 65,000 (default 540)

> Determines the amount of time (in "ticks") that SPX will wait without receiving a response before it terminates a session.

SPX VERIFY TIMEOUT = 1 to 65,000 (default 54—about three seconds)

> Adjusts the time interval at which SPX sends an "I'm alive" packet to the other side of a connection if no other traffic for this connection appears.

SPX LISTEN TIMEOUT = 1 to 65,000 (default 108)

> Determines the length of time that SPX will wait without receiving a packet on any particular connection before requesting one from the other end. SPX will send an "I'm alive" packet and indicate that a response is expected.

Shell Options (NETx.COM)

CACHE BUFFERS = (default 5)

> Sets the number of 512-byte buffers the shell will use at a workstation for buffering nonshared files.

SHOWDOTS = on/OFF

> For compatibility with DOS subdirectory view which shows "." and ".." for the parent structure. Default is OFF.

FILE HANDLES = (default 40)

> Determines how many files a workstation can have open at the same time.

EOJ = ON/off

> Turns on or off the automatic closing of files and removal of locks and semaphores when a program is finished. Default is ON.

HOLD = on/OFF

> If Hold is ON, all files opened by a program will be held open until the program terminates. This may be needed to work around some programs that close data files at the wrong time and thereby allow other users to change data. Default is OFF.

SHARE = ON/off

> If Share is ON, any child process of a running program will inherit the same file handle as the parent. If OFF, a new file handle is created. Default is ON.

LOCK RETRIES = (default 3)

> The number of times the shell will attempt to get a lock on a network file before giving up.

LOCK DELAY = (default 1)

The amount of time in "ticks" that the shell will wait between retries.

SEARCH MODE = 0 to 7

The default mode is 1, which indicates that if a full path is not speci-fied for a data file, the default drive and all search drives will be searched for that name.

MAXIMUM TASKS = 8 to 50 (default is 31)

The maximum number of tasks or programs that can be active at the same time.

TASK MODE = 0 or 1

For compatibility with early versions of MS Windows. If set to 0, the shell will not check for Windows virtual tasks. If left at the default value of 1, it will check.

APPENDIX: XEROX NETWORK SYSTEMS (XNS)

Some of the greatest contributions to the local area network business have been made by the Xerox Palo Alto Research Center (PARC). In this fast-paced world, it is interesting to see how far back some of these developments extend. One obvious contribution is the Ethernet hardware, developed in 1972. However, Xerox research and design didn't stop with the hardware. It also extended through what is now all seven layers of the OSI protocol stack. The reference model didn't exist at the time so the Xerox descriptions tend to lump several layers at a time together.

7	Application	many
6	Presentation	Courier
5	Session	
4	Transport	Internet
3	Network	
2	Data Link	Ethernet
1	Physical	

The Ethernet specification covers the lower two layers: Physical and Data Link. A specification called Internet covers the Network and Transport Layers. The Courier specification covers Session and Presentation. At the Application layer, a large number of specifications exist to cover document, graphics, mail, and gateway access to name a few. The philosophy was to cover every aspect of business and office interconnection without limiting it to any one local area or host processor. In fact, the design will handle worldwide communications.

The entire philosophy is referred to as Xerox Network Systems (XNS). Xerox will license all or part of this system to interested commercial operations. Novell,

3Com (in its earlier days), and Ungermann-Bass, for example, license the Internet Protocol portion of XNS for use on their networks.

Although this makes the three manufacturers very similar at layers 3 and 4, they differ widely in their higher layers and in their implementation of the file and user control programs that run on the server.

The big attraction of the Internet Protocol is, as its name implies, that it defines a mechanism for sending packets through multiple networks and over diverse media. In other words, it offers a path for future growth.

One of the competitors for the Internet Protocol is IBM and Microsoft's implementation of NetBIOS (NETBEUI) and LLC, which we have already discussed. Remember that this is the core of the Local Area Network Program from Sytek Corporation.

The real alternative to the Xerox Internet Protocol and Novell's IPX is the moderately similar Internet Protocol (IP) from the Department of Defense (DoD) and the National Bureau of Standards (NBS), now heavily used in UNIX environments. IP is described in the following chapter.

This isn't a competition, and there won't be a winner. Various protocols must coexist, as will be discussed in Chapter 12.

REFERENCES

1. Rose, Charles G. *Programmer's Guide to NetWare.* New York: McGraw-Hill, 1990.

2. *Novell API Reference.* Vols. 1 and 2. Provo, Utah: Novell, Inc., 1992.

3. *C Language Interface.* Provo, Utah: Novell, Inc., 1992.

4. *Inside NetWare for UNIX v3.11.* Novell Research Report 164-000031-013. Provo, Utah: Novell, Inc., February 1992.

Chapter 11
TCP/IP

Protocols generally referred to as TCP/IP are widely used in a number of computing environments—especially UNIX. Transmission Control Protocol (TCP) and Internet Protocol (IP) are but two components of the full "Internet protocol suite" (see Figure 11.1) The suite was initially developed for the Department of Defense (DoD) and the original defense research network—ARPAnet.

In addition to UNIX, many of the protocols within TCP/IP are included within the VINES network operating system from Banyan Systems, Inc. TCP/IP support is available for NetWare by loading an extra Network Loadable Module (NLM) at the server and adding multiprotocol drivers at the workstations.

The TCP/IP suite does not define layers below what we now refer to as the "transport layer." In a typical situation, this would often be **X.25** or Ethernet, although ARCnet and Token Ring can certainly be used.

ORIGINS

Some of the descriptions in this chapter will make more sense if we keep the origins of these protocols in mind.

The TCP/IP suite was originally developed for a telephone line network—not a high-speed LAN environment. ARPAnet consisted of a variety of host computers and communications services with wide geographic separation. They were linked with leased, high-speed phone links which typically ran at 56K bits per second. Some basic communications links supported packets of only 128 bytes whereas others were capable of 64,000 bytes. There were also many alternate paths between the source and the destination. TCP and IP had to accommodate these variations.

The role of hosts and terminals has also changed over the years—a difference that affects addressing, to be discussed later. As originally designed, the host machine was a minicomputer with users accessing it via terminals. Only the host needed a network address since the terminals rely on dedicated RS-232 lines, ports, and asynchronous protocols. In newer UNIX environments, the trend is toward self-contained UNIX workstations interconnected via Ethernet. The host and terminal merge.

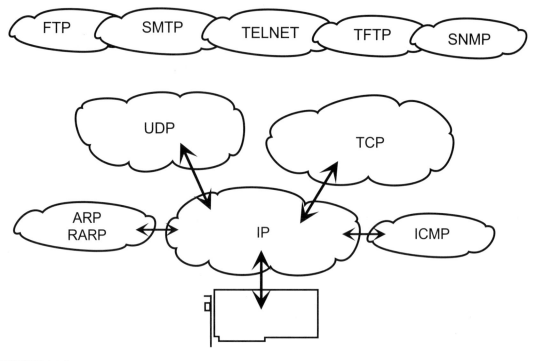

FIGURE 11.1
Full Internet protocol suite contains many layer options. Two "side" packages assist with addressing control.

Note that many descriptions of TCP/IP will include references to the "Internet"—with a capital "I." The original ARPAnet has evolved into the Internet, which is a collection of university, research, and government contractors using TCP/IP to communicate. However, many other installations use the TCP/IP protocols for their own purposes without ever touching the Internet. For them, the word "internet" (lowercase "i") simply means a connection of two or more networks—possibly one in the warehouse and one in the office. It is important to remember the distinction between the two.

Other distinctions, such as the words "packets" and "frames," are also important within the TCP/IP community. Following is a list of associations used in this chapter.

FRAME	Data with an adapter header, used in Ethernet, etc.
IP PACKET	Some data with an IP header
UDP DATAGRAM	Data with a UDP header
TCP SEGMENT	Data with a TCP header

INTERNET PROTOCOL (IP)

The basic packaging and routing mechanism (an approximation to the OSI Network layer) is the Internet Protocol (IP). An IP "packet" can carry up to 64,000 bytes of

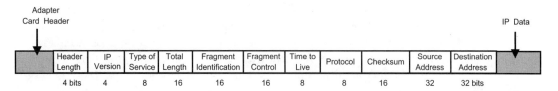

FIGURE 11.2
IP packet structure. Fields are in the order transmitted, starting with Header Length.

data but typically is set to a much lower limit. The actual packet size is determined by the lower-level carrier system. This could be a leased phone link, or it could be LAN adapter cards. At a minimum, the lower layers must somehow be capable of carrying 576 bytes—the same requirement as Novell and Xerox-XNS. If packets are larger than what lower layers can handle, they may have to be fragmented (cut into shorter pieces) and reassembled.

IP, like Novell's IPX, is termed an "unreliable/connectionless" protocol—it doesn't care if your packets aren't delivered. Within any one frame, some checking, of course, will be available with the CRC provided by the lower-level adapter cards. However, there is no checking for missing or out-of-sequence packets. Further error control is built into layers above IP.

The IP header typically contains 20 bytes but might be four bytes longer if some testing features (Options and Padding) are added. The header is shown in Figure 11.2, and each item is further described in the following sections.

IP Header

All 16- and 32-bit values within the header are held and transmitted as high byte first. This is not the natural order for Little Endian machines, such as Intel or DEC products. Order in the data portion is not defined and is controlled by the user.

Pay attention to three fields in particular: Header Length, Version, and Fragment Control. Each contains components less than a byte in length. Both in Figure 11.2 and in the description that follows, fields are shown in the order they enter the network (cable order). Remember that (for Ethernet) the least significant bit of each byte goes first. However, within a program, you would tend to read a byte or word at a time. Within the first byte of the header, Length would be at the least significant end—on a programmer's "right-hand" end. Version would be on the most significant or "left-hand" end. Some books interchange the order of these two fields in drawings similar to Figure 11.2. The third field with a similar problem is the 16-bit Fragment Control field. The three least significant bits of this field are individual control bits. Again, if read as a 16-bit word, these bits are on the programmer's "right-hand" (least significant) end.

Header Length (4 bits)—Indicates the size of the header in four-byte increments. Normally set to 5 (0101) for a 20-byte header.

Version number (4 bits)—Typically set to 4. This is the current (1990) version number of the IP protocol.

Type of Service (8 bits total)—Includes Precedence (3 bits), Reliability (Normal or High), Delay (Normal or Low), and Throughput (Normal or High). These bits form a request to the underlying carrier for a specific type of service. However, many lower-layer services don't provide any choices so this field is often ignored. Some routers may use these bits to select a preferred path.

Total Length (16 bits)—Indicates the total length of the packet in bytes. The measurement includes both the header and data sections.

Identification (16 bits)—Used for sequence control of fragments. If a longer packet requires fragmenting, all portions will be given the same identification number.

Fragment Control (16 bits)—Provides information for the destination on how to reassemble packets that were fragmented. This only happens when a larger packet must squeeze through a limited system. The bits within this field will be described shortly.

Time to Live (8 bits)—Set to a particular count when the source machine creates a packet. As the packet moves through the network, the count is decremented. When it reaches Zero, the packet dies even if it hasn't been delivered (IP is unreliable). This feature prevents packets from endlessly moving around the continent looking for someone who isn't there. The actual count can't really be a measure of time but is often described as such (Time to Live). Packets halfway down a telephone cable cannot be altered, and packets sitting in storage could be altered but aren't because of excessive processing overhead. The decrement occurs, not once each second, but rather each time an IP header is routed by some machine.

Protocol (8 bits)—Identifies which protocol above IP is being used. In decimal, 01 = ICMP, 06 = TCP, 17 = UDP.

IP Header Checksum (16 bits)—Adds all header numbers 16 bits at a time using one's complement arithmetic (assuming the checksum position itself is 0000h) and then forms the one's complement of the result. Note that this checksum does not include the data portion.

Source Address and Destination Address—Each is 32 bits, but several options exist (see Addresses).

Options and Padding—Not often used. Options are added only for network testing. When used, they increase the header by four bytes. Because the IP header is sized (using IHL) in increments of four bytes, padding with extra Zeros might be required.

Fragmentation needs a little more explanation. Remember that IP is an "unreliable" protocol, and so no attempt is made to number sequential IP packets during, for example, the transfer of a large file. That task belongs to TCP. However, IP packets could still extend to 65,535 bytes. If a lower layer finds it necessary to cut an IP packet into fragments, the IDENT and FRAG fields come into use. Each fragment will have the same general format as the original, and their IDENT field will contain the same number. Only the 16 Fragment Control bits will change.

The least significant of these bits is undefined and always stays at Zero. The next bit, if set, prohibits fragmentation (NF). The third bit is called the "More" bit. If set to One, it indicates there are more fragments to follow. If Zero, it indicates this is the last or only segment. The remaining 13 bits, called "offsets," indicate the fragment position, in multiples of eight bytes, within the original message.

0000000000000 M NF Ø

INTERNET ADDRESSES

All IP addresses are 32 bits (four bytes) long. For ease, they are often written in "decimal dotted form." This simply involves writing the equivalent decimal number for each of the four bytes with a period (dot) between. For example, address

1100 0000 0100 1011 0100 0111 0100 1111

would normally be written as "192.75.71.79".

The 32-bit IP addresses are divided up into a network portion and a host (or workstation) portion. There are three ways this can be done. These choices accommodate some users who have many hosts but only a small number of networks (often only one) at their facility and other users with the reverse. The distinction between address type depends on the first one, two, or three bits (see Figure 11.3).

Class A addresses always begin (the most significant bit of the first byte) with a Zero. The remaining seven bits of the first byte are used for a network number. The next three bytes are used for host numbers on that network. Two of these numbers (0 and 127) are reserved. This results in 126 different Class A host addresses. Very few organizations are large enough to deserve a Class A internet address.

Class B addresses begin with the most significant bit set to One and the next bit Zero. The following 14 bits are used for the network number and the remaining 16 bits for the host. Permissible first bytes are 128 through 191.

| Class A | 0 | n n n n n n n | s s s s s s s s | s s s s s s s s | s s s s s s s s |

| Class B | 1 0 | n n n n n n | n n n n n n n n | s s s s s s s s | s s s s s s s s |

| Class C | 1 1 0 | n n n n n | n n n n n n n n | n n n n n n n n | s s s s s s s s |

n = network,   s = host or workstation

FIGURE 11.3
IP address variations.

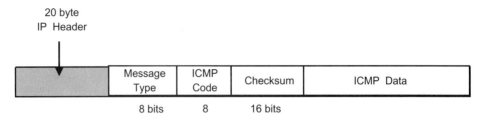

FIGURE 11.4
ICMP message structure.

Class C addresses begin with 110. The rest of the first three bytes are used for the network number and the last byte for the host. This suits smaller corporations with only a few host machines. Class C network numbers (first byte) can range from 192 to 223. The remaining numbers are reserved.

Some of the network–host number combinations are reserved. Any network number of Zero refers to "this network." A network and host/workstation number of all Ones is a broadcast. A network number of 127 is an internal loopback within a host.

The IP protocol has been accepted by the OSI Standards committee as one choice for ISO Layer 3—the Network Layer. The other choice is the High Level Data Link Control (HDLC) portion of X.25. OSI did make one change to the IP protocol. They allow the address portion to be a variable length instead of limiting each to 32 bits.

ICMP and Flow Control

If the IP layer at a destination is receiving packets at a rate too high, it will send an Internet Control Message Protocol (ICMP) message back to the source asking it to slow down. This slow-down request is called "Source Quenching."

ICMP is not a separate protocol. It is simply the control system within the IP protocol. Source Quenching is but one of 13 different messages carried by ICMP. The form of these messages is shown in Figure 11.4 and consists of a few extra bytes added after an IP header. The IP protocol number is set to 01 to indicate ICMP. The "data" portion of the ICMP message often contains the first 64 bits of the packet that originally caused the problem. The source may then extract something useful from it.

Following are the 13 different ICMP message types:

  0   Echo Reply

  3   Destination Unreachable

  4   Source Quench

  5   Redirect a route

  8   Echo Request to a remote station

11   Time exceeded for datagram

12   Parameter problem with a datagram

13   TimeStamp request

14   TimeStamp reply

15   Information request

16   Information reply

17   Address Mask request

18   Address Mask reply

The Echo Request and Reply determine if a remote station is reachable. Redirect is used by routers. Time-exceeded messages are sent back to a source when a router or other device kills an IP packet that has exceeded its Time to Live. Time-Stamps are used to estimate the time required to reach a remote station. Address Masks are used in definitions of subnetworks.

The content of the ICMP Code field depends on the ICMP Type field. It generally provides more detailed information. Here are a few sample codes:

For DESTINATION UNREACHABLE

Code = 0   Network Unreachable

1   Host Unreachable

2   Protocol Unreachable

3   Port Unreachable

4   Fragmentation Needed

5   Source Route Failed

For a REDIRECT message from a router back to a host

Code = 0   Redirect for Network

1   Redirect for Host

2   Redirect for Type-of-Service and Network

3   Redirect for Type-of-Service and Host

A suggested new address is included within a redirect message so that a machine can update its routing table.

HIGHER-LEVEL PROTOCOLS

In the next layer above IP, several choices are possible. The two more common are TCP and UDP.

Transmission Control Protocol (TCP)

Transmission Control Protocol (TCP) is used when long messages must be moved reliably from one machine to another. The most common example would be the movement of a large file. TCP will break a long byte sequence into whatever size is

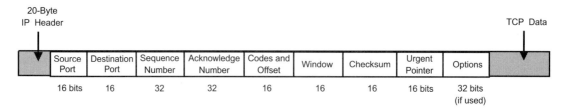

FIGURE 11.5
TCP header fields are shown in the order transmitted.

necessary to do the job. It then adds its own 20-byte header to each piece of data and passes the combination down to the lower IP layer (see Figure 11.5). The combination of the header and some data is referred to as a TCP segment.

At the remote end, TCP will put the original file back together. It will watch that everything is back in sequence and that there are neither duplicates nor missing segments. TCP adds reliability through the use of "connections" in the same sense that SPX does, but there are differences.

Since TCP is a connection-oriented protocol, some negotiating is done before data starts to move. When TCP gets a local request to send a file to a remote site, it first sends a connection request to the remote computer. The request indicates the source port to be used and how many bytes at a time the local machine can handle. The remote TCP will reply with its own logical port number and its largest data size. The source machine then determines which is the smaller segment size and uses that for the duration of the connection.

> *Source and Destination Ports* (16 bits)—The "socket numbers" used to identify individual higher-level users, terminals, and applications on each machine.
>
> *Sequence Number* (32 bits)—Used to put the packets of the original file back in sequence. TCP numbers individual bytes, not packets as does SPX. This is the position number of the first byte in each message. The very first frame in a session would start with byte 0000 and so set the sequence number to Zero. If that first frame carried 500 bytes (numbered 0–499), the next frame would use sequence number 500.
>
> *Acknowledge Number* (32 bits)—Indicates the next byte that is being expected and so, in effect, acknowledges the quantity correctly received.

The next 16 bits contain several fields made up in the following order:

$$msb \rightarrow OOOO\ 000000\ UAPRSF \leftarrow lsb$$

> *Offset* (4 bits)—Because a TCP header length can change if options are used, there has to be a mechanism to say where the data portion begins. Offset is measured in four-byte chunks and, for the normal 20-byte header, will have a value of 5–0101.

Reserved (6 bits)—Set to Zeros.

Code (6 bits)—Operating as individual control bits.

U (URG)	Urgent Pointer field is valid
A (ACK)	Acknowledgment field is valid
P (PSH)	"Push" or flush any data buffers
R (RST)	Reset the connection
S (SYN)	Synchronize sequence numbers
F (FIN)	End of the total message

The "FIN" bit is the least significant bit of the 16-bit offset/control field and is the first bit of this field to enter the network.

Window (16 bits)—A number sent from the destination back to the source. It indicates how many bytes can be sent before the next acknowledgment should be expected. The source can then either speed up or slow down.

Checksum (16 bits)—Covers the TCP header (in a prototype form) plus all data.

Urgent Pointer (16 bits)—Allows one end to tell the other to skip ahead in its processing by a specific number of bytes. This wouldn't normally be done during a file transfer. It may mean that the person at the keyboard is trying to exit the process by hitting the "break" key.

Sliding Window

The "sliding window" is TCP's compromise on flow control. It is more efficient than having every segment acknowledged, which could involve long waits on the part of the source machine. The other extreme is to have the source simply keep sending, but that is also wasteful if the destination machine cannot keep up.

When a virtual circuit is first established, information on capabilities is exchanged. This determines, in part, how many bytes can be sent before the receiver has to answer back indicating that data was correctly received. This number is referred to as the window size.

As the source sends each successive segment of a large file, it includes byte counts in the Sequence field of the header. The destination machine doesn't have to respond immediately, and the source keeps sending. It can continue sending until it reaches the end of its "window." At some point, one of two things must happen. The preferred reaction is for the destination to send back an acknowledgment saying that everything up to, perhaps, byte 5999 was correctly received, that byte number 6000 is the next one expected, and that another 4000 bytes (the window) can be handled. These next 4000 bytes would likely be sent in many separate segments.

The other possibility is that the source has been keeping track of time and has sent all the bytes in its window, had no acknowledgment back, and a timer has expired. The source will then start resending everything from the last acknowledged byte.

```
0000     00 00 C0 34 78 30 00 00     C0 C9 78 30 08 00 45 00
0010     00 31 00 15 00 00 FF 06     B5 CB 80 12 34 56 80 12
0020     34 57 67 DB 02 00 00 13     45 5D 00 14 4C C2 50 18
0030     10 00 4E 0C 00 00 .. ..     .. .. .. .. .. .. .. ..
0040     .. .. .. .. .. .. .. ..     .. .. ..
```

```
Adapter
  Destination:    00 00 C0 34 78 30
  Source:         00 00 C0 C9 78 30
  EtherType:      0800h  (IP)

IP
  HeaderLength: 5    Version: 4    TypeOfService: 00
  Length:  0031h     ID:  0015h    FragOffset:  00    Flags:  0
  TimeToLive:   FFh   NextProtocol:  6 (TCP)  Checksum:  B5CBh
  Source:         80 12 34 56
  Destination:    80 12 34 57

TCP
  SourcePort:         67DBh
  DestinationPort:    0200h
  SequenceNumber:     0013455Dh
  AcknowledgeNumber:  00144CC2h
  Codes:  .AP...      Offset:  5      Window:   1000h bytes
  Checksum: 4E0Ch     UrgentPointer:    0000
```

FIGURE 11.6
Hex dump and decoding of a segment carried on Ethernet with IP and TCP headers.

When the full file has been sent and acknowledged, a disconnect request is sent, and confirmation is returned. The virtual circuit has then ended.

Figure 11.6 is a memory dump of the first portion of a TCP/IP segment. Note that the bytes are in "memory order" and not in "cable order."

User Datagram Protocol (UDP)

User Datagram Protocol (UDP) is the programmer's interface to an unreliable/connectionless mechanism (IP should not be used directly by applications). It adds an eight-byte header before passing data down to the lower IP layer. Messages must already be broken up into a convenient size before being passed to this layer. Actually, if it is necessary to break up a message for this protocol, the wrong protocol is probably being used. Since there is no sequence numbering within UDP, it is not suitable for things like file transfer unless sequencing is added at a higher level. The IP header protocol number for UDP is 17 (11h).

The UDP header is shown in Figure 11.7 and consists of the following fields:

Source Port (16 bits)—Can be left at Zero if no replies are expected (replies are not automatic).

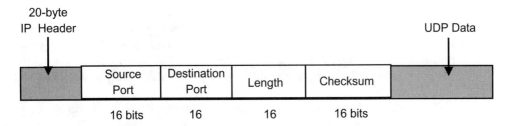

20-byte
IP Header   UDP Data

Source Port	Destination Port	Length	Checksum	

16 bits   16   16   16 bits

FIGURE 11.7
UDP header and data.

Destination Port (16 bits)

Length (16 bits)—Indicates the length in bytes of the header plus data portions.

Checksum (16 bits)—Covers the UDP header and any data. Note that the checksum within the IP header only covers that header and not any included data. Can be set to Zero to indicate "not calculated."

A few well-known Port numbers used with UDP are:

    5   Remote Job Entry (RJE)
    23   TELNET
    25   Simple Mail Transfer Protocol (SMTP)
    69   Trivial File Transfer Protocol (TFTP)
    161 Simple Network Management Protocol (SNMP)
    162 SNMP Trap (Chapter 14)

ADDRESSES AND ROUTING

Routing is required when several networks are interconnected. IP routing is based entirely upon the network number in the Destination Address of the IP header.

All TCP/IP hosts maintain a "little black book." This is a local table of addresses of other hosts frequently called. Entries in this book "age" so that the table doesn't keep growing indefinitely.

When a computer wants to send a message, it first checks to see if the IP Destination Address is on the local network. If not, it tries to find a router number in its table that provides entry to the other network. If an entry exists on the local host, the message is sent. If no particular route is found, the message is simply sent to the default gateway/router.

Gateways and routers are smart enough to answer back (using ICMP messages) that this isn't the best route and to try "xyz" instead. If such a response is received, the local table can be updated so the next transmission will be more efficient.

In addition to routing, hosts will also have to translate 32-bit network–host messages into the 48-bit (or whatever length) hardware addresses used on their cabling system. The Address Resolution Protocol (ARP) helps with this task.

ARP allows one machine to find the physical address (e.g., Ethernet or Token Ring address) of another machine given the two-part internet address. ARP requests are sent as broadcasts out of necessity. These tend to load the system, so they must be minimized. The destination machine will send a response directly back to the specific Ethernet address, and this will contain the physical and internet addresses of both machines.

When a machine is first turned on, it broadcasts its physical and network–host address pair. Being a broadcast, any interested machine can pick it up and use the information to update its local routing tables.

The reverse task is to find a corresponding 32-bit network–host address given the Ethernet or Token Ring adapter address of a station. The Reverse Address Resolution Protocol (RARP) is used to perform this operation.

UNIX and TCP/IP are very fond of broadcasts which tend to load a network in certain cases. The "little black book" also consumes local memory and processing time for maintenance. On DOS-based machines, these all become serious problems. However, with more capable hardware and operating systems, the problems diminish.

REFERENCES

1. Comer, Douglas. *Internetworking with TCP/IP*. Englewood Cliffs, NJ: Prentice Hall, 1988.

2. Stevens, Richard. *UNIX Network Programming*. Englewood Cliffs, NJ: Prentice Hall, 1990.

3. Miller, Mark A. *Troubleshooting TCP/IP*. San Mateo, CA: M&T Books, 1992.

Chapter 12

Multiprotocol Drivers

In previous chapters, we described a register-level programming interface for a variety of network boards. Each board had to be handled in a different way with no standard approach.

Until very recently, any protocol code working with the board had to be rewritten for each major variation of ARCnet, Ethernet, or Token Ring card. This also meant that one protocol would own the board and exclude all others.

This chapter shows several attempts at standardizing the board level interface. Each allows several higher-level protocols to share a card and permits multiple cards to coexist.

MULTIPLE PROTOCOLS

Network system software has traditionally been designed to handle only one protocol. Developers created software as if it were the only one that would be interacting with the adapter card. In other words, a machine would work only with a single protocol stack. The stack could accommodate a variety of cards but would have to know who was using the card.

This approach is no longer acceptable. It is now common for a user to require simultaneous connections to, for example, a UNIX machine via TCP/IP and a Novell server via IPX (see Figure 12.1).

Novell, as with many other vendors, has always had a solution to the common-interface-to-the-board problem. Partial copies of IPX.COM code are prepared for each card by the board manufacturer, which is linked to the NetWare portion of IPX at the time of installation. This form of "delayed linking" (not the proper use of the term) allows IPX versions and drivers to be maintained independently. However, the resulting combined IPX.COM file is still the sole user of the adapter card and expects to see NetWare-only protocols pass through it.

There are three current multiprotocol board-level interfaces.

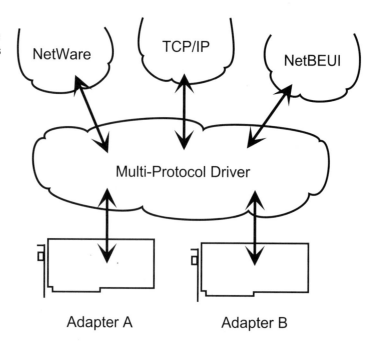

1. Microsoft/3Com Network Driver Interface Specification (NDIS)
2. Apple/Novell Open Data-Link Interface (ODI)
3. FTP Software Packet Driver Specification

All three techniques add a distinguishing set of numbers to the packet header to indicate for which higher-level protocol a message is intended. Because a matching multiprotocol driver will also be used at the Receive end, it can strip these numbers out before any higher-level protocol ever knows they were used.

Now, the question is, who wants to write programs to this level? Many standard networking protocols already exist—IPX, SPX, NETBEUI, IP, and TCP. "Yet Another Protocol" really isn't needed. Most programmers should be interfacing with those higher protocols, not at the driver level. Some programmers working with drivers described in this chapter are probably rewriting existing protocols—a very big task.

However, there is always room for experimenting. One possible reason for programmers to work with these drivers is to develop diagnostic tools and network management aids.

PACKET DRIVERS

The term "Packet Driver" may seem to be rather generic, but it does refer to a very specific board interface technique.

A Packet Driver is a small piece of software that works closely with the adapter board and must be written specifically for each new board. It does not come in two parts as does the traditional IPX file or as do some of the competing drivers.

A Little History

Packet Drivers were originally developed by John Romkey in 1986 when he was at FTP Software. The concept allowed FTP's PC/TCP product to coexist with other network protocol stacks. The driver specification was made freely copyable, and a group of volunteers now write Packet Drivers for the wide variety of adapter cards on the market. The central collection point for these drivers was Clarkson University in Potsdam, New York. These drivers became the "Clarkson Collection." In 1992, Russell Nelson purchased the rights to the driver collection from the university, and they are now available from Crynwr Software.

The advantages of a Packet Driver are its small size, fast processing, and ease of attaining by mail or through the Internet. The drivers are well documented (source code is available in many cases), and support is available via the Internet.

Packet Driver Installation

Driver loading is performed by simply typing the file name, and the driver then becomes a memory resident program (TSR). In many cases, default settings are adequate, but specific values can be included. For example, the following command:

    3C503 0x65 2 0x300 1

loads the driver for the 3Com Ethernet card using software Interrupt 65h for driver access, IRQ 2 for communication between board and driver, and 300h in the PC's range of port addresses for the adapter's registers. The final One indicates that the coaxial connector on the back of the Ethernet board will be used for the network connection instead of the 15-pin AUI connector.

Software Access

Once loaded, the Packet Driver is accessed by other software by loading a desired function number into the processor's AH register and then using one of the PC's software interrupts. In principle, this is very similar to using the INT 21h DOS functions.

The big difference is that the programmer may not know which software interrupt to use. DOS enjoys the luxury of always using INT 21h. However, add-on software, such as Packet Drivers, doesn't have a reserved interrupt. If, for example, INT 65h was arbitrarily assumed for Packet Driver use, there is nothing to prevent another software product from selecting the same interrupt. Those two products could not then coexist on the one machine. Therefore, no specific interrupt can be assumed. Instead, the driver will install itself using the first empty interrupt starting with vector 60h (INT 60h) and searching as high as vector 80h. The various software running above the driver then has the initial task of locating the interrupt in use. Fortunately, this isn't as difficult as it may sound.

The entry point for Packet Driver code is assumed to start with three bytes of executable code. This can either be a three-byte jump instruction, or a two-byte jump followed by an NOP. These three bytes must, in turn, be followed by the null-terminated ASCII text string "PKT DRVR", 0x00, a total of 12 bytes.

To find the interrupt being used, an application must scan through the response code for vectors 60h through 80h until it finds one with the "PKT DRVR" string in the first 12 bytes indicated by the entry point. If found, the application knows the interrupt vector being used.

The following program will locate that interrupt number.

```
/* ------  PACKET_D.C  ----------------------------------------- *
 *      For use with a Clarkson Packet Driver              *
 *      Finds driver Interrupt 60h - 80h                   *
 *      J.K. HARDY     March 24, 1994                      *
 * ----------------------------------------------------------- */

#include <stdio.h>
#include <dos.h>

int check_signature(unsigned char far *Address);

void main()
{
    int i, Intno, success;
    unsigned char far *Address;
    printf("Looking for PACKET DRIVER signature\n");
    for (Intno=0x60; Intno<=0x70; Intno++) {
        Address = (long)getvect(Intno);
        printf("INT %02Xh Vector %08lXh\n", Intno, Address);
        Address = Address + 3;
        success = check_signature(Address);
        if(success){
            printf("We have a match at INT %02Xh\n", Intno);
            break;
        }
    }
}

// Check for a signature match in nine bytes.
// -------------------------------------------------------------
int check_signature(unsigned char far *Address)
    {
    int i = 0;
    char signature[] = "PKT DRVR";
    while ( i<8 && (*Address==signature[i])){
        if (i == 7) {
            return(1);
        }
        i++ ;
        Address++;
    }
    return(0);
}
```

Packet Driver Functions

The full set of functions available to Packet Driver users follows. However, not every Packet Driver will respond to all functions. Packet Drivers can have three levels of complexity depending on which functions are made available to higher-level programs. The number of levels included in any particular driver will depend on the adapter itself and the amount of coffee available at the time the driver was written.

All Packet Drivers must provide the functions listed as "basic." These provide minimal features such as the ability to send, broadcast, and receive packets. A second, optional, group of functions are categorized as "high-performance" functions. These duplicate some of the basic functions but add features and performance improvements. The third optional group adds "extended" functions. These support less commonly used operations of the network interface such as adapter address changes and multicasting. Of course, not all adapter cards will permit these operations. One other extended function gathers statistics on the use of the interface and makes these available to the application.

Programs wishing to use either extended or high-performance functions should first use the driver_info( ) function (a basic level function) to determine what other levels of support are available. Depending on the underlying adapter card, most recent Packet Drivers will typically respond to this function with an indication that all three levels are available.

Class, Type, and Interface

Three integers must be known when a Packet Driver is being accessed. All three numbers can be found with the driver_info( ) function yet to be described.

The first integer is the interface Class. This is an eight-bit integer that tells what kind of media the interface supports—DEC/Intel/Xerox (DIX) Ethernet, IEEE 802.3 Ethernet, IEEE 802.5 Token Ring, etc. Having the Class number is very important because layers of software above the Packet Driver still must know on what general type of network they are running. They need to know maximum packet size and byte order for integers, for example. This means that a Packet Driver doesn't totally isolate upper layers from the network media.

Some typical Class numbers are

Class

1   DEC/Intel/Xerox Ethernet
2   ProNET-10
3   IEEE 802.5 Token Ring
4   Omninet
5   Appletalk
6   Serial line

     7   Starlan

     8   ARCnet

    11   IEEE 802.3 with 802.2 headers

    12   FDDI with 802.2 headers

    13   Internet X.25.

The second number describes the Interface Type. This is a 16-bit integer which specifies a particular brand of adapter card within the general class. Within Class 1 or Class 11, depending on the Ethernet headers used, a 3Com 3C503 board would have an assigned Type = 12.

The third and final value that must be known is the eight-bit Interface number. If a machine is equipped with more than one adapter card of a given Class and Type, they must be numbered to distinguish between them. The first card will be Interface = 0; the next, 1, etc.

Class and Type constants are managed by FTP Software. Contact FTP to register a new Class or Type number. The third number is selected by the software automatically.

Be aware that the word "type" is used in two different contexts. The first has just been described as interface type. The second use refers to the multiplexing/demultiplexing technique needed to accommodate multiple protocols. "Type," in this case, takes its name from the Type/Length field in the Ethernet header. In the abbreviated descriptions that follow, this second use of the word has been changed to "Mux_Type."

In spite of the Interface number, one Packet Driver can only handle one adapter card. For multiple cards, multiple drivers will be required. In a multiprotocol, multi-card environment, protocol software must look for a suitable card. During the initial checking, the Class and Type number for a driver/card combination must be examined to ensure suitability for the desired cable media and packet format. If a Packet Driver is found that is not of the correct Class, the search should continue since multiple drivers for multiple cards may exist.

The Functions

Packet Drivers are not as dependent on command blocks as are NetBIOS and IPX/SPX. Pointers to data buffers are still needed, but most other pieces of command-related information go into the processor's registers. Although somewhat less versatile, this is faster than using a command block.

The content of the AH register selects the desired function. In all cases, when the function returns, the processor carry bit should be clear, indicating that all went well. If the carry bit is set, something went wrong, and the DH register will contain an error code.

The following list of functions, while complete, lacks detail. Programmers experimenting with the Packet Drivers should always get the full descriptions. This list is just a starting point.

Group I—Basic Functions

driver_info()

> AH = 1
>
> AL = 255

This function returns the three essential interface numbers plus some other information. The functionality value returned in AL indicates which of the three function groups are supported.

Values returned (if carry clear):

> BX = Code revision number
>
> CH = Class number
>
> DX = Type number
>
> CL = Adapter number 0, 1, . . .
>
> DS:SI = Pointer to ASCII string "driver name"
>
> AL = Functionality

1	Basic functions supported
2	Basic and extended functions
5	Basic and high-performance
6	Basic, high-performance, extended
255	No driver installed

access_type()

> AH = 2
>
> AL = Class number
>
> DS:SI = Pointer to "Mux_Type"
>
> BX = Interface type number
>
> CX = "Mux_Type" length
>
> DL = Interface number
>
> ES:DI = Receive handler

Returns (if carry clear):

> AX = Handle

This function is used to "register" or establish a working relationship between a higher-level program and the driver. The argument Mux_Type is a pointer to a protocol stack multiplex specification. It must match the underlying generic adapter type, i.e., the adapter class must be known before this function is used. This determines how the Packet Driver will determine for whom an incoming packet is intended.

The returned handle number is used for all subsequent communications between the application and the driver.

The "receive handler" address is a pointer to a subroutine that is called when a packet is actually received, similar to a POST address in NetBIOS.

release_type()

> AH = 3
>
> BX = handle

Returns Carry clear if successful.

This function ends access to the driver associated with a specific handle. Subsequently, that handle will no longer be valid, and packets received for that application will be lost.

send_pkt()

> AH = 4
>
> DS:DI = Far pointer to a buffer
>
> CX = Length of buffer in bytes

Returns Carry clear if successful.

This function transmits the number of bytes as specified by the CX register. The application must supply the entire packet, including "Class"-specific network headers and demultiplexing information. The high-performance function as_send_pkt() provides improved throughput for back-to-back packets.

terminate()

> AH = 5
>
> BX = Handle

Returns Carry clear if successful.

This function terminates the driver associated with the handle. If a second application is using the driver and has an open handle, the terminate will fail.

get_address()

> AH = 6
>
> BX = Handle
>
> ES:DI = Pointer to a buffer
>
> CX = Size of buffer

Returns Carry clear if successful.

> CX = Number of bytes copied

This function copies the current local adapter address, or its substitute (see Set_Address()), into a buffer. The initial buffer length is passed in the CX register.

In most cases, six bytes are adequate. The actual number of bytes copied is returned in CX.

reset_interface()

> AH = 7
>
> BX = Handle

Returns Carry clear if successful.

This function resets the interface associated with a handle to a known state. Any transmissions in process are aborted, and the adapter address is reset to the ROM value.

Group II—High Performance Driver Functions

get_parameters()

> AH = 10 (decimal)

Returns Carry clear if successful.

ES:DI = Pointer to parameter list

This is an enhanced version of the driver_info() function. It returns a description of the driver's and underlying adapter card's capabilities. This information could then be used to improve performance if the card indicates it is capable.

as_send_pkt()

> AH = 11
>
> DS:SI = Pointer to a buffer
>
> CX = Buffer length
>
> ES:DI = Pointer to second routine

Returns Carry clear if successful.

This is a Packet Send function with an added feature. The ES:DI pointer identifies a second routine entry point that is called when the application's data has been copied out of the buffer. The second routine can then safely re-use that buffer.

Group III—Extended Driver Functions

set_rcv_mode()

> AH = 20
>
> BX = Handle
>
> CX = Mode

Returns Carry clear if successful.

If the adapter card is capable, set_rcv_mode( ) sets various options for packets to be received based on destination addresses. Most Ethernet cards, for example, support multicast addresses. ARCnet cards do not. Mode 3 is the default. The following values are available:

1	Turn off receiver
2	Receive only packets sent to this card
3	Mode 2 plus broadcast packets
4	Mode 3 plus limited multicast packets
5	Mode 3 plus all multicast packets
6	All packets

get_rcv_mode()

AH = 21

BX = Handle

Returns Carry clear if successful.

AX = Receive mode

This function returns the current Receive mode of the interface associated with that specific handle. The mode numbers are the same as for set_rcv_mode( ).

set_multicast_list()

AH = 22

ES:DI = Pointer to an address list

CX = Total length of list

Returns Carry clear if successful.
For adapter cards that support multicast addresses, this function passes a list of acceptable addresses to the driver.

get_multicast_list()

AH = 23

ES:DI = Pointer to an empty buffer

Returns Carry clear if successful.

CX = Buffer length

This function should return a list of multicast addresses currently in use.

get_statistics()

> AH = 24
>
> BX = Handle
>
> DS:SI = Pointer to an empty buffer

This function returns a pointer to a table of statistics for the interface. This table will contain seven values stored as normal 80 x 86 32-bit integers, i.e., least significant byte first.

Non-error return:

Carry flag clear

DS:SI = Pointer to the following structure:

```
struct statistics {
    unsigned long    packets_in;
    unsigned long    packets_out;
    unsigned long    bytes_in;
    unsigned long    bytes_out;
    unsigned long    errors_in;
    unsigned long    errors_out;
    unsigned long    packets_lost;
};
```

set_address()

> AH = 25
>
> ES:DI = Pointer to the "new" address
>
> CX = Number of bytes in new address

Returns Carry clear if successful.

CX = Number of bytes copied

Some adapter cards read their serial number from a ROM and then hold it in a writable register. For those cards, this function will change that address. Such a change is often of interest during network monitoring or troubleshooting. There are also situations in which network operating systems, such as DECnet, require this ability.

Example

The following brief program uses the get_driver_info( ) function to retrieve some numbers from the driver. As written, it assumes the driver was installed at software Interrupt 0x60. The previous program can be used to verify that. Obviously, the two programs could be combined.

```
// ----------------------------------------------------------------------
//  Retrieve Packet Driver information
//  J.K. Hardy                           May 10,1994
// ----------------------------------------------------------------------
#define  INTNO 0x60
#include <stdio.h>
#include <dos.h>

main()
{
  unsigned char function_groups, A_number, D_class;
  unsigned int D_type, version;

  asm {
     push es; push ds
     mov ah, 0x01        // function 01 = get driver info
     mov al, 0xFF
     int INTNO
     pop ds; pop es
  }
  version  = _BX;
  D_class  = _CH;
  D_type   = _DX;
  A_number = _CL;
  function_groups = _AL;

  printf("Driver version = %4d\n", version);
  printf("Class number = %6d\n", D_class);
  printf("Type Number = %7d\n", D_type);
  printf("Adapter number = %4d\n", A_number);
  printf("Functions supported = %2d\n", function_groups);
  printf("01=Basic 02=Basic,Extended 06=Basic,Ext,HiPerform\n");
}
```

Error Codes

When a Packet Driver function works correctly, it returns with the processor's Carry bit clear. However, should an error occur, the Carry bit is set instead, and the DH register then contains an error code.

The following codes are defined:

1	BAD_HANDLE	Invalid handle number
2	NO_CLASS	No interfaces of specified class found
3	NO_TYPE	No interfaces of specified type found
4	NO_NUMBER	No interfaces of specified number found
5	BAD_TYPE	Bad packet type specified
6	NO_MULTICAST	This interface does not support multicast

7	CAN'T_TERMINATE	This Packet Driver cannot terminate
8	BAD_MODE	An invalid receiver mode was specified
9	NO_SPACE	Operation failed because of insufficient space
10	TYPE_IN_USE	The driver had previously been accessed and not released
11	BAD_COMMAND	The command code was not implemented
12	CAN'T_SEND	The packet couldn't be sent (usually a hardware error)
13	CAN'T_SET	Adapter address couldn't be changed
14	BAD_ADDRESS	Adapter address has bad length or format
15	CAN'T_RESET	More than one handle was open

To obtain Packet Drivers, contact

Russell Nelson
Crynwr Software
11 Grant St.
Potsdam, NY 13676
nelson@crynwr.com
Voice (315) 268-1925
Fax (315) 268-9201

FTP Software, Inc.
26 Princess St.
Wakefield, MA 01880-3004
(617) 246-0900

OPEN DATA-LINK INTERFACE (ODI)

The ODI specification was jointly created by Apple and Novell as another solution for a multiprotocol adapter interface.

The lower software layers now consist of two executable files instead of a single one as used by the Packet Drivers. Of the two, the focal point is the Link Support Layer file— LSL.COM. When loaded into memory, this file becomes a **TSR** and acts as a multiplexer for multiprotocol, multidriver operations.

The second file is a driver written specifically for the adapter board being used. Multiple adapter cards are permitted, and each will have its own driver. However, there will always be only one LSL.

Drivers designed for use with ODI are generically referred to as Multiple Link Interface Drivers (MLIDs). Drivers written to the ODI specification are said to be ODI compliant (see Figure 12.2).

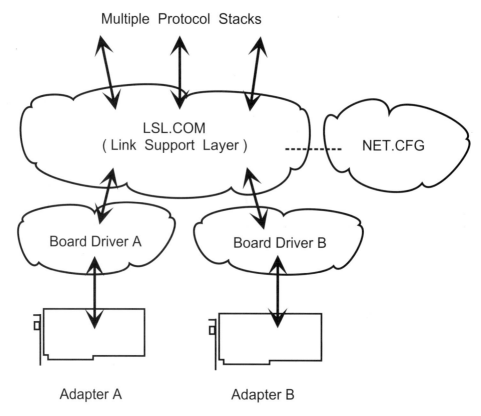

Multiple Protocol Stacks

LSL.COM
(Link Support Layer)

NET.CFG

Board Driver A

Board Driver B

Adapter A

Adapter B

FIGURE 12.2
Apple-Novell ODI system.

The LSL provides

- multiprotocol to multidriver steering or multiplexing
- event scheduling and timing
- centralized queuing, buffering, and memory management for these.

A third file—NET.CFG—is a text file carrying configuration options. An example of such a file might be

```
# sample NET.CFG file
Link Support
    Buffers 3 653
    MemPool 1K
Link Driver ARCnet
    INT 2
    MEM D00000
    PORT 2F0
```

The LSL.COM file is loaded into memory first, followed by the board driver(s) and the protocol stack(s). As the board drivers and protocol stacks are loaded, they must each initially find the code entry point for the LSL program. This is the same general problem that faces Packet Driver users, but the technique is different. ODI drivers are ultimately accessed with a "call" to a specific address rather than through a software interrupt. The task then is to find this address.

The DOS INT 2Fh multiplexer function is used to locate used registration numbers. For each multiplexer registration, a search is made for code with the ASCII characters "LINKSUP$". This second step is very similar to the Packet Driver "PKT DRVR" search.

Once this entry point is found, a driver calls the entry point and gives the LSL three addresses: the driver's Send Entry Point (Packets are sent by the LSL to this address), the Control Entry point, and the address of the driver's internal configuration table.

LSL will reply with a Driver Support Entry Point address, a board number, and the maximum buffer size to be used. The Driver Support entry is then used for subsequent communication between the driver and the Link Support Layer.

Protocol stacks register with LSL in a similar fashion but are given a different entry point.

The Link Support Layer has four entry points:

1   Initialization (found with INT 2Fh)
2   Driver Support Entry Point (16 functions)
3   Protocol Support Entry Point (25 functions)
4   General Services Entry Point (6 functions)

NETWORK DRIVER INTERFACE SPECIFICATION (NDIS)

The NDIS specification from 3Com and Microsoft takes a somewhat different approach to multiple protocols and multiple cards. It assumes that the card drivers and the protocol stacks are perfectly capable of talking directly to each other without extra help. However, help is needed in the initial linking between a protocol and a card driver and later with the disconnect.

The NDIS specification describes the form that direct communications between protocol and adapter drivers should use. It also describes an initial setup or "binding" operation that involves a separate Protocol Manager (see Figure 12.3).

This Protocol Manager program is loaded before the protocols or the board drivers. Its job is to read configuration information out of the PROTOCOL.INI file and make this available to the other software to be loaded. With DOS, the Protocol manager consists of two files: PROTMAN.DOS and PROTMAN.EXE. The PROTMAN.DOS file is loaded with the line "device=protman.dos" in the computer's CONFIG.SYS file. If needed, this may cause the corresponding PROTMAN.EXE file to be loaded.

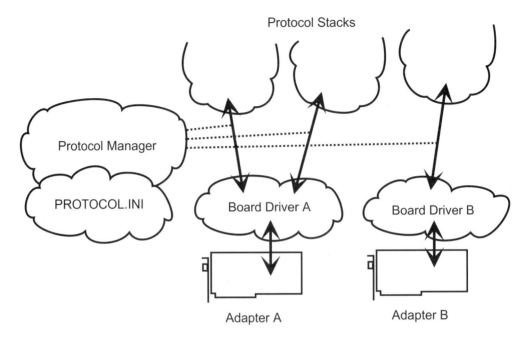

FIGURE 12.3
NDIS uses a Protocol Manager program to connect or bind protocols with board drivers.
Setup information is held in a PROTOCOL.INI text file.

Once loaded, the first task of the Program Manager is to locate the PROTO-COL.INI text file, read its contents, parse (cut up) into a usable form, and then create a memory resident image for later access. As each protocol or board driver loads, it asks the Protocol Manager for the memory address of the text file image. It searches through this "file" for any relevant setup information. It then identifies itself to the Protocol Manager by providing a Module Name and Characteristic Table. In effect, a module says, "Hello, my name is NETBIOS and my characteristics are in a table at address xxxx."

Finally, before two modules can communicate, they have to be bound together. Binding involves exchanging characteristic tables so that each is known to the other. This includes specific parameters and code entry points.

Characteristic Tables

Each driver holds a characteristic table within its code file. The table contains a 16-byte module name, an indication of how this driver module interfaces with other software above and below it, i.e., Session interface via NCB at the top and MAC interface at the bottom. It will also contain long (32-bit) addresses for its various internal entry points. The table also defines the protocols supported (802.3, .4, .5, DIX, ARCnet, etc.) and gives driver-specific information such as broadcast, multicast, promiscuous address, source routing supported? (Yes/No).

PROTOCOL.INI File

The PROTOCOL.INI file is a text file with several entries similar to the following. Some lines will be used only with protocol stacks; others, only for adapter drivers.

```
[NETBIOS]
Drivername = NETBIOS$
Bindings = ETHERCARD       only for protocol modules
Dynamic = YES              protocol can be disconnected
BindStatus = YES
MaxNCBs = 32
MaxSessions = 32
MaxNames = 16
```

After an adapter driver loads, it calls "GetProtocolManagerInfo" for access to the text file. It then calls "RegisterModuleInfo" to exchange characteristic tables.

As with all multiprotocol drivers described in this chapter, the NDIS adapter and protocol drivers have the initial task of locating the previously loaded Protocol Manager (PROTMAN.DOS, etc.). In a DOS environment, this is accomplished by loading AH = 44h, AL = 02h, and then issuing INT 21h. The DS:DX register pair returns holding the address of a Reply Block, which, among other information, includes a direct entry address.

As indicated, NDIS specifies the command for direct communication between adapter driver and protocol driver. As of early 1994, about 35 commands were available. Each involves pushing a set of values onto the stack and then making a direct CALL to the other protocol.

NDIS also specifies ten commands for Driver-to-Protocol-Manager communication. These can be accessed either using the initial AH = 44h, INT 21h technique previously described or, if the direct address is known, by a PUSH and CALL operation. The commands themselves and any needed information are assembled in a request block.

Protocol Manager Interface Commands are

GetProtocolManagerInfo	Returns a pointer to the PROTOCOL.INI memory image
RegisterModule	A driver passes the address of its characteristic table to the Manager and requests registration
BindAndStart	Initiates protocol binding
GetProtocolManagerLinkage	Requests the direct entry point of the Manager for subsequent CALLs
GetProtocolIniPath	Returns the path for the PROTOCOL.INI file

RegisterProtocolManagerInfo	Updates the address of the protocol.ini memory image if it has been altered
InitAndRegister	For OS/2 versions only
UnbindAndStop	Modules that are "dynamic" can be terminated (unbound)
BindStatus	Returns a description of current driver modules and their characteristics
RegisterStatus	Asks whether a specific driver is currently registered

REFERENCES

1. Doupnik, Joe R. *Packet Drivers Made Simple.* Logan: Utah State University, January 9, 1990.

2. *Packet Driver Specification,* Version 1.09. Wakefield, MA: FTP Software.

3. *Apple/Novell Open Data-Link Interface Developer's Guide.* APDA M0355LL/A. Cupertino, CA: Apple Computer, Inc., 1989.

4. *3Com/Microsoft Network Driver Interface Specification*, Version 2.01. Available from either 3Com or Microsoft.

Chapter 13

AppleTalk

Developed in the early 1980s, AppleTalk was one of the first peer-to-peer networking protocols. It is used to interconnect Macintosh computers, servers, and printers. However, AppleTalk is not restricted to peer operation nor to the MAC environment. Its higher layers can also interconnect with the UNIX, MAC, and DOS worlds.

AppleTalk Phase II, which added enhancements to the original definition and support for the Token Ring system, was published in June 1989.

AppleTalk is a complete protocol stack—stretching from filing system messages at the top, down to connectors and cables at the bottom. At the physical layer, several choices are available. An installer can use the built-in LocalTalk® capabilities of all MACs. For greater speed, ARCnet, Ethernet (EtherTalk®), or Token Ring (TokenTalk®) can be used. The latter three will require add-in adapter cards.

PROTOCOL SUITE

The full suite is shown in Figure 13.1. In the sections that follow, we will explore a few of the specific protocols, but space does not permit a description of the full set. The next few paragraphs contain very brief descriptions of each before we move into more detail on some.

As mentioned, AppleTalk will support Ethernet, Token Ring, and LocalTalk. A separate Link Access Protocol (LAP) is defined for each of these: TokenTalk (TLAP), EtherTalk (ELAP), and LocalTalk (LLAP), respectively.

The Datagram Delivery Protocol (DDP) is the only protocol described for layer 3. DDP can include network as well as station numbers and is thus a routable protocol.

Four different protocols are described at layer 4. Each has its own purpose. The Routing Table Maintenance Protocol (RTMP) is used for communications between routers and is further described in Chapter 14. The AppleTalk Echo Protocol (AEP) is essentially a test to see if a station is alive and reachable and how long the communication takes. The AppleTalk Transaction Protocol (ATP) adds reliability and time-

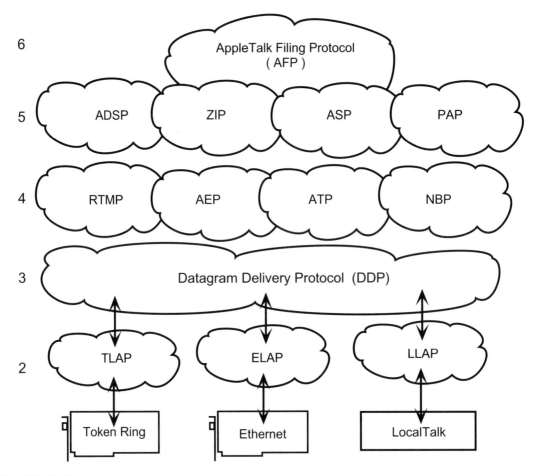

FIGURE 13.1
Full AppleTalk protocol suite. The correspondence with OSI layers is very approximate.

out checks to the basic DDP service. It is a one-way service. The Name Binding Protocol (NBP) searches for links between character string names and internet addresses.

In the fifth layer, which roughly corresponds to the session layer, AppleTalk has four protocols. The AppleTalk Data Stream Protocol (ADSP) is a full duplex (two-way), connection-oriented, and therefore "reliable," protocol. The Zone Information Protocol (ZIP) maps zone names to network numbers. The AppleTalk Session Protocol (ASP) opens, closes, and maintains sessions. The Printer Access Protocol (PAP) is for Postscript printing.

The AppleTalk Filing Protocol (AFP) resides in the top layer. It is the "language" that communicates with remote servers and stations about disk directories and the opening, closing, and sharing of files.

LOCALTALK

Out of the three lower-layer protocols supported by AppleTalk, we will concentrate on LocalTalk because Token Ring and Ethernet have already been described. LocalTalk is the physical connection protocol that is built into every MAC. Compared to other local area network physical protocols, it is relatively slow at 230.4 kilobits/sec. For a speed comparison, the floppy drives on a DOS machine typically transfer data at 200 to 400 kilobits/sec. LocalTalk's low speed is offset by its low cost and the ease with which a small network system can be set up and used.

LocalTalk stations and printers interconnect on a single twisted pair of wires—a linear bus. A maximum of 32 devices can be connected to one bus segment, and a segment can have a maximum end-to-end spread of 300 meters. The actual connection between the MAC and the twisted pair is made with the AppleTalk adapter, which consists of two connectors for the twisted pair wire and a small transformer. "Daisy chain" cables run from one adapter to the next.

The final two ends of the twisted pair must be terminated with 100-ohm resistors (see Figure 13.2). If no cable is connected into the second connector of the adapter, a parallel resistor automatically takes its place to form the termination.

The transformer maintains the "balanced" state of the twisted pair so that neither wire is grounded. This is an essential condition for low noise pickup.

Cable voltages are a differential waveform following the RS-485 standard. RS-485 is essentially the same as RS-422 but allows multiple connections instead of only two. Both standards are very different from RS-232, which allows one wire to be grounded. The differential nature of the wiring means that neither wire is grounded and that noise pickup and radiation should, therefore, be minimal. No shielding is used on the cable so the installer must be careful of the immediate environment.

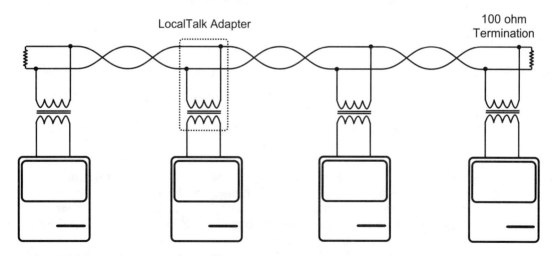

FIGURE 13.2
Bus topology for LocalTalk uses a single 100-ohm twisted pair. Each station connects with a small transformer.

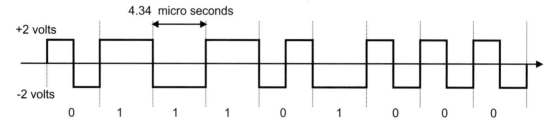

FIGURE 13.3
LocalTalk cable waveform. A data bit of Zero is transmitted with a change in the middle of
the time slot. A data value of One holds its level for the full time. Both bits include a
change to the opposite level at the end of their time slot.

Cables should be kept away from high-noise sources, not coiled excessively, with no
staples used to hold the wires.

Encoding

At 230.4 kilobytes/sec, each data bit lasts 4.34 microseconds. To ensure that timing
pulses are included, data is encoded with a type of frequency modulation. This also
happens to make the average cable voltage Zero over the long term—a requirement
of the coupling transformers. A data value of One holds a voltage at one level or the
other for the full 4.34-microsecond time slot. A data value of Zero makes a change
in the middle of the slot. Both values make a change to the opposite voltage level at
the end of their time slot (see Figure 13.3). This is somewhat similar to differential
Manchester encoding used on the Token Ring. The difference is that the words
"middle of time slot" and "end of time slot" must be interchanged.

LINK ACCESS PROTOCOL

Each of Apple's physical transmission systems has a corresponding link access pro-
tocol. EtherTalk uses the EtherTalk Link Access Protocol (ELAP); TokenTalk uses
TokenTalk Link Access Protocol (TLAP). The operation of LocalTalk is managed by
Apple's LocalTalk Link Access Protocol (LLAP).

The protocol header for LLAP is shown in Figure 13.4 along with a LocalTalk
header and trailer. The LLAP portion begins with the Destination ID and ends with
the last byte of data and the FCS. Code running on the MAC's 68000 family processor is used to implement the LLAP protocol. The LocalTalk portion is controlled by
hardware centered around a Zilog 8530 chip, which implements the Synchronous
Data Link Control (SDLC) protocol.

In both headers, all 16-bit values are sent most significant byte first. In fact,
because the Motorola 68000 processor family is "Big Endian," even the data will
likely be most significant byte first.

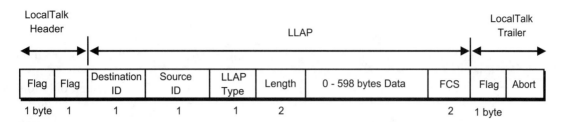

LocalTalk Header | LLAP | LocalTalk Trailer

Flag	Flag	Destination ID	Source ID	LLAP Type	Length	0 - 598 bytes Data	FCS	Flag	Abort
1 byte	1	1	1	1	2		2	1 byte	

FIGURE 13.4
LLAP packet with LocalTalk encapsulation. The LLAP portion starts with "Destination Node ID."

The LLAP packet contains the following fields:

2 or more flag bytes set to 01111110 (7Eh)

8-bit DESTINATION NODE ID number

8-bit SOURCE NODE ID number

8-bit LLAP TYPE indicates what is in the data portion

16-bit LENGTH (first 6 bits = 000000)

0–598 bytes of data

16-bit FCS uses CRC-**CCITT**

8-bit flag (7Eh)

minimum 12 abort bits

Addresses

LLAP addresses are eight-bit values that are set dynamically. This means that a machine's ID number could change from day to day. Use of dynamic node ID assignment bypasses the problem of having to set DIP switches inside each computer to a different station number. In contrast, ARCnet requires the installer to set an eight-bit number either with DIP switches or via software. Ethernet and Token Ring use factory-controlled 48-bit numbers to avoid any setup problems.

In selecting a node ID, a MAC makes an initial guess at an eight-bit number when it is turned on and sends several LLAP Enquiry Control Packets (ENQs) out to that address. If another station acknowledges, the new station knows that number is already in use. The station simply picks another number and tries again. It keeps trying until a vacant number is found. To minimize future network loading, most stations have the ability to store that number for the "guess" used at the next startup.

Not all Node IDs are available for station use. ID Zero is not used, 255 is used only for broadcasts, and the numbers 128 to 254 tend to be used only for server devices. A normal station is, therefore, restricted to addresses within the range 1 to 127. This is an adequate set since only 32 devices in total can be connected to any one segment.

LLAP Types

For data packets, the Type number within the LLAP header is set to either 1 or 2. The specific value depends on whether short or extended DDP headers are used inside LLAP.

Control packets use Type numbers between 80h and FFh, although only four types are currently defined. Two of these—ENQ and ACK packets—are used during dynamic node assignment, which has already been described. The remaining two—RTS and CTS packets—perform an initial handshake between stations prior to the exchange of data. Their use will be described shortly. The four control Types are:

81h = Enquiry packet (ENQ)

82h = Acknowledge packet (ACK), response to ENQ

84h = Request to Send (RTS)

85h = Clear to Send (CTS), response to RTS

Control packets do not contain length or data fields.

Bit Stuffing

After the LLAP portion of any packet has been assembled, a 16-bit CRC is calculated, and the LocalTalk header and trailer are added. However, there is a possibility that bytes in the LLAP portion will look the same as the 01111110 flag byte used by LocalTalk. Therefore, just prior to adding the header and trailer, the full bit sequence is examined, and an extra Zero is inserted after every five consecutive Ones. This "stuffing" is done after the Length and CRC have been calculated. With the extra Zeros added, the overall packet on the cable may grow in physical length by several bits and thus will not always be an exact multiple of eight bits.

At the receiving end, after the header and trailer are stripped off, these extra Zeros are removed. CRC and length calculations are done after the removal and won't even be aware that extra Zeros existed. The insertion and removal is done by the Zilog 8530 chip or its equivalent.

AppleTalk's frame check sequence at the end of the packet uses the CRC-CCITT equation to calculate a 16-bit value. It covers all parts of the LLAP portion from the Destination Node ID through to the end of the data.

Cable Access

LocalTalk accesses the shared cable via CSMA/CD using techniques somewhat similar to Ethernet. This is a random access system that doesn't wait for a token to be passed. However, once access is gained, an initial handshake occurs before data packets are transferred. This is similar to ARCnet's "buffer-free" enquiry. There is no similar operation with Ethernet.

Here is how the cable is accessed. Prior to transmitting any data, LocalTalk listens for a quiet gap of 400 microseconds. Once found, it waits an additional random length of time, which reduces the chance of multiple stations starting at the same instant. The maximum random time value is increased during periods of heavy traffic and decreased during light traffic.

The first transmission is a single one-bit "synchronizing pulse." This is followed by a quiet period of at least two bit times. The pulse and delay sequence should force all receivers to lose clock synchronization. If they don't, they know that the twisted pair line is being used by someone else.

The message that follows could be directed to a single station or a broadcast to all stations.

Directed Message

If the line is clear, a short Request-to-Send (RTS) packet is sent to the intended destination node ID. That destination must return a Clear-to-Send (CTS) packet within 200 microseconds—the interframe gap time. Upon reception of a valid CTS, the original source can start sending data packets but must do so within another 200-microsecond time limit. Several data packets can be sent end to end as long as the gap between them doesn't exceed 200 microseconds. When finished, a gap of more than 400 microseconds is left (the Interdialog Gap) before starting a new dialog. Again, this starts with a synchronizing pulse and the RTS control packet.

This unusual sequence makes collisions most likely to occur within the RTS and CTS packets. Because these packets are short, little time will be lost as a result.

If collisions are detected, a transmitter must "back off" and wait an increasing random length of time in the same way that Ethernet does. LocalTalk will make 32 attempts at transmitting before giving up and passing control back to higher layers.

Broadcast Message

Broadcasts are handled in a slightly different manner from directed packets because there is no way to perform a handshake with all stations on the cable. Once a station senses that the line is free for 400 microseconds, it waits an additional random time length and sends an RTS control packet to Destination FFh. No CTS is expected in return. Other stations will recognize that a broadcast is about to occur and should stay quiet. The source machine waits an additional 200 microseconds to be certain that no collisions occurred with the RTS packet and then sends the broadcast message. Once again, the Destination Node ID is set to FFh.

Receiving

Stations accept a packet either if it is a broadcast or if the Destination Node ID matches their own. When an RTS packet appears with a matching Node ID (not a broadcast), a station will respond with a CTS packet as long as it feels able to process the data which will follow. The source station will then send one or more data packets.

Valid data packets will have an overall length of 5 to 603 bytes and have a valid CRC. Data packets are not acknowledged by the LLAP protocol.

DATAGRAM DELIVERY PROTOCOL (DDP)

Datagram Delivery Protocol (DDP) is to Apple what IP is to UNIX and IPX is to NetWare. DDP is a network layer (layer 3) protocol. This protocol is used by all three lower-layer Apple protocols. Remember that DDP is not part of LocalTalk. DDP will cooperate with Ethernet, Token Ring, or LocalTalk.

As with IP and IPX, DDP is an "unreliable" protocol. Again, this only means that there is no automatic acknowledgment, sequencing, or retransmission of packets built into the protocol. Higher layers can certainly add that if they wish.

DDP adds the possibility of network numbers to a packet. We say possibility because there are two forms of packets that are allowed within DDP. If a single network segment (no routers) is being used, no network numbers are needed; thus a shorter, more efficient header is used. For internetwork use, an extended header accommodates routers.

The DDP header follows immediately after the link layer header. The Type byte in that lower-layer header will be set to 1 or 2 to indicate DDP in the next layer. What follows could either be a short (LLAP Type = 1) or extended (LLAP Type = 2) DDP header. In either case, the maximum length of the data portion of a DDP packet is 586 bytes (see Figure 13.5).

In the DDP short header:

Length (16-bit value)—The first six bits are always set to Zero. The remaining ten bits indicate the length—to a maximum of 591, which includes the DDP header plus data.

Destination Socket and Source Socket (8-bit values)—To be described shortly.

DDP Type (8-bit value)—Describes what is inside the data portion—most likely another, higher-level, protocol.

Data—Maximum 586 bytes.

The extended header must be used with interconnected networks (see Figure 13.6). In the DDP Extended Header:

Length (2 bytes)—The first two bits are permanently set to Zero. The next four bits are used as a "Hop Count" by routers. This limits packets to crossing a maximum of 15 network boundaries before being discarded.

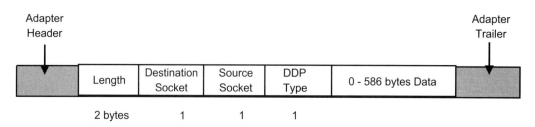

FIGURE 13.5
DDP short header.

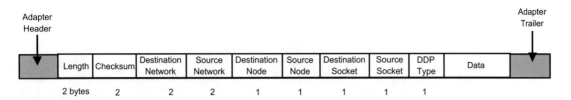

FIGURE 13.6
DDP extended header.

DDP Checksum (2 bytes)—If checksum is calculated, the procedure resembles that of XNS with a rotate after each 16-bit addition. If the checksum is not calculated, the two bytes carry Zeros.

Destination Network (2 bytes)

Source Network (2 bytes)

Destination Node ID (1 byte)

Source Node ID (1 byte)

Destination Socket (8 bits)

Source Socket (8 bits)

DDP Type (8 bits)

With the Phase II definition of AppleTalk, one network can now use several network numbers. Using LocalTalk connections, this was never necessary because only 32 attachments could be made to any one segment. However, with Ethernet and Token Ring, several hundred connections are possible, in which case the eight-bit Destination Node ID in the extended header would not have been sufficient. Allowing multiple network numbers for one network solved the problem. The numbers must be consecutive and are often referred to as a network range.

Network numbers should not use 00. This essentially means "unknown."

DDP Type byte indicates what higher-layer protocol is contained after the DDP header:

01 = RTMP response or data

02 = NBP packet

03 = ATP packet

04 = AEP packet

05 = RTMP request packet

06 = ZIP packet

07 = ADSP packet

DDP Sockets

Several programs or tasks could be running simultaneously on any one computer. These won't necessarily be end-user application programs. They could be other components of the protocol stack. If each wants to use the network, some means must exist to identify the correct source and destination program. This is the purpose of the eight-bit socket number. Socket numbers 0 and 155 are reserved. This leaves 254 available numbers for each machine. The values 1–63 are reserved for Apple's use, 64–127 are for experimental use, and 128–254 can be dynamically assigned by DDP. Within these limits, the source and destination programs coordinate socket numbers.

For the programmer, DDP supports only four interface operations. Three of these concern sockets.

1. Open a statically assigned socket (1–127)
2. Open a dynamically assigned socket (128–254)
3. Close a socket (1–254)
4. Send a datagram

APPLETALK FILING PROTOCOL (AFP)

AppleTalk Filing Protocol (AFP) is the message system that communicates between users and servers concerning remote files, etc. Remember that with a peer system, a server could be almost anyone. AFP is similar in intent to Server Message Block (SMB), Novell's NetWare Core Protocol (NCP), and Sun's Network File System (NFS).

Volume, directory, and file names within the AFP filing system are more elaborate than that of DOS but not much different from those used in UNIX, OS/2, and MS Windows NT. Like NetWare, Macintosh disks are identified with a volume name which can be up to 27 characters long. Novell uses SYS:, VOL1:, etc. In contrast, MS/PC DOS uses exotic volume names such as A:, B:, C:, etc.

Within an AFP volume, directories and files use names of up to 31 characters. Spaces can be used within a name, but the colon and the null character (0x00) cannot. The null character is used as the separator between directories, known as folders on the MAC Finder screen. Files and other directories within any one directory are referred to as the "offspring" of that directory.

Because the null character is used as the separator, null-terminated strings for a directory path cannot be used as in a DOS path reference. Instead, path strings take a Pascal-like form with the first byte indicating the length. A sample DOS-to-AFP path string conversion is included in the following program example.

Another major AFP difference appears inside of a file. MAC program files, of course, carry code for the 68000 family of processors instead of the 80 x 86 family used in the DOS world. MAC programs, therefore, won't inherently run on DOS machines without translation. Data files are much more transferrable; their content depends more on the commercial software used than on the processor.

The key difference between Macintosh and other file systems is that there are two essential parts to every file regardless of whether it is a program or data.

Data Forks and Resource Forks

Every Macintosh file contains two parts or "forks." The first portion—the Resource Fork—contains an icon, executable code, and other things specific to the Macintosh system. The second part is the Data Fork. It is often much larger in size and contains data from the wordprocessor, etc., that was used to create the file.

If a data file was created on a MAC and then used by a DOS client, the Resource Fork can be safely ignored. If created on a DOS machine and then used on a MAC, a generic Resource Fork will be automatically added. A third situation carries an element of danger. If the DOS COPY command is used to move MAC files around to different server subdirectories, the Resource Fork could be lost. For that reason, the NetWare NDIR and NCOPY commands are much safer.

When the NetWare for Macintosh Network Loadable Module (NLM) is added to a NetWare file server, it expands the directory description of all its files so they are available to both MAC and DOS users. In effect, it creates a shadow directory or separate name space for Macintosh files (see Figure 13.7). Macintosh clients read the one side; DOS clients, the other. The DOS side will have abbreviated names, fewer dates, and fewer attributes.

AFP defines approximately 50 client–server messages. Here are a few examples:

Get Server Info

Login

Logout

Get Server Parameters

Open Volume

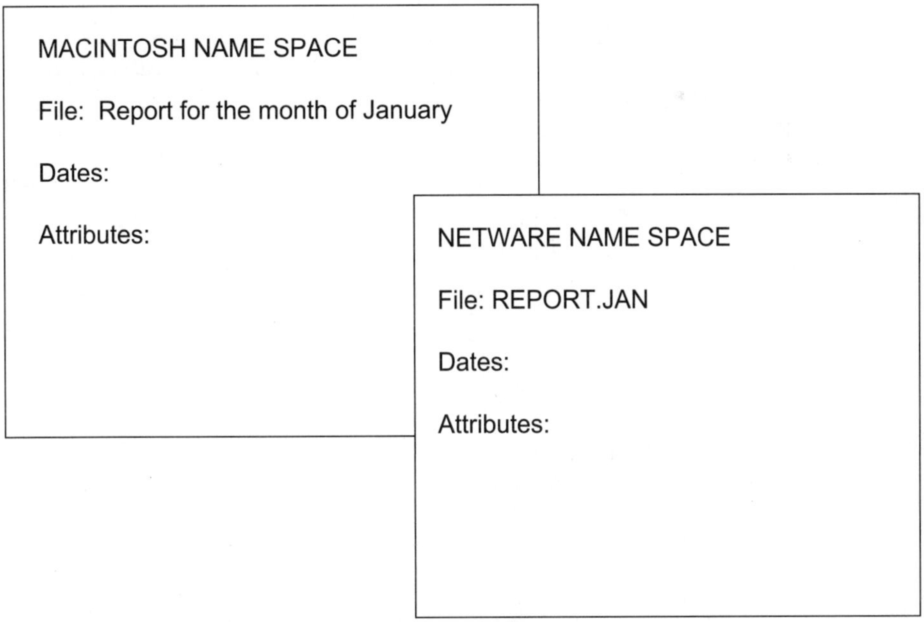

```
┌─────────────────────────────────────────────┐
│                                               │
│   MACINTOSH NAME SPACE                        │
│                                               │
│   File:  Report for the month of January      │
│                                               │
│   Dates:                                       │
│                  ┌──────────────────────────────────┐
│   Attributes:    │                                    │
│                  │   NETWARE NAME SPACE               │
│                  │                                    │
│                  │   File: REPORT.JAN                 │
│                  │                                    │
└──────────────────┤   Dates:                           │
                   │                                    │
                   │   Attributes:                      │
                   │                                    │
                   └────────────────────────────────────┘
```

FIGURE 13.7
Separate name space for Macintosh files is a parallel directory to the normal DOS/NetWare directory on the file server.

Close Volume

Create File

Copy File

Open Fork (Data or Resource)

Close Fork (Data or Resource)

Read

Write

Program Example

NetWare provides support for a limited number of the AppleTalk Filing Protocol functions. The following example uses one of these—Get AFP File Information. It reads the MAC name space on the server for information on a selected file.

Like many other network programming examples, a 12-byte request block is assembled, and processing is initiated with a software interrupt. The second field in the request block carries function code 05 which, along with the specific AH and AL register values, define this as "Get AFP File Information."

If all goes well, a reply will be sent back in a second block containing a 116-byte AFP description of the selected file. For comparison, a corresponding DOS description would be less than 32 bytes.

```
// Read a Macintosh file entry
// from MAC server name space.  April 26,1994
// -----------------------------------------------------------------------
#include <stdio.h>
#include <dos.h>

typedef unsigned char BYTE;
typedef unsigned int  WORD;
typedef unsigned long LONG;

struct RequestBlock {
  WORD  BlockLength;            // Structure length - 2
  BYTE  Function;
  BYTE  VolNumber;
  LONG  EntryID;
  WORD  RequestBits;
  BYTE  PathLength;
  BYTE  MAC_Path[255];
} Request ;

struct ReplyBlock {
  LONG  EntryID;
  LONG  ParentID;
  WORD  Attributes;
```

```
  LONG   DataForkLength;
  LONG   ResForkLength;
  WORD   NumberOffspring;
  WORD   CreateDate;
  WORD   AccessDate;
  WORD   ModifyDate;
  WORD   ModifyTime;
  WORD   BackupDate;
  WORD   BackupTime;
  BYTE   FinderInfo[32];
  BYTE   LongFileName[32];
  LONG   OwnerID;
  BYTE   ShortFileName[12];
  WORD   AccessRights;
} Reply ;

main()
{
  BYTE DOS_Path[254] = "MAC:3270\\CONFIG.TEL";
  BYTE DOS_Length;
  int i, result;

// -----------------------------------------------------------------------------
Translate into a MAC path
  DOS_Length = strlen(DOS_Path);
  printf("DOS path length = %d (decimal)\n", DOS_Length);
  Request.MAC_Path[0] = DOS_Length + 1;
  for (i=0; i<DOS_Length; i++) {
     if (DOS_Path[i] == '\\'){
        Request.MAC_Path[i+1] = 0x00;}
     else {
        Request.MAC_Path[i+1] = DOS_Path[i];
     } // End If.
  } // End For.

// -----------------------------------------------------------------------------
Fill in the request block.
  Request.PathLength = DOS_Length + 1;
  Request.RequestBits = 0x3FFF;    // Request all
  Request.EntryID = 0 ;
  Request.VolNumber = 0 ;
  Request.Function = 0x05 ;           // Get File Information
  Request.BlockLength = Request.PathLength + 9 ;

// -----------------------------------------------------------------------------
Request AFP information
  _SI = FP_OFF((void far *)&Request);
  _DS = FP_SEG((void far *)&Request);
  _DI = FP_OFF((void far *)&Reply);
  _ES = FP_SEG((void far *)&Reply);
```

```
    _CX = Request.BlockLength + 2 ;   // Request Buffer Length
    _DX = 114 ;                       // Reply Buffer Length
    _AH = 0xF2;
    _AL = 0x23;
    geninterrupt(0x21);
    result = _AL;

// ------------------------------------------------------------------------------------
Display the Information
    if (result == 0x9C)
        printf( "MAC path is wrong!\n");
    else if (result == 0x00){
        printf("Attributes - %04X\n", Reply.Attributes);
        printf("Data Fork Length - %08lX\n", Reply.DataForkLength);
        printf("Res. Fork Length - %08lX\n", Reply.ResForkLength);
        printf("File Creation Date - %04X\n", Reply.CreateDate);
        printf("Last Access Date - %04X\n", Reply.AccessDate);
        printf("Modified Date - %04X\n", Reply.ModifyDate);
        printf("Backup Date - %04X\n", Reply.BackupDate);
        printf("Long Name - %s\n", Reply.LongFileName );
        printf("Short Name - %s\n", Reply.ShortFileName );
        printf("Owner ID - %08lX\n", Reply.OwnerID);
        printf("Access Rights - %04X\n", Reply.AccessRights);
    }else
        printf("Something went wrong!\n") ;
    return ;
}
```

AFP Fields

The returned information fields need to be explained because there are differences from the usual DOS fields. The first issue concerns byte order.

On the Macintosh, as we have already indicated, word and long word values are represented in Big Endian form. However, the C compiler doesn't know this and assumes we have intel order. As a result, the "printf" function interchanges bytes within 16- and 32-bit values before displaying them. To keep it short, our sample program has made no attempt at correcting the display order—that will be a good exercise for the programmer.

Our second difference concerns the AFP encoding of date and time values. AFP dates are assigned four-byte values that represent the number of seconds before and after midnight, January 1, 2000. With 32 bits, dates can stretch approximately 68 years either side of the year 2000. As an example, July 1, 1993, would have a date value of approximately 0xF3C58E40.

Figure 13.8 describes the bit pattern inside two of the returned fields. Again, remember that the hex printout of these fields will have the Hi and Lo bytes transposed.

Access Rights

| M | S | P | D | C | O | W | R | – | – | – | – | – | – | – | – |

Attributes

| S | – | A | Sub | X | S | H | R | Wa | Ra | I | T | – | S2 | S1 | S0 |

FIGURE 13.8
AFP Access Rights and Attribute field bits within 16-bit integers. The most significant bit is on the left.

REFERENCES

1. Sidhu, G. S., Andrews, R. F., and Oppenheimer, A. B. *Inside AppleTalk,* 2nd Ed. Reading, MA: Addison-Wesley, 1990.

Chapter 14

Hubs, Bridges, and Routers

Although hubs, bridges, and routers may seem to be unrelated, each of these devices can participate in the remote management of a network. In this chapter, we will discuss the devices first and then examine their control possibilities near the end of the chapter.

NETWORK EXPANSION

Each LAN technology, i.e., Ethernet, Token Ring, etc., has a limited distance span and a maximum number of connections. To extend these limits, networks can be joined. This, unfortunately, isn't as simple as splicing cables. Instead, it involves adding an intelligent network box—a bridge, router, or some variation.

Even if distances and number of users aren't excessive, there are other reasons for interconnecting segments. Bridges and routers are used to filter packets, passing only ones destined for stations on the other side. Careful splitting of a segment and insertion of one or another of these devices reduces traffic on the individual segments. Each segment has its own server, but users are still able to access resources on other segments. If traffic previously was heavy, doing this helps eliminate delays.

Of course, if not properly planned, performance with an added bridge or router can also be worse. Because both involve considerable internal processing, there are limits to the number of packets per second that can be handled. It is, therefore, important to identify the heavily used workstation–server pairs and keep them on the same side of the connecting device. That way the bulk of their packets won't have to cross the bridge (see Figure 14.1).

Another form of networking "black box" that will be mentioned only briefly is the Gateway. It is used to connect systems with totally different architectures, i.e., LAN to X.25 public packet switched network or LAN to mainframe. The use of a gateway isn't as discretionary as we have suggested for bridges and routers. If you need to connect to a mainframe, you won't have a choice. Gateways perform a tedious protocol conversion function.

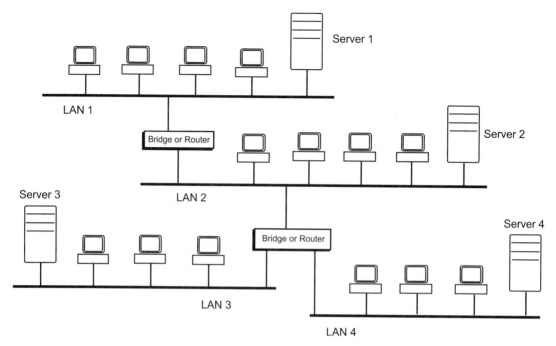

FIGURE 14.1
Four network segments connected together with bridges or routers (they look similar).

BRIDGES

The distinction between a bridge and a router depends on how far into the packet header the device reads. Bridges operate in the lower portion of OSI layer 2—the Data Link layer. This is the region that defines the "adapter card header" of a packet. A bridge uses only the source and destination addresses within that header. From that, it must decide whether to pass the packet to an adjoining network or not. It operates strictly on a pass–discard basis. A bridge does not touch anything in the data portion of a packet and normally does not alter the DLC header.

A typical bridge has only two ports, although more are certainly possible (see Figure 14.2). Bridges are most often used to connect networks with similar lower-level protocols together. For example, two Ethernet segments can be joined, or two Token Ring segments can be joined. However, bridges are also available to interconnect Ethernet, Token Ring, and ARCnet. In this case, the box must translate one header into the other and vice versa. Even when conversions are being made, the bridge uses nothing more than the normal "adapter" headers.

Learning

Unlike a workstation, a bridge must examine the header of every packet on each of its connected networks. A workstation, in contrast, is only watching for its own

FIGURE 14.2
Block diagram of a bridge.

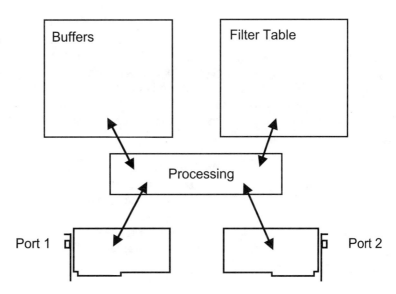

address (aside from broadcasts and multicasts). A bridge must, therefore, be a promiscuous device.

Early bridges were static devices. A knowledgeable administrator had to load a filter table and then modify it every time something in the network changed. Newer bridges build their filter tables dynamically. They watch all the source addresses in packets and, from that, learn who is on one port or the other. A bridge builds a table with that information and works continually to keep it up to date.

Along with learning, a bridge "ages" its table entries. Perhaps every 20 seconds or so, each entry is made "older." Should a particular source address be heard again, its age is taken back to Zero. If the age should reach a critical value, the entry is removed from the table (see Figure 14.3).

Most bridges do their learning quietly. They do not solicit information. In Ethernet, for example, there is no provision within the DLC layer to ask a station if it is alive.

Filtering

The learning operation is a nonstop process. However, the main task of a bridge is to use this information to filter and forward packets. While filtering, the bridge exam-

FIGURE 14.3
Short example of a filter table for a two-port bridge. Only six stations exist in total.

ADDRESS	PORT	AGE
0C00004567	1	0
000B003245	2	0
000C567987	1	0
0000012345	1	1
0C00435671	2	0
0000B234B3	2	0

ines all destination addresses of packets circulating on both networks. It compares them to its table to see whether they should be forwarded or not. If a destination address matches a workstation or server on the other side, the packet is passed through. The content of the packet is not changed.

If the destination address is on the input side, the bridge simply stops further processing. It doesn't destroy the packet—it simply doesn't pass it through to the other network. This is commonly known as "discarding." The term is correct as long as it is understood that the original packet isn't damaged. Even discarded packets are examined to see if their source address matches an up-to-date entry in the filter table. On a Token Ring, the bridge always allows a packet to continue around the source ring whether it is being forwarded or not.

If no match for a destination address can be found in the table, the packet is normally forwarded just to be safe. If the assumption was correct, there will probably be some reply from that "unknown destination," and the bridge can then update its table.

Broadcast and multicast messages can be forwarded if that feature has been turned on by the installer.

Workstations do not address a packet to a bridge. They have no knowledge that a bridge is operating—unless, of course, it is operating too slow and packets begin to get lost. The workstations simply use the address of the final destination.

During the filtering process, packets are held in a memory buffer inside the bridge. When ready, they are transmitted through another port. As a result, there is no problem with packet collisions and timing between the two connected systems or with maximum cable length between the two sides of the bridge. A bridge can, therefore, extend a network.

A bridge, as we have seen, has a considerable workload. It must examine source and destination addresses of every packet on each network. It must maintain its filter table and make forward/discard decisions. These introduce delays. Bridges, therefore, have a limited throughput, although this can be improved with faster (and more expensive) internal processing. Typical throughput is 10,000 to 15,000 packets per second. Bridges generally have a higher throughput than routers.

Spanning Tree Algorithm

This protocol is part of the IEEE 802.1d specification and relates to bridges. As more segments are bridged together, the possibility of multiple paths increases. While not fatal, this will allow multiple copies of a packet to pass from source to destination. Normal packets will not circulate endlessly because their destination address is always being checked. However, broadcasts are often just passed through to "the other side." If a second path exists, broadcasts through Bridge Two will appear as an input to Bridge One and be passed back onto the originating network. This is referred to as a "broadcast storm." Since bridges are supposed to reduce traffic, this is counterproductive.

Sometimes, however, multiple paths are created intentionally. Even in the simplest situation, two bridges can be used in parallel to join two networks. The second acts as a backup and provides increased reliability. It listens for a periodic status message from its twin. If it doesn't appear on time, the backup takes over.

The IEEE Spanning Tree Protocol can be used to define a preferred route and thus prevent loops. The protocol builds a logical map with only one path through all interconnected networks. Other bridges still function but not as the main highway. They only pass packets into local branches of the internet.

With Spanning Tree, bridges now communicate with one another—something they normally wouldn't do. They exchange table information but include only stations that they are supposed to reach rather than those they can reach.

ROUTER

Routers operate at OSI layer 3, the Network layer. They require a common protocol at this level. A router reads further into the packet than a bridge does, hence the requirement for the common protocol. For example, NetWare uses IPX routers, UNIX uses IP routers, and AppleTalk uses DDP routers.

Unlike bridges, routers are "visible" on an interconnected network. They have specific Data Link layer addresses and other stations send packets to these addresses. Once received at this DLC address, the router reads the network layer header. Depending on the exact protocol, the network header typically defines a separate network number and station number (see Figure 14.4).

Routing Tables

Routers maintain routing tables with the DLC addresses of adjacent routers and the network numbers that can be accessed through them. Unlike the filter table in a bridge, however, this table does not contain the specific address of individual workstations.

When a router receives a specifically addressed packet, it checks the destination network number in the Network layer header. It then consults its routing table for a port number, distance, and router DLC address. If an entry is found and the distance is Zero, the router knows that the destination station is on the immediately adjacent network. In this case, the router copies the station address from the Network header into the DLC header and sends it through the appropriate port.

This copying of addresses isn't always simple. Depending on the DLC and Network level protocols, some processing work could be required. IPX on ARCnet, for example, uses 48-bit station addresses in the network header but only eight-bit addresses in the adapter card header.

In a larger network, the router may find that the entry in the routing table has a distance greater than Zero. This means there are more routers to go through before

Adapter Header   Network Header

DLC Addresses	NET_NUMB.STATION_NUMB	. . . data . . .

FIGURE 14.4
Routers use the network layer information which appears after the adapter card header.

NETWORK	DISTANCE	PORT	NEXT_ROUTER	AGE
0045	2	1	002C560B	2
0013	1	1	0B005702	1
0007	0	1	00000000	1
0102	0	2	00000000	0
0345	0	3	00000000	0

FIGURE 14.5
Sample routing table for a three-port router.

the destination network is reached. It, therefore, modifies the DLC destination address for the appropriate router and sends the packet on its way (see Figure 14.5).

Table Aging

As with bridges, routers also age their table entries. This prevents tables from growing indefinitely. Routers are more active devices than bridges and communicate with each other regarding table contents. To use a specific example, XNS performs a table broadcast every 30 seconds. If no update is received for an entry within 90 seconds, it is marked as "suspect" and is not used. Entries not updated for three minutes have their hop count set to infinity ("Infinity" = 16). An entry is usually not deleted for another 60 seconds. When it is deleted, the changes made to the local table are sent to adjacent routers so they can update their tables.

A new router could take interval*maxhop (seconds) to fully update its table. "Interval" is the router broadcast interval in seconds (usually 10 to 30), and "maxhop" is the number of routers between this router and the farthest network.

If a router goes down, all other routers will have their tables up to date within the "aging time"—the time during which no routing information was received, and so they mark an entry as "suspect." During transitions, some message packets may get bounced around. As long as their hop count or Time to Live is being incremented/decremented, they will eventually cease to exist.

Because packets are addressed to specific routers, part of a router's workload is reduced. It can look only at packets sent to it and ignore all others. Although this helps to reduce a router's workload, throughput will be lower than for a bridge because it has other tasks to do. For a less expensive router, throughput between any one pair of ports will typically be 2000 to 5000 packets per second for short 64-byte packets and 700 packets per second for longer packets. Higher-performance routers can move close to 15,000 short packets (64-byte Ethernet) per second or 800 long packets (1500-byte Ethernet) per second.

A high-end router will typically contain a Motorola 68040, 10 megabytes of RAM used mainly for packet buffers, and several megabytes of rewritable ROM to hold the filter table. Highest-performance routers use multiple processors, some of which may even be RISC processors.

IBM's definition of NetBIOS (NETBEUI) unfortunately can't be routed because it doesn't include a definable Network protocol. The solution is to use either bridges or protocols, such as NetBIOS on IPX or NetBIOS on TCP/IP. Similarly, DEC's Local Area Transport (**LAT**) protocol cannot be routed. Bridges or gateways must be used instead.

Routers constantly communicate with each other. This requires a specific protocol. The exchange typically occurs once every 10 to 30 seconds. In some cases, especially with Wide Area Networks (**WANs**) connected with medium-speed phone lines, this exchange can become a significant portion of the overall traffic. Slower updates help in this case.

TCP/IP Routing

Most TCP/IP routers use the Routing Information Protocol (RIP) to periodically broadcast their routing tables. The RIP message contains a series of "tuples"—network number and hop count pairs. Each RIP message can contain up to 25 pairs. Messages are broadcast from/to UDP port number 520.

RIP has its faults. The hop count can only climb as high as 15; a count of 16 indicates "unreachable." This may be inadequate for very large networks. Table changes also propagate very slowly through a large network. Until all tables are up to date, which could take a few minutes at the extreme, some loops could exist.

Instead of RIP, some routers use the newer Open Shortest Path First (OSPF) protocol. OSPF routers maintain an internal "map" of the network and exchange information about the current state of each link as soon as a change occurs. Whereas RIP defines "reachability" as hop count (the number of routers that sit between two nodes), OSPF defines it more realistically in terms of expected time delays.

One more comment on TCP/IP routers—many UNIX host machines perform their own routing; thus, separate boxes are not always needed. The UNIX commands ROUTE, ROUTED, and GATED are involved. However, host-based routing does use up a computer's resources. To prevent this performance loss, a separate routing box may still be used.

IPX/SPX Routing

Novell uses a variation on TCP/IP's RIP. The end result is still called RIP but is slightly different. RIP communicates with well-known routing information socket 01 on each machine. XNS routing assumes that only a few hundred networks, at most, are interconnected. This makes it possible for each router to know about all of the others and get the total picture. At least in early versions of XNS, routing by area or hierarchical routing was not used.

XNS RIP packets (see Figure 14.6) start with an IPX header. The IPX Type is set to 01. Following the header the fields are:

```
Operation code (16 bits) 01 = request, 02 = response
First Tuple:
     Network Number (32 bits)
     Hop Count (16 bits)
Next Tuple:
     Network Number (32)
```

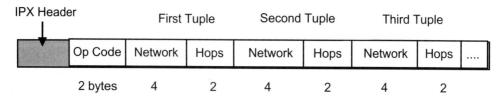

FIGURE 14.6
NetWare router updating packet.

```
            Hop Count (16)
     Next Tuple:
          ....
```

The pairs of Network Number and Hop Count are referred to as a "tuple," and many tuples are sent to convey all the information in the routing table of one router. A request (01) operation code is used as an interrogation. The source router will typically set the Hop count to 16 (decimal) for an interrogation. The response packet will contain the correct count.

AppleTalk Routing

Apple's routing changed somewhat with the definition of AppleTalk Phase II in 1989. Prior to this, a maximum of only 254 (numbers 00h and FFh are excluded) workstations, servers, etc., could exist on any one segment. However, with larger segments based on Ethernet or Token Ring, this became too restricting. AppleTalk Phase II solved this by allowing multiple, consecutive network numbers (a range) to be assigned to one segment. For routing table maintenance, these range numbers will be exchanged. These consist of two 16-bit network addresses—a range start and a range end. Each network number can have a maximum of 253 machines because Node ID FEh is now also reserved when this extended network addressing is used (see Figure 14.7).

AppleTalk network numbers can be any value from 0001h to FEFFh.

For a two-port router, each port will have a separate Network and Node ID. Regardless of the adapter type used, these Node IDs are the dynamically acquired eight-bit values.

AppleTalk routers use RTMP messages to maintain their routing tables. For each network in the internet that can be reached within a 16-hop limit, a router

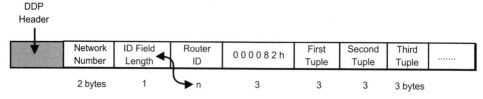

FIGURE 14.7
AppleTalk router updating packet.

holds one entry. Each entry includes the Network and Node ID of the next router, this router's port for that router, and the distance measured in hops. All routers on the internet will have similar, but not identical, entries. The hop count and port numbers will change with exact router position.

Approximately once every ten seconds, each router will periodically broadcast an RTMP data packet through each of its ports. These packets inform other routers of the originator's Node ID and network number for this port. A list of network numbers and hop counts for each entry in the local router follows. Again, these are referred to as tuples. All receiving routers can adjust their tables accordingly—hop counts must be adjusted, of course.

RTMP uses four kinds of packets: Data, Request, Route Data Request, and Response.

```
RTMP data packet (nonextended networks)
Data Link header (specifies overall length)
+ DDP header (Type set to 1)
16-bit router network number
1-byte Node ID length measured in bits (08 for LocalTalk)
Router Node ID (one or more bytes)
18-bit version indicator (00 00 82h)
First Tuple:
     16-bit network number
     3-bits = 000 (nonextended network)
     5-bit distance in hops
Next Tuple:
     16-bit network number
     ....
```

AppleTalk routers age their entries every 20 seconds. After three agings with no updates, an entry is declared bad. RTMP will then inform its neighbors that a table entry has expired by setting the "distance" value to 31. This is faster than letting the other routers find out for themselves.

AppleTalk routers perform a second function—the maintenance of zone names. Each network can be known by one or more zone names. These are maintained by the ZIP protocol, and each router holds a zone name table.

Zone names are provided for user convenience and show up on the Macintosh CHOOSER screen. They allow a user to send a print job, for example, to Printer 3 in zone Accounting.

Point to Point Protocol (PPP) standardizes the signaling that occurs between multiple routers. This allows routers from various suppliers to communicate.

BRIDGING TOKEN RINGS

Although Ethernet systems normally use a transparent bridge, IBM's Token Ring most often uses a more sophisticated bridge—a Source Routing Bridge, which is almost a router. When internetworking Token Ring, the user has three choices: source routing bridges, routers, and source routing transparent.

Source Routing Bridges

Source routing is an IBM-created and IEEE-endorsed method of routing from one node to another. It is Token Ring's method of extending the number of workstations on a network beyond the maximum 72, 96, or 260, depending on cable type. In its final IEEE-approved form, source routing has changed slightly from the original definition.

In transparent bridging, as often used for Ethernet, the internetworking takes place at the MAC sublayer of layer 2—the Data Link layer. When bridging with source routing, the internetworking occurs one half-layer higher, at the Logical Link Control (LLC) layer. This layer is now hardware independent and has a longer, more flexible header with which to work.

If the IEEE standard is followed, a destination can be up to 13 rings removed (14 rings in total including the originating ring). The original IBM standard limited this to seven bridges.

With source routing, unlike transparent bridging, the sending and receiving stations control the route a packet will take through the network. The source station, not the bridge, is responsible for placing it there—hence the name. However, the source station must determine the route before it can send the message, thus increasing its workload.

The route is discovered through initial broadcasting of packets between source and destination. Once a path is found, it is used for the duration of a session. Source routing is efficient if long sessions are used that make the initial setup time (route determination) worthwhile. However, if a path change is required because of a sudden failure, the session fails and must be reestablished.

Source routing becomes inefficient if sessions are short or if a large network has heavy traffic peaks. During one of these peaks, a route might be selected which could then prove to be less than optimum when the peak passes. With source routing, the selected route lasts for the duration of the session. Transparent bridging selects a new route for each packet.

Source routing uses distributed routing tables rather than a centralized one. Source routing bridges do not keep routing tables—ring stations do.

With source routing, each frame carries a full description of the path it must follow. This routing information is acquired by the source station using a previous transmission of TEST and XID (exchange identification) frames. These are types of data frames, not MAC frames.

Source routing adds an extra 4 to 30 bytes of addressing information just after the source address and before any LLC or Data portions of the frame.

To indicate that source routing information is contained in a Token Ring frame, the very first bit of the source address is set to One. Remember that Token Ring sends the most significant bit of each byte into the network cabling first—unlike most other local area networks. As a result, a source address of 0----------------------- (binary) would be sent as 8----------------------- (hex).

Source routing information consists of a 16-bit routing control field followed by as many as fourteen 16-bit Route Designators (see Figure 14.8).

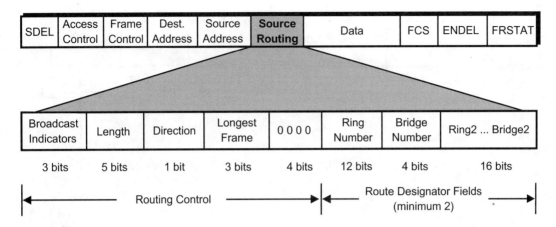

FIGURE 14.8
Token Ring frame with source routing added. This could be a MAC frame or a normal data frame. Source routing information is placed after the modified source address and before any LLC or data information.

Broadcast Indicators (3 bits)—Indicate the control placed on path selection. In large, multibridged systems, this could prevent multiple copies arriving at a destination. Also called frame type.

> 110 = Single Route Broadcast (SRB)
> xxx = All Routes Broadcast (ARB)
> 000 = Specifically Routed

Length (5 bits)—Overall number of bytes in the routing code (maximum 30 bytes).

Direction (1 bit)—Controls the order in which the bridging station interprets the routing information—forward or backward.

Longest frame (3 bits)—Valuable when different types of networks are bridged. For example, Ethernet-to-Token-Ring bridges would use 001 to indicate the longest frame that can be exchanged is 1500 data bits. An 011 would indicate a possible 4472 data bytes between two Token Ring segments.

Reserved (4 Zero bits)

Route Designator Fields

Each ring requires one Route Designator Field. There can be 2 to 14 of these fields, which will allow a frame to cross from 1 to 13 bridges. IBM's original definition only allowed seven bridges (eight rings). Each Route Designator Field is a 16-bit value made up as follows:

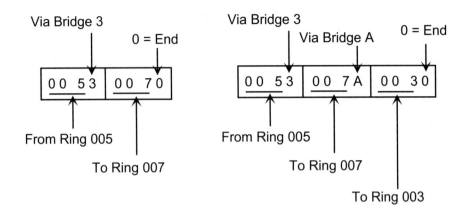

(a) Two Route Designator Fields   (b) Three Route Designator Fields

FIGURE 14.9
Example of reading route designator fields. The last four bits must be Zero.

Ring number (12 bits)

Bridge Number (4 bits)

Rings are numbered 001–FFFh. Bridges are numbered 1–Fh. Bridge numbers do not have to be unique unless two are directly in parallel, which is sometimes done for reliability.

Any two consecutive route designators are read as "from Ring number 5, across Bridge 3, to Ring 7." The "bridge number" of the very last route designator is set to Zero to indicate the end of the path (see Figure 14.9).

Route Determination

Two types of route discovery packets can be used: All-Routes Broadcast (ARB) and Single-Route Broadcast (SRB). We will start with ARB packets and explain the use of SRB later.

1. The source station prepares an ARB. This will have two bytes of routing information and no route designator fields.
2. The first bridge adds a four-byte route designator field—the first field—as in the first example in Figure 14.9. Of course, the "size" value within the route information header and the token ring header must be changed.
3. The next bridge and all subsequent bridges add two more bytes and adjust the sizes as necessary.
4. Finally, the destination station receives the route discovery packet(s). Using ARB broadcast, the same number of packets will reach the destination as there are possible routes to the destination.

5. Destination answers back using a Specifically Routed Packet—using the same routing code but with direction bit reversed.

ARB packets wander through all possible routes between rings. As we will see, they are smart enough (because of the longer header structure) not to repeat a path. SRB packets take only one route (they need some advance information to determine this).

The station wishing to determine a route sends an ARB. Multiple copies (depending on the number of paths) will float around the interconnected system. As a packet crosses a bridge, the bridge will insert its own bridge number and the numbers of the two rings attached on either side into the header. The header grows as a result.

The originating station receives one ARB packet back for each possible path from the source to the destination. The originating station then selects the most efficient path based on this information: timing, hop count, and maximum packet length. For the duration of the current session with that destination, the route is now fixed.

When packets contain a route, the Routing Information Bit is set Hi. Source Routing bridges watch for packets with this bit set and perform filtering on them. They then pass packets destined for the network on the other side. However, the bridge first sets other bits to indicate that the packet has passed through that bridge and shouldn't try again. If the bit is not set, the bridge ignores the packet.

A source routing bridge can be set up (configured) as a single-route broadcast bridge (usually the default) or as an all-routes broadcast bridge. The bridge can also be allowed to configure itself by negotiating with other bridges on the network.

If set up as a single-route broadcast bridge, the following frames will be forwarded to the next ring:

- All routes broadcast
- Single route broadcast
- Specifically routed

If set up as "all-routes broadcast," single-route broadcasts will not be forwarded.

"All-routes" broadcasts will not circulate endlessly because a bridge will not forward a frame that has an earlier route designator field already indicating that ring.

A recent alternative to routing, in a source routing environment, is Source Routing Transparent (SRT). It provides a way for Token Ring and Ethernet to interconnect. The IEEE is currently studying this. An SRT bridge allows both source routing and nonsource routing (transparent) packets to pass through.

SRT defines three packets that can be used for route discovery.

1. *All-Route Explorer (ARE)*—Equivalent to source routing's ARB packet.
2. *Specifically Routed Frame (SRF)*—Issued in response to ARE.
3. *Transparent Spanning Frame (TSF)*—Performs the same function as source routing SRB but doesn't contain routing information.

SRT allows the destination station to determine the route; source routing doesn't. SRT also allows end stations to hold backup routes in their routing tables.

NETWORK MANAGEMENT

At its simplest, network management involves gathering statistics on packet counts and errors. However, network management can also extend to sending commands to change things—configuring, turning on and off. The extent of management will depend on both the intelligence of the devices being managed and the amount of concern installers and supervisors have about system security.

Managed devices are typically routers, bridges, and concentrators that inherently have some internal processing. Although adapter cards in individual personal computers can be controlled, this is rarely done.

Management of a device can be either by "in-band" or "out-of-band" methods. These are terms carried over from telephone use and aren't really being applied correctly. Out-of-band control simply means that there is a separate connector, usually an RS-232 serial port, on the router box to which a terminal or spare PC can be attached. This is good for initial setup and troubleshooting, but the user must be physically close to the controlled device.

For long-term management, it is easier (but less secure) to communicate with the device through normal network cables using standard protocols. This is what is meant by in-band management. The managing person can be as far away from the device as the network cabling allows.

Each controllable agent holds counts of different events and errors that have occurred in a Management Information dataBase (MIB). The standardized form of the MIB will be described shortly. The manager communicates with entries in this agent MIB.

The following three high-level protocols facilitate in-band monitoring and control. Only SNMP will be described in detail.

1. *IBM's Netview*—Requires SNA
2. **CMIP** *(Common Management Information Protocol)*—Part of OSI. Very exotic. Expected to eventually replace SNMP in the long run. Some specific variations are:

    CMOT—CMIP over TCP/IP

    CMOL—CMIP over LLC. Somewhat better for mixed networks.
3. *SNMP (Simple Network Management Protocol)*—SNMP is defined in RFC 1155, 1156, and 1157. This is currently the most popular control method.

Simple Network Management Protocol

SNMP is a two-way protocol for communicating in-band network management information over a LAN between a controllable device and a central location. SNMP grew out of the TCP/IP and Internet worlds. It is a descendant of Simple Gateway Management Protocol (SGMP).

SNMP defines five message types:

0	GetRequest	Read information
1	GetNextRequest	Read a table of information
2	GetResponse	Message from Agent to Manager
3	SetRequest	Send changes for reconfiguration
4	Trap	Unsolicited message from a controlled Agent

These messages move between "Manager" software and "Agent" software. The manager process typically runs on some centralized workstation where a system administrator occasionally works. To look impressive, this station will usually have a graphic map of the network on its screen. The Manager software spends most of its time gathering statistics on packet counts and error counts, etc. Sometimes it may make a preprogrammed decision, or it may flash a warning to the system administrator.

At the opposite end, Agent software tends to be ROM-based code running inside, for example, a 10BaseT wiring hub. For devices that are controllable but haven't learned to speak "SNMP," Proxy Agents can be added. This is usually a separate box connected between the network and perhaps an RS-232 port of the non-SNMP speaking device. The connected device still must be controllable; there is no mechanism to make noncontrollable devices controllable.

For most communications, SNMP uses polling to send a question from the Manager to the Agent and solicit a response. For the question, the Manager program can use either GetRequest or GetNextRequest packets—GetNextRequest being used for extended queries of Agent data. The answer will come back from the Agent as one or more GetResponse packets.

If the Manager has to change a setting in the controlled device, it will send a SetRequest packet and likely expect a GetResponse in return. The SetRequest starts to be dangerous because wrong settings here can seriously upset the network. For security, some controllable devices will only accept setting changes from a direct console, an out-of-band connection.

The fifth message type is Trap. This is an unsolicited message from the Agent to the Manager. It usually occurs when something has gone wrong inside the controlled device—too many packet errors, for example.

SNMP can use various transport protocols. However, lower-layer protocols are preferred because they are closer to the bottom (obviously) and, therefore, less dependent on other layer failures. Use of a connection-oriented protocol would increase traffic. Besides, if a device is failing and communication is erratic, it will be almost impossible to open and maintain a session.

With a TCP/IP network, the layer of choice is UDP. In this case, SNMP will use UDP port number 161 for all Get and Set messages and port number 162 for trap messages.

The two packet forms used by SNMP are shown in Figure 14.10. Trap messages have a special format. All other communications use a common Get/Set format.

SNMP **Get/Set** Protocol Structure

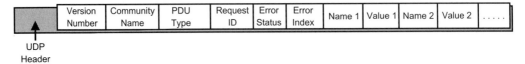

UDP
Header

SNMP **Trap** Protocol Structure

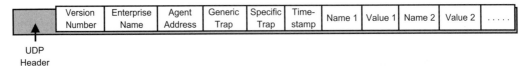

UDP
Header

FIGURE 14.10
Two SNMP message structures.

Each of the SNMP message structures is divided into fields, which is quite normal. What is unusual is that many of the fields have a variable length. Therefore, the first byte of these fields is a length value. The second byte indicates, in part, the data type. Figure 14.11 is an example of an SNMP message.

Three fields occur at the front of all SNMP messages. The first two form what is often called the "authentication header," and the third field defines the type for the rest of the message:

Version—The SNMP protocol version number used to check that both Manager and Agent are using similar protocols. Usually contains the single byte 00h.

Community—An ASCII character name

PDU Type—Determines the message type

  0 = GetRequest
  1 = GetNextRequest
  2 = GetResponse
  3 = SetRequest
  4 = Trap

The remaining fields depend on which of the two message types is being carried.

SNMP Request-Response Messages

PDU Type = 0, 1, 2, or 3

Request ID—To correlate requests and responses, the Agent will respond with the same "message number" as used in the request.

Error Status—Agent can place an error code here such as 04—I cannot process your SetRequest, or 02—I don't understand that variable name. Most of the time the Error Status should be Zero.

```
        0  1  2  3  4  5  6  7    8  9  A  B  C  D  E  F
0000   00 C0 15 00 15 92 00 C0   15 00 15 93 00 00 45 00
0010   00 9B 7F A1 00 00 FE 11   48 04 C0 99 B9 3C C0 99
0020   BA 3C 00 A1 00 A1 00 87   79 B7 30 7D 02 01 00 04
0030   06 70 75 62 6C 69 63 A0   70 02 02 01 B5 02 01 00
0040   02 01 00 30 64 30 12 06   0E 2B 06 01 02 01 10 08
0050   02 01 02 BC 27 F3 7F 05   00 30 12 06 0E 2B 06 01
0060   02 01 10 08 02 01 04 BC   27 F3 7F 05 00 30 12 06
0070   0E 2B 06 01 02 01 10 08   02 01 05 .. .. .. .. ..
```

```
SNMP
    Length: 7Dh
    Version: integer, 1 byte, 00
    Name: string, 6 bytes, "public"
    Type: integer, 02 (Get Response)
    ID: integer, 2 bytes, 01B5h
    Error Status: integer, 1 byte, 00
    Error Index:  integer, 1 byte, 00
    Variables/Values:   (1.3. prefix assumed)
        6.1.2.1.16.8.2.1.2.....
        6.1.2.1.16.8.2.1.4.....
        6.1.2.1.16.8.2.1.5.....
```

FIGURE 14.11
SNMP message carried in an IP–UDP packet. The SNMP portion begins at byte 002Ah.
The message is between UDP Ports 161 and 161.

Error Index—Indicates which of the following values has caused an internal error.

The rest of the message will consist of pairs of variable names and corresponding values from the MIB.

SNMP Trap Messages

PDU Type = 4

Enterprise—Indicates the type of management system located in that Agent.

Agent Address—Typically the Ethernet card number or the IP network.station number that generated this trap message.

Generic Trap Type and Specific Trap Type—Define the reason for the message.

TimeStamp—Indicates when the failure occurred.

The rest of the message will consist of pairs of variable names and corresponding values from the MIB.

Management Information Base

The Management Information Base (MIB) is a small database inside the managed object that holds error counts, statistics, and operating parameters. To be a bit more correct, the MIB is distributed over all the managed objects—each holding only relevant values. Over the years, various manufacturers held these values in totally incompatible ways, making central data-gathering difficult. More recently, they have cooperated to standardize the MIB structure.

The original definition was made in 1987. MIB version II (RFC 1213) was introduced in 1991. It adds many types of additional devices which can be managed. These include some features that were previously proprietary to specific vendors.

Each object in the MIB has a unique identification number. This numbering system, if drawn out on paper, would appear structured as a hierarchical tree and is often described this way. In reality, a controlled device simply holds a pile of numbered objects in its memory. Figure 14.12 shows one portion of the standard MIB tree. The first set of three branches at the top defines different standards organizations and the definitions and numbers each controls.

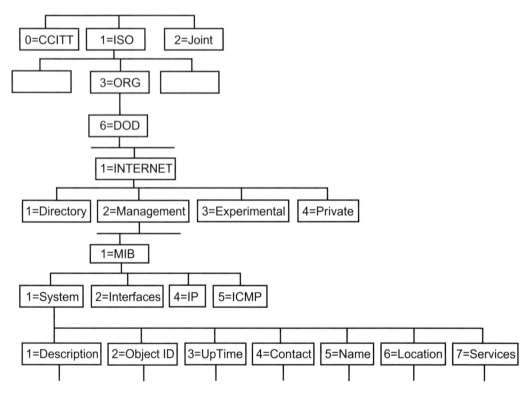

FIGURE 14.12
MIB object tree.

Through software in the manager workstation, these ID "numbers" can be translated into descriptive characters as long as they are unique. The Information Sciences Institute in San Diego controls the numbering system and descriptions and monitors specific extensions made by vendors.

As an example of locating an object, the sequence 1.3.6.1.2.1.1.1 points into the System Description area of the MIB. If the manager were to send the SNMP message GetNextRequest 1.3.6.1.2.1.1.1 to a particular device, it would expect several messages in return describing the manufacturer, serial numbers, software version numbers, etc.

Security Concerns

SNMP, as initially defined, had very little built-in security, and routers, etc., could be accidentally or intentionally shut off or reconfigured. For this reason, many manufacturers do not allow SNMP "Set" functions to be used over the network. The equivalent operation would have to be performed by direct console. The Internet Engineering Task Force has developed a secure version of SNMP, which, unfortunately, is not compatible with the original definition. The protocol packets now contain user authentication features and the ability to encrypt the data being carried. The use of all these features has raised the complexity considerably and also placed a heavier load on the network traffic.

10BaseT Hub Management

To provide an idea of what is available for remote reading, we present a list of numbers that are gathered by a typical 10BaseT Ethernet hub. The numbers can be read either with a direct out-of-band terminal connection or in-band via SNMP.

The hub accumulates numbers in several different ways. Some counts are held as totals that start at Zero when the device is reset and then just keep accumulating for days. Other counts are based either on an interval of time or a quantity of frames handled, e.g., 50 collisions in any ten-second period or 50 collisions per 1000 frames. The initial setup by the installer determines the method. Within these time or frame slots, the hub records both averages and peak counts. For time-based measurements, statistics are gathered every 2.5 seconds.

Triggers can be set on many of the counts. For example, a trap message could be sent if more than 65 errors were to occur in any ten-second period (sliding ten-second window) or when the total number of collisions reached 5000.

Measurable Parameters

FCS Error—Wrong frame check sequence

Collisions—Transmit collisions

Excessive Collisions—More than 31 consecutive collisions on any one port

Late Collisions—After 512 bit-times

Runt Frames—Collision fragments longer than 96 bits but shorter than the minimum legal frame size (longer than a pygmy but shorter than a legal packet)

Pygmy Frames—Collision fragments shorter than a runt frame (less than 96 bits). Usually indicates an external noise hit on the cable

Jabber—A single transmission of more than 65,000 bits causes the hub to "auto-partition"

Alignment Errors—Frames that don't contain whole bytes

Source Address Changes—Number of times the source address has changed. Indicates that multiple users are running on the one port for some unusual reason

Frames Too Long—Number of frames with an overall length greater than 1518 bytes

Number of Broadcast Frames

Number of Frames Received OK

Number of Multicast Frames

Source Address of the Last Readable Frame

Automatic Actions

10BaseT specifies a number of actions that a hub can perform on its own to keep a network operating. Should the need arise, a hub will disconnect a station through an action called auto-partitioning.

Auto-partitioning of any one port will take place if a collision situation exists for more than 1024 bit-times or if a shorter collision situation reoccurs on each of 32 consecutive attempts to transmit to that port. Once partitioned, the hub will continue to pass external packets to that station and listen for transmissions from it but will not pass those transmissions to other stations.

When partitioning occurs, the hub will notify the remote management software using a trap message and continue to monitor the port. It will be automatically reconnected if a legal data packet longer than 512 bits is received from the port without a collision.

The wiring concentrator also performs a continuous testing of each station-to-hub wiring link. Single-polarity Link Integrity Pulses, also known as "I'm Alive" pulses, are sent by adapter and concentrator if nothing else has been transmitted for the last 16 milliseconds. The receiving end of each pair watches for periodic activity. If nothing has been received for more than approximately 100 milliseconds, the port will be "failed." Both adapter and concentrator will, however, continue to send periodic link test pulses. A failed device will be removed from this state after either four consecutive link test pulses or a data packet is received.

In addition, because the Link Integrity Pulses are only one polarity, the adapter on the other end of the cable can check the polarity of its wiring and, if necessary, automatically reverse terminals to compensate for a wiring mistake.

REFERENCES

1. Sidhu, G. S., Andrews, R. F., and Oppenheimer, A. B. *Inside AppleTalk,* 2nd Ed. Reading, MA: Addison-Wesley, 1990.

2. *IBM Token-Ring Network*. Architecture Reference. Research Triangle Park, NC: International Business Machines Corporation. SC30-3374-02, September 1989.

3. *Xerox Network Systems Architecture*. General Information Manual XNSG-068504. Sunnyvale, CA: Xerox Systems Institute, April 1985.

4. *Internet Transport Protocols Guide XNSS-028112.* Sunnyvale, CA: Xerox Systems Institute, December 1981.

The Seven Layers
of ISO-OSI

Most LAN textbooks start with a description of the OSI seven-layer reference model. This book, to be obstinate, finishes with it. My reason is that a description of the model is not a good starting point for the initial understanding of LANs. However, the model and its standards are important and must ultimately be understood by all who are deeply involved in networking.

The total field of data communications covers a very broad area. It includes telephone links, dedicated cables, and satellite channels with many data rates and a variety of fixed, switched, and virtual circuits. Data communications also includes local and wide area networks for offices and factories.

In an effort to standardize the total field, the International Standards Organization (ISO) and CCITT cooperated to develop the Open Systems Interconnection (OSI) standards for data communications. In 1984, they adopted the seven-layer reference model mentioned in earlier chapters. Each layer in this model is accompanied by a general description of what it does.

Various committees have and continue to fill out the details of each layer. The lower-layer standards were completed a while ago whereas the higher layers are more recent. Many of the resulting standards aren't really new. They are just formalized descriptions of existing techniques. However, one of the advantages of the process is that terminology is now at least consistent.

All of the layers offer choices. The result is a good, controlled shopping list so that network purchasers can piece together a stack of protocols with characteristics that suit their individual needs.

The major impact of these standards, especially for DOS-based workstations, is still in the future. More powerful workstations with more capable operating systems already have OSI-compatible software available from a number of manufacturers.

The seven layers of the reference model are:

User's Application Program

Layer 7	Application
Layer 6	Presentation

Layer 5	Session
Layer 4	Transport
Layer 3	Network
Layer 2	Data Link
Layer 1	Physical

Notice that the user's application program is separate from the layers of communications.

Each layer is defined so that some easily described operation is performed, and the software or hardware that is responsible can be identified.

Each layer thinks it is communicating with an identical layer on another machine and has little concern for what occurs within adjacent layers. Each layer must know, of course, what form the adjacent layers use when passing data back and forth, but they don't need to know what goes on inside. The direction of passing depends on whether the message is being sent (down through the layers) or received (up). On sending, each layer will perform some function, add an identifying header to the incoming data, and pass the modified message to the lower layer. On receiving, the process is reversed. In theory, we could have up to six added headers. The physical layer does not add a header.

The bottom two layers are of greatest interest to electronics people since wires, voltages, and integrated circuits are involved. The layers above this are all software. The lower layers are most concerned with the specific details of the network cards and cables whereas the higher layers become progressively more concerned with the user's program and complete files.

The following descriptions attempt to relate the seven layers to local area networks. Keep in mind that the fit with existing technology is only approximate.

From the bottom, up:

Level 1—Physical

Describes the connectors, cables, voltage levels, and timing used. All of level 1 can be analyzed either visually or with an oscilloscope. Using "thin" Ethernet, for example, we would find 50-ohm coaxial cable (RG-58) using BNC connectors. The cable voltage would reach a high of Zero volts, a low of −2 volts, and would change every 100 nanoseconds.

Level 2—Data Link

In a typical LAN, the cable described in layer 1 will be shared by many users. This layer describes the fighting that takes place when several users try to use the cables at the same time. Before the information being sent gets down to this level, it has already been broken into chunks of, perhaps, 500 or 1000 bytes each. This level then converts the information chunks into frames or packets by adding headers with destination addresses and trailers with error-checking codes. At the receiving end, this layer can extract the information bits and determine if any errors have occurred. To arbitrate cable access, some networks pass a token; others use CSMA/CD. Most of this layer is determined by integrated circuits on network adapter boards. Also included in this layer are various attempts at creating a standard interface to the hardware. Some examples are LLC, ODI, NDIS, and Packet Drivers.

Level 3—Network

Most concerned with addresses and routing. Information has already been cut into packets before it reaches this layer, and full network source and destination addresses are added. The protocol chips at the lower layer also add addresses, but there could be differences. ARCnet, to cite the greatest difference, uses only eight-bit addresses in the frame header. The network layer of NetWare adds 96-bit addresses that define the network, the station, and the process within a station. When multiple networks are linked together with routers, this layer decides if the frame must pass into an adjacent network. In some very simple networks, this layer could be missing, and the addresses in the adapter card frame header used instead.

Level 4—Transport

This is the most vital layer for local area networks. It controls the flow of data up and down the layers and over the network. The transport layer usually knows when the other station is ready to send and receive and what sizes of data the lower layers can handle. It cuts the local data into chunks before sending and puts received chunks back together into complete messages. One of the options in this layer is full end-to-end error checking. Layers above this don't have to know anything about the network itself.

Level 5—Session

This layer is above the packet level and is concerned with larger chunks of data and their integrity. It may choose between optional "virtual circuit" or "datagram" services provided by the layers below. It may also allow the user to substitute "alphabetic" names for their workstation. One machine might then be known as the unique individual "Charlie" and at the same time be a member of a group of machines named "Accounting."

Level 6—Presentation

On local networks between machines of the same type, this layer often isn't needed. In a more general situation, the layer handles data encryption for security, file conversion (i.e., ASCII to EBCDIC), and modifications for terminal emulations.

Level 7—Application

This isn't the user program (i.e., database or spreadsheet) itself. Instead, the application layer provides services to the user program such as retrieving files, reading keyboards, and displaying items on the screen. This layer is typically MS-DOS or PC-DOS plus the network redirector.

How important is this reference model?

The answer is: very important, but mainly for the future. It is a poor starting point for the individual trying to understand how networks work. One of the major problems at the present is the DOS-based personal computer. Although these machines can be fitted with plenty of memory chips and modules, it is difficult to allocate much of that to running programs. Fully defined OSI protocol stacks tend to require more memory space, which just isn't available on these machines.

Common DOS network software still combines the operation of two or three of the layers into one executable file. The justification for this present state is that it works and, especially with multi-protocol drivers, satisfies the user's requirements.

For the purposes of this book, the key word is "reference" model. At a minimum, the names and order of the layers should be memorized, as they are constantly used in descriptions.

RELIABLE NETWORKS

Many descriptions of the OSI layers will make continual reference to the "reliability" of lower layers. This probably conjures up images of warnings printed on the packaging of each network product:

Caution: This product is only 85% reliable. Use could endanger the health of your network.

Fortunately, it means nothing of the sort.

Each design of network card includes a CRC check on the data within its packet. This provides very good control against transmission errors within individual packets. The "reliability" being discussed involves packets that might get sent out of sequence or might be missing altogether. This causes errors in large messages that must be cut into packets for transmission. The possibility of this happening increases with network loading and when multiple networks are interconnected.

The designer of the complete set of network software (the protocol stack or suite) must decide how these errors are going to be detected and which layer will have the responsibility. This is why a general description of what each of the seven layers does is somewhat difficult.

Most protocol suites will allow the programmer either to use the automated "reliability" checks or to bypass them as desired. Therefore, most suites offer both a "connection-oriented" service, which includes the checking, and a "datagram" service, which adds no checking of its own. In the latter, the programmer either isn't concerned with the correct order of packets or has decided to do the job manually.

With both NetWare and the Department of Defense TCP/IP, the main end-to-end error checking is available at the Transport level. All layers below that are, therefore, considered to be "unreliable." If desired, the Transport layer will keep copies of every message and set individual timers for each. If messages are not acknowledged by lower layers as having been properly received within a specific time, they will be retransmitted.

IEEE LAYERS

Specifically for Local Area Network use, the IEEE modified the lower two layers of the OSI model, creating three layers. The IEEE descriptions better define the typical split between adapter card hardware and higher-level software.

LLC—Logical Link Control layer	A uniform software interface to lower hardware.
MAC—Media Access Control layer	Defines hardware that arbitrates access to a shared cable.
Physical	Defines cabling and connectors. Note that the physical layer as defined in the IEEE standards is more specific about cables and connectors than is the OSI definition.

The related standards are:

IEEE 802.1	Presents an overview of the IEEE definitions and discusses network management and bridging.
IEEE 802.2 (ISO 8802/2)	Logical Link Control. A uniform interface to adapter cards and dedicated line networks.
IEEE 802.3 (ISO 8802/3)	CSMA/CD definition. Essentially Ethernet with some changes.
IEEE 802.4 (ISO 8802/4)	Token-passing bus used by the Manufacturing Automation Protocol (MAP).
IEEE 802.5 (ISO 8802/5)	Token-passing ring used by IBM.
IEEE 802.6 (ISO 8802/6)	Metropolitan Area Networks.

◼ GLOSSARY

PART I: NETWORK- AND COMPUTER-RELATED TERMS

1Base5 StarLAN® network operating at one megabit per second over twisted pair wiring.

10Base2 Thin coaxial Ethernet.

10Base5 Ethernet with thick cable and separate transceivers.

10BaseT Ethernet on unshielded twisted pair.

AUI Attachment Unit Interface. Used in thick cable Ethernet.

backbone A central cable used to interconnect several smaller networks. Where possible, the data rate of a backbone will be higher than for other systems.

baud A measurement of how fast voltages change on a cable. This is the same as bits per second if the cable only uses two voltage levels. However, for networks and modems that use multiple levels it will be considerably less than the data rate.

bps Bits per second.

bridge Joins two network segments but only passes selected packets.

broadcast A single packet addressed to every network station.

byte A combination of eight bits. Also called an octet.

CCITT Consultative Committee on International Telephony and Telegraphy.

CMIP Common Management Information Protocol.

CMOT CMIP over TCP/IP.

collision Two Ethernet packets that are transmitted at approximately the same time.

concentrator A wiring box that joins cables together. See Hub.

CRC   Cyclic Redundancy Code. Usually a 16- or 32-bit value computed from packet contents and designed to check for transmission errors. Also known as a Frame Check Sequence (FCS).

CSMA/CD   Carrier Sense Multiple Access with Collision Detection, as used in Ethernet and Apple's LocalTalk.

datagram   A complete message in one packet or frame. Does not rely on two or more packets to be correctly sequenced.

DCE   Data Circuit Terminating Equipment. A device (like a modem) on one end of an RS-232 cable. (Pin 2 receives data and pin 3 transmits.)

DTE   Data Terminal Equipment. A computer or terminal on the other end of an RS-232 cable. (Pin 3 receives data and pin 2 transmits.

EMI   Electro-Magnetic Interference.

EPROM   Erasable Programmable Read-Only Memory. A memory "chip" that holds its content when the power is removed and can also be rewritten, but not rapidly. Erasure may be with ultraviolet light (EPROM) or electrically (EEPROM).

FCS   Frame Check Sequence. Provides a very strong possibility of detecting errors in a packet or frame.

HDLC   High-Level Data Link Control. A layer 2 protocol commonly used over dedicated lines. Very similar to IBM's SDLC (Synchronous Data Link Control) and DEC's DDCMP (Digital Data Communications Message Protocol).

hub   A connection point for wiring. Some hubs are nothing more than four resistors. Others include a good deal of electronics and processing.

IEEE   Institute of Electrical and Electronic Engineers.

internet   Could refer to any collection of network segments joined by routers. Could also refer to "the Internet," which is a connection of university, corporation, and government computers covering much of the world.

IP   Internet Protocol.

ISO   International Standards Organization.

LAT   Digital Equipment Corporation's Local Area Transport Protocol.

MAU   Multistation Access Unit. Part of the IBM Token Ring cabling system.

multicast   A packet sent to a group of users but not necessarily all users.

NIC   Network Interface Card.

RAM Random Access Memory. Values in this type of memory can be both read and changed at high speed, but when the power goes off, they immediately lose everything.

routers Devices that connect two or more network segments and use network layer information to control the movement of frames between segments.

SNMP Simple Network Management Protocol.

STP Shielded Twisted Pair of wires.

TCP Transmission Control Protocol.

TSR A DOS program which is loaded into memory and then immediately Terminates but Stays Resident in memory for future use.

UTP Unshielded Twisted Pair.

WAN Wide Area Network.

X.25 A CCITT protocol for public packet switching network. The definition covers OSI layers 1, 2, and 3. RS-232 is used for the user interface, and High-Level Data Control (HDLC) is used for the data link operations. Much of the interface strongly resembles IEEE 802.2 LLC.

PART II: ELECTRICAL TERMS

ac Alternating Current. In spite of the word "current," the letters ac are often used to describe both voltages and currents. An alternating voltage or current continuously makes changes in level and polarity. A good example is the 50 or 60 Hz electrical power system for lights and refrigerators, etc.

capacitance Determines how strong an electric field will be when voltage appears between two objects. Like inductance, capacitance stores energy for later use and does not waste it. Measured in farads, microfarads, and picofarads.

current The electrical stuff that flows along copper wires. Consists of a movement of clouds of electrons. Measured in amps and milliamps.

dc Direct Current. Also used to describe both voltages and currents. A dc voltage or current holds a constant value over a long period of time.

impedance A catch-all term that includes resistance, capacitive reactance, and inductive reactance. It may or may not represent a loss of energy. Measured in ohms.

inductance   Determines how strong a magnetic field will be when current flows through a wire or other component. An inductance does not waste energy as does a resistor. It stores it for later use. Measured in henries, millihenries, and microhenries.

reactance   Capacitance and inductance can have an impact on changing voltages and currents, and the effect changes with frequency. Reactance is a calculation of this impact. The reactance of an inductor increases with frequency; that of a capacitor decreases with frequency. Reactance is measured in ohms, but, unlike resistance, this does not represent a loss of energy.

resistance   The property of a material that determines how much current can flow through it. Copper wires have a low resistance, and so currents can flow easily with little voltage needed to push. Plastic insulation, on the other hand, has a very high resistance, and so very little current flows for a given voltage. As current flows through a resistance, it loses energy and a slight heating occurs. Resistance is measured in ohms.

transformer   An electrical device with at least two sets of wires wound together. There is no electrical connection from one to the other. Energy moves from the primary set to the secondary set using a magnetic field. This provides electrical isolation and also creates the possibility of increasing or decreasing voltage levels. There is no free ride, and current levels will change by a corresponding amount in the opposite direction.

voltage   The electrical force that pushes electricity through wires. Measured in volts.

■ Index